Information Age
Journalism

05- 63

22.00

Information Age Journalism

Journalism in an International Context

Vincent Campbell

ARNOLD

First published in Great Britain 2004 by
Arnold, a member of the Hodder Headline Group,
338 Euston Road, London NW1 3BH

http://www.arnoldpublishers.com

Distributed in the United States of America by
Oxford University Press Inc.
198 Madison Avenue, New York, NY10016

The advice and information in this book are belived to be true and
accurate at the date of going to press, but neither the author nor the publisher
can accept any legal responsibility or liability for any errors or omissions.

British Library Cataloguing in Publication Data
A catalogue record for this book is available from the British Library

Library of Congress Cataloging-in-Publication Data
A catalog record for this book is available from the Library of Congress

ISBN 0 340 76349 3

Typeset in 9.5/13 New Baskerville by Charon Tec Pvt. Ltd, Chennai, India
Printed and bound in Malta

What do you think about this book? Or any other Arnold title?
Please send your comments to deedback.arnold@hodder.co.uk

Cover Image: PA PHOTOS/EPA: US Navy picture obtained Saturday 29 March 2003
shows Spc. Bernard S. Wiess, a journalist assigned to the 22nd Mobile Public Affairs
Detachment, getting a close shot with his camera of an oil fire at the Ramaila Oilfield,
Iraq, 28 March. Kuwaiti firefighters are fighting the oil blaze, set by Iraqi military forces,
as part of their support of Operation Iraqi Freedom.

Contents

List of Figures

List of Tables

The editor rules the world; he receives ministers of other governments and settles international quarrels; he is the patron of all the arts and sciences; he maintains all the great novelists; he has not only a telephone link to Paris but a telephote line as well, whereby he can at any time from his study in New York, see a Parisian with whom he converses.

Advertisements are flashed on the clouds; reporters describe events orally to millions of subscribers; and if a subscriber becomes weary or is busy, he attaches his phonograph to his telephone, and hears the news at his leisure.

The Electrical Review, 1889

Acknowledgements

I'd like to thank a number of people who've helped me in the preparation of this book, in a range of different ways. First and foremost I want to thank my wife, Jenny, for all the emotional support she constantly provides. I'd like to thank Bob Franklin who encouraged me to pursue the idea of writing a book in the first place, and gave me my first opportunity to teach journalism studies at the University of Sheffield. I wouldn't have been able to even begin this book without the opportunities provided by the Department of Film and Media Studies at Stirling University and I'd like to give particular thanks to Mike Cormack, Raymond Boyle, Brian McNair, Peter Meech, Jacquie L'Etang and Gillian Doyle, and the rest of the department for the invaluable experience I gained there. Thanks also go to those who've shared office space, and thus had to put up with me over the years, including Rodney Fairley, Amir Saeed, John Casey, and Sharon Lockyer. This book has evolved over the years of its writing in no small part due to the many undergraduate and postgraduate students I have taught journalism studies to, principally at the Universities of Sheffield and Stirling, so thanks also to all of them. I would also like to thank the people that I was taught by as a schoolkid and undergraduate who made me realise the joys of studying a subject you're interested in regardless of what others think, particularly Richard Dyer at the University of Warwick, and Dr Terence Edwards at Maidstone Grammar School. I'd like to thank the editors at Arnold for their patience and tolerance in dealing with me. Finally, my academic career might not have happened if it wasn't for the help of my parents at key moments in my life, and I owe a lot to them for that.

Vincent Campbell, May 2003

Chapter One

THE CONTEMPORARY CRISIS ☐ IN JOURNALISM

It could be said that in the contemporary world nothing is more important than information. For at least 400 years, journalism has occupied a pivotal place in the transmission of information in societies all around the world, and yet, as we enter the twenty-first century the status and nature of journalism, perhaps surprisingly, is unclear. Social, economic, political, and technological changes over the course of journalism's history have constantly shifted the context in which it operates, the methods used and the end products. The lack of universal notions of what journalism is, despite its global presence and long history, is evident in contemporary commentaries. John Hartley, for example, reflected this uncertainty in his comment in the launch issue of an academic journal on journalism in 2000:

> What is it that journalism does? News organisations exist where there is democracy and where there is not. They exist where government is largely open and where decision-making is largely secret. They can be found where parties are strong or weak, where public ownership of communications media is powerful or absent. How journalism differs in these various settings should be a subject of journalism studies around the globe. This requires broad historical and comparative perspectives that are so far underdeveloped in the typically nation-centred studies of the press.
>
> (Hartley, 2000: 56)

Hartley is right in saying that most studies of journalism eschew international comparisons, but new technologies directly impinging on journalism are allowing ways for researchers to begin to examine issues in journalism studies within a far more international context than previously. Journalism organisations, public and private, commercial and academic, mainstream and alternative, now offer a welter of data and information for researchers and students to draw on over the Internet, whether it is in the form of economic data on media markets, news content from around the world, or critical analyses of news media issues conducted by people both inside and outside the profession.

This book reviews a range of the dominant theoretical debates around journalism as they currently stand at the beginning of the twenty-first century. It does so with the express intent of drawing on new sources of information to provide as international as possible consideration of the core concerns in journalism studies. The availability of information varies wildly from nation to nation, so detailed systematic analysis of every nation with journalism simply isn't possible. By reviewing some of the most significant empirical data, exploring some of the paradigmatic theoretical frameworks, and using examples from around the world as illustrations, it is hoped that the reader will get a wider sense of the issues of contemporary journalism in the information age.

THE INFORMATION AGE

This book's title invokes one of the common themes of social and cultural commentary of the last 25 years or so. There is a widespread perception that the contemporary period is the beginning of a new phase in human society, with industrial society being replaced by what is most commonly called the information society. This notion has some problems, however, particularly in terms of attempts to apply it in a literal sense, rather than a metaphorical one. In other words, calling any particular country an information society is fraught with problems as to what characteristics determine the definitional boundary between an industrial society and an information society. As such, writers on the subject have been sceptical over its merits, one suggesting 'the information society has remained little more than a catchphrase or a slogan, more a matter of rhetoric than of reality' (Martin, 1995: 1).

By using the term Information *Age*, this book addresses this problem in a straightforward way. To historians, speaking of ages involves not so much defining specific places and time periods by certain criteria, but of offering a broad categorisation of behavioural trends over time (McQuail, 2000: 123). To give an example, there are still today a few isolated tribes who live via the hunter-gatherer lifestyle that the earliest modern humans lived by. Whilst much of the globe saw the emergence of agriculture many thousands of years ago (estimates suggest around 12,000 years or so), there was no simple cut-off point between hunter gathering and farming. Similarly, the transition from the Bronze Age to the Iron Age was no single event, but a gradual process of change. By using the term Information Age, then, what is being suggested is that we are possibly at the beginning of an era of transition from societies organised around industrial development to societies organised around information. One area where this process of transition can be seen most overtly in professional discourses is in journalism.

It's worth pointing out that in some ways, terms like information age or information society are misnomers. Modern humans are almost defined in relation to other animals by our capacity for the generation, transmission and recording of information. Current views about human evolution suggest that modern humans survived where Neanderthals became extinct, not because they were better adapted to the environmental conditions

2

around 50,000 years or so ago, but because they had a greater intellectual capacity, and crucially a greater capacity for communication between individuals. Modern humans have succeeded biologically because they are information-rich animals. The complexity of rituals and belief systems amongst hunter-gatherer tribes still extant today demonstrates the intricacy of human interpersonal and social communication, even without any media to record information. Some authors have gone further, arguing there is perhaps a genetic predisposition towards an interest in giving and receiving information, and we could therefore regard humans as being, in a very loose sense, 'hardwired for news' (Shoemaker, 1996). In this sense, the apparent desire for news and information humans exhibit in all kinds of different social systems is understandable, with only the degree and direction of our interests being shaped by the societies in which we live. It is also important to recognise that the roots of the current information age were sown a long time ago in the origins of humans learning how to represent information in recordable forms.

A BRIEF HISTORY OF HUMAN INFORMATION

Artefacts from the earliest humans give tantalising clues as to how those people lived and thought, but our efforts to decipher the meaning of notches and carvings on bone are generally speculative. By at least 37,000 years ago, though, early modern humans in southern Europe were painting the walls of caves, mostly with images of animals. Again the exact meanings of these paintings are uncertain, although archaeological evidence, along with some of the more unusual images (for example of half-human, half-animal figures), leads the current consensus to suggest that they are related to rituals probably to do with the hunter-gatherer lifestyle of people of the time. Cave art was unlikely to be just for aesthetic purposes, instead serving important social needs for Stone Age communities.

The progress to writing took at least another 30,000 years, with the earliest known appearing in Sumer around 3000 BC. By this time agriculture had been discovered and the nomadic hunter-gatherer lifestyle that early modern humans used was being gradually replaced by an agrarian, settled lifestyle. The first cities produced the first complex political and economic systems, and writing developed primarily to aid these systems. Something like 95 per cent of the writing found in ancient Sumer concerns trade (Wood, 1999: 30). Sometimes talk today of the information society relates it to the growing economic worth of information systems, but the earliest emergence of writing some 5,000 years ago is quite evidently demonstrating a fundamental relationship between economics and information.

Writing technologies developed relatively slowly, with stone and clay being eventually replaced by papyrus, then parchment, and eventually paper (arriving in Europe via the Silk Road in the eighth century AD). Printing technology followed in China and Korea in the eleventh century, but did not become widespread until the Europeans discovered it in the fifteenth century. Used first for printing books, then occasional pamphlets, it wasn't until the early seventeenth century that the first newspapers appeared in Europe. They spread to the New World at the end of the seventeenth century, but it wasn't until the nineteenth and early twentieth century that many other parts of the world saw their first newspapers.

What gives the idea of an age of information such potential power is the rapidity with which information and communication technologies (ICTs) have advanced over the last 150 years or so, compared to the last 5,000 years. Although people found different materials to write on (and write with, once ink was invented), the means of gathering and disseminating information were still extremely limited. Even when printing arrived, little changed in terms of gathering or transmitting information over any distance. Information, and post-printing, journalism, could only be transmitted as fast as a horse could run, a bird could fly, or a ship could sail.

If one were looking for a starting point for the information society, a good candidate would be the development of the electric telegraph in the mid-1800s. By this time the industrial revolution was in full flight, and there were therefore the means to develop new ideas and technologies in ways never previously possible. Already inventions like steam-powered transport, the railroad and steamships were shrinking the geographical gaps between communities, nations, and continents. With the telegraph, there were equally major social changes as a result of its rapid information transmission capabilities. Today, the impact of the telegraph is often forgotten, superseded by later inventions like radio, the telephone, television, and the Internet, but in its heyday, the global rhetoric about the telegraph was remarkably similar to contemporary rhetoric about the Internet (see Standage, 1998, for an interesting overview of this period).

For journalism, the impact of both new transportation technologies and the telegraph revolutionised the way news was made. It is no accident that the global news agencies that still dominate the world, Reuters, Associated Press and Agence-France Press, had their origins in the nineteenth century (the former two associations began in direct relationship to the new telegraph technology). Although it is much debated, there is also an indication that the technology of the telegraph contributed to changes in both journalism style, and journalists' self-perception as to their roles and responsibilities, particularly in the USA.

The telegraph did not become a news medium in itself, with a few notable exceptions, but later technologies would afford journalists new media through which to ply their trade, not least radio and film, which for the first half of the twentieth century at least began to play an increasingly significant role in news provision in the developed world at least. Both of these media added important new audio and visual dimensions to the provision of news, but radio prospered because of its potential for immediacy and live broadcasting. When television began properly after the Second World War (having appeared first in the late 1930s in Britain), it took away the newsreels' main selling point, as a medium of visual record, and also had the addition of radio's immediacy. Yet while the newsreels died out, their importance and audience appeal, both before and during the Second World War when they reached hundreds of millions of people weekly, should not be underestimated.

Television developed relatively rapidly, within a few short decades offering the possibility of live broadcasts via satellite of events on and even off-world (with the 1969 moon landing) that could be broadcast all over the world. But in this recent period when television news increasingly began to take on a global outlook, a new medium began to take off with audiences that both offered new opportunities, and undermined the existing spheres of authority for traditional news media. Computers, developed during the Second World War as code-breaking machines began to impinge upon routine work practices by the 1970s, and into people's homes, mainly through games consoles, in the 1980s. It was at this point that some authors began to talk about the emergence of the information society, such as John Naisbett in his 1982 book *Megatrends*.

At the start of the 1990s, the network of computers linked by telecommunication lines that for many years had been sole preserve of the US military, and a few scientific associations, began to come into public use. The Internet, as it was dubbed, with its potential for multi-format capacity (for text, sound, still and moving images), and with its interactivity, suddenly gave audiences a degree of autonomy and potential authorial control that no previous news medium had allowed. Moreover the rate at which this new technology has begun to reach audiences is unprecedented. As one practising British journalist pointed out:

> It took 38 years for radio to amass 50 millions users. It took 13 years for television to do it. The Internet has done it in just 4.

> (Yelvington, 1999: 16)

The extent to which any one nation may have begun to restructure itself socially, culturally, politically and economically in relation to the growth of information and communication technologies is difficult to measure in any absolute way, although one could safely argue that no nation has yet become a genuine information society. What can be said, however, is that nations and supranational bodies like the European Union, have come to regard the information society as part and parcel of the policy agenda for the future. As the technologies are becoming more widespread, and political and economic agendas become dominated by ICT-related concerns, one can also say that the age of information is definitely upon us, even if a true information society is not with us yet.

THE CURRENT CRISIS

It may sound from the brief history of information outlined above that contemporary journalism should have the greatest potential it has ever had and that humanity now has the greatest ever range of communication tools. It may seem strange then that despite all these technological developments that have enabled and shaped journalism's development, concern about the future of journalism has arguably never been more vociferously presented than at the present time. Serious criticism of journalism has occurred throughout its history and is nothing new, what is different, or at least what appears to be different, is the nature and extent of contemporary criticisms that seem to have spread outside particular national systems and are being voiced in similar ways across the globe. The particular concerns of what could be dubbed the contemporary crisis in journalism have mostly been articulated in developed nations, although many of the concerns relate to journalism globally. These criticisms are not just the complaints of idealistic academics, or disgruntled senior journalists, although both of these groups are well represented in the debate, but have become major talking points in mainstream journalism and in popular debates.

In some countries the rhetoric is apocalyptic, with British writers talking about the 'death of news' (for example Cohen, 1998). In Britain, with a rampantly commercial newspaper market and a broadcasting industry in the throes of fundamental transformation from a decades old traditional analogue system to the new multi-channel digital future, debates about news media have been high profile for at least a decade. Senior journalists and academics have been writing with concern about trends in journalism at least since the 1980s, with recent works such as Bob Franklin's *Newszak and News Media* (1997) and Steven Barnett and Ivor Gaber's *Westminster Tales* (2001), for example, raising the critical stakes by talking explicitly about crises and fundamental shifts in journalism standards.

In the USA, despite the news media always having operated in a largely commercial environment, debates about journalism standards have been equally vociferous, if not more so in recent years. Senior journalists have participated in the US version of the debate, notably James Fallows whose 1996 book *Breaking the News* is explicit in its criticisms of the standards and status of contemporary US journalism. William Hachten chipped in with his 1998 book *The Troubles of Journalism*, and some authors have written books that go back to basics in their critique of the state of US journalism, such as Jay Rosen's *What Are Journalists For?* (1999). Rosen and others have advocated what has come to be called public or civic journalism, a pro-active effort from journalists to regain a social and political function and to revitalise America's apathetic democracy (more on this in Chapter 8).

In France, the prominent sociologist Pierre Bourdieu gave lectures on television and journalism that not only articulated very similar concerns to those expressed in Britain and the USA, but generated a major public debate about the state of French news media through both the broadcasting of his talks, and their publication in *On Television and Journalism* (1998). Even in countries where such debates have not been significantly raised, their presence in nations traditionally dominant in global news hierarchies, like Britain, the USA, and France, has prompted researchers to investigate whether the same trends are evident in other countries also, for example, in Germany (for example Esser, 1999).

The more one looks around at journalism across the globe, the more one sees the notion of crisis, or at the very least notions of uncomfortable transition, apparent in many nations. The crises of journalism in developing nations are in many ways very different, having more to do with basic rights of journalists being able to do their job without fear of intimidation, arrest, and even torture and murder. Nonetheless, there is an internationally recognised set of concerns about the role of journalism in societies that are being raised, albeit in different ways in different countries.

It may seem strange to equate the crises of developed world journalism with the often life or death concerns of journalists in the developing and non-democratic nations, or even to use the term crisis at all in the context of developed democracies. But in order to effectively examine the issues of journalism in the information age the key elements of the contemporary crisis in parts of the developed world need to be outlined, so that debates about specific aspects of journalism's organisation, practice and influence can be judged within contemporary attitudes to the profession as whole.

DECLINING AUDIENCES

Perhaps the biggest shock to the system for journalism organisations in many developed nations has been the decline in audiences for traditional news media, particularly in the newspaper industry. The status of audiences amongst traditional news media lies, in some ways, at the core of the rhetoric of crisis and is a useful place to begin unravelling this clamour of concern. Newspaper industries that expanded their audience reach for decades, in some cases even centuries, have found themselves approaching the millennium in a brave new world. There has been a significant degree of industry rhetoric expressing concern about declining newspaper markets, both within individual countries and coming from international bodies such as the World

Association of Newspapers (WAN) and the International Newspaper Marketing Association (INMA). Earl Wilkinson, the Executive Director of INMA, summed up the broad market position of newspapers in a presentation in August 1999:

> Depending on your source of information, newspaper circulation has been in steady decline or stagnant in most Western countries since the 1970s. As a percentage of population, paid circulation has been in decline in many countries since the 1950s.
>
> (Wilkinson, 1999: 2)

As one might expect, however, the real picture is more complicated than a simple case of uniform audience decline. In some markets signs of decline are pretty marked, whilst in others audiences not only remain buoyant, but are also on the rise. There's little doubt, though, that many nations are experiencing problems, including many in the English speaking parts of the world. Wilkinson went on to give examples of declining audiences in the 1990s, with countries such as Australia (2 per cent), Canada (9 per cent), New Zealand (5 per cent), Britain (5.5 per cent), and the USA (5.25 per cent), all experiencing declines between 1994 and 1998 (1999: 2). In the frequent *World Press Trends*, produced by the WAN, evidence suggests similar trends across many European nations in the 1990s (summarised in Papathanassopoulos, 2001: 111, who offers an analysis of the declining newspaper audience in Greece).

The last ten years or so may simply be the tip of the iceberg for a newspaper industry in an uncertain future. Recent declines need to be put into longer term contexts in each nation to genuinely explore whether the disappearing audience aspect of the crisis is real or not, global or not. One way to do this is to explore a few nations in a bit more detail. Picking representative nations is not easy but good places to explore, perhaps, would be some of the most prominent nations, economically, politically, and also in media terms. If amongst the global leaders there are signs of decline and crisis, then arguably there may at least be the roots of long-term problems for news media around the globe. For the purposes of this illustration, four nations have been chosen that represent the historical, political and economic forces that have dominated the globe over the last century or so: Britain, the USA, Germany and Japan. Daily newspaper circulations for roughly the last 30 years or so are presented in Figures 1.1 to 1.4, and the subsequent sections discuss the trends apparent in these figures.

Britain

Britain's newspaper market has experienced the most persistent and drawn out downturn in newspaper readership of any of the major newspaper nations, as shown in

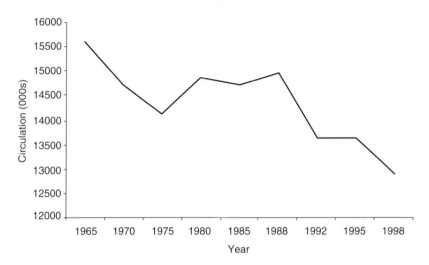

Figure 1.1   British national daily newspaper circulation 1965–1998. Source: Seymour-Ure, 1991. Used with permission from Blackwell Publishers Ltd.

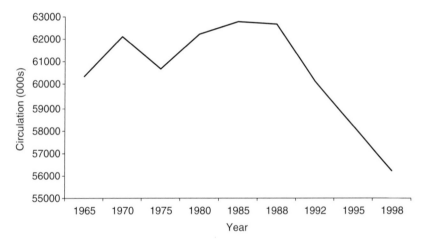

Figure 1.2   US national daily newspaper circulation 1965–1998. Source: *Editor and Publisher* Magazine, New York.

Figure 1.1. The structure and organisation of British media in both the press and broadcasting have served as models for many other nations to follow, but few other nations of such status have seen their newspaper industries decline in terms of audience appeal as has occurred in Britain.

British newspaper readership is quite distinct in comparison to other European nations, in that the majority of newspaper sales occur amongst national newspapers, produced

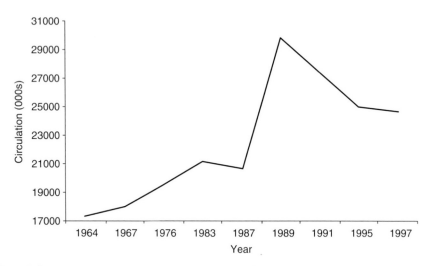

Figure 1.3   German national daily newspaper circulation 1964–1997. Source: Media Perspektivan.

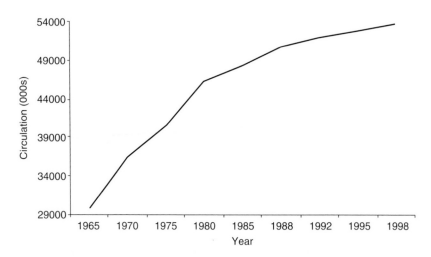

Figure 1.4   Japanese national daily newspaper circulation 1965–1998.

in London, and distributed across the whole of Britain. National newspapers first overtook regional titles in terms of sales in the 1920s and have remained dominant ever since. However, since the mid-1950s when national newspaper circulation peaked there has been an overall and largely consistent decline amongst national newspaper audiences. The one blip in this period when newspaper sales appeared to recover some-what was during the so-called 'newspaper revolution' in the mid-1980s. A combin-ation of aggressive re-organisations of industry working practices initiated by the likes of Rupert Murdoch and backed by the government, coupled with the introduction of new production technologies, saw a flurry of new national newspapers launched from 1986. The respite from decline was short-lived, however, as the majority of these papers failed to achieve commercial viability, with only two titles from that era currently surviving.

The decline of the national daily press is mirrored in other parts of the newspaper industry, and the decline in national Sunday newspapers has been even more marked. Across the same period as displayed in the figure above, national Sunday newspapers in Britain declined in circulation from just under 24 million sales in 1965 to just over 14 million in 1998. Indeed, from a peak of around 30 million sales in the mid-1950s, audiences have more than halved in the intervening time (for early figures see Seymour-Ure, 1991; more recent figures from the British Audit Bureau of Circulation).

Britain's regional press, meanwhile, has exhibited two slightly contradictory trends in the post-Second World War period. There has been evidence of declining audiences in some areas, but there have been some significant variations complicating the picture. Paid-for regional daily newspapers, for example, have generally been declining in circulation from sales of around 11 million at the beginning of the 1960s, dropping to around 5 million by the end of 1995 (Franklin, 1997: 104). In recent years there has been a lot of movement in the regional newspaper market, with some markets expanding, such as in Scotland where newspaper consumption has largely been very distinct from the rest of mainland Britain (see Meech and Kilborn, 1992, for a discussion of the Scottish media landscape).

Another significant trend has been the growth in free newspapers, funded entirely by advertising and costing readers nothing, that have increasingly replaced paid-for regional newspapers. In 1975 there were 185 free regional newspapers (Franklin, 1997: 104), whilst by 2001 there were over 600 free weekly newspapers (overtaking paid-for weeklies), 9 free Sunday titles, and 7 daily morning free papers (Newspaper Society, 2001). The move into the daily markets by free newspapers in recent times has arguably bolstered daily circulation figures, which including the free titles stood at an average of around 6.3 million per day at the end of 2000 (ibid). On the surface with total weekly circulation of almost 72 million copies, across nearly 1,300 titles, Britain's regional press would seem to be relatively healthy. We'll return to Britain's regional press in relation to another part of the crisis that brings this 'healthy' state into question.

USA

In the last decade, audiences for traditional news media in the USA have been declining in significant proportions (see Figure 1.2). Unlike Britain, US newspaper readership peaked a lot more recently, in the 1980s, but the current downturn in daily news-paper sales sees circulation at the lowest point since the 1940s. Furthermore, US newspaper circulation has clearly risen and fallen over the last 30 to 40 years or so, but looking at consumption trends another way shows that circulation in the USA has grown barely 4 per cent in the last 50 years in comparison to an 81 per cent increase in popu-lation (Wilkinson, 2000: 1). Most of the overall increase represented by this figure has occurred in the increasing audience for Sunday newspapers, but whilst there are an awful lot more Americans out there than in 1940, large proportions of them are not reading daily newspapers.

A pretty clear indication of this comes from surveys examining the frequency of news-paper readership amongst readers. There has been a significant decline in the num-bers of Americans claiming to read a newspaper every day. In 1975, for example, surveys suggested that around two-thirds (66 per cent) of Americans read a newspaper every day, but by 1996, this had declined to only 42 per cent (Schoenbach et al., 1999: 231). Further analysis of readership against sociodemographic factors suggests that there is a relationship between the frequency of newspaper reading and age, with older readers tending to read more frequently (ibid.: 35). Concerns about the media use or lack of it amongst the young is a notable factor in another aspect of the crisis argument, that of civic decay (see below).

Other survey research in the US has shown that this move away from traditional media outlets is also impacting on television news. Again, younger viewers tend to watch tele-vision news a lot less frequently that older viewers (Pew Research Centre, 2000), but across all age groups attention to network news programmes has declined significantly in the 1990s. As recently as 1994, some 74 per cent of Americans reported watching a news programme the previous night, but this had fallen to a figure of 55 per cent by 2000 (ibid.), with only 30 per cent claiming to regularly watch network news, and with only 23 per cent of respondents claiming to have spent an hour or more watching TV news each day. In local news too regular programme viewing dropped in the last decade, from some 77 per cent in 1993 to 56 per cent in 2000 (ibid.). Partly, such trends have to do with the fragmentation of the audience, due to the rise of cable net-works, and subsequently the Internet – by 2000 some 54 per cent of Americans reported going online, compared to just 21 per cent in 1996 (ibid.). The threat of new technology is another factor in the crisis argument.

Germany
Similarly to the USA, the German newspaper market expanded through much of the post-war period, peaking in the late 1980s only to begin falling in the 1990s, even after unification between West and East Germany in 1990 (see Figure 1.3). Of course,

the context of news audience trends in Germany is very different to that of either Britain or the US. For a start, in the immediate post-war period it was the occupying Allied nations that fundamentally restructured the German press, aiming to ensure both pluralism and a move away from state controlled media (see Humphreys, 1994 for a detailed discussion). Newspaper audiences continued to rise until the middle of the 1980s when a decline first appeared. Reunification at the end of the 1980s saw a sudden expansion of the press as the East German press was integrated into the Federal Republic's media system. It did not take long for the decline to reassert itself, however, and if anything accelerate slightly as the old East German press was subsumed into the West's media companies.

Although absolute circulation appears to be on the decline, unlike the USA there has yet to emerge evidence of a similar decline in the frequency of regular newspaper reading. The proportion of respondents declaring themselves as reading newspapers 'regularly' stood at 74 per cent in 1974, and stayed around this level into the late 1980s, dropping in the mid 1990s to 68 per cent (Schoenbach *et al.*, 1999: 231). Schoenbach *et al.* went further in reporting changes in newspaper readership patterns in Germany and the US, exploring whether socio-demographic factors accounted for differing trends in newspaper consumption, particularly the differing rates of decline. Although the researchers failed to find any strident demographic determinants of newspaper consumption they did note that in both countries older people with higher paying jobs tended to read more newspapers than other groups, but whilst in the US education and gender also seemed to relate to greater propensity for newspaper readership, in Germany they were less important than social factors like marital status, and the size of community (ibid.: 237). Linking to this possible importance of community, one important factor within the German newspaper market may explain the more general audience decline in relation to another trend in the German newspaper industry, and the next key aspect of the crisis thesis, declining diversity.

Before moving on though, it's worth reiterating that to a greater or lesser extent in Western Europe and North America at least, many mature environments like the US, Britain and Germany are experiencing varying degrees of audience decline, at least in the newspaper sector. Looking further afield, the developing world is far more difficult to judge, as there are still many countries that do not have the infrastructure to support significant newspaper industries, and many also retain authoritarian regimes that restrict what news is available, and therefore possibly the potential for expanding audiences or for that matter audience decline. In post-Soviet Russia, for example, once widely read papers like *Pravda*, which many people read to look like good citizens, rapidly lost their audience and went out of business to be replaced by new nominally independent titles. In some developing nations, however, newspaper readership has been increasing as standards of living and literacy have increased. In India, for example, newspaper readership has expanded five-fold as literacy rates have increased from around 50 million people in 1951 to some 352 million in 1991, according to the Census of India 1991.

If that suggests that the declining audience problem is a symptom of a developed nation's media consumption there are exceptions here too. In Scandinavia, for example, newspaper readership remained high throughout most of the second half of the twentieth century, with only small signs of possible declines in the last few years of the century (for example in Norway no decline appeared until 1995, Eide, 1997: 173). In terms of large nations, Japan would seem to offer a particularly good example of a mature media environment that showed no sign, at least up until the turn of the millennium, that its media industries were in a crisis over audiences.

Japan

Like Britain, Japan has a mixed market of very successful national titles as well as a regional market. Unlike Britain, though, the Japanese newspaper market is robust. Japan is also very different to the USA, with newspaper production having outstripped population growth by 3 to 1 (Hamilton, 2000: 94). Like Germany, allied occupation immediately after the war saw deliberate efforts to instil a Western free press model on the Japanese news media, but unlike Germany there's little sign as yet of decline. Surveys indicate a pretty consistent figure of around 80 per cent of people reading a newspaper daily, with a proportion of 1.13 newspaper subscriptions for every one of the 47 million households in Japan according to the Japan Newspaper Publishers and Editors Association (http://wwwpressnet.or/jp). As shown by Figure 1.4, since 1965, daily newspaper circulation has been on a continual rise, only levelling out in 1997 to 1998.

Some sources put absolute circulation higher than the figures here, at over 70 million newspapers daily (Cooper-Chen, 1997: 52; Hamilton, 2000: 94). Certainly newspaper readership is endemic, with the national titles accounting for at least 50 per cent of daily newspaper circulation, and having individual circulations that dwarf the largest newspapers in Britain, Germany, or America. The *Yomiuri Shimbun*, for example, was selling around 14 million copies per day, and *Asahi Shimbun* was selling around 12 million copies daily in 1999 (ibid.: 96), at least three times the circulation of leading titles *Bild Zeitung* in Germany (achieving about 4 million sales), or *The Sun* in Britain (about 3.5 million), or America's leading title *USA Today* (on a little under 2.5 million).

So Why the Declines?

Newspaper industries in these and other nations are clearly experiencing distinct trends relating to the particular socio-cultural and politico-economic conditions of each country. It is certainly premature at this point in time to argue that a global trend for declining audiences in traditional news industries is apparent. Nonetheless, it would be difficult to disagree that in some nations at least, certain sectors of the traditional news media are indeed in a genuine crisis in relation to audiences. But declining newspaper audiences, on their own, do not tell us very much about the contemporary state of journalism. They have to be seen in the context of a range of other aspects which declining audiences are both a possible cause and a likely consequence of. In order to understand possible reasons for these audience trends, and industry and academic rhetoric of crises in journalism, these other elements needs to be outlined as well.

DECLINING DIVERSITY

Whatever the overall trend in audiences may be, even in nations where audiences are stable, or rising, another trend features in expressed concerns about journalism's contemporary crisis. Declining audiences in some markets puts pressure on news organisations that make them vulnerable to takeover or closure within those markets, and also encourages media organisations to look abroad for new opportunities for profit-making. Expanding markets in other countries attract the attention of global media players looking to expand operations and improve profit margins. The extent to which news media ownership is increasingly being characterised by the dominance of global organisations, and how national systems are being directly or indirectly affected as a result of these corporate giants would appear to be a development distinct to the modern era. Amongst the various concerns about this trend that have been expressed perhaps the most persistent and widespread is the concern over diversity.

The diversity question relates strongly to issues around the social role of journalism and what organisational structures best allow journalism to fill that role effectively. These issues will be discussed in more detail in the next two chapters, as will the extent of change in the contemporary news media market. For now, a commentary relating to the 1999 merger between CBS and Viacom, two of the world's largest media companies at that time, offers a neat summary of why diversity should be an issue at all. Commenting more directly on the US Federal Communication Commission's contemporaneous decision to relax its rules on local broadcasting ownership (that had prevented companies from owning two stations in the same market), Jerome Barron identified three core elements of what he calls the rationales for diversity (2000: 557). He states:

> The *first* is to encourage greater gender, ethnic, and racial diversity in the ownership of broadcast stations. The *second* is to limit multiple ownership of the media in order to maximise diversity of viewpoint in programming. The third is based on the idea that media deconcentration rules will prevent 'undue concentration of economic power contrary to the public interest'.

> Limiting concentration minimises the ability of a small group of corporate
> media to dominate the local opinion process.
>
> (Original emphasis, Barron, 2000: 557)

Diversity then is seen to play a crucial role in providing a range of viewpoints, a limiting of concentration of influence within too few hands, and ensuring a range of groups within society get access to media production. These are pretty typical ideas underlying debates in many countries about the need for, and concerns about the decline in, the diversity of news media outlets audiences have access to.

It is perhaps in broadcasting where the most obvious and dramatic developments have occurred relating to issues of diversity, both on the national and international levels. In the developed markets of North American and Western Europe, regulatory and market structures have been in a period of major change over the last decade or so, bringing this issue of diversity and public interest to the fore. Some of these developments in broadcasting will be discussed in more detail in the next couple of chapters, particularly Chapter 3. By way of some illustration of the diversity concerns for this introduction, re-examining some of the newspaper markets described provides evidence of trends that have caused concern in these terms, irrespective of whether audiences have been declining or increasing.

Looking again at Germany, for example, whilst audiences continued to rise through much of the post war period, the range of newspapers audiences had to choose from reduced. In absolute terms, before unification to some extent artificially restored the figures, the number of editions being produced in Germany went from 1,500 in 1954 to 1,273 in 1985 (*Media Perspektiven Basisdaten* 1999: 45). Alongside this, the number of publishers declined across the same period from 624 in 1954 to 382 in 1985, and unlike the number of editions this has continued to fall post-unification to a figure of 355 in 1999 (ibid.). The German method of newspaper production, however, means that editorial content is not produced directly by publishers, but by independent editorial units (*Publizistische Einheiten*), whose content is then spread by publishers across many different regional and local editions. These independent editorial units have also declined since the 1950s, with 225 in 1954, reaching a low of 119 in 1989, and after unification levelling out at 135 between 1995 and 1999 (ibid.). In effect then whether audiences have been increasing or declining in the German newspaper market, concentration of ownership and a narrowing of diversity and choice have increased.

In the US, trends of ownership and range of outlets in the newspaper industry are slightly more complicated. Overall numbers of daily titles hovered in the 1700s from the end of the Second World War to the beginning of the 1980s, before beginning to decline to a figure of some 1489 titles as of 1998 (*NAA*). Within that decline, though, there has been a significant shift in the balance between morning and evening titles. Morning titles have gradually increased since the war, from some 330 in 1945, to more than double that with 721 in 1998 (ibid.). Evening titles, on the other hand, have been going in the other direction, from some 1419 in 1945 to just over half that number, 781 in 1998 (ibid.). Matching the overall increase in circulation, Sunday newspaper titles have largely increased also, going from some 485 in 1945 to 898 in 1998, although as with circulation, there are signs that the Sunday newspaper market is currently levelling out (ibid.). In terms of ownership the US press is arguably not as dominated by a few companies as other countries' newspaper industries, or the US broadcasting industry, although some 80 per cent of the USA's daily titles are in the hands of 129 companies and trends for concentration of ownership appear to be accelerating (Hachten, 1998: 74–5). Currently though, even the biggest publisher, Gannett, owns only about 7 per cent of the daily titles and achieves about 14 per cent of total daily circulation (for more on Gannett see Chapter 3).

Mixed messages then appear to come from the US newspaper market, but looking at trends in newspaper ownership in another way reveals a more worrying development in terms of diversity. In 1965, some 70 US cities had competing daily newspapers, owned by different companies, and some 150 cities at least had two daily titles, even if the same company owned them. But 30 years on, only 36 cities still had competing daily titles, and only 26 still had two titles owned by the same company (Katz, 1995: 15). Even in the largest US cities the decline in competition in news is startling, for example, New York once had 14 competing daily newspapers (Hachten, 1998: 74). Now it has three, and according to journalist and commentator Howard Kurtz 'the only reason you have two tabloid newspapers in New York is that you have two rich men with large egos who are prepared to subsidise them' (in Katz, ibid.). Quite clearly these kinds of developments narrow the range of choice for US newspaper readers, and may be a factor underlying declining newspaper audiences. On the other hand, economic pressures in a market with declining audiences means that group ownership makes sense. Despite his reservations about group ownership Hachten points out that in the US press at least group ownership is very profitable, providing economic stability, and arguably keeping some titles afloat (1998: 76).

In Britain, the issue of concentration of ownership and declining diversity has been a major issue throughout the post-war period in both the national and regional press, and this conflict between what may make economic sense in terms of profitable business, and what's in the public interest, is much more pronounced. To give an illustration that compares interestingly with the US and German newspaper markets, Britain's regional newspaper market is heavily dominated by a small number of companies, some of which have become part of global concerns. As of 2001, the top 20 publishers accounted for 85 per cent of all titles (that's some 1086 titles out of a bit under 1300) and 96 per cent of the total weekly circulation (some 69 million out of 72 million copies). In some parts of the regional market the dominance of the leading companies is strident. The leading 20 companies are responsible for all of the regional Sunday newspapers and 93 of 99 daily titles, accounting for some 98 per cent of regional daily circulation (based on data from the Newspaper Society (2001)). Of those 20 companies the top 5 companies alone control over half the titles (57.4 per cent, 737 titles), and over two-thirds (70.6 per cent) of total weekly circulation (ibid.).

These companies are clearly not satisfied and want to expand further, and have been lobbying hard in recent years for relaxation of media ownership restrictions, but these efforts have been met by some vocal opposition, including former national newspaper editor turned media analyst, Roy Greenslade, who commented:

> Papers have always straddled the line between public service and private profit, finding a way to make them mutually compatible for the benefit of both the reader and the owner. The balance between the two is delicate. What I fear is the tearing asunder of all regulations will create an imbalance which could, in the long run, destroy our national network of local and regional newspapers. In the long term, profit will eclipse all sense of public purpose.
>
> (Greenslade, 2000: 7)

For some then, diversity is something more than simply an issue of economics and relates far more to the social function of journalism, whatever that might be. In some European countries efforts at limiting declining diversity has been far more pro-active than in Britain, with systems of press subsidies to support diversity and representation, with varying degrees of success (the role of state subsidy systems will be discussed in the next chapter). Whether states have engaged with this issue in a regulatory capacity or not, the tenor of debates about diversity remain remarkably consistent from country to country, and Greenslade's comment here is typical of many expressed across the globe.

Some of these industry developments are merely continuations of pre-war trends in commercially run news media markets. What does appear to be a distinctly new feature of contemporary media, and one of the reasons for the consistency of expressed concern, is the trend for increasing multi-national control of media, including news media. One of the best known commentators on the growth of multi-national corporate control of the media is Ben Bagdikian, through his seminal work *The Media Monopoly*. In an extract from the latest edition on US public broadcaster PBS's website, Bagdikian indicates just how rapid changes in ownership have been since the first edition of his book:

> When the first edition of this book was published in 1983, fifty corporations dominated most of every mass medium and the biggest media merger in history

was a $340 million deal ... By the time the second edition was published in
1987, the fifty companies had shrunk to twenty-nine. By the third edition in
1990, the twenty-nine had shrunk to twenty-three, by the fourth edition to
fourteen. By the fifth edition in 1997, the biggest firms numbered ten and
involved the $19 billion Disney-ABC deal, at the time the biggest media
merger ever. But the 'biggest' of 1983, worth $340 million, would give way
seventeen years later to AOL Time Warner's $350 billion merged corporation,
more than 1,000 times larger ... But today there is an even smaller number
of dominant firms – six (even excluding the AOL-Time Warner deal) and
those six have more communications power that all the combined fifty leading
firms of sixteen years earlier.

(Bagdikian, 2001)

This trend for the growth of media companies into global companies with massive
assets and vast markets is at the heart of many debates not only about the state and
nature of contemporary journalism and the media, but also about the emergence of the
information society. The AOL Time Warner deal was not only the biggest media merger
in history, but was one of the biggest merger deals in any industry sector. Media companies have increasingly become amongst the most powerful and important corporations in the global economy, and because the products they control relate to culture and
information, it could be said that these companies have potentially the greatest amount
of power and influence in contemporary society.

Concentration and conglomeration of ownership has consequences for the working
practices of regular journalists, to be discussed later in the book, and may also be impacting on the consumption habits of news audiences. Academic and political concerns
about diversity in the news audiences receive may be reflected in the declining audience
trends, as citizens reject the corporate approach to news production. When readers only
have one local paper to choose, and if it follows an editorial line dictated from a headquarters in another part of the country, or even on another continent, it is little wonder
that there seems to be a simple relationship between the spread of corporate control and
the decline in audiences' consumption of news. What is remarkable about this trend,
perhaps, is that the major corporations seem blind to this, consumed as they are by the
pursuit of new acquisitions and greater market share, at the expense of citizen's satisfaction, with their only solution to declining audience satisfaction to be to increase certain
kinds of (presumed to be) popular news content in a process dubbed tabloidization.

TABLOIDIZATION

Tabloidization, sometimes more colloquially referred to as 'dumbing down', refers to
a number of characteristics of contemporary journalism linked to a particular kind of

journalism, tabloid journalism, that does appear, or is at least assumed to be, a successful strategy for maintaining or increasing audiences. What this actually means, though, is more complicated than one might think, as is judging the global extent of tabloidization.

Originating from the term for a particular size of newspaper format (roughly half the size of a conventional newspaper), the concept of tabloid news has grown to refer to far more than simply a particular size of newspaper, to cover issues of content (for example the use of photographs), style and trends in broadcast journalism. Colin Sparks suggests three aspects of the tabloidization thesis (2000). First, in both print and broadcast journalism, tabloid news is distinct in it emphases, which can be summarised as the devoting of 'relatively little attention to politics, economics, and society and relatively much to diversions like sports, scandal and popular entertainment' and the devoting of 'relatively much attention to the personal and private lives of people, both celebrities and ordinary people, and relatively little to political processes, economic developments, and social changes' (Sparks, 2000: 10). Quite clearly expressions of concern here relate to normative decisions about what are appropriate targets for journalists to pursue, with politico-economic and social issues deemed by critics more appropriate than sport and human interest.

Second, and a slightly broader feature, is 'a shift in the priorities within a given medium, away from news and information towards an emphasis on entertainment' (Sparks, 2000: 10–11). In this sense tabloidization is not simply about what the news does, but how 'news' is treated in the broader media landscape. For example, in British television where satellite and more recently digital television channels have begun to seriously fragment audiences, channels have been engaged in a widely criticised rescheduling of news and current affairs programmes in order to try and maximise audiences, with entertainment programming replacing news and current affairs. One example of this has been the debate over the moving of *News At Ten*, for some 40 years a flagship prime-time news programme on the main commercial terrestrial channel, ITV. The broadcasters lobbied the regulator for permission to move the news programme (to later in the schedule) in order to screen entertainment programming to retain audience share. Political opposition, and falling ratings for the replacement broadcasts, saw the regulator require the channel to reinstate the programme, but before it returned the BBC switched its prime-time news programme from 9pm to the 10pm slot, so now the news programmes of the two main channels on British television are in direct competition. The BBC, itself suffering from falling audience share, has also introduced controversial changes to its news and current affairs output, not least moving its prime-time news programme, but also in funding its 24-hour digital news channel out of existing news budgets without supplying additional resources, and in moving its flagship current affairs strand *Panorama* to a weekend late primetime slot.

These are just recent examples of changes in the British news media landscape in the last decade or so that have provoked some remarkably strident critiques. Bob Franklin's analysis of the state of contemporary news media in Britain, dubbed contemporary news as 'newszak', the informational equivalent of muzak. He states:

> Newszak is news converted into entertainment. The institutions of news media and practices of news journalism are more then ever coming to resemble a finely tuned piano which is capable of playing Bach or Beethoven, but too frequently insists on playing chopsticks ... The task of journalism has become merely to deliver and serve up whatever the customer wants; rather like a deep-pan pizza.
>
> (Franklin, 1997: 5)

Sparks' third sense of how tabloidization is articulated is that area where one begins to find opposition to criticisms such as Franklin's about the negative consequences of tabloidization. Sparks describes the third usage of tabloidization as denoting the 'shifting boundaries of taste within different media forms' (2000: 11). The particular targets here lie mainly in broadcasting trends for talk radio shows, confessional television talk shows, and most recently 'reality' TV shows, and contains a core critical presumption. Sparks offers a particularly useful insight into this particular criticism in saying that what is distinctive about these trends is 'that the wrong kinds of people (who are not accredited experts) talk about the wrong kinds of topics (their deeply private dilemmas and experiences) in the wrong kind of atmosphere (that of the game show) ... it is the populist tone and the rightist content that are being denounced' (ibid.).

Defenders of tabloids in the academic arena often point to this aspect as being too proscriptive and elitist (e.g. Fiske, 1989, see also McNair, 1998a, 2000). In the views of such authors, alternative subjects, topics, and modes of expression may have democratising consequences as previously marginalised topics and people are given a site that legitimates these concerns in a way that conventional non-tabloid journalism has simply refused to acknowledge. At the very least, if discussion of the way issues and people are represented in such new formats reaches the mainstream news media, that alone is enough to legitimate these new forms. (Discussion of some of these alternate forms of tabloid broadcasting appears in later chapters.) If working out what tabloidization *is* has its problems, then considering whether it is actually happening or not in any given country is really quite difficult to do.

In Britain, tabloidization is perhaps most clearly underway in the literal sense of many post-war newspapers switching to a tabloid format. Towards the end of the Second World War in 1945, British readers of national newspapers largely read broadsheet papers and there were only two tabloid papers. Since then, surviving newspapers have frequently changed to a tabloid format (e.g. *The Sun* in 1969, *The Daily Mail* in 1971, and *The Daily Express* in 1977), and many newspapers launched in the post-war period have been tabloid in format (for example the *Daily Star* in 1978, and the *Mail on Sunday* in 1982) (for more details see Seymour-Ure, 1991: 32–3). Even within the broadsheet press, tabloidization has occurred in this simple sense, with several papers converting sections of the paper to a tabloid format (the pioneer was the *Guardian* in the late 1980s, with others following in the 1990s). Britain traditionally had a very distinct national newspaper market where the division between popular tabloid newspapers and serious elite broadsheet newspapers has been very clear. In broadcasting too, there have been clear distinctions between public service and commercial broadcasters and the news they provide. Books like Franklin's offer detailed analysis of how these distinctions between serious and tabloid in both print and broadcasting have begun to dissolve, and not merely due to changes in production format (1997; see also Curran and Seaton, 1997).

In the US, on the other hand, the daily press is largely without the kind of tabloid newspapers seen in Britain. As mentioned, the largely monopolistic situation that particularly metropolitan newspapers have in their own markets, creates much less pressure on US newspapers to move towards tabloid strategies, as they do not have to compete for audiences. Instead, tabloidization appears to be a feature in one small but not insignificant area of the print media, the so called 'supermarket' tabloids like the *National Enquirer*, and more widely in broadcasting, particularly television. Scathing attacks on the tabloid news values of US TV news are widespread. Matthew Kerbel's *If It Bleeds, It Leads*, an innovative critique of US TV news using the content of actual stories to hoist the journalists by their own petards, offers a highly cynical view of the approach to news (2000). In one section he talks about the annual ratings 'sweeps' that occur every few months, and are significant for broadcasting stations' market share and thus ad revenue. To get the best results during the sweeps, Kerbel says:

> ... means rolling out the most gripping, the most exciting, the most entertaining news shows of the year. A crime that would merely 'rock a normally peaceful neighbourhood' in April would 'leave residents reeling in disbelief' in May. A 'potentially dangerous' January snowfall would 'pack a punch perhaps potent enough to be the storm of the century' if it had the good fortune to strike in February. A warehouse fire is 'dramatic' in October. In November, it's 'dramatic and suspicious'.
>
> (Kerbel, 2000: 51–2)

In Latin America, similarly, there has been a lack of mass market newspaper trends of tabloid news, but on television tabloid style news and current affairs programmes are rife (Hallin, 2000: 268). 'La Nota Roja' as it's known in Mexico, for example, consists of large numbers of both current affairs and news programmes using sensationalised and dramatic styles of presentation and proving both highly popular and controversial, so much so that two of the most popular programmes in the 1990s, *Ciudad Desnuda* (Naked City) and *Fuera de la Ley* (Outside the Law), were eventually cancelled by their channels (ibid.: 268).

What such nations share, regardless of where tabloidization emerges or in what forms, is the general concern over negative consequences of such forms of journalism. In other countries, however, the basic logic of the tabloid model is turned on its head. In Norway, for example, popular tabloids have emerged in recent decades (particularly *VG* and *Dagbladet*) but analysts suggest that tabloids in Norway are more often simply tabloid in format and that the associated style is not present (Eide, 1997: 181). In Germany, whilst the best selling national paper *Bild* is a tabloid (within most understandings of that term), attempts to use tabloid styles to improve audiences in the local press have largely been unsuccessful, in one author's view because audiences for local newspapers in Germany want information not entertainment (Schönbach, 2000: 72). Meanwhile in Japan, the dominant newspapers (*Yomiuri* and *Asahi*) were originally the Japanese equivalent of tabloids (known as Ko-shimbun, or 'little' papers), and their large circulation is seen there as evidence, not of dumbing down for a mass audience (as might be perceived in Europe), but of high quality journalism (Hayashi, 2000: 149).

Those who favour the more positive appraisal of tabloid news would point to the success of tabloid news outlets in print and in broadcast media when compared to more serious forms of news (e.g. McNair, 1998a, 2000). Mass audiences undoubtedly seem to prefer tabloid news, and this may reflect their greater accessibility and consonance with public concerns. Critics, on the other hand, point to tabloidization as a causal factor in the overall decline in newspaper audiences. Newspaper audiences are falling because of perceived falling standards in the news which tabloidization represents (e.g. Franklin, 1997).

Either way, tabloidization is rather a broad-brush kind of criticism incorporating many elements. It is difficult to empirically assess criticisms of tabloidization in some regards, because they often amount to aesthetic criticisms – distaste for a style of news, akin to distaste for certain modes of film-making or art. But in some areas it is more possible to get an indication of changes in journalism, particularly in terms of the maintenance of standards that can be assessed to some extent through the activities of regulatory bodies. Esser's comparison of tabloidization in Britain, the USA and Germany included a comparison of complaints made to regulatory bodies in Britain (The Press Council up until 1990 and Press Complaints Commission subsequently), and Germany (the Presserat) (1999). Esser found that in Britain, 6 times as many complaints were received on average between 1988 and 1997 as in Germany, with

Britain generating an average around 2000 complaints per year, compared to 330 being made to the Presserat (Esser, 1999: 231). Making broader international comparisons is difficult without easy access to the data, but drawing on data from the Australian Press Council across roughly the same period, 1988–1999, the Australian body received an average around 400 complaints per year (APC, 2001).

Does this mean that the British press is 5 times worse than the Australian and 6 times worse that the German press? Or does it simply mean that British audiences are more sensitive and/or more proactive in their complaints than German or Australian audiences? This is very difficult to say with any certainty, but the high profile restructuring of the British press complaints body at the start of the 1990s may have been a factor, as could the British libel laws which are regularly and routinely used by celebrities and politicians unhappy at press treatment of them. In other words a culture of complaining about the press may exist in Britain that simply doesn't occur in many other countries. In Sweden, the Press Council was similarly restructured at the end of the 1960s, and after that time complaints to that body did increase significantly from a very low base to around 350 a year in the 1980s (Weibull and Börjesson, 1992: 131). Of course, this figure is still a long way off the British figures, and it would be difficult therefore to refute the notion that something must be evident in British press to generate these kinds of complaints to such a degree above those of other nations.

NEW TECHNOLOGY AND CIVIC DECAY

Another reason for the decline of conventional media audiences has been the emergence of new forms of information provision, forms which have the potential to so radically transform information production, dissemination and reception, it is little wonder that their inventions have been met with a mixture of delight and fear. All media have gone through similar periods when they first emerged. But the global reach of first satellite television, and then most recently the Internet, has raised the stakes yet again for those concerned about the social impact of the mass media. Unlike other mass media to have emerged, new ICTs seem to challenge all the basic assumptions about journalism. These issues will be explored at points throughout the book, and in detail in Chapter 10, but a useful summary here comes from John Pavlik, who suggests that new technologies affect journalism in at least four key ways. He states:

> Technological change affects: (1) the way journalists do their job, (2) the nature of news content; (3) the structure and organisation of the newsroom and the news industry; and (4) the nature of the relationships between and among news organisations and their many publics, including audiences, competitors, news sources, sponsors and those who seek to regulate or control the press.
>
> (Pavlik, 2000: 229)

In short, all aspects of journalism are transformed by new ICTs. Whether those transformations are positive or not is very much up for debate, particularly since they remain largely speculative at this stage. The transformations are happening, but their long term consequences on both the professional practice and social role of journalism are as yet unknown. Some writers, like Pavlik, are remarkably positive about these developments, whilst others move from caution to hostility over the potential negative consequences of new technologies.

One area where there has been a consistent thread of expressed concern is in the impact of ICTs on civil society within developed democracies. New media technologies are sometimes feted for offering ways to offset the concerns expressed about declining diversity. Satellite and cable television, for example, provide space for dozens of channels, as opposed to the handful that existed in the first phase of broadcasting in Europe and elsewhere, and new digital broadcasting technologies offer the potential of hundreds of channels for audiences to choose from. The Internet offers even more choice, with audiences able to choose from a multitude of online news sources from around the globe, as well being able to access information they previously would have had to get indirectly through the news media, whether that be government statistics, corporate or pressure group information, or even the views of participants in major global events (for example, during the Kosovan War of 1999, the International War and Peace Reporting website carried an open forum where citizens of the nations involved, including Serbs in bunkers whilst being bombed, gave their views on the conflict).

Such potential must be viewed within general trends of declining audiences for news. It is not simply that the audience is fragmenting between all these various new outlets, although that is happening, but also that audiences are turning away altogether from news. Multi-channel television and the Internet are replete with much more than just news, and it is entertainment programming and web content that is attracting audiences to these new outlets, not news. Breaking down the trends in declining audiences, discussed above, a bit further it can be seen that it is amongst the young in the developed world where news consumption is at its lowest. In the USA, for example, surveys suggest that only 17 per cent of people under the age of 30 regularly watch network news programmes, less than a third read newspapers on a daily basis, and only a third of that age group claim to enjoy keeping up with the news (Pew Research Centre, 2000). In terms of newspaper readership this trend is apparent in other countries as well, such as Germany (Schoenbach *et al.*, 1999: 235) and Greece, (Papathanassopoulos, 2001: 119–120).

The central concern over the lack of engagement with news amongst the young is what impact this will have on democracy in the long term. In the USA, Britain and the

European Union, declines in turnouts at elections, particularly amongst the young, have been seen as a consequence of, amongst other things, a failure of news media to adequately engage audiences with public and political affairs. These inadequacies have largely been seen, in turn, as a consequence of the other trends identified above, particularly tabloidization, with events like the Bill Clinton/Monica Lewinsky scandal offered as examples of a political press obsessed with personal scandals and sensationalism rather than serious representation and debate of issues of public importance.

In Britain, concerns about the impact of changes in journalism, and in government relations with journalism, have been persistently expressed and analysed in some detail (e.g. Franklin, 1994, 1997). One recent analysis of political journalism in Britain, argued that it was clearly in crisis, brought about by four key factors – the relationship between journalists and their political sources (to be discussed in more detail in Chapter 4), the impact of media ownership, the impact of increased competition produced by the arrival of new media outlets for news and fourth, the changing nature of the news profession (Barnett and Gaber, 2001: 4–9). These trends are seen as detrimental within the position that journalism, in all its forms:

> ... play[s] a fundamental role in relaying information which citizens require in order to make informed judgements about their political leaders and participate effectively in the proper functioning of a democratic state. Furthermore, thriving news media do not just relay but uncover relevant information: by so doing, they act as a check on government and inhibit abuse of political power.
>
> (Barnett and Gaber, 2001: 1)

Such a view reflects a very different set of assumptions about the role of journalism from those mentioned at the beginning of this section on the crisis in journalism. Within the industry itself, commercial imperatives see the primary concern being declining audiences for news in terms of declining profit margins. In this view the concern is about the impact on democracy, with declining audiences seen as a product of the tendency for the news media industry to focus on profits before the public interest. This conflict between perceptions of journalism as serving a social function and journalism as merely another business within the information society, is a vitally important aspect of debates within journalism studies and needs to be explained and explored more fully in order to begin to evaluate contemporary journalism. These notions of journalism also need to be put in the broader context of journalism that exists outside of the liberal capitalist democracies in which most of these debates have been formulated, to see if it is possible to resolve, or perhaps further complicate, the issues surrounding what journalism is, what it does, and what for.

OVERVIEW OF THE BOOK

This chapter has outlined some of the key question marks over contemporary journalism in the modern era, as well as indicating the broad conceptual framework within which debates about contemporary journalism are placed. Issues in journalism of the information age relate to core ideas about the social functions, production practices, and even the very nature of journalism. Through the course of this book, these core concerns will be examined, highlighting the central theoretical positions, and discussing these via a range of examples from all over the world in order to illustrate the state of modern journalism.

The book is broadly divided into three sections, the first dealing with what might be called external influences on journalism. Two chapters examine journalism in terms of the politico-economic factors that shape the journalism profession, principally the state and the market, looking at the fundamentally oppositional attitudes towards journalism as introduced above. The second section of the book looks more at the internal influences on journalism, inside the production process if you like, looking at a range of concepts that model journalistic practices. In this middle section, four chapters explore notions of the role of sources in the news, news selection processes, professional ethics in journalism, and the professional ideology of objectivity. The final section of the book considers questions of the fundamental nature of journalism in the context of current anxiety-filled debates about the changes within journalism. It does so by exploring a range of journalism and factual media content often ignored or avoided by journalism scholars, including the alternative aesthetics of literary journalism, and the organisation, style, and content of other alternatives to mainstream journalism. This final section also explores some neglected genres of journalism that have been expanding in recent decades such as sports writing and lifestyle journalism. The book rounds off with a discussion of the potential future of journalism in the context of the major technological changes that have radically altered the environment for journalism in the twenty-first century, not least global television news and the rise of the Internet.

Chapter Two

☐ JOURNALISM AND THE STATE

In this chapter and the next the aim is to examine a range of structural elements that influence the production of journalism. Separating the state and the market in this way is really a false distinction, since the two are inherently inter-related, but the intent is not to argue that such a distinction actually exists. Politico-economic influences on news production are absolutely unavoidable, affecting the basic resources journalists have available to them, and setting the boundaries of what journalists can print and broadcast. One central reason for dividing such a discussion along the lines of state and market, is to address a central belief present in many free-market liberal democracies that the less the state intervenes in news production, and the more the free market is left to structure the news media, then the less restrained journalists will be in doing their jobs. As the next two chapters will show, many have critiqued this assertion from the point of view that the restrictions on news production do not so much diminish when state control is replaced by free market control, but simply change their form. In this chapter we shall also explore the assumption that state involvement with journalism necessarily has negative consequences.

DEFINING THE STATE

In journalism's 400-year history, it has existed within a wide range of political systems. The early development of the press in many European nations was stifled by monarchies and empires suspicious of a medium offering the people they ruled information about what was going on in the world. Even before newspapers appeared, concerns about the uses of printing saw the introduction of the laws that remain at the bedrock of media legislation, such as the famous British monarch Henry VIII's introduction of the first British libel laws in the sixteenth century. Journalism in Europe and elsewhere has developed amidst revolutions, be they political (playing a key role in both the US war of independence, and the French Revolution for example), or economic (first in the industrial revolution, and latterly in the emergence of information technologies). Today, much of the literature on the relationship between journalism and the state tends to concentrate on the role of the government, reflecting the dominant Western perspective running through journalism studies. As Colin Sparks points out, however, even within Western developed democracies the government is only one small part of that larger body of institutions comprising the state:

> The government is a fairly small, although very influential, body of people.
> The state, on the other hand, is very large indeed. It is staffed by 'professional'
> people who owe their position not to any election, popular or otherwise, but to
> the allegedly rational internal bureaucratic norms of the sector of the state for
> which they happen to work.
>
> (Sparks, 1996: 84)

In most democratic nations it is the government that has the biggest impact on journalism within the range of institutions that comprise the state, and therefore governments have rightly been the central focus of much of the research literature.
However, if we are to apply theories of journalism and the state more widely, then we
need to remember that a whole range of other institutions comprise the state, and
depending on where you are in the world, these other institutions may be of particular importance. Many countries, for example, retain monarchies that have varying
degrees of political authority and varying relationships with the news media of those
countries. In some countries, monarchs are still regarded as having privileged status
and the news media are very circumspect in their treatment of royalty. In Thailand,
for example, newspapers are noted for their tendency for sensationalist reporting of
crime that has been dubbed 'chop-chop' journalism, after the regularity of stories
about machete wielding gangs, producing lots of gory photographs of lopped off
limbs (Coleridge, 1993: 432). But when it comes to the monarchy and the Crown
Prince, the tone changes completely as Nicholas Coleridge explains:

> [T]he royal family is a non-subject in Thailand ... This is a country in which to
> discuss the Crown Prince rudely in your own home is an offence. Foreigners in
> Bangkok refer to him by the letters CP, and tell you the story of the expatriate
> dinner party raided by Thai police after guests had been shopped by a servant
> for making jokes about the King.
>
> (Coleridge, 1993: 433)

The status of the press in Thailand has been improving since major social and
political reforms in 1992, but the monarchy remains an important part of the
Thai state, clearly not a target for the more sensational style of news prevalent in the
Thai press.

Some countries today are run as theocracies, where the senior religious figures have
in effect the real political authority, such as in the Islamic states of Iran, or until recently,
Afghanistan under the rule of the Taliban. Theocracies' attitudes towards news media

can vary dramatically. In the examples mentioned very different applications of Islamic law have been applied. In Iran, whilst under strict requirements to conform to Islamic law, the press still operates and has been at the forefront of calls for reform since the death of the Iranian revolution leader Ayatollah Khomeini. Such 'reformist' material has caused controversy with the religious authorities in Iran, however, and their have been many closures of newspapers by the religious courts in recent years, including the closure of 16 newspaper and magazines in 2000, after the religious leader Ayatollah Khamenei accused them of 'undermining Islamic and revolutionary principles' (in Campagna, 2000). The Taliban's interpretation of Islamic law has been even more hard-line, resulting in the near complete close down of news media in Afghanistan (more of which later in the chapter) during their time in power. Even where government and religion have formally been separated, as in European countries, the extent of influence of the religious authorities should not be underestimated, whether that be the Catholic church in countries like Italy, or the Orthodox church in parts of Eastern Europe.

The machinery of even largely secular states comprises many more elements that may have an impact on journalism. The judiciary, for example, can play a crucial role in determining the limits on journalistic practice, either through acting as a guardian of constitutional law, as in the US Supreme Court, or through particular court decisions that impact on journalism practice, and the limit of state influence on journalism practice. A good example of this in the USA would be the 1931 trial '*Near Vs Minnesota*', when a newspaper had been prevented from being printed and distributed because it routinely criticised Minnesota politicians. The court ruled that this kind of pre-publication censorship on the grounds of the political views being expressed was an illegitimate restraint on press freedom, and ruled against the Minnesota state officials (Hachten, 1998: 42). The case set a precedent that still applies in the US, preventing pre-publication censorship. It also shows how different parts of the state, in this case local government versus the judiciary, can be in conflict, so the state should also not be seen as a set of institutions sharing a uniform position with regard to the news media.

Given the many different kinds of states that exist around the world, and given the inherent complexities of trying to map out the relationship between journalism and any one state, it may seem that trying to model journalism/state relations is an impossible task. Yet that is exactly what a range of different scholars have attempted. Not surprisingly perhaps, attempts at categorising different nations' journalism and placing them within some kind of comparative framework has produced some very different approaches to describing and evaluating the organisation of journalism around the globe. Some approaches have been qualitative, categorising systems by the overriding ethos evident in the organisation of journalism, whilst others take a more systematic and quantitative approach, measuring nations on scales of freedom and control. Yet another approach has looked at individual systems to develop models of the range of relationships a state may have with journalism and such models might be useful in comparing states. This chapter explores some of these varying models, using examples from a range of nations to explore the different relationships between journalism and the state.

'FOUR THEORIES OF THE PRESS'

One of the most important theoretical approaches in modelling the relationship between journalism and the state was published in 1956 in America. Since then, Siebert, Peterson and Schramm's *Four Theories of the Press*, as it was straightforwardly entitled, has become a benchmark for debates about the social function of journalism, although much of the discussion of this model has involved strident criticism of its assumptions and arguments. Many of these criticisms are extremely strong, particularly those that point out the model's shortcomings in relation to journalism today as opposed to the profession's status in the 1950s. Nonetheless it remains a useful starting point for a number of reasons. First, as mentioned, it represents an early paradigm of theories of journalism and the state. Second, it reflects one of the many ways to approach a comparison and categorisation of different national systems of journalism. Third, the theories' shortcomings in terms of contemporary developments help us to focus more clearly on some of the features of journalism that are substantively different today from when the theories were first presented in the 1950s.

The 'four theories' model is also useful because the starting assumption is one that remains perfectly reasonable for a discussion of why journalism is as it is today, the same basic question the model's authors were trying to answer (Siebert, Peterson and Schramm, 1956: 1). That assumption is that 'the press always take on the form and colouration of the social and political structures within which it operates. Especially it reflects the system of social control …' (ibid.). They go on:

> To see the differences between press systems in full perspective, then, one must look at the social systems in which the press functions. To see the social systems in their true relationship to the press, one has to look at certain basic beliefs and assumptions which the society holds: the nature of man, the nature of society and the state, the relation of man to the state, and the nature of knowledge and truth. Thus, in the last analysis the difference between press systems is one of philosophy.
>
> (ibid.: 2)

One might expect from such broad components seen to be contributing factors to the organisation of journalism, that the authors' comparative analysis might have produced a complex set of approaches to journalism with subtle variations from country to country. In fact, while they outline four theories, reductive enough one might think, they say straight away that there are really just two theories of the press, *authoritarian* and *libertarian*, which the latter two theories, *social responsibility* and *soviet communist*, are merely extensions of (ibid.: 2). They present analyses of each of the theories in the order the theories historically emerged.

THE AUTHORITARIAN THEORY

Historically speaking, as mentioned above, the earliest state responses to journalism fit into the theory dubbed by these authors as the 'authoritarian' theory. Siebert's chapter on the authoritarian theory explores the historical and philosophical roots of this approach to journalism and argues that:

> It is the theory which was almost automatically adopted by most countries when society and technology became sufficiently developed to produce what today we call the 'mass media' of communication. It furnishes the basis for the press systems in many modern societies; even where it has been abandoned, it has continued to influence the practices of a number of governments which theoretically adhere to libertarian principles.
>
> (Siebert *et al.*, 1956: 9)

Siebert suggests that historically it has been the dominant approach to controlling the media, the basis from which subsequent theories follow, and at the centre of the theory is the notion that 'the press, as an institution, is controlled in its functions and operation by organised society through another institution, government' (ibid.: 10). In this model the state supersedes the rights of the individual, as most people are deemed to only be able to thrive through the protection of the state, otherwise incapable of running their own affairs and needing the firm hand of a benevolent state. This conception of the role of the strong state Siebert traces all the way from Plato, through Machiavelli and the European monarchies in the early years of the newspaper, to Hegel and twentieth-century fascism.

In the authoritarian model 'the units of communication should support and advance the policies of the government in power so that this government can achieve its objectives' (ibid.: 18). The main ways of achieving this are to restrict access to the means of producing media content, and state institutions taking over control of media production, both of these possible in the early days of a mass medium when the technology is scarce and easy to physically control. In the early days of the newspaper in Europe, for example, printing technology was not widespread, so the authorities were able to control who had access to it. As mass media technologies become more widespread and thus more difficult to control in this kind of way, different methods of control become more significant, such as strict licensing systems, or using legal provisions to control the content produced around areas such as treason, sedition and libel (ibid.: 19–22).

What is crucial to understand here is that the authoritarian model is premised on the attempt to essentially preserve the status quo, to preserve the institutions of the state, maintain the existing social hierarchies, and prevent efforts at dissent, reform or change. This was certainly the line taken by most European monarchies when printing technology first appeared, reflected in the heavy restrictions placed on publishers through most of the seventeenth and eighteenth centuries. A good contemporary example of this kind of approach to journalism would be the Afghan media under the rule of the Islamic fundamentalist group, the Taliban. The Taliban's hard-line interpretation of Islamic law saw them radically restructure the already heavily compromised news media in Afghanistan when they took power in 1996. This is how one Afghan-born journalist described news media under the Taliban in 1999:

> In line with the Islamic ban on human representation, [Afghan newspapers']
> pages are free of pictures. News is limited to official announcements,
> accounts of Taliban military victories, and anti-opposition propaganda. And
> there are no newsstands in Afghanistan: the papers are distributed mainly to
> government offices ... Bereft of music, Radio Kabul (now known as Radio
> Voice of Islamic Law) is heavily oriented towards religious topics ... While
> there is no explicit ban on independent journalism, state-owned publications
> and radio stations dominate the nation's media.
>
> (Farivar, 1999: 2)

Television was banned under the Taliban, and even statues were destroyed for breaching their interpretation of Islamic ideas about representation. The Taliban's Afghanistan stands as a good example of the archetypal authoritarian approach to journalism, an approach within which journalists have very little freedom of expression and independence, with their jobs heavily controlled and constrained by the institutions of the state.

THE LIBERTARIAN MODEL

The libertarian model stands in stark contrast to the authoritarian model. According to Siebert *et al.*, the libertarian approach to journalism owes most to the political ideology of liberalism, and also to aspects of Christian theology (1956: 39–41). Seen as a product of the social changes of the sixteenth, seventeenth, and eighteenth centuries, primarily in Europe, the libertarian model in many ways completely reverses the role relationship between journalism and the state. It is also, interestingly, identified by Siebert as a particularly Anglo-American approach to the state/press relationship (ibid.: 57).

The new approach to political and social progress rested not in the absolute power of the authorities (be they the monarchy, clergy or whatever), but instead on the absolutes of reason, rational debate, and freedom of speech (ibid.: 44). The period known as the Enlightenment reflects this new idea that, in the end, the progress of humanity can only occur through the freedom to present, pursue, and discuss new ideas. Increasingly the newspaper, the only modern mass medium around at that time, was seen as absolutely central to this goal, with key figures like John Milton in his *Areopagitica* (1644) and Thomas Paine in his later *The Rights of Man* (1792) beginning to see press freedom as being an important part of the process of social progress.

In the libertarian model 'the functions of the mass media of communication are to inform and to entertain' (Siebert *et al.*, 1956: 51). Siebert *et al.*, explain further:

> Basically the underlying purpose of the media was to help discover truth, to assist in the process of solving political and social problems by presenting all manner of evidence and opinion as the basis for decisions. The essential characteristic of this process was its freedom from government controls or domination ... Thus there developed a refinement of the function of the press as a political institution. It was charged with the duty of keeping government from overstepping its bounds. In the words of [Thomas] Jefferson, it was to provide that check on government which no other institution could provide.
>
> (ibid.: 51)

In order to act as a genuine check on government, the press needed to be free from government influence. At the core of the libertarian argument is the contention that 'the less government becomes involved the better' (ibid.: 53). Only with minimal, or even no government interference, can the press act as a check on the government, or as it has also been referred to, as a 'Fourth Estate'.

This does not mean that a libertarian system is one without any kinds of controls or statutory influence, but the extent of those controls and influence is, in principle at least, kept to a minimum. State influence in such systems largely involves those areas where the right to freedom of speech clashes with other freedoms deemed as equally fundamental, such as questions of individuals' privacy and reputation and issues of taste and decency. The other main area where a libertarian press system succumbs to statutory control is in matters of national security, say, during wars. In the US, this difficult position of balancing press freedom against national security was clarified by the events of the two World Wars, between which the Supreme Court ruled that there would be grounds for state interference in the dissemination of news if a 'clear and present danger' to national security could be demonstrated (ibid.: 58). In Britain too, wars brought media restrictions, for example, the Second World War saw the closure of the nascent television service and radio and newspapers' content being subject to vetting from the Ministry of Information.

The press system in the minds of the four theories authors that perhaps best represented the libertarian model was undoubtedly the USA, described as one of 'chief custodians of libertarian principles', alongside Britain (ibid.: 67). The struggle for political independence from Britain, and the role the press played in that struggle meant that in the founding of the new nation the press was central in the minds of the founding fathers. The First Amendment of the US Constitution provides for the right to free speech and press freedom. European commentators visiting the USA by the middle of the nineteenth century often highlighted the role the press played in the development of the USA. Alexis de Tocqueville, in his great work on *Democracy in America*, for example, wrote in 1840 of newspapers that:

> To suppose that they only serve to protect freedom would be to diminish their importance: they maintain civilisation ... The effect of a newspaper is not only to suggest the same purpose to a great number of persons, but to furnish means for executing in common the designs which they may have singly conceived.
>
> (deTocqueville, 1945: 111)

Today, the news media continue to operate within the assertions of the first Amendment, and with the clarification of the boundaries of press freedom outlined by several Supreme Court rulings, including those already mentioned. The Freedom of Information Act (FOIA) introduced in 1966, and amended to include electronic information in 1996, has also been particularly important in allowing members of the public but also journalists access to information. A good example of this would be in the aftermath of the 1990 to 1991 Gulf War. Reporting the Gulf War proved very difficult during the conflict, as the US government and military tried to heavily control journalists' access to events, mainly attempting to avoid the PR/media disaster that the Vietnam War had been for the US authorities. The compliance of US journalists to their military in the Gulf drew some criticism from their European counterparts as John Eldridge explains:

> Journalists were assigned to pools, which were essentially corralled by the military ... Journalists not in the pool who tried to act autonomously were labelled 'unilateralists' and this could be a point of friction between journalists. When Robert Fisk of The Independent tried to report the battle

of Khafji, which the Iraqis briefly held, the NBC correspondent, Brad Willis reported him to the United States marines ... In the same place a French film crew obtained pictures which they were prepared to provide to others, as distinct from the official pool pictures. As Clive Ferguson of the BBC described it: 'They were spotted on the road and an American television reporter said: "Hey! They're not members of the combat pool, arrest them." So when you get your own journalists acting against you in such situations it doesn't make life easy'.

(Eldridge, 1993: 12)

After the war, however, the tables were turned as US journalists trying to find out what had really gone on, were able to use the FOIA to view the records of the kinds of bombs used, including, for example, confirmation that the US used nearly 500 napalm bombs, despite official statements denying this (O'Kane, 1995: 16). Meanwhile British journalists were stifled by Britain's lack of a Freedom of Information Act at that time. Even though FOI legislation has emerged in recent years in the UK, its scope is much more limited than in the US, and it has been compromised by extensions to the rights of state institutions to monitor things like private e-mail messages in the course of investigations. Also, unlike the amended FOIA in the US, there are no formal require-ments for government departments and agencies to make their statistics publicly avail-able in electronic form.

THE SOCIAL RESPONSIBILITY MODEL

One of the central problems with the libertarian model, from the point of view of its critics, is that with the absence of state influence the news media have few or even no controls on what they do. Whilst the changes from authoritarian to libertarian attitudes were arguably dramatic, one consistent element to both is the notion of the genuine importance of the news media in the effective functioning of society. Whilst authoritarian states view the media as a threat to social stability that needs to be con-trolled, libertarian states view free news media as essential to social stability. Whilst the authoritarian model evidences distrust in the news media's capacity to be compliant without interference, the libertarian theory presumes that a free news media will ful-fil the desired goals of acting, as the US approach would put it, as a 'free marketplace of ideas'. Yet in systems where the news media have been given a largely free reign to develop and act as they choose, concern has increasingly grown that 'the press has been deficient' in that role (Siebert *et al.*, 1956: 74).

Again, the authors of the four theories model suggest the social responsibility model to be a largely Anglo-American concept (ibid.: 75), and to have emerged at a time when the largely free newspaper industries were expanding into a true mass medium of millions of readers, and new media technologies of film, radio, and later television, increased the potential reach and impact of the mass media. Here, in the emergence of the idea of social responsibility, comes the first indication of the problems of the free market (although the four theories authors do not make a major issue of the role of private finance in the standards of the press, something that their critics have highlighted, see below).

The concept began to emerge out of how the press, and the new media, operated. With the absence of state controls and financing, newspapers rapidly became essentially another part of the free market, subject to the same forces of commercialisation, conglomeration, and so on, as any other product. In Britain, state licensing of newspapers had continued into the middle of the nineteenth century, designed to try and stop the many politically radical titles, seen by the state to have contributed to much of the civil unrest that occurred in the early part of that century. These restrictions, dubbed the 'taxes on knowledge', were removed by the end of the 1860s but as the press became more commercial, with ever increasing production costs and the growth of reliance on advertising revenue, the radical press disappeared in favour of a more populist and largely depoliticised press. By the 1920s, when public radio broadcasting was beginning to appear, the British newspaper industry was dominated by a small number of regional and national newspaper chains, dominated by a number of high profile owners such as Lord Northcliffe, owner of the *Daily Mail*, the first really successful populist newspaper in Britain. Owners like Northcliffe were dubbed the 'press barons', were widely criticised for their use of their newspapers as vehicles for their own political ends, and also proved the inspiration for Evelyn Waugh's famous satire on newspapers *Scoop* (much as William Randolph Hearst would later prove the alleged inspiration for Orson Welles' celebrated film *Citizen Kane*). Even the Prime Minister of the time, Stanley Baldwin, was moved to comment that 'what these proprietors exercise is power, and power without responsibility' (in Curran and Seaton, 1997: 42).

The concentration of newspaper ownership into the hands of politically motivated owners wasn't the only concern. It was also felt in both the US and Britain, that commercial pressures brought about by the need to maximise sales and advertising revenue were leading newspapers downmarket, away from the noble aims of a fourth estate, pandering instead to popular tastes and commercial imperatives – the very arguments that are a major feature of the climate of crisis apparent today.

The social responsibility model involved a number of ways in which the state could attempt to play a role in attempting to ensure that news media fulfilled their social obligations, whilst at the same time trying to retain the independence of journalism, and freedom of speech. One response has been to draw up codes of practice

(Siebert *et al.*, 1956: 86), many voluntary and self-regulatory, although on occasion some have had statutory force. Across different media at different times codes of practice had limited the scope and nature of media content, supposedly in order to protect the public interest (things such as the Hays Code in 1930s Hollywood). In terms of journalism, codes of practice have also reflected attempts to develop professional standards and ideals of practice, such as the principle of objectivity. Both codes and objectivity will be discussed in more detail later in this book.

A second response, not seen in either the US or Britain but used extensively in mainland Europe, has been the use of state subsidies to newspapers in order to try and ensure pluralism. Like in Britain, rather than opening up diversity in many European countries, market forces have been seen to narrow the public's choice. A common response has been to use state money to support newspapers in order to retain a diversity of political, religious, regional and ethnic viewpoints in situations where the market cannot support such a wide range of views. Of course, once the state becomes explicitly involved in financing the press the problem of excessive state interference emerges, and thus there is an equal onus on the state to act responsibly as much as the press, in actively promoting press freedom (ibid.: 95).

Subsidy systems in Europe have had varied success. In some countries there have been occasions when the subsidy and licensing systems have been used to restrict politically radical newspapers. In France, for example, there have been attempts to balance the press towards the left (in the late 1940s), and seizures and censorship of left-wing newspapers during the Algerian crisis (Humphreys, 1996: 47). Moreover, whilst the political interference in newspapers may have subsided since the 1940s and 1950s, there are some who criticise whether the French subsidy system actually does very much to counter the negative impact of the market. French subsidies are now designed simply to ensure that the overall number of titles available remains reasonably high, and are targeted primarily at newspapers of general political interest, rather than those that may address minority communities or reflect different political viewpoints, so the issue of diversity remains (see Murschetz, 1998 for a comparative discussion of European subsidy systems).

In other countries subsidy systems have been seen as successful attempts to halt the negative impacts of the market, such as in Norway (Skogerbø, 1997). The terms of the Norwegian press support system, established in the 1960s, were designed to address the sharp post-Second World War decline in newspapers. Norwegian newspapers have traditionally been closely associated with political parties, and this fall in the number of newspapers was seen as a threat to the balanced flow of information for all parties and thus for all citizens. So subsidies were seen as a legitimate way to ensure the survival of a pluralist political press (ibid.: 102). In addition, the provisions for receiving subsidies are not seen as curtailing editorial freedom. Newspapers receive subsidies only in order to ensure that communities have a choice of a newspapers, and that distinct ethnic groups, like the Saami (or Lapps as they are more widely, and incorrectly, known), have newspapers that address them in their own language (ibid.: 105). Critics have argued that such state patronage is open to abuse of the freedom of the press, but studies of newspaper reporting in Norway argue that the opposite is in fact the case. Skogerbø cites one native study that examined the journalism of Norwegian papers and concluded that 'journalists working in subsidised newspapers produce far more original news stories than journalists in non-subsidised newspapers. The former ones thus contribute more to the total news menu than the latter' (Sivertsen in Skogerbø, 1997: 111; translation by Skogerbø).

Public Service Broadcasting: Social Responsibility Writ Large

Subsidies for newspapers, then, are an explicit example of social responsibility although they are a distinctly non-British and non-US approach, neither of those countries using such systems. In broadcasting, a wider example reflecting this idea of state influence in order to ensure the media operate responsibly in the public interest, is the concept of public service broadcasting. Many nations, including the USA, have some kind of conception of public broadcasting – broadcasting for the citizens of a country, often with citizens directly paying for such broadcasting. In Europe, however, approaches to broadcasting from its origins in the 1920s were far more involved than, say, the Public Broadcasting Service of the US.

Public Service Broadcasting historically has involved a philosophy of the social role of the media that has impacted on the financing, organisation, content and regulation of broadcasting, and here Britain does offer one well-established and widely copied system. The birth of British broadcasting occurred at a time of particular social and political concerns about the increasing role of existing media (in the form of the politically motivated press barons mentioned earlier, and the impact of film newsreels, particularly during the First World War) and the potential impact of new media. The experience of the USA, where the early radio environment was basically a mess of bitter competition, was also a factor. The combination of these factors saw radio (and roughly a decade later television) being introduced in a highly regulated manner, nominally in the public interest. The resulting organisational structure of broadcasting in Britain was designed to reflect a number of key ideas about the social function of broadcasting. Whilst the organisational framework has changed over the years, particularly in recent years with the growth of satellite, cable, and digital broadcasting, nominally at least, these principles of Public Service Broadcasting are still at the forefront of British broadcasting philosophy.

In the mid-1980s, at the beginning of the current period of major technological change in British broadcasting, the Broadcasting Research Unit was commissioned to find out what these principles were (as they hadn't been set down in any particular way). Their study, a product of document analysis and interviews with broadcasting professionals, produced a list of eight criteria that offer a neat indication of how a concept of the social responsibility of the media was operationalised in the introduction and running of a broadcasting service in Britain. The eight principles were:

> Geographic universality – broadcast programmes should be available to the whole population; universality of appeal – broadcast programmes should cater for all interests and tastes; minorities, especially disadvantaged minorities, should receive particular provision; broadcasters should recognise their special relationship to the sense of national identity and community; broadcasting should be distanced from all vested interests, and in particular from those of the government of the day; universality of payment – one main instrument of broadcasting should be directly funded by the corpus of users; broadcasting should be structured so as to encourage competition in good programming rather than competition for numbers; and, that the public guidelines for broadcasting should be designed to liberate rather than restrict the programme makers.
>
> (BRU, 1985)

Whether British broadcasting has been able to live up to these aims (or even should live up to these aims) is a subject of continuing debate. For the purposes here, though, it is enough to illustrate how some countries have attempted to put ideas about socially responsible media into practice, with a mind to balance methods of control to ensure responsible practice with the independence of media organisations from the state.

THE SOVIET COMMUNIST MODEL

Perhaps the most obviously dated of the four theories is the Soviet communist theory of the press. Clearly demonstrating a Western 1950s Cold War bias towards Soviet approaches to news, Wilbur Schramm's chapter in the book offers many contentious ideas. Schramm argues that within Marxist communist ideology[1] the press could 'not function as a Fourth Estate ... Rather, the Communist press would be conceived as an instrument to interpret the doctrine, to carry out the policies of the working class or the militant party' (Siebert *et al.*, 1956: 110). For Schramm, the Leninist application of Marxist attitudes to the media in the Soviet Union was based on the view that 'the media should be instruments of social change and social control, in a tightly unified, closely drawn frame of reference' (ibid.: 116).

---

[1] One of the problems here is the extent to which Schramm conflates terms like communist, Marxist, Soviet and so on in a way difficult to accept today, and in a way that has been called 'unfair' (Nerone, 1995: 125).

Whilst the details of the Soviet Union's media system are now an historical artefact, the distinctions drawn by Schramm between Soviet Communist approaches and authoritarian systems are worth recollecting. Schramm offers a number of supposed differences between the Soviet Union and authoritarian systems. Amongst these the notion that the press play a significant and positive role in the promotion of social change is marked as one distinction. Whereas in more conventional authoritarian states where the authorities claim their right to rule through divine right, a communist state derives its authority through its assertion of acting as an agent of the class struggle, and thus as being representative of the people and not separate from it (ibid.: 140–41). To give an example of this, we can look to China which, while operating its own particular brand of communism, certainly displays this kind of attitude in terms of its treatment of the media. In 1985, Party Secretary Hu Yaobang, gave a speech entitled 'On the Party's Journalism Work', in which he stated:

> The party's journalism is the party's mouthpiece, and naturally it is the
> mouthpiece of the people's government, which is led by the party ... In our
> socialist motherland, the interests of the party and the government are identical
> with those of the people and the party's newspapers are the people's newspapers.
>
> (in Jakobson, 1990: 4–5)

So rather than being seen as a potential threat to the authority of the state by giving subjects access to information that might undermine their compliance to the state's demands, in a soviet-like state journalism is seen as an ideological tool to be used to promote the state to its citizens. One could go further and say that the news media are seen as having a duty to act as an instrument of the state, party, and thus by association the people. Indeed, journalists in some communist states, such as China, often indicate that this is exactly how many of them in such regimes view their work. As such the kinds of political control over editorial content that is routine in countries like China, and which are seen as wholly illegitimate in the West, is not only tolerated but also seen as legitimate by many journalists in those countries.

In some of these systems, traces of this 'theory' of the press can still be seen. One of these, North Korea, remains one of the most secretive and closed societies on the planet. Krzysztof Darewicz gives a remarkable insight into the control and ideology of the press from his time in North Korea, as a correspondent from Poland (2000). The ideological role of journalism, that the four theories authors referred to, is reflected strongly by the official North Korean text about journalism, called *The Great Teacher of Journalists*, the great teacher being the then leader of North Korea Kim Jong II. In that text it states:

> The Great Leader, the Dear Comrade Kim Jong II is always among journalists
> and teaches them (about) every detailed problem arising in their activities,

and kindly leads them to write and compile excellent articles that arouse the sentiment of the masses in keeping with the Party's intentions. He also brings up journalists to be the Party's reliable writers under his wings and takes meticulous care of every facet of their life and activity ... The love and generosity he confers upon the journalists is indeed boundless.

(in Darewicz, 2000: 139–140)

The levels of control of journalism in North Korea are to the point where one can see little difference between it and the likes of the Taliban's Afghanistan, save perhaps in state institutions' rhetoric about why the system is organised that way. This in itself raises the issue of how one regards a state's relationship to journalism – in terms of its declared (or perceived) attitudes towards the press, or in terms of what really happens in practice? Nonetheless, what this model offers, for all its flaws, is the possibility of a different ideological position in which there can be authoritarian control of the media coupled with a rhetoric of press freedom, with the two things not being seen as contradictory, not only by the political authorities, but by most of the journalism organisations and their journalists as well.

PROBLEMS

Whilst no model is free from criticism, the four theories model has been critiqued over the years from a number of perspectives (a good overview of those criticisms and revisions is offered by Nerone, 1995). Of course, many of the assumptions the authors make are no longer valid at the beginning of the twenty-first century, even if they were apposite to the mid-twentieth century. Also, many of the comments about the philosophical and organisational features of different press systems have been criticised, even the very claim that the models outlined are *theories* (Nerone, 1995: 18). At this point, these kinds of criticisms are not really of concern, but one of the challenges to the four theories approach is worth mentioning, as it is significant for the consideration of the role of the free market discussed in the next chapter.

The Mythology of Social Responsibility?

One of the most persistent critiques of the four theories model, and one that perhaps best reflects the range of problems identified with the model, especially within US journalism studies, has concerned the viability of the concept of social responsibility. The four theories authors undoubtedly view press systems through a liberal capitalist perspective, and an Anglo-American one on top of that. In doing so, however, they arguably ignore significant features of how power and control operate in the press, particularly in so-called libertarian or social responsibility systems. Herbert Altschull, for example, accuses the four theories authors of essentially ignoring the issue of press finance and the issue of profit (1995: 373). For Altschull, 'social responsibility' is an absurd, meaningless term, particularly in the context of economic power over news organisations, whether that power is in the hands of state or private institutions (ibid.: 446). For Altschull the first 'law' of journalism is that:

> In all press systems, the news media are agents of those who exercise political and economic power. Newspapers, magazines, and broadcasting outlets thus are not independent actors, although they have the potential to exercise independent power.
>
> (ibid.: 440)

His second 'law' goes on to say that 'the content of the news media always reflects the interests of those who finance the press' (ibid.: 440). Social responsibility in this framework is thus a 'masquerade', within which journalists act knowingly or otherwise as agents of social control neatly avoiding the realities of their economic position (ibid.: 446).

Here, Altschull demonstrates how the political and economic forces in journalism can't really be separated, even in theoretical models that attempt to do so. But as well as critiquing the capability of the press to act independently and responsibly when controlled and financed (directly or indirectly) by the state, he also raises concerns about the capability of privately owned news media to act independently or responsibly. This is precisely the concern that will be picked up in the next chapter.

FREEDOM HOUSE'S PRESS FREEDOM SURVEY

If the four theories model can be critiqued for being conceptually problematic, other models offer diametrically different approaches to evaluating and comparing nations' journalism. Since 1979, a US organisation known as the Freedom House has provided an annual assessment of the levels of press freedom around the world, presented as a numerical ratings scale in which high scores denote low press freedom and vice versa (available at http://www.freedomhouse.org). The most recent analysis for 2001 included 187 countries from all around the world.

The criteria used by Freedom House relate to the range of provision within a state for meeting Article 19 of the United Nations Declaration of Human Rights, which states 'Everyone has the right to freedom of opinion and expression; this right includes freedom to hold opinions without interference and to seek, receive and impart information and ideas through any media regardless of frontiers'. The survey authors explain:

> To deny that doctrine is to deny the universality of information freedom –
> a basic human right. We recognise that cultural distinctions or economic

under-development may limit the volume of the news flow within a country. But these or other arguments are not acceptable explanations for outright centralised (governmental) control of the content of news and information. Some poor countries provide diverse reports and viewpoints; some developed countries do not allow content diversity. We seek to distinguish the reality in all countries.

(Sussman and Guida, 2001: 10)

The system used examines four key criteria, within a 100-point scale (outlined in Sussman and Guida, ibid.). First, the laws and administrative decisions and their influence on journalism are measured. Second, the extent of political influence or control over news content is measured, including things such as attempts at news management (basically where state institutions try to influence the subjects the news media cover, and the way they cover them). Third, the extent of economic influence and control is examined, including economic control from state institutions and private corporations. The fourth category looks explicitly at the extent of incidents of violations against the news media 'including murder, physical attack, harassment, and censorship' (ibid.). Print and broadcast media are measured separately for each country, and the cumulative score indicates the extent of press freedom, with low scores indicating greater freedom and higher scores indicating lesser freedom.

Figure 2.1, below, collates data from the 2001 survey, showing the proportion of states in different regions of the world with a free press.

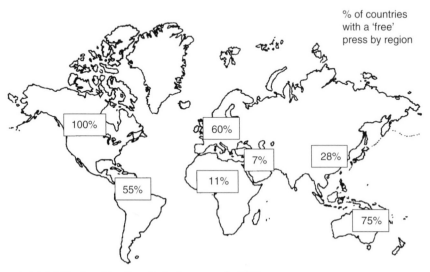

% of countries with a 'free' press by region

100%

60%

7%

28%

11%

55%

75%

In total 39% of world nations had a free press in 2001

Figure 2.1   Map of press freedom 2001.

What the figure illustrates is an apparent relationship between the level of economic and political development and the extent of press freedom, with the economically under-developed and politically more authoritarian parts of the world having smaller proportions of press freedom than in the developed world. To put this another way the survey results for 2001 places 1.2 billion people in countries with a free press (approximately 20 per cent of the world's population), compared to 2.4 billion (43 per cent) with a partly free press, and 2.2 billion living in nations with a press that is not free (36 per cent).

THREE CATEGORIES OF NATIONS: 'FREE', 'PARTLY FREE', 'NOT FREE'

The survey divides nations into three broad categories. The first of these are 'Free' nations that score between 0 and 30. In fact, no nations score '0' that presumably would indicate an entirely free press, the lowest score for 2001 being achieved by Norway with a rating of 5. It is interesting that in contrast to the four theories' presumptions of the libertarian model being a kind of ideal system for providing press freedom, it is in fact a system reflecting the social responsibility model that scores lowest in the Freedom House survey. As mentioned Norway has a well-established subsidy system in the newspaper industry and retains a public service broadcasting system not unlike that in Britain.

Most of the nations in the 'free' category are developed democracies and in the Western world. In Europe, for example, the overall share of 'free' nations hides a clear difference between the former Soviet states in Eastern Europe, many of which are struggling to develop liberal press systems, and Western European nations (all of which are rated as 'free', with the exception of Turkey). The four theories authors persistently refer to Britain and the USA as models for press systems, yet neither of these nations are considered to be the most free by Freedom House, with the USA scoring 15 in 2001, and Britain scoring 17. In the US case part of this is due to concerns about the extent of corporate control on the news media, whilst in Britain the propensity for state regulation and influence on news production contributes to its score.

Whilst no nation on the Freedom House survey scores the perfect zero, at the other end of the scale more than one nation has received the score of 100 indicating a complete absence of press freedom. In 2001, three nations had the dubious honour of achieving this score, namely Iraq, Burma, and the previously discussed North Korea, whilst other nations like Afghanistan scored in the high 90s.

Attempting to convey the difference in journalism from country to country along a numerical scale in this way couldn't contrast more dramatically with the four theories approach. Offering a quantitative measurement of levels of press freedom is inherently problematic, given the complexity of perceptions of what press freedom actually means, let alone how it does or doesn't function in any given country. Nowhere is this clearer than in the problematic middle part of the scale where many nations reside. Nations scoring between 31 and 60 are dubbed as being 'Partly Free'. A lot of the nations falling into this category in 2001 were developing nations in the throws of political transition, including nations in Latin America (like Argentina, Ecuador, and Mexico), Asia (including India, Bangladesh, and Indonesia), and Africa (including the likes of Nigeria, Gabon, and Morocco). Some former Soviet states also feature in this category and one good illustration of this would be Russia.

Russia: A 'Partly Free' Press Nation?

Since the fall of the Soviet Union, the new nations that once comprised it have taken different roads to new systems of government. Russia was one of the first of the new states to tackle the issue of the media, and a key aim was to try and make the news media independent along a Western model of press freedom. In terms of the state, Price says that the aims of a new media law introduced in 1991 was 'to involve the state as little as possible, to move towards autonomous information providers that have rights against the state, rather than the other way around' (Price, 1995: 108–9). The reality of the first decade of the new Russian media, however, has seen extensive state interference in the media. One key reason for this has been the continued political and economic uncertainty in post-Soviet Russia, with economic conditions being very unstable and political power struggles being an everyday feature of Russian life.

Despite proclamations about the independence of journalism in post-Soviet Russia, the legacy of strong-arm Soviet attitudes towards journalism has persisted through the presidencies of both Boris Yeltsin and current leader Vladimir Putin. By the time Putin took office in 2000, only one national TV station in the whole of Russia was independent of government ownership and control (Bivens, 2000). NTV has made a reputation for itself as an ardently independent station, for example, reporting the war in Chechnya extensively and openly.

The democratically elected political authorities in Russia have used dramatically undemocratic tactics to try and stem dissent and independent journalism, whilst their rhetoric remains pro-press freedom. For example, a routine of journalism in Russia is to have raids by armed and hooded 'tax police', who storm news organisations, rifle through their records, and often demand and take money found on the premises. Such a raid occurred at NTV days after Putin took office and subsequently the owner of NTV's parent company Vladimir Gusinsky was arrested and jailed. The authorities also went as far as having one prominent journalist who reported openly on Chechnya, Andrei Babitsky, kidnapped (ibid.).

Yet despite such acts, often provoking international condemnation, the authorities in Russia persist with their rhetorical support of press freedom. Part of the problem of this contradiction between practice and rhetoric lies in the political and economic instability of the country. Many of the journalists working in Russia today remember the days of trying to work in the Soviet Union, and despite the controls regard a return to communist rule as the greater threat than current restrictions. In the 1996 presidential election campaign, for example, opposing Boris Yeltsin's candidacy was an unreconstructed communist, Gennady Zyuganov, who wanted to return to the days of the Soviet Union. As such the news media went out of their way to not give Zyuganov equal, fair, or even accurate coverage. Matt Bivens, editor of the English language *The Moscow Times*, recounts one instance where a speech given by Zyuganov to appreciative students was reported by the local radio station as having been cut short by students booing Zyuganov offstage, a complete fabrication (ibid.). These complexities in systems like Russia and elsewhere can hardly be accurately reflected in a numerical scale, and suggest that perhaps what is needed to explore the relationship between journalism and the state is a typology of the different kinds of relationship state institutions can have within in any one system. Perhaps such a framework can accommodate the contradictory trends, evident in many countries, between independence and control, and freedom and responsibility.

SPARKS' MEDIA/STATE MODEL

Colin Sparks, talking ostensibly about Britain in the mid-1980s, a period when a right wing Conservative government was radically altering the British environment including the media, offers a model of this kind (1996). Despite very much reflecting the pessimism of commentators of that time in British history, this model remains useful for assessing journalism/state relations. This is not so much in terms of where a particular nation's state and journalism sit in relation to other nations, but more in terms of the possible range of relationships that can exist within one country. He suggests six possible roles the state takes in relation to the media: The patron, the censor, the actor, the masseur, the ideologue, and the conspirator (Sparks, 1996).

Sparks describes the role of *patron* as being the state as 'the direct economic benefactor of the media' (ibid.: 85). Most obvious in state-run media systems, state patronage is also evident in other systems. In British broadcasting, as indicated above, the state has played a role in the financing of media organisations through its setting and collection of the licence fee that has funded the BBC since the 1920s. But patronage needn't only mean financial influence. Just as potentially contentious is the capacity in some nations for states to play a role in the appointment of senior figures in news media organisations, particularly in broadcasting. Towards the end of 2000, this kind of issue was dramatically demonstrated in the Czech Republic when the Council of Czech TV appointed a new head of the television service who had strong ties to one of the main political parties in the Republic. The journalists working at the station objected to his appointment, which they saw as politically motivated, and were fired. They refused to leave their offices, their sit-in brought people onto the streets in support, and it was some weeks before the appointment was repealed after massive public pressure to dismiss the political appointee provoked the Czech parliament to step in and take temporary authority away from the TV Council.

The *censor* role involves the restriction of information either in terms of availability or presentation (ibid.). Again, there is no simple relationship between apparently democratic and free nations, and the occurrences of censorship, and systematic censorship too, not merely individual cases (save perhaps that authoritarian and dictatorial regimes practise censorship more routinely in all areas). A further complication can occur in that even if state institutions do not engage in overt acts of censorship, the mere potential of such acts can foster a climate of censorship in a country. Journalists may also find themselves engaging in acts of self-censorship in advance of state censorship, a risk that has been particularly evident and well documented in Hong Kong since the handover from British to Chinese rule in 1997 (e.g. Cohen, 1997). At the time of writing, since the beginning of the 'war on terrorism' US networks have willingly censored video material being produced by Osama bin Laden without the need for official state intervention.

Sparks suggests that the state as *actor* has a routine effect on journalism – particularly in Britain (1996: 85). This role is the one of the state as a primary news source. Government and Parliamentary activities, court proceedings, police investigations, activities of royal families/celebrities, and so on make up the routines of regular daily journalism. Sparks argues that this close relationship means there is 'a convergence between the actions of the state and the norms of modern journalism' (ibid.). A good example of this lies in the routines of political journalism. Helen Thomas is one of the USA's best known and longest service political journalists, having been part of the White House Press Corps since 1961, reporting for United Press International. Her career has seen ten different presidents so far, and as such her understanding of the machinations of US politics is arguably unsurpassed. Thomas is as clear as anyone could be about the relationship between the US president and journalism, talking about the White House Press Corp:

> [Journalists] were there because, plain and simple, the president makes the news. His agenda dominates, from his annual State of the Union address to his budget, from his state visits to his policies, from his re-election to his inauguration to his martini mixing. From the New Deal to the Great Society, from Vietnam to Watergate to Iran-Contra to Whitewater to White House interns.
>
> (Thomas, 1999: 128)

Following on from this routine reliance on state institutions and figures for news, there is the potential for the State to act as a *masseur* trying to influence the way information is presented in the news media. This idea raises the issue of the relationship of journalists and their news sources and will be explored in Chapter 4.

The *ideologue* role is a rather more complicated one, and depending on one's point of view, a more insidious role, which comprises two elements. First, is the idea that 'the media adopt the definitions made by the state' (Sparks, 1996: 88), primarily as a result of regarding state institutions and figures as the most significant actors in events, and being (wittingly or otherwise) subject to those actors managing the information disseminated to journalists. Second, and relating to this, the journalistic ideology of a clear separation of fact from opinion makes journalism subject to manipulation by spokespeople for the state (ibid.). Both of these points are very important when trying to evaluate the practices and outcomes of journalism and will be explored at length later in the book.

Finally, in the *conspirator* role the media act in concord with the state, not because of some literal conspiracy between state and media, but because they are organised in the same way and the people in charge come from the same stock. Most media organisations are hierarchical, just like the institutions of the state (like government, the military etc.). In authoritarian countries the relationship between state institutions and media institutions is usually overt, and direct – for example the central government control of news media in China is such that editors will openly talk of getting approval from party officials before publishing stories. In supposedly more liberal systems, however, there can be remarkably close personal links between members of state and media institutions. In a country like Britain, for example, the still existing class system (despite claims to the contrary from recent prime ministers) has a significant impact on the key figures in senior positions in those media institutions that the state has an impact on. In both public organisations, like the BBC, and especially in many of the regulatory bodies responsible for the media in Britain, different studies over the years have shown that people who end up in these positions frequently share the same social, educational, and professional backgrounds as the politicians who appoint them (e.g. Collins and Murroni, 1996: 199–212).

THE PROBLEM OF 'OCCIDENTAL COSMOLOGY'

One of the central problems with all of the approaches outlined above rests in the central criteria that are used. Even with the apparent acknowledgement of economic development being an important issue in achieving press freedom, there does seem to be a clearly Western notion of what constitutes press freedom – notably that in general the less state influence in the news media the freer the press. The four theories model and the Freedom House ratings schema suffer from what has been referred to as an 'occidental cosmology' (Galtung and Vincent, 1992; see also, Gunaratne, 1998). In other words, Western, liberal democratic notions about the role of the press in relation to the state, and what is *meant* by press freedom, are being used to judge the press in other parts of the world, and such criteria may not be appropriate to apply to non-western, non-democratic systems. Sparks' model is inherently pessimistic about the role of state influence on the media in Britain, but in some parts of the world state influence on the news media is seen as having a necessary and constructive role to play in society. Attempts to model news media systems outside of the liberal capitalist dominant paradigm (or the opposing communist ideological models), have produced a couple of non-Western theories of journalism/state relations.

DEVELOPMENT JOURNALISM AND 'ASIAN VALUES'

One much-debated term relating to the new media in developing nations was coined in the late 1960s. Alan Chalkley, in a speech to economic journalists in the Philippines in 1968, introduced the idea of the 'development journalist', one whose responsibility involves not only informing audiences of the facts and offering context and interpretations (seen as the tasks of all journalists), but also involves promotion (Gunaratne, 1998: 293). He said:

> You must get your readers to realise how serious the development problem is, to think about the problem to open their eyes to the possible solutions – to punch that hole in the vicious circle.
>
> (in Gunaratne, 1998: 293)

Exactly how one interprets the concept of development journalism relates a lot to how one perceives the role of state influence on journalism. A key criticism has been the idea that this kind of journalism would inevitably involve inappropriate state influence, through efforts being made to ensure that the press are supportive of and report positively state development programmes. Hachten, for example, argued that development journalism would result in, or would require, state institutions controlling news media organisations, and that as a result the capacity to challenge or question those institutions would be significantly diminished (1992). In many European nations, however, this kind of control has existed, and in places continues to exist, such as in the introduction of broadcasting in Britain already mentioned. In other words, seeing development journalism as some kind of authoritarian system might not be appropriate, as any state influence that does occur might be more along the lines of acting in the public interest to ensure a socially responsible press. Gunaratne offers a comment from a Sri Lankan political scientist pre-dating the development journalism concept, but ably demonstrating the relationship between development and a socially responsible press:

> [I]f freedom of the press tends to disrupt national unity, if such freedom is
> utilised to promote civil commotion and conflict between communities,
> religious or racial, it might become necessary for the state to introduce
> restrictions which might help toward restoring order or promoting unity.
>
> (Wilson in Gunaratne, 1998: 300)

Chalkley himself certainly did not view development journalism as government-controlled, rather seeing it as a critical and evaluative form of journalism (Chalkley, 1975). Other proponents have also pointed out this difference saying that development journalism requires a particular focus on the social, political, and economic programmes in a developing nation with proper scrutiny of things such as the 'relevance of development projects to national and local needs, on the differences between planned schemes and their actual implementation, and on the differences between projects' actual impacts on people and the impacts claimed by government officials' (Gunaratne, 1998: 294). The central ideas of development journalism fed into the debates about the need for better and more equitable information flows in the developing world, that produced the calls for a new world information and communication order (NWICO) in the 1970s, and this will be revisited at the end of the book.

Nonetheless, concerns about what might really be meant by development journalism have persisted, not least because of the way some developing nations appear to have treated news organisations whilst maintaining claims of support for press freedom. Particularly in Asia, aspects of development journalism have arguably been distorted by some regimes and conflated with the particular cultural and historical traditions of those countries to create what has become dubbed 'Asian Values' theory, most notably being utilised in Singapore, Malaysia, and Mainland China. Take, for instance, this comment from former Singapore Prime Minister Lee Kuan Yew, who said that journalism's responsibility was:

> [T]o inform the people of what was happening in Singapore and in all parts
> of the world, of events relevant to Singapore, educate them not just in the
> three Rs, but continue the schooling process, inculcate values which would
> make Singapore a more cohesive society and viable nation.
>
> (in Seow, 1998: 26)

On the surface such comments fit into the development journalism schema of a press committed to the social and economic progress of a developing nation and equally working towards the goal of development. But Lee's comments also reflect the more strident and authoritarian attitudes of Asian values theory as it has been applied in

51

nations like Lee's Singapore. Whilst there are subtle variations in the way the theory has been presented from country to country there are four core claims of the Asian values model (see Li, 1996, and Mendes, 2001 for explanations and discussions). The first of these was summed up by a document produced by the Chinese government in the wake of international condemnation over the Tiananmen square massacre of 1989. The 'Human Rights in China' White Paper states clearly that 'owing to tremendous differences in historical background, social system, cultural tradition and economic development, countries differ in their understanding and practice of human rights' (in Li, 1996).

Second, in Asian culture the community is deemed to take precedence over the individual. This notion that duty to the community and state overrides individuals' rights, comes into direct conflict with the principles applied by Western theoretical models of the press, like those discussed in the rest of the chapter. A core principle used by the Freedom House to judge press freedom, for example, is that 'the starting point is the smallest, most universal unit of concern: the individual' (Sussuian and Guida, 2001: 10). Presented by several states as a cultural justification for the denial of individual rights, including freedom of speech and freedom of access to information, this has been challenged as a genuine reflection of Asian philosophical and cultural attitudes towards the state and the individual (see Mendes, 2001).

Third, rights to do with social and economic development take precedence over civil and political rights. For states like Singapore and Malaysia, which have had remarkable economic growth and success in recent decades, a stark contrast exists between their economic successes and what they perceive as the economic decay of the West. Proponents like Lee in Singapore, and Prime Minister Mahathir of Malaysia, perceive this decline of the West as a product of the individualism of Western nations, and the success of the East as a product of their cultural values. Yet such perceptions do not take into account the massive social changes occurring in the tiger economies of South-East Asia, and in some views over-simplifies the situation dramatically (Mendes, 2001). Nevertheless this argument persists in places like mainland China where economic growth has occurred at such a rate since the 1980s that many there apparently accept the notion that economic development can occur without the political freedoms that are seen in the West as essential for economic development.

Finally comes the idea that rights are subject to national sovereignty, the internal responsibility of a nation, and are not international or universal standards to be imposed on nations from the outside. In the idea rests a difficult dilemma for international proponents of press freedom. 'Universal' ideas about press freedom are anything but that, having been developed by and continually promoted by Western nations. Opposition to Western diktats as to how to run news media as much reflects the legacy of opposition to colonial rule as it does genuine affirmations of national sovereignty. But the valid arguments about sovereignty and cultural difference should not be confused with cultural relativism, the concept by which there are no moral or ethical absolutes, all are culturally determined, and different cultures are entitled to their differences. The problem with cultural relativism is that anything can therefore be seen to be legitimate, protected by the cloak of cultural 'difference'.

CONCLUSION

Whether one accepts the Asian values model, and many do not, it does at least highlight the issue of where the current dominant ideas about the rights and roles of journalism came from. In other words, whilst many may now regard the dominant ideas about journalism's relationship to the state as universal absolutes, it should not be forgotten that they originated out of very particular socio-cultural and historical developments in particular nations, and have spread around the globe not necessarily because of their universal truth, so much as because of the politico-economic dominance of Western European and North American nations over the last 200 years or so. Even within Western nations, perceptions of the positive or negative influence of the state on journalism vary.

Chapter Three

☐ JOURNALISM AND THE MARKET

What the various models of journalism–state relations argue, either implicitly or explicitly, is that the greater the state's involvement in news production the more restrictions journalism has upon it (although they disagree as to whether this is a good or bad thing). Within the dominant Western perspective is the notion that systems with the least statutory influence would have the most free news production. Yet, as the discussions in Chapter 1 indicated, within many of the countries containing journalism systems seen as 'free' (according to the Western paradigm), the absence of state controls doesn't mean the *total* absence of controls, particularly in terms of economic control.

The consequences of private economic control in the free market provoke as much, if not more, concern as state control. The characteristics of the effects of the free market are distinct in nature, if not in their consequences, from the effects of state influence on news production. One key difference would be that whereas state influence is generally frowned upon (in non-authoritarian societies at any rate), the free market has often been promoted as the saviour of press freedom. Why this assumption should be so routinely made needs to be explored first, before we can endeavour to explore the particular ways in which aspects of the free market impact on journalism, and why this has generated significant criticism in its own right.

PRESS FREEDOM AND THE MARKET: A DEBATE

It is worth briefly introducing the central arguments relating to journalism and the market. On the one hand, supporters of the role of the market argue that the free market is essential for a free press and free speech, which are the cornerstones of democracy. On the other, critics argue that the press does indeed play a crucial role in democracy, but that the market 'is systematically at odds with the values of journalism' (O'Neill, 1992: 21).

William Hachten outlines the basis of the market-driven system in the USA:

> A democratic society, it is argued, requires a diversity of views and news
> sources available – a marketplace of ideas – from which the public can
> choose what it wishes to read and believe about public affairs. For no one

or no authority, spiritual or temporal, has a monopoly on truth. Underlying
this diversity of views is the faith that citizens will somehow make the right
choices about what to believe if enough voices are heard and government
keeps its hands off the press.

(Hachten, 1998: 37)

The reasoning behind the value of the free market then, relates strongly to ideas
about democracy. In a democratic system, the primary function of the media is to
act 'as a watch-dog on government' (O'Neill, 1992: 21). This is the idea of the press
as the 'Fourth Estate', an independent check on the activities of the key institutions
of the state, particularly government. In the pro-market argument, this is only
deemed possible if media organisations are free from economic and political control
by the state.

A second element to the values of the free market is that democracy, based as it is on
the will of the people, is also deemed to only work effectively if citizens are able to
make judgements on issues of importance from an informed position. In the mass
democracies of the modern era, countries of millions of citizens, it is argued that 'the
press is a necessary condition for an informed and critical citizenry' (ibid.). In other
words, the very existence of news media is required for mass democracy to function,
and it can only function properly if the news media are free. Part of the requirement
of being informed is access to a diverse range of viewpoints, and as has already been
mentioned in Chapter 1, diversity is a primary issue in contemporary journalism. The
pro-market argument suggests that only through the market can the full range of
viewpoints be represented, as state run or state influenced media would of necessity
follow a narrow agenda determined by the state whilst audiences in the free market
are free to disseminate and consume whatever viewpoints they like.

The problem is that *all* of the claims of the pro-market position have been stridently
challenged. The best way to examine the problems of free market journalism is to
look at some of the most fundamental challenges to this position in a bit more detail.
Analysis from both theoretical and practical perspectives provides substantive evidence
undermining the rhetoric of the pro-market position. This chapter will look at four
key areas: the audience, advertisers, ownership, and professional competition.

AUDIENCES: CITIZENS OR CONSUMERS?

One of the central contentions of market-driven journalism in the USA is that the
First Amendment, providing for free speech and a free press, is 'an individual right'
(Hachten, 1998: 39), protecting individual citizens as much as large news media
organisations. Critics say, however, that the market fails audiences in a number of

ways. The main way in which market-driven news media are deemed to fail audiences is in their fundamental treatment of audience members as consumers rather than citizens. This concern involves a number of aspects, relating to questions of choice and access, diversity and representation, and paternalism versus populism.

Defenders of the market say people must be allowed to choose what they want, that in itself is democracy in action, and attempting to dictate what people should use is paternalistic, even patronising. A good example of this comes from the early days of British broadcasting. As mentioned in the last chapter, the development of broadcasting in Britain was shaped by a range of factors coalescing over the years into the concept known as public service broadcasting. Probably the most important figure in the early development of this concept was John Reith, the first director general of the BBC, and fortunately for media scholars he was very overt in expressing opinions about what broadcasting should be doing. He wrote in 1924, acknowledging accusations of paternalism that already were apparent:

> It is occasionally indicated to us that we are apparently setting out to give the public what we think they need – and not what they want, but few know what they want, and very few what they need. There is often no difference.
>
> (Reith, 1924: 34)

This comment has been used by later authors to demonstrate the paternalism of the early BBC (e.g. Franklin, 1997: 123–24). Yet quoted this way the comment is incomplete. In the next sentence he says 'better to over-estimate the mentality of the public than to underestimate it' (Reith, 1924: 34). As Hachten's quote above indicated, the market argument rests on the 'faith' that citizens will be able to make choices in their own interests, and here lies one of the primary contentions. Just how able are audiences to choose media content that serves their interests as citizens of a democratic state, and who decides what constitutes 'correct' and 'incorrect' choices?

As the discussion of tabloidization in Chapter 1 indicated, critics of the market argue that the choices audiences appear to make suggest that Reith's view, even if paternalistic, might be quite legitimate. Generally speaking, audiences around the world seem disinclined to be interested in serious news media, tending to prefer news with at least an element of entertainment in it. Where choices are offered between entertainment-oriented and 'serious' news, audiences often seem to prefer the entertainment-based output, whether that be in the form of tabloid newspapers, magazine-style current affairs programming, or even entirely non-factual material.

A situational problem for market-based news organisations in such an environment is that 'to survive within the market place, the press has to satisfy the preferences of its consumers' (O'Neill, 1992: 22). In other words, when reliant on the retention of audiences for revenue (either directly through sales, or through advertising – see below), news organisations must follow the demands of the audience, even if those demands are incompatible with the public interest. This happens either simply through organisations trying to give audiences what they want, or by them trying to change aspects of their serious news output in order to try and attract or retain audiences.

In Britain this has led to changes in terms of layout, design, and editorial content in broadsheet newspapers, and the re-formatting and re-scheduling of news and current affairs programmes increasingly outside of prime-time slots. All of this change has contributed to the clamour of anxieties about the standards of journalism in Britain (e.g. Sampson, 1996). In the place of serious current affairs programmes, prime-time audiences in Britain have seen a flood of so-called 'docu-soaps' in recent years. These programmes have garnered large audiences, have made unwitting stars of their subjects, but have been criticised for failing to provide any kind of socio-political context or analysis to the lives of the people that they depict. (More on docu-soaps in later chapters.) Trends like these arguably turn one of the free market's central claims on its head. Rather than offering a wider range of choice and diversity of viewpoints through not having state controls imposed, the market itself can produce a decline in diversity and choice, as news media organisations are forced to follow audience tastes in order to remain economically viable. For those with mainstream views this is not necessarily a problem as there will likely be a large audience to generate revenue from, but for minority viewpoints the costs of production may likely restrict the possibility for those views to be expressed in news media. Other features of the market, such as the impact of advertising and ownership, only compound this problem further.

One of the caveats to this critique about dumbing-down due to market demands for news organisations to follow audience tastes rests on the often swift dismissal of mass audience choices. Some say that mass audience choices are products of the market 'rooted in the political and cultural conditions of a market democracy' (Sparks, 1992: 45), reflecting the economic realities of the consumer culture that has emerged in post-Second World War developed nations (Rooney, 2000). Others say, however, that these choices need to be explored to see what people are getting from these sources that 'serious' journalism doesn't appear to offer them. Proponents of this view argue that even given the trends apparent in market-driven news, audiences may still be able to use contemporary news formats in constructive ways. Indeed, some go further and argue that what is often interpreted as dumbing down could also be seen as the democratisation of news, as complex socio-political issues are represented in ways which allow a wider range of people to engage with those issues, something which the highbrow, serious news media can't achieve (e.g. Bird, 1990, 2000; McNair, 2000).

One example of this would be the predominance of scandals in market-led journalism involving politicians, celebrities, and even ordinary people. Critics point to these scandals as evidence of the sensationalism and prurience of market-driven news, but such a view doesn't really address the question of why audiences become so interested in particular cases. One argument is that these scandals offer examples of the testing of social standards in an accessible way that allows people to engage with particular social problems, even if that is often in an oblique and indirect manner (Tomlinson, 1997). Cases in recent years to have captured audiences' attention actually reflect a range of concerns that mainstream news media have often been criticised for failing to address. The O.J. Simpson trial, for example, became a focus for issues about race in the US. The Monica Lewinsky scandal raised issues of fidelity and trust in the most powerful job in the world. The case of Elian Gonzalez raised the long-ignored issue of Cuban-American relations and the issue of Hispanic Americans, a highly marginalised and politically invisible group in US society. Cases like these can be international in their reach, or even be international in their consequences, such as the case of the babies bought over the Internet that became headline news in both Britain and the USA in 2001. What distinguishes such scandals in terms of their representation of social concerns is a level of personalisation that 'can enable political insight and understanding through, rather than in spite of, their affecting qualities' (Macdonald, 2000: 264).

Another issue in the relationship between news audiences and the market rests on the question of access for audiences. There is a clear paradox here in the different interpretations of individual freedom between free market and public service news media. In the free-market model, audiences should be free to use news outlets that express whatever range of opinions and perspectives people may have. There should be no restrictions in the 'marketplace of ideas'. In the public-service model, freedom for audiences is interpreted as the freedom for every member of the public to have access to information. Both models require finance, but the latter model says that people should not be disenfranchised from access to information, whereas the former implicitly has this at its heart. In the free market, you can buy whatever news you want, but you have to be able to pay for it. In developed nations, where the costs of newspapers, radios, televisions, and even computers are small enough for the vast majority of members of the public to access information in this way, this isn't always a major problem. In the developing world, however, where incomes are significantly lower than in the developed world, access to information becomes an expensive luxury. Even in developed nations though, there are some consequences of market-led news provision based around costs to audiences, and the most significant of these is the fragmentation of the audience, itself compounded by the role of advertisers.

ADVERTISERS: INDIRECT AND DIRECT INFLUENCE

In the early days of newspapers advertising was not a major feature, although it didn't take long for people to recognise the commercial potential for placing ads in newspapers (the first advertising-led newspaper in Britain, the *Public Adviser*, appeared in 1657). Similarly, in European broadcasting at least, advertising did not have an immediately strong influence, with many of the public service broadcasters being completely free from adverts altogether (as the BBC in Britain continues to be to this day). Advertising only really began to have a major impact on news media when markets began to be opened up, but the consequences of the increasing importance of advertising in journalism have been testing to say the least. Advertising affects the production of news in two distinct ways. First, the reliance of news organisations on advertising revenue can have a detrimental effect on news diversity. Second, advertisers have increasingly attempted to influence the editorial content of the news publications their ads appear in. In news media that are entirely funded by advertising, particularly commercial broadcasting, the role of advertising is of utmost importance, but even in media forms where other sources of revenue are available, advertising can have significant effects.

The extent of news organisations' reliance on advertising revenue has historically emerged in systems where political controls have been relaxed in favour of market controls. To take Britain as an example, for much of the early history of the British newspaper industry strong state controls existed seriously hampering the economic situation of newspaper publishers. The stamp duties, or 'taxes on knowledge', that lasted in various forms from the early eighteenth century to the mid-nineteenth century, included taxes on the number of pages and the number of adverts printed. As campaigners against the taxes began to succeed in getting them reduced and eventually abolished, significant changes occurred in the British newspaper market spurred by the rise in advertising revenue this allowed. Curran and Seaton summarise these changes:

> This [change] financed bigger papers, more staff, and the introduction of sale-or-return arrangements with distributors. It also helped to underwrite a further halving of the price of most popular papers ... in the late Victorian period.
>
> (Curran and Seaton, 1997: 34)

On the surface then, this period was an emancipatory time for the newspaper industry with more resources for newsgathering and so on, but the increasing role of advertising as a prime form of revenue had another set of more negative consequences. The stamp duties were introduced and maintained for such a long period of time because of the political authorities' concerns about their potential use as a means of political opposition. An entire network of politically radical newspapers sprang up in the late eighteenth and early nineteenth centuries, with titles like the *Poor Man's Guardian*, articulating and representing the attitudes of the emerging working classes. Heavy state controls were often unsuccessful in stopping these papers, as they refused to pay the taxes (they were dubbed the unstamped, or pauper press), whilst the politically acquiescent titles paid the heavy duties and thus were at a major financial disadvantage. Curran and Seaton argue that removing the taxes on knowledge simply replaced an overt form of control over radical newspapers, with a more subtle, yet far more effective form of control – advertising (ibid.).

The basic reason why advertising proved an effective means of curtailing the radical press was due to the way advertising revenue in the press is generated. Basically what is happening in newspaper advertising (and in other media forms also) is that the newspaper is selling the 'presumed attention' of its readers to advertisers (see Sparks, 1992: 39). Now the attention of readers of different kinds of papers is not necessarily equally desirable for advertisers to reach. In the years after the taxes on knowledge were repealed there was already a clear range of different types of newspaper. There were the major establishment papers that had always stayed on the side of the political authorities and were read by the political elites (papers like *The Times*). There was also a range of popular but essentially non-political newspapers, the so-called penny press, which were often criticised for their sensational treatment of things like crime, but were popular with the mass audience. There were also the surviving politically radical titles, like *Reynolds News*, but titles like this found it increasingly difficult to retain a distinct political line, representing the interests and attitudes of the working classes in an advertising-led market. This was due partly to a lot of politically motivated advertisers at that time, often refusing to advertise in papers that pursued particular political campaigns, but perhaps even more fundamental was the problem of the attractiveness of the audiences for radical titles. The generally small but wealthy audience for titles like *The Times* were inherently more attractive to potential advertisers than the often large, but essentially poor audiences for titles like *Reynolds News*. Even though standards of living and literacy increased massively amongst the working class in the latter half of the nineteenth century, the audience for politically-minded popular papers was never particularly attractive to advertisers. Besides, the advertising revenue being generated by other kinds of popular newspapers that emerged in this period (the best example being the *Daily Mail*, which is often seen as the first modern tabloid in Britain) had the consequence of making newspaper production an incredibly expensive exercise, and one that could not be sustained on sales alone.

Perhaps the best example of this trend would be *The Daily Herald*, a left-wing newspaper that for a time in the 1930s was the largest circulation newspaper in the *world*, with some 2 million readers. But its very success in terms of sales was its economic downfall, as it could not generate sufficient revenue from advertising to sustain production in this period. Readers were drawn to the paper in the 1920s in their droves, particularly when it was accused of being financed from Moscow, but despite this audience interest, the only way it could survive without ad revenue was to become owned by the Labour Party and the Trades Union Congress (TUC). This change from independent to institutional control did little to offset the paper being run at a loss, a situation that continued even after the Second World War when the disposable income of the working class began to improve, making them potentially more attractive to advertisers. Eventually the paper was essentially closed down and re-launched as what has become the stereotype of the modern British popular newspaper, the *Sun*, in the 1960s. *The Daily Herald* was one of the last politically radical titles to have existed in the British newspaper market. Curran and Seaton summarise the factors that contributed to the demise of the politically radical press in Britain:

> In short, one of four things happened to national radical papers that failed to meet the requirements of advertisers. They either closed down; accommodated to advertising pressure by moving up-market; stayed in a small audience ghetto with manageable losses; or accepted an alternative source of institutional patronage.
>
> (Curran and Seaton, 1997: 37)

Today, the print media remain heavily reliant on advertising revenue, which has arguably polarised the British press. In Britain, the national newspaper market is broadly divided between populist tabloid newspapers that rely on advertising for somewhat under half their revenue, making them required to attempt to retain or increase a large readership, and 'quality' broadsheet newspapers that gain up to two-thirds of their revenue from advertising, due to the nature of their smaller, yet more affluent audiences (ibid.: 97). The problem here then is that advertising can contribute to a fragmentation of the audience in terms of the news outlets available to them and the kinds of content they are likely to receive in those news outlets. This fragmentation due to advertising influence is seen by many as an inevitable result of the force of the market being left to control news media production. After the collapse of the Soviet Union, for example, many predicted that the introduction of market forces in former Soviet states would see these kinds of trends emerge in those states' media systems (e.g. Sparks, 1992). Evidence from some of those states would appear to support this claim (e.g in Hungary, Gulyás, 2000).

In the US, daily newspapers rely on advertisers for up to 80 per cent of their revenue and the magazine and broadcasting sectors are also highly dependent on ad revenue

(Altschull, 1997: 264). For US broadcasters the financial power of advertisers is massive; by the late 1980s, Herman and Chomsky suggested that a mere 1 per cent fall in the Nielsen ratings could cost a network up to $100 million in lost ad revenue (1999: 172). When this situation occurs of advertisers being the primary, or even sole, form of finance for a news organisation, the potential for direct influence on editorial content is very high. News organisations become 'interested in attracting audiences with buying power, not audiences per se' (Herman and Chomsky, 1999: 171), and as a consequence it is the advertisers who can exert influence on news content over and above audience interests/needs. After all, as a report into the pressures on US journalists produced by Fairness and Accuracy In Reporting (FAIR) indicated 'what most of us think of as the *content* of news media, sponsors see primarily as the context in which their ads appear' (original emphasis, 2000a: 2).

A number of surveys conducted into the attempts by advertisers to influence US news media, show the practice to be widespread in both print and broadcast media, and also at national and local level (Soley, 1997; FAIR, 2000a; PEJ, 2001). Soley's survey of 241 television journalists in the US, showed that almost three-quarters of journalists had experienced efforts by advertisers to try and influence content. These efforts take the form of tactics such as threatening to or actually withdrawing advertising, 'recommending' ideas for conducive stories about the products being advertised, and meeting with senior figures in news organisations to try and exert pressure at that level (Soley, 1997). Some 40 per cent of those surveyed said that their organisations had capitulated in such instances, and there was evidence of pressures from within news organisations themselves to please advertisers, with some 56 per cent indicating this had occurred (ibid.). A survey by the Project for Excellence in Journalism in 2001 concurred with these findings, showing that some 53 per cent of the 118 TV news directors surveyed in that study had experienced efforts by advertisers to influence editorial content.

Even the most established news media outlets in the USA can be subject to the pressures of advertisers. Soley (1997) notes that *Sports Illustrated* lost around $1 million from golf ball companies after running a story about lesbian golf fans. Some of the biggest advertisers and sponsors in the US make extraordinary demands of the news media they advertise in. The Chrysler Corporation, a major car manufacturer, sent a memo via its ad agency to US magazines that the corporation should be informed in advance of:

> Any and all editorial content that encompasses sexual, political, social issues or any editorial that might be construed as provocative or offensive ... in order to give Chrysler ample time to review and reschedule if desired.
>
> (in Baker, 1997: 30)

In the top five largest advertisers in the US at the time, spending around $270 million on magazine advertising alone in 1996, Chrysler's demands caused a major panic in the magazine industry. The policy evidently influenced some editorial decisions, such as the killing of a short story *Esquire* magazine planned to run about a gay student who wrote college essays in exchange for sex (Baker, 1997: 32; Soley, 1997). Will Blythe, literary editor of the magazine at the time, quit because he felt that magazines were now 'taking marching orders (albeit, indirectly) from advertisers' (in Baker, 1997: 32).

Proctor & Gamble, another major advertiser spending hundreds of millions of dollars each year, has been making demands of news organisations for decades. One senior executive expressed concern in the 1960s about the representation of big business as 'cold, ruthless, and lacking all sentiment or spiritual motivation' (in testimony to the Federal Communications Commission (FCC) in Soley, 1997). More recently executives have stated that the company doesn't want its ads appearing near anything about 'gun control, abortion, the occult, cults or the disparagement of religion' (Baker, 1997: 31).

At a more local level, news organisations also find themselves at the whims of advertisers. Car dealers appear to be a particularly powerful group at the level of local news media. In the early 1990s, a survey of local print journalists conducted for *Advertising Age* indicated car dealers were aggressive advertisers, one editor saying:

> They want all stories involving auto sales to have a rosy outlook, and they whine about negative economic stories, even if they're on a national level from [Associated Press].
>
> (in Soley, 1997)

The PEJ survey in 2001 showed that nearly a decade later little had changed, with reporters saying 'we don't aggressively go after car dealers' and negative stories about car dealers being killed (PEJ, 2001: 2). In small communities, where the survey suggests these kind of pressures are felt most strongly, the potential for in-depth, critical reporting of local companies that effectively fund local news media appears to be seriously compromised.

It is because of the combination of the systemic effects of advertising on news media markets, and the everyday effects on editorial decision-making, that people like Herman and Chomsky, and Curran and Seaton view advertising as a core problem of the free market approach to the organisation of news media. For Curran and Seaton, advertising's progressively important role in the British newspaper industry has contributed directly to what they see as the de-politicisation of the British press (1997: 95).

63

For Herman and Chomsky the reliance of news organisations on advertising revenue makes them liable to direct influence on content through needing to accommodate the needs and interests of advertisers more than the democratic needs of the audience. (For a detailed exposition, see their 1988 classic *Manufacturing Consent: The Political Economy of the Mass Media.*)

OWNERSHIP

Arguments about the impact of ownership take us back to a core presumption of the pro-market position. This is that a free press is essentially the same as free speech. The American Constitution demonstrates this clearly by including the two in the same clause, the First Amendment, which states that 'Congress shall make no laws ... abridging the freedom of speech or of the press'. The previous chapter introduced Altschull's 'second law' arguing that news content reflects the interests of those with economic control (1995: 440), and others have pointed to this as a core distinction between free speech and a free press. O'Neill argues, for example, that in practice press freedom can in fact be seen as synonymous merely with the freedom exercised by those with ultimate editorial control over a news organisation's output (1992: 18). At the end of the day the privately owned news organisation is the de facto 'private property' of the editor (acting on behalf of their employer) who has the right to choose who has access to that newspaper. Although in principle anyone is entitled to start their own newspaper, or produce their own broadcast news, the economics of mainstream news production prohibit most people from doing this. So in this sense then, press freedom is not in practice about free speech per se, but about giving editors the right of control over free speech by allowing them the right to manage who can or can't have access to the news. Depending on the level of influence owners thus have on the editorial content of a news organisation's output, one could argue that journalists in privately owned news organisations are not 'free' but instead are subject to the authority of the editor, and ultimately the owner 'of the organisation.

For O'Neill press freedom, meaning in effect editorial freedom, need not be a problem as long as it is exercised according to what he calls the 'internal goods' of journalism (ibid.). In other words, as long as editors retain the authority to judge access to news, based upon the established principles and practices of journalism, then this may only be a minor detail. In this view the editor should be free to decide the value of events and opinions in relation to these principles and practices of journalism, based on their presumed experience and expertise, which should ensure a diverse and balanced range of views gaining access to the news. But central to debates about the impact of news media ownership within a free market system, is the concern over the ability of editors to function according to purely journalistic standards within the constraints imposed upon them by owners.

OWNERS

Owners have two kinds of control over the media, according to Graham Murdock, one is the direct personal control over the organisation and operation of their media, and the other is the influence on their competition (1996: 95). In the latter sense, these influences are more pronounced and more obvious in the trends of concentration and conglomeration that will be discussed shortly. The personal influence of owners on their own organisations, however, has been of persistent historical interest and concern. There have been phases in which that influence has been very pronounced, such as the era of the press barons (like Northcliffe, Beaverbrook, and Rothermere) in Britain between the World Wars. In the US, press influence has been more diffuse, but that didn't stop some newspaper owners achieving notoriety, perhaps most famously William Randolph Hearst's prominence in the US press of the 1930s (despite having a share of only 13.6 per cent of national circulation at his peak, Hachten, 1998: 54).

In Britain in the 1960s a study of the newspaper industry by the Economist Intelligence Unit stated:

> When all allowances have been made for variations within the industry, its most striking feature, and possibly its greatest problem, is its dominance by a small number of highly individualistic proprietors with their own personal interests and philosophy of management.
>
> (in Tunstall, 1996: 89)

There is a clear distinction here between the issue of dominant individuals in entertainment media organisations (Disney, for example) and news organisations (although the two are increasingly combining, see below). The central concern in news organisations is that owners may undermine editorial independence by dictating or influencing editorial policy. Examples abound of owner influence, both recent and historical, particularly but not exclusively in the newspaper industry where significant influence has been exerted, in some cases by generations of owners.

The *New York Times* is one of the world's most established newspapers, a significant paper of record having existed for some 150 years. For most of the last 40 years or so the paper has been in the hands of the Sulzberger family, beginning with Arthur Hays Sulzberger, followed by Arthur Ochs Sulzberger Senior, nicknamed Punch, and most recently Arthur Ochs Sulzberger Junior (dubbed Pinch by some, although not to his face). The middle name Ochs comes from A.O. Sulzberger's mother's maiden name, the daughter of another former *New York Times* publisher Adolph Ochs. In the early 1990s Nicholas Coleridge interviewed a number of the world's leading newspaper owners, including the latter two Sulzbergers (1993), whilst Daniel Chomsky undertook a detailed analysis of internal communications at the paper during the era of Arthur Hays Sulzberger (1999).

The combination of these works indicate decades' worth of clear owner influence on editorial content at the paper that proclaims it presents 'All the news that's fit to print'.

In his early days in charge A.H. Sulzberger read and approved of every editorial before it went to press (Chomsky, 1999: 580). Eventually he employed senior editorial staff who shared his outlook reducing the need for him to look at editorials in such detail. He wrote in internal documents that it was understood by senior staff that 'there was no question but that on *The New York Times*, the publisher was responsible for the editorial policy' (A.H. Sulzberger in Chomsky, 1999: 581). He did continue, however, to make comments about the paper's line on a range of issues from the unions to the Soviet Union, urging editors and senior journalists to push the US case in the Cold War and to demonise the USSR. He directed resources for stories conducive to his own and his friends' political and corporate interests, such as in Guatemala where he personally dispatched reporters to cover stories (ibid.: 586).

By the days of Arthur Ochs Sulzberger Senior, not a great deal appeared to have changed. Interviewed by Coleridge, 'Punch' Sulzberger outlines how he did what his father never did – attended the daily news conference:

> I like to go to the news conference every day at five o'clock to hear what's going on. Not that I take a particularly active role in it, I like to stand way at the back, get a feel for what they're thinking. And I go to the editorial type lunch everyday when we invite outside guests in. I think the journalists are used to me being around now. They're quite comfortable with it. They know the final word on editorial opinion is mine. That's been tested.
>
> (in Coleridge, 1993: 35)

Staff speaking to Coleridge indicated that Punch Sulzberger was not necessarily a particularly forceful, or intimidating owner (1993: 49), but Chomsky identifies a management strategy at the paper whereby 'management generally gets the coverage it wants quietly through gentle persuasion and "polite suggestions". Reporters understand the message and promptly comply with the bosses' wishes' (1999: 587). If reporters fail to feel the pressure of persuasion and suggestions then, knowingly or otherwise, it's likely that they are a product of management's other strategy, which is to use the power of hiring and firing. Chomsky says 'the recruitment of ideologically compatible reporters can help assure that management's views are reflected in the news pages' (1999: 592).

The kind of control owners can exercise, subtle or otherwise, is well documented in a number of countries, and many media owners have a high public profile precisely because of their interventionist style, for example, CNN's Ted Turner (Küng-Shankleman, 2000: 82). In Britain, there is a welter of evidence of interventionist proprietors in the national press, stemming from both academic analyses (e.g. Franklin, 1994, 1997; Eldridge, Kitzinger and Williams, 1997; Curran and Seaton, 1997) and the recollections of former Fleet Street editors (e.g. Evans, 1984; Neil, 1996). Because of the significance of the national press in British political affairs, due to its large and concentrated audience, the influence of the owners of the small number of titles causes persistent concern in Britain. As mentioned above, in many ways owner intervention is what you would expect given that the news organisation belongs to the owner. But the level of influence is of particular concern in the British press because of the question of motivations for interference.

What can be dismissed pretty easily is the possibility that owners intervene for purely journalistic reasons. After all the journalistic responsibilities lie ultimately with the editor, and a simple and evident trend in the British press is for owners to use the hire and fire strategy if they are unhappy with the work of editors. In other words there's no need for owners to get involved in editorial decisions when all they need do is hire a compliant editor who does the job the way the owner wants it done. One model organisation that shows this largely to be the case is the Scott Trust, the organisation that runs the *Guardian* newspaper in Britain. Following the precedent and principles established by its long time editor C.P. Scott, the *Guardian* remains a benchmark for many journalists of the right way to run a newspaper, with editors appointed by the Trust and then left to run the paper the way they see fit. In the USA, James Fallows mentioned the Scott Trust's approach as a model in his diatribe against US journalism (1996: 47).

But the Scott Trust's approach is the exception rather than the rule in Britain. In terms of the more typical approach to newspaper ownership in Britain there is something of dispute in interpretation over whether the primary motivations for owner intervention are driven by political or economic goals. Few dispute that before the Second World War, the 'press barons' that dominated national newspaper ownership, the Lords Northcliffe, Rothermere, and Beaverbrook, utilised their papers for political ends. Indeed, their promotion of political viewpoints oppositional to the government of the time prompted Prime Minister Stanley Baldwin's famous 'power without responsibility' comment mentioned in the last chapter.

In the post-war period, some have argued that this kind of deliberate intervention in editorial decisions for political motives has largely disappeared, replaced by a new breed of owners more interested in profits than politics (e.g. Koss, 1981, 1984). Tunstall argues, for example, that unlike the press barons of the pre-war period, modern media moguls are primarily profit-oriented rather than politically oriented. The ownership of media outlets is not a means to an end, political influence or power, but is an end in itself. The primary goal of the media mogul, according to Tunstall is *acquisition*, buying more media outlets and producing greater profits

(Tunstall, 1996: 80). Part of this argument stems from the emergence of non-British owners, like Canadian Conrad Black and Australian-born Rupert Murdoch, whose interests are often global, and thus their attention to the domestic politics of any one nation is likely to be small. This does not mean that owners have become apolitical, however, just that political influence is expedient to the interests of growth in any particular market. Some would see this as evident from the decline in the amount of political coverage in the British press, particularly the popular press, a trend going back at least to the launch of Northcliffe's *Daily Mail*, but accelerated in the post-Second World War era.

Other authors fundamentally disagree with this view (Curran and Seaton, 1997; Franklin, 1997). Evidence exists of clear efforts of owners to play a role in the political environment of countries where they have media interests, including Britain. Often the profit-motives of news media owners require them to actively engage in the domestic politics of nations where they have commercial interests. Rupert Murdoch's influence on the British newspaper industry has been profound since he entered the market in the 1960s, and many of his activities have explicitly involved collusion with politicians. The political line of the *Sun*, for example, was switched from being left wing to right wing in the 1970s (despite its audience being primarily made up of left wing readers – the legacy of its former incarnation as *The Daily Herald* mentioned earlier). Throughout the 1970s and 1980s, Murdoch's papers avidly supported the right-wing government, and in turn he was 'rewarded' by help from the Thatcher administration.

One of the most notorious examples of this occurred in the early 1980s when Murdoch moved to buy *The Times* and *The Sunday Times*. Opposition to this across the industry was rife, for a number of reasons. First, Murdoch's strategy at the *Sun* and the *News of the World* (Britain's best-selling Sunday newspaper) was seen to be about dragging the titles downmarket. Through the introduction of tabloid news styles and, most controversially, photos of topless models (the infamous 'Page 3' girls which survive to this day), the *Sun* had rapidly picked up readers to become the big success story of the otherwise declining newspaper market. Critics worried that he would use similar tactics on *The Times* titles. A second concern was that this buy-out would result in Murdoch having a massive dominance of the British newspaper market in terms of audience share. Murdoch managed to avoid a referral to the Monopolies and Mergers Commission that might have blocked the deal, by giving assurances to Prime Minister Margaret Thatcher that he would not interfere in editorial matters at *The Times*. The editor of *The Times* when Murdoch took control tried to assert some editorial independence from the new owner in the belief that he was secure because of Murdoch's promises. He later summarised his perception of how it really worked in practice: 'Murdoch went to see the Prime Minister, Mrs Thatcher. They shared a problem: it was me' (Evans, 1984: 17). Evans' tenure as editor ended after less than a year and very acrimoniously, and not long after his counterpart at *The Sunday Times* was recommended to retire. After that, *The Times* titles ardently supported the Thatcher administration and there were few editorial problems for Murdoch to deal with. Murdoch also used his close personal relationship with Margaret Thatcher in 1986, when he introduced new production practices despite the opposition of newspaper unions (for a discussion see Eldridge, Kitzenger and Williams, 1997). In the 1990s, the gradual re-emergence of the Labour Party as a political force saw a gradual mutual wooing campaign occur between Murdoch and the Labour Party leaders. In the mid-1990s, senior figures in the Labour Party, including prime-minster-to-be Tony Blair, attended conferences organised by Murdoch companies. In 1997, the *Sun* switched its political allegiances to the Labour Party shortly before the general election, which Labour went on to win.

The close personal relationship between news media owners and politicians is not restricted to Britain, with concern about this kind of collusion between politicians and supposedly 'independent' news media expressed in many countries (e.g. in Turkey, Dolay, 1997). To return briefly to the Sulzbergers at *The New York Times*, Punch Sulzberger commented on one of the difficulties of owning a newspaper:

> You know the only time this friendship business is difficult is when one of your friends is running for office. Or, worse, if a *couple* of your friends are running for the *same* office – that does make it difficult. They ring up and ask you, 'Punch, are you supporting me?' and then the other fellow, your other friend, rings up too asking the same question: it can be awkward.
>
> (original emphasis, in Coleridge, 1993: 34)

Another point against the idea that modern media owners are purely economically motivated is that some media moguls are overtly ambitious politically. Silvio Berlusconi is an excellent example here. The Italian owner of private TV channels as well as the paper *Il Giornale*, and AC Milan football club, is, at the time of writing, in a second period of holding senior political office in Italy. Despite continuing changes to TV ownership laws in Italy, these seem to have had only a superficial impact on Berlusconi's political influence. Indeed, whether after political office, or merely corporate gain, the ability of modern media owners to play the political game is evident in the extent to which they have been able to circumvent, or get changed, countries' regulations on media ownership as seen in the case of Murdoch in Britain, but also in the cases of people like Robert Herseant in France and Leo Kirch in Germany.

CONCENTRATION

Active owners may exacerbate two further trends of market influence on the media. One is the trend for concentration of ownership. The reason for this is simple. Competition drives innovations, such as better printing, news from more parts of the world etc., which pushes up start up costs of newspapers and TV channels. Increased costs means fewer people can afford to start media companies, and also that buying another media company is cheaper than starting from scratch. Concentration of ownership occurs where the market is lightly regulated, if regulated at all, and of course, in terms of providing a diverse range of views for democratic purposes this would seem to be a major problem. The operation of the media for profit by acquisition-minded owners, it is argued, actually narrows rather than increases the diversity of voices that have access to the news media by leading to concentration of ownership. The impact of concentration of ownership on diversity in journalism can be seen in two key ways; first in the stifling of competition, and second in the undermining of editorial independence in favour of corporate editorial lines.

In some parts of the world, corporate control of struggling news media is seen as an inevitable or even positive trend. The argument goes that in an ever more expensive and competitive market, concentration of ownership into the hands of corporate giants will save many struggling news outlets from being closed. In the USA, where the principles of the free market are very much a part of media organisation, concentration of ownership is often met without much criticism. Hachten refers to the Gannett organisation in the USA: The largest newspaper publisher with some 98 daily newspapers across the US, as of 2000 (see Figure 3.1 below).

Hachten indicates that the market logic of concentration of ownership in the US press has become an accepted part of the modern industry:

> Gannett's earlier purchases of respected family-owned papers had raised the issue of whether good journalism and corporate ownership can coexist. Now the question does not seem to come up.

(Hachten, 1998: 75)

98 daily titles in
mainland USA

Figure 3.1   Gannet daily newspapers, 2001. (Note: newspapers depicted by state, not exact location).

Gannet's overall significance in the US market in terms of ownership should not be overstated, as these titles amount to only 7 per cent of all daily titles and only 14 per cent of total daily circulation. However, in 1999 Gannet bought out one of Britain's leading regional newspaper publishers, Newsquest, owner of some 300 local and regional newspapers in Britain, so their corporate strategy is being exported globally. In Gannett's case, the corporate strategy employed with regard to competing newspaper titles has come under significant public scrutiny. Small town independent publishers, who have struggled to survive against Gannett's bulldozing efforts at monopoly, have initiated lawsuits against the corporate giant, details of which have been recorded in Richard McCord's *The Chain Gang* (1996).

At the core of documented attempts by Gannett to cripple competitor newspapers lay control over the all-important local advertising revenue. By explicitly targeting the local advertisers of rival papers by offering incentives and using pressure tactics Gannett-owned operations sought to push their rivals out of business. In Salem, Oregon, Gannett was successful in pushing a small local paper, the *Community Press*, out of business. The owners of the paper tried to sue Gannett under US anti-trust laws and, despite settling out of court, information about Gannett's strategies got into the public domain due to Richard McCord's fortuitous accessing of the depositions and evidence compiled for the case. Amongst the varied internal Gannett documents that indicated what corporate control meant for local competition, came a memo from the local Gannett publisher Buddy Hayden, after the folding of the Sunday edition of the *Community Press*. He said 'rather than rest and smirk, we will move forward with an eye to eliminate the *Community Press* from the market altogether' (in McCord, 1996: 60). McCord's release of such information helped prevent Gannett employing the same tactic against his small independent paper, but Gannett did continue to use aggressive strategies against its competition in other parts of the US.

For competitors then, concentration of ownership can be damaging as large companies can throw their weight around to ensure their dominance. Internally, though, with companies becoming so vast, the possible hands-on influence of the owner, chief executive, or the board of directors on the everyday activities of individual employees may seem to be potentially diminished. After all unlike Punch Sulzberger, the chief executive of Gannett can't attend the daily news conferences of 98 newspapers across America. Some argue that corporate control, of the kind that companies like Gannett have, can't therefore be all that damaging to individual journalists' daily routines.

Yet there is evidence that there can be editorial consequences of becoming part of a corporate news media organisation. Late in 2001 in Canada a public controversy arose between journalists and owners in CanWest Global Communications. Can West is one of Canada's largest media organisations with some 120 newspapers across the country, including 14 major metropolitan titles and the *National Post*, a national title. They also own a number of television stations in Canada and some in Australia, New Zealand, and Ireland. The controversy arose after CanWest executives, including Israel Asper (a member of the company's founding family), sent a directive to its newspaper editors that on national matters, local editors had to run company approved national editorials. Asper said 'we firmly believe that on some major issues, our readers deserve and will welcome a national point of view and not merely a local or parochial perspective' (in Cribb, 2002). Internal efforts by journalists to argue for the role of local newspapers offering local viewpoints were met by warnings that criticising management decisions was a firing offence. Both the Canadian Association of Journalists and the Newspapers Guild have become involved in the controversy, which continued throughout 2002 and was further fostered by Asper's efforts to restrict the company's journalists from writing critical material about Israeli and US policies in the Middle East. The crisis at CanWest typifies the arguably hidden potential consequences of concentration of ownership for editorial freedom.

CONGLOMERATION AND SYNERGY

CanWest is also a good example of the fundamentally different nature of contemporary news media organisations. In having interests in newspapers, radio, television, and the Internet, CanWest is a typical example of the new breed of media conglomerates. Whilst concentration of ownership in one medium, newspapers say, might have consequences in that medium, the trend for media organisations in different media to come together in huge conglomerates offers its own problems for journalists. As stated earlier, owner influence in entertainment companies is arguably not as significant as owner influence in news companies, but what happens when a major entertainment company buys a news company? This has happened on numerous occasions in recent years, with the biggest deals occurring in the US, between Disney and ABC, CBS and Viacom, and AOL and Time Warner (the latter for $350 billion). There are few other players of equivalent size, but there are some whose influence is arguably just as pervasive, not least Rupert Murdoch's News Corporation (see Figure 3.2 below).

What are the consequences for journalists within such massive, multi-media, multi-national conglomerates? Two potential problems emerge, largely due to the phenomenon dubbed 'synergy' by the business community. Synergy is about ensuring that all parts of a conglomerate are working together, in a consistent and complementary way. For journalists in such organisations this can lead to the narrowing of the investigative agenda as subjects that involve the parent organisation's interests become out of bounds or very difficult to report. It can also mean that instead of critical, investigative reporting, journalists may end up being involved in little more than cross-promotional advertising dressed up as journalism.

Evidence of these kinds of impacts does exist. In Britain in the early 1990s, Rupert Murdoch's newspapers were criticised for uncritical reports of the Murdoch-owned Sky TV network of satellite channels. Also in the 1990s, critical reporting of human rights violations in China saw Murdoch remove the BBC's World Service Television channel from its Asia-serving Star satellite network (*Columbia Journalism Review*, 1997). Murdoch's effort to keep the potentially lucrative market of China open was also seen in the late 1990s, when the last Governor of Hong Kong's memoirs were vetoed by the publishers, Murdoch-owned HarperCollins, because of criticism of China in the book. Whilst the furore over this was widely reported in other British broadsheet newspapers *The Times* titles were unusually quiet on the matter.

In the US, the most explicit examples of problems developing from synergy have been identified at ABC news, in the wake of their takeover by Disney ($19 billion in the mid 1990s). Commentators have noted how ABC news programmes have

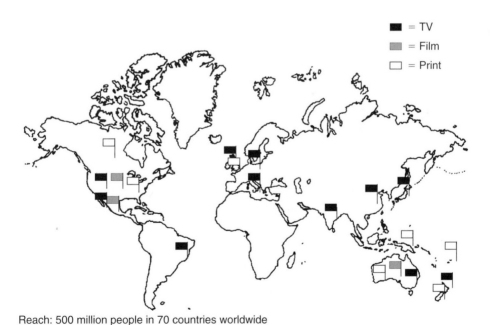

= TV
= Film
= Print

Reach: 500 million people in 70 countries worldwide

Figure 3.2   News corporation 2001.

increasingly been filled with promotional pieces for other Disney products, particularly films (Glaser, 1998). Howard Kurtz cited the example of an entire 2-hour edition
of *Good Morning America*, celebrating the twenty-fifth birthday of Disney World, which
was full of commentary like 'Probably the greatest man-made vacation centre that has
ever been built' (in *Columbia Journalism Review*, 1997: 50). At the same time as this
kind of promotional activity, evidence has emerged of ABC news chief David Westin
killing negative reports about Disney, including stories on sweatshop labour in the
developing world and a story about possible paedophilia at a Disney theme park
(FAIR, 2000b).

In the case of CanWest in Canada, the company has been criticised for using its newspapers to lobby against the retention of a public broadcaster in Canada, the removal
of which would benefit the commercially driven stations run by CanWest (Saunders,
2002). These and other examples of the ways in which news organisations become
merely avenues for product promotion for parent companies, is one of the primary
concerns about corporate control. In late 2001, the US FCC indicated plans to further liberalise the restrictions on cross-media ownership, possibly indicating removal
of the restrictions on ownership of broadcast and print media outlets in the same
community.

JOURNALISTS: PROFESSIONAL COMPETITION

Defenders of the free market and its trends for concentration of ownership and
conglomeration would argue that the kinds of influence from owners outlined above
are far from everyday occurrences, the exceptions rather than the norm. Defenders
point to the comparative resources and technology available to news organisations
today when compared to a decade or two ago, and to the massive growth of global
television news provision. But such arguments look at the issue of the impact of the
market in too direct a manner, either in terms of the amounts of money spent on
news production, or on overt influence of owners and advertisers on editorial content. There is, however, an aspect that is often overlooked in both defences and
critiques of market-based journalism. The effects of a competitive and market-led
environment on journalistic routines and practices impacts on how journalists perceive their roles, and it is evident that competition is a key factor. News organisations
compete for audiences, but also for professional status. Rivalry is a big part of news.
Matthew Ehrlich argues that, in the USA at least, an 'ethic of competitive individualism' runs through journalism practice (1997: 304). He provides some examples of
this ethos as expressed in America including this comment from an insider's guide to
journalism 'Good journalists want to win. They want to handle it so well that their
competition *cries*' (original emphasis, in Ehrlich, 1997: 303). Another example

Ehrlich gives comes from a document from the Radio–Television News Directors Association:

> News is a competition. From deadlines and budgets to ratings and shares, every day we run the race that determines who's the best. It takes skill and experience to win.
>
> (in Ehrlich, 1997: 304)

Ehrlich suggests that this ethos of competition 'may inadvertently serve corporate interests and legitimate the status quo' (ibid.). Ehrlich's work focused on the effects of this competitive ethos on local television news production in the US, building on previous work also indicating market pressures on the way journalists work and the kind of news that is produced. In a study originally published in 1980, researchers argued that:

> The demands of profits, consultants, producers, and technology combine to constrain the type of product a news organisation produces. The emphasis is on technically uniform, visually sophisticated, easy-to-understand, fast-paced, people-oriented stories that are produced in a minimum amount of time ....'
>
> (Bantz, McCorkle and Baade, 1997: 273)

Ehrlich argues that these effects of the market on television news can be categorised in four main ways (1997: 310–11). First, competition leads to 'cheap and viewer-friendly news' (ibid.: 310). Stories with good visuals that are cheap and quick to produce are favoured over complex stories, resulting in news stories of little obvious importance to the audience. John McManus's study of television news in the US concurs with this view, arguing that:

> If the news is a commodity only, the production of news narratives should follow market logic. Given scarce resources of time and capital, rational media firms should provide the least expensive mix of content that is hospitable to advertisers and investors and generates the largest audience those advertisers want to reach.
>
> (McManus, 1994: 93)

McManus's study found evidence that the routines of newsgathering in television news stations in the US indeed involved a favouring of easy to produce reporting (1994). Ehrlich goes a bit further in stating that part of the reason for this is the competitive desire within a news organisation to get to the audience-friendly news first, regardless of its social significance, citing an example of reporting traffic accidents (1997: 310).

Second, is the accusation of the 'homogenisation of the news' (Ehrlich, 1997: 310–11). The pressure not to be beaten to a story becomes more important than producing original news, the end result being news output that is more similar rather than more diverse. Organisations watch their competition, but not to ensure they're doing something different, only that they're not getting beaten on stories. Other studies concur with the homogenisation argument. Kimball's examination of national television news in the US, for example, concluded that 'the contents of the news programmes on the three major networks usually resemble each other to a larger degree than they differ' (1999: 212). Matthew Kerbel's diatribe against US television news, cleverly utilising actual news reports to illustrate his points, centres on this tendency for news to follow particular formulas undermining the capacity of market-driven news to achieve independence and diversity (2000). He states:

> Every day the particulars of television news – the news stories – are
> different, but the tone and feel of the newscast remains the same. Even
> though news events are a variable entity, television news requires consistency
> to build and hold your loyalty. If you know what to expect from a newscast,
> you'll become comfortable with it. Producers hope you'll even become a bit
> dependent on it. They try to achieve that objective by delivering the same type
> of news stories in the same format with the same personalities every day.
>
> (Kerbel, 2000: 130)

Ehrlich's third consequence of competition between journalists, concerns not content so much as the issue of power and control within a news organisation. From the point of view of journalists in the newsroom, there is the issue of the 'control of labour costs' (Ehrlich, 1997: 311). The poor financial rewards for journalists at the bottom end of the news organisation's hierarchy creates internal competition, as journalists fight to move up the ladder or move on to bigger stations. Personal progress becomes more important than noble journalistic principles, and that means covering the stories you're told to cover rather than following your own interests. As Daniel Chomsky's analysis of Sulzberger's *New York Times* discussed above showed, for individual journalists trying to keep in favour, conformity rather than dissent can be a major factor in shaping the overall news agenda. On top of that, the pressures of the production environment create a factory like atmosphere constraining and routinising the approach to news (Bantz, McCorkle and Baade, 1997: 282).

Finally, in Ehrlich's categorisation of the problems of journalistic competition, there is the issue of the 'perpetuation of the ratings system' (1997: 311). Editors and managers in the end define their success in terms of beating the competition, by how well they are doing in the audience ratings. Size of audience, i.e. having a bigger audience than your competitors, becomes the most important factor in television news success. As mentioned in Chapter 1, some critics of US television news point to the change in tone of reporting around the time of the 'sweeps', the periodic detailed measurement of audiences (Kerbal, 2000).

In the ever more competitive market of British television, the ratings have become of utmost importance to broadcast journalists. Ratings, or the lack of them, have been central to the reorganising of the decades old system of prime-time national news programmes in the late 1990s. These changes, primarily moving the flagship prime-time news programme *News at Ten*, caused a great deal of public controversy, and after failing ratings for the rescheduled alternatives the channel was forced to bring it back, only to have the BBC move its prime-time programme from 9 o'clock to 10 o'clock in direct competition. More fundamentally though, British broadcast journalists are now far more sensitive to ratings success or failure. One executive at ITN (the company responsible for news programme on three of the main terrestrial channels in Britain) indicated this:

> I'm much more analytical now in terms of ratings. I mean I have ratings information coming out of my ears overnight. I know on a minute by minute basis what time people turn off and on during the previous night's news. I'm having that developed into a schematic analysis for the production team to see, so we are more and more focused on the maximisation of the audience ratings.
>
> (in Franklin, 1997: 256)

On the surface this attention to ratings might be seen as appropriate attention to audience response, but as this chapter has already outlined, attention to ratings (or sales in newspapers) is just as likely to be focused around delivering audiences to advertisers, and many would argue it to be more likely to be for the benefit of advertisers. What is key here is that the competitive nature of market-driven journalism feeds through into how journalists operate on a day-to-day basis. Regardless of whether or not owners or advertisers make overt and direct attempts to interfere in news production, the competitive environment socialises journalists into focusing on minimising costs and maximising audiences. This can be seen as a conflict between what McManus calls 'market logic', the logic of cheap production costs reaping maximum audience ratings, and 'journalistic logic', the logic of professional standards of journalism in the public interest (1994). Like O'Neill's concern about owner influence, McManus expresses concern that the production process favours this market logic over journalistic logic, or the 'internal goods' of journalism (O'Neill, 1992: 18; McManus, 1994: 108).

CONCLUSION

Market-driven trends in journalism are increasingly pervasive around the world and are seen as fundamentally negative, particularly in the developing world (e.g. Randall, 1993; Çatalbas, 2000). Critics of the market's influence on journalism tend in the end to point to the lowering of standards in journalism by appealing to the lowest common denominators demanded by advertisers, profit-oriented owners, and a highly competitive professional environment. A key problem here is that the 'worst' examples of this kind of news are also often the most popular with the mass audience. As such there seems to be something of a conflict between what academics think audiences should be receiving in their news and what audiences appear to want in their news. Audiences can only choose from what's available of course, and it is argued that the market has reduced the choice audiences have. In many ways then, the concerns about the negative impacts of the market on journalism are pretty similar to the concerns about state influence: that vested interests take precedence over the public interest, that diversity is diminished not enhanced, and that journalistic independence is undermined rather than supported. What becomes clear is that whilst news organisations operate in environments that vary in the degree to which state institutions and the free market have influence, there are some features of any journalist's working environment that put pressures on their capacity to fulfil the social roles that society expect them to fulfil.

Chapter Four

NEWS SOURCES AND SOURCE STRATEGIES

In 1997, Nicola Horlick, an economist at Deutsche Morgan Grenfell, hit the headlines in the British news media after being sacked. Normally, people in the financial sector are rarely seen on newspapers' front pages or leading television news bulletins, and even then it's normally in relation to some major scandal or crisis (e.g. the accountants in the Enron affair). Horlick had featured in the press before as her being not only a woman but also a mother of several children, made her high position particularly out of kilter with the staunchly patriarchal nature of British high finance. As such, on the day of her sacking, photographers and camera crews waited outside her home, in a conventional 'doorstep' exercise.

The normal response of people who are door-stepped is to try and avoid being photographed by dashing down the street, or into a car, and offering little in the way of comment to shouted questions. After all, coming out of your home to find a barrage of cameras and journalists in your face is unlikely to be a pleasant experience, especially if they're there because you've just been publicly sacked. Horlick's response, however, was crucial in her story going from the city pages to the front page. Instead of trying to avoid the journalists by running to her car and speeding off, she did something quite unusual. She not only posed for photographs and spoke to journalists of her plans to see her boss and ask for a face-to-face explanation of her dismissal, she *invited the journalists along with her.* The journalists willingly followed her all the way into her offices and then, when her boss was nowhere to be found, they went with her by plane to Germany as she chased after her elusive employers. Later on in the week, Horlick allowed the press to take photos of her with her children, contributing to her being dubbed 'superwoman' by parts of the press (for being a woman able to have a career and a family).

This book has already demonstrated how the institutional and economic framework in which journalism operates can have significant consequences for what journalism actually means in any particular nation or culture. Another more universal element of journalism practice is the importance of sources. Without people willing to talk, journalists are severely hampered in their ability to report the news. Yet the relationship between journalists and their sources is a complicated one, and can have profound implications for the nature of news production. Indeed, the relationship between journalists and sources could be seen as the key to understanding how and why the news is the way it is. Certainly, at the institutional level, the concerns of the last two chapters have shown how the relationships between news organisations and state institutions and/or private companies, significantly influence the environment in which journalism operates. For some authors, particularly those of the critical political economy school of thought, there's almost no need to investigate further. For others, however, there has been an interest in how these relationships and pressures impact at a micro level, in other words, at the level of journalists in the newsroom and the sources they interact with in the process of news making. The views of such authors, not atypically, offer a varied range of theories.

This chapter considers journalist–source relations in terms of some of the core theories that raise questions about how journalism production works in practice, but also about the status of journalism in relation to other professions. Much of the dominant work on sources has centred on the production of crime news (e.g. Hall *et al.*, 1978; Schlesinger and Tumber, 1994). The communication of political affairs is also an area where journalist–source relationships have been much discussed (e.g. Kurtz, 1998; Barnett and Gaber, 2001). Often problems in the representation of subjects such as these in the news media are seen as due to the manipulation of journalism by sources, whether at individual or institutional levels, and theories have emerged to account for this. Some subjects, however, arguably emerge from disciplines whose cultures and practices fundamentally jar with the culture and practices of journalism. In this sense the misrepresentation of a subject may not be so much the fault of incompetent journalists or insidious sources, but of inherent disciplinary differences. This chapter will illustrate this latter point with a discussion of the relationship between science and journalism.

GETTING ACCESS

The case of Nicola Horlick reflects a complex to and fro between journalists and their potential sources. Two things appear to be clear though. First, journalists rely on people to talk to them in order to get their job done – journalists need sources. Second, a wide range of people and organisations often seek news coverage, or more accurately *positive* news coverage. Herbert Gans' seminal study of news making suggests that:

> The source–journalist relationship is therefore a tug of war: while sources attempt to 'manage' the news, putting the best light on themselves, journalists concurrently 'manage' the sources in order to extract the information they want.
>
> (Gans, 1979: 117)

Ericson *et al.*, distinguish here between *coverage* and *access* (1989: 5). News organisations can report on people and organisations without those individuals/bodies influencing content. This is *coverage*, whereas *access* means that a source has influenced the production of news items involving that source in some way or other, possibly resulting in 'favourable representations' for the source (ibid.: 5). The success or failure of any source in achieving access then, is based on four criteria, according to Gans: '(1) incentives; (2) power; (3) the ability to supply suitable information; and (4) geographic and social proximity to the journalists' (1979: 117). The *incentives* for sources to access the news may be many and varied, but certainly some individuals and organisations seek to gain access to the news more than others. Some victims of crime or disasters, for example, want nothing to do with the media after their traumatic experiences, while others court media coverage. People do this for a range of different motives, from personal financial gain, to wanting to offer warnings to other potential victims about the risk involved in some practices (e.g. drug taking), whilst public figures, like celebrities, seek access to build and maintain reputation.

For organisations and institutions, some may need news coverage to promote their activities (e.g. charities, or scientific research bodies), whilst others might be very reluctant to be in the news (e.g. arms companies, or security organisations like the CIA or MI5). In government institutions, access to the news can often be seen as an absolute necessity. This was a conclusion reached by a government-commissioned review into government communications in the UK in 1997:

> The effective communication and explanation of policy and decisions should not be an after-thought, but an integral part of a democratic Government's duty to govern with consent.
>
> (in Barnett and Gaber, 2001: 118)

Whatever the motives for wanting access to the news, as a very general rule 'eager sources eventually become regular ones, appearing in the news over and over again' (Gans, 1979: 118). The more recalcitrant a source then the less likely it is to feature, especially if it has the means to withhold access to journalists (ibid.: 118–19). Having said this, the second of Gans' criteria potential sources must fulfil to gain access offers numerous exceptions to this general rule.

Power amongst sources is important in relations with journalists, and in Gans' view the hierarchy of news sources broadly reflects the hierarchies of wider society (ibid.: 119). This means that the institutional authorities in society gain access to the news more frequently and more routinely than those with less power, even if the less powerful are eager for access. In some ways this seems self-evident, for example, as indicated in Chapter 2 the US president effectively *is* the news as far as the White House Press Corp are concerned (Thomas, 1999). For people further down the hierarchy of the White House staff, it becomes less and less possible to get access to the news, although it's not impossible, as the case of White House intern Monica Lewinsky showed. This basic feature of the differential levels of access between the powerful and the non-powerful, is a central part of critical theory of the journalist–source relationship. Although Gans himself doesn't stress this point, other authors have focused their analysis of sources in this area and are discussed in more detail later in the chapter. In relation to the incentives criteria, powerful sources are also more able to deny journalists access to themselves, where the less powerful often have little capacity to do this. Victims of disasters, for example, are often in the media spotlight before they even know what's happened to them (for more on this, and its ethical implications, see Chapter 6).

One of the reasons why powerful sources come to apparently command so much of the news is their *ability to supply suitable information* (Gans, 1979: 121). In many areas the flow of information between sources and journalists has become a routine process, with people on both sides employed solely to interact with their opposite numbers. The most obvious example of this would be the journalists assigned to follow politicians at the centre of government such as in the White House Press Corp in the USA, or the Westminster Lobby correspondents in Britain. In both those institutions, the politicians in turn have dedicated teams of professionals whose job it is to liaise with these specialist journalists, the most prominent of which are the press spokespeople, the White House Press Secretary in the US case, and the Prime Minister's Press Secretary in the British system. The power of sources in the area of democratic politics is one of the most heavily documented and debated, often precisely because of the perceived power of these figures. Alastair Campbell, press secretary to British prime minister Tony Blair until 2001, had a very high profile in the British media and was described by one biographer as 'the second most powerful man in Britain' (Oborne, 1999).[2] Aside from specialists in media relations, skilled in dealing with journalists, sources can gain access to the news through routines of press releases, press conferences, and 'media events' – events orchestrated in order to generate news media interest, perhaps providing good photo-opportunities (Gans, 1979: 122–3).

The final aspect indicated by Gans as important to sources' success in getting access is *geographic and social proximity* (ibid.: 124). In a very literal sense, at the time Gans was writing, journalists had to be at or near locations to report events. In order to report events more widely, say for a national news media outlet, or to report foreign news, news organisations relied on bureaus placed around a country (and for large organisations, around the world). Alternatively, especially for smaller news organisations, 'stringers' are used – journalists not necessarily attached to a particular news organisation, who work

[2] Partly because of his high profile, seen to be distracting the media from reporting government initiatives, Campbell stepped out of the press secretary role in 2001, and became Director of Communications at No. 10 Downing Street until 2003. Since taking office in 1997, the new Labour government has been in the process of reorganising government communications, and the current set-up looks increasingly like that of the White House (see Barnett and Gaber, 2001).

freelance. In the age of Internet communication both the reliance on geographical proximity and the reliance on stringers may decline, although the main global news agencies currently retain their far-reaching network of bureaus (for more, see Chapter 10).

In terms of social proximity, however, Gans is essentially referring to questions of social status and class (ibid.: 125). Arguably this aspect is as relevant today as it was in the 1970s, and is perhaps best seen not in mainstream news but in the emergence of daytime TV talkshows. Powerful, educated, and authoritative people end up dominating mainstream news, with 'ordinary' people often being marginalised because they lack expertise, authority, and power. Whilst daytime TV talkshows like *Oprah* and *Jerry Springer* have been subject to a high level of criticism for allegedly exploiting people, a defence of such programmes is that they give a marginalised, even disenfranchised group of people (in terms of access to mainstream news) access to the media to articulate concerns important to them in their own way (Grindstaff, 1997). (See later chapters for discussion of TV talkshows.)

FROM ACCESS TO INFLUENCE

In the struggle between journalists after information and sources after positive coverage (or no coverage), who comes out on top? The complexity of the relationship between journalists and sources is described by Gans as resembling:

> a dance, for sources seek access to journalists, and journalists seek access to sources. Although it takes two to tango, either sources or journalists can lead, but more often than not, sources do the leading.
>
> (Gans, 1979: 116)

Gans' contention, that sources are dominant in the relationship is central to many of the theories that have emerged about their role in news production. There are several reasons why sources have been seen to have the power in the relationship. One of these follows on from the debates in the previous chapters about the influence of states and markets on news production. Ericson *et al.*, explain that:

> the media elite is not separate from the elites who control many of the government and corporate bureaucracies that are reported on ... They interlock with these organisations in ownership, management participation, and social participation.
>
> (Ericson *et al.*, 1989: 5)

It is difficult to independently investigate organisations that may own the news outlet a journalist works for, or individuals who are close personal friends with senior figures in your organisation. If an individual or institution has some kind of influence, polit-ical or economic, over your organisation's operation, again investigative reporting can be very difficult. And yet, at the same time, these individuals/organisations might be very important potential news sources, so they cannot be entirely ignored. This is most evidently true of politicians in a country with state-run news media, but can also apply to journalists in a multi-national corporation, and is illustrated by the examples of ABC News' treatment of Disney mentioned in the last chapter.

'GOING NATIVE'

One significant way in which sources may have a straightforward advantage over jour-nalists involves routine practices of newsgathering. Even at the level of small, local news media, routines of newsgathering can have consequences for the relationship between journalists and sources. One of the key criticisms about chain ownership is that there can be a loss of understanding between a local news outlet and its community. For some journalists the point here is as much about access to key figures in the local com-munity as it is about audiences. Journalists, who are part of the local community rather than outside appointees from corporate HQ, will probably have developed close rela-tionships with key aspects of the local environment through the routine of news 'beats'.

The assignment of journalists to particular subjects, or *beats*, has become a central part of contemporary journalism at all levels. Beat journalists will have particular responsi-bilities for subject areas like politics, crime, sport, etc. The routine of covering this area will result in the journalist becoming ever more familiar with the practices and indi-viduals in that area. A crime reporter, for example, will become familiar with police officers, crime scene investigators, prosecutors and defence lawyers, and possibly with recidivist criminals. In some areas, beat journalists might even be afforded their own space within an organisation, as is the case of the White House Press Corp and the Westminster Lobby correspondents. The advantages of this for the journalist are that they are more likely to get inside information, and be more able to read between the lines of official statements through their familiarity with the people giving those statements. But there is a major potential downside:

> On beats, journalists are not only physically part of the source organisation, but over time become part of it socially and culturally. They become socialised into the occupational culture of sources on the beat to the point where the relation between their understanding and values coheres with that of their sources.
>
> (Ericson *et al.*, 1989: 7)

Herbert Gans describes this process more simply as 'going native' (1979: 144). The jour-nalist becomes, consciously or otherwise, more sympathetic to source organisations through their personal relationships with members of that organisation. In some areas this becomes informally codified amongst the journalists and sources in the same beat. Amongst the Westminster lobby of some 200-odd journalists from varied news organisations, who report on the activities of the British government and parliament, there is a group dubbed the 'white commonwealth', an even more select group of journalists who get better access to government sources, for being seen as sympathetic to the government (Barnett and Gaber, 2001: 112–13; see also Jones, 1997).

This process is potentially exacerbated by the practices of developing relationships with sources used by journalists. In Canada in 1999, a row erupted over a CBC (a public service broadcaster roughly like the BBC) journalist's strategy in interacting with a source in which e-mail messages suggested the reporter did not act impartially in gathering information. The journalist, Terry Milewski, was suspended, as a result of a complaint made to the CBC by the Canadian prime minister's director of communications. In defence of the journalist some argued that offering sympathetic comments to potential sources was not an indication of the journalist's real sympathies, but merely a technique used to get sources to open up and reveal more information. Fellow Canadian reporter Yen To, explained:

> It is called establishing a rapport. Sucking up to your source. Buttering up an interviewee. A harmless way to obtain important information. Most working journalists use this technique and it is common practice throughout the media. A journalistic convention. A method that has been used since the conception of the reporter–source relationship.
>
> (To, 1999)

Arguing further, Yen To states that using such techniques has no impact on the way stories are reported, but clearly the CBC, under government pressure, didn't agree in this case. Another journalist, Donald McDonald, summed up the problem neatly:

> The objective public-affairs reporter ... must develop a relationship with his source that is intimate enough to generate confidence and yield information but detached enough to enable him to be truthful in his writing even when the truth may not flatter the source of his information.
>
> (in To, 1999)

The capacity of journalists to achieve this tightrope walk of engagement and distance with sources they interact with on a regular basis might seem difficult enough on routine newsbeats such as crime or politics. In the extreme conditions of a war-zone the relationships between troops and the journalists accompanying them are strained even further. Morrison and Tumber offer an incisive analysis of how British journalists accompanying troops in the Falklands War of 1982 became thoroughly socialised to their military surroundings and openly admitted to their experiences shaping their reporting (1994). They quote one journalist, David Norris, who states:

> I found I was referring to 'us' collectively when we were on shore: not on the ships [when] I still felt a little divorced from the whole thing ... But I think once they were on shore and fighting, and we were with them, I couldn't help but think of myself as part of the operation.
>
> (in Morrison and Tumber, 1994: 221)

Since the reporters during the Falklands War had to accompany the troops to witness events, they ended up sharing tents, food, and experiences with the soldiers and as a Press Association journalist admitted 'the more insights you have, the more sympathetic you tend to be ... it's difficult when you are being shot at by the other side not to refer to them as "the other side"' (ibid.).

PRIMARY DEFINITION

The consequences of interactions between sources and journalists in terms of this prob- lematic of journalists, wittingly or otherwise, 'going native' have generally been seen to be pretty negative. A dominant model of these consequences and other factors on news production was suggested in the 1970s by a group of authors led by the noted British media sociologist Stuart Hall. Dubbed the model of 'primary definition', its basic premise remains central to debates about sources in journalism studies to this day (Hall *et al.*, 1978).

In this model it is argued that certain institutional sources, like the government, are able to access the news more frequently and more effectively than other groups and the public at large. They do so for reasons already outlined – that they have authority within the hierarchies of society and also have the resources to regularly produce information in a form suitable for the news media. But Hall *et al.*, go further, declaring that:

> This is what Becker has called the 'hierarchy of credibility' – the likelihood that those in powerful or high-status positions in society who offer opinions about controversial topics will have their definitions accepted, because such spokesmen are understood to have access to more accurate or more specialised information on particular topics than the majority of the population.
>
> (Hall *et al.*, 1978: 58)

This then is a subtle difference to other statements of institutional authority, as it sug- gests not only that the powerful get better and more frequent access, but that the consequences of that access are that the interpretations and definitions offered by the powerful will be more readily accepted and adopted by the journalists (and, possibly therefore, by news audiences). Hall *et al.*, state 'effectively then, the primary definition *sets the limit* for all subsequent discussion by *framing what the problem is*' (original emphasis, 1978: 59).

To give a recent example, within hours of the September 11 attacks on America the news media were naming Osama bin Laden as the number one suspect, following the initial views of the US authorities. As the US, British, and other Nato nations stepped into line with the perception that bin Laden/al-Qaida were responsible for the attacks, discussion of potential alternative suspects was non-existent in much of the Western news media. When anthrax attacks began a few weeks later in the US, the initial presumption of a culprit from the same group was quickly taken up by the media, only for investigation to reveal the source of the strain of anthrax being used to have come from a US lab (see Chapter 7). The concern of the primary definition model is thus that news media audiences, many of whom may not have direct experience of the events being depicted, are being potentially misinformed by journalists favouring the powerful both in terms of access, and also in terms of 'official' definitions of events.

The context of the development of this theory was the analysis by Hall *et al.*, of the representation of crime. They argued that:

> Crime, then is 'news' because its treatment evokes threats to, but also reaffirms, the consensual morality of the society: a modern morality play takes place before us in which the 'devil' is both symbolically and physically cast out from the society by its guardians – the police and the judiciary.
>
> (Hall *et al.*, 1978: 66)

For these authors crime news represented a clear area in which the role of the media in reproducing the consensual definitions of 'correct' and 'deviant' behaviour offered by the powerful is most evident. The language used in the above quote may seem emotive, but the high profile of a number of crimes in countries around the world, and the media's focus on them, would seem to substantiate this claim. Many countries have crimes and criminals that have become etched in the public consciousness, with mention merely of the names of those involved being instantly recognisable: in the US cases like those of O.J. Simpson, Jonbenet Ramsey, Lisa Gier King; in Britain those of Jamie Bulger, Myra Hindley, Stephen Lawrence; in Belgium, Marc Detroux, the lists go on in each country. (Some of these cases will be referred to in more detail later in this, and later chapters.)

Hall *et al.*'s contention is that in the area of crime, journalists are particularly suscep-tible to the influence of institutional sources – in Britain at least. They state:

> The police, Home Office spokesmen and the courts form a near-monopoly as sources of crime news in the media. Many professional groups have contact with crime, but it is only the police who claim a professional expertise in the 'war against crime', based on daily, personal experience. This exclusive and particular 'double expertise' seems to give police spokesmen especially authoritative credence.
>
> (original emphasis, Hall *et al.*, 1978: 68)

Primary definition occurs through a combination, therefore, of the privileged access powerful sources have to information and events that reporters are distanced from, and through the necessary development of close relationships between journalists and powerful sources, that may see the journalists 'go native'.

SPIN: THE TACTICS OF THE POWERFUL

Before looking at critiques of the model, it is worth considering some of the evidence for this interpretation of the journalist–source relationship. Since Hall *et al.*'s work, other studies have offered critiques of both the model and its relationship to crime reporting, but in the area of politics there is arguably a significant amount of evidence indicating the level of influence political authorities have over news media, even in systems like the USA and Britain, which are generally thought to have independent news media. In Britain and the USA (and in some other countries) the extent to which governments and political parties have developed sophisticated methods for dealing with the news media is something of a persistent concern.

In the early years of US independence, presidents operated without any support staff, and some actively avoided the newspapers. Thomas Jefferson, for example, wrote that a key aim of his was 'to avoid attracting notice and to keep my name out of newspapers' (in Nelson, 1998: 3). Through much of the nineteenth century, presidents had to persuade Congress to even get basic secretarial support, but as the twentieth century approached, the informational environment the US government found itself in had changed dra-matically. The population was many times larger than it had been at independence, was spread across the continent, and there were now many hundreds of newspapers, connected by an extensive telegraph network, and with ever-improving transportation links also. It was President McKinley who first allowed journalists into the White House itself (the origins of the White House Press Corp), and under McKinley the entire White House staff reached the dizzy heights of 18 people. By the time of Bill Clinton's presi-dency, a century later, the staff of the West Wing amounted to around 400 people, with a budget of many millions of dollars (ibid.: 16).

This historical, gradual evolution of the president's support staff has meant that over time successive administrations have developed ever more sophisticated tools for interacting with the news media and getting out the message to the American public. By the time of the Clinton administration, which successfully saw off an impeachment and other investigations against it, the skill of what could be dubbed their primary definition techniques were widely acknowledged. Howard Kurtz, in a book about the Clinton 'propaganda machine', wrote of Clinton's ability to maintain a high popularity rating throughout the troubles of his second term:

> It was a carefully honed media strategy – alternately seducing, misleading, and sometimes intimidating the press – that maintained this aura of success. No day went by without the president and his coterie labouring mightily to generate favourable headlines and deflect damaging ones, to project their preferred image on the vast screen of the media establishment.
>
> (Kurtz, 1998: xvii)

The strategies of information management used by the Clinton team already had a name: *spin*. A term originating in the US in the 1980s, spin essentially referred to the strategies of governments (and others) in trying to ensure positive news coverage, or ensure primary definition. Maltese says that 'spinning a story involves twisting it to one's advantage, using surrogates, press releases, radio actualities, and other friendly sources to deliver the line from an angle that puts the story in the best possible light' (Maltese, 1994: 215). A less pejorative term for this is *news management*, which can be defined as 'the attempt by an organisation or individual to systematically influence the coverage of the news media through: [1] the planned production of information and events and/or [2] the creation of a manipulative relationship with journalists and media executives' (Tulloch, 1993: 367).

There is a range of specific tactics used in political news management (outlined in detail in Barnett and Gaber, 2001: 102–113). Essentially news management involves strategies in areas of the timing, content, and presentation of information. Governments now utilise large amounts of public money for promotional information and advertising. In Britain, the government has been amongst the top spenders on advertising, in the election year of 2001 spending some £192 million advertising, making it the biggest single spender on promotion in that year – bigger than even the largest corporate advertisers like Proctor and Gamble (Cozens, 2001). Governments, then, already have a major advantage over other potential sources of political information due to the tremendous resources they have available to produce press releases, advertising, promotional materials, and publicity events geared towards gaining news media access.

Most major democratic government institutions now have dedicated teams of journalists working the beat such as the White House Press Corps, the Westminster Lobby correspondents, and the Brussels Press Corp (who report on the European Union institutions). Much of government news management activity is directed at these select groups of journalists. The most direct forms of contact are regular briefings of these journalists, which can occur in both on-the-record forms, as in White House Press Briefings (that are not only on-the-record, but are routinely filmed by broadcasters), and off-the-record briefings. Briefings are opportunities for directing journalists towards some subjects and away from others, but off-the-record briefings are even more useful for government sources as they can be used to manipulate journalists in a number of ways. Proposals for new policies can be tested out, known as 'flying kites', and if media/public responses are particularly hostile then the policy can be denied as ever having been a genuine consideration with the claim that otherwise it would have been announced officially. Similarly, information can be 'leaked' to journalists, perhaps to boost a government announcement, build expectations, or undermine opposition activities (for a more detailed list of motives for leaks see Tiffen, 1989: 105–115).

Until the late 1990s, all official briefings to the Westminster lobby by the prime minister's press secretary were off-the-record and, as such, British journalists were not allowed to name the press secretary as the source of their information, leading to the use of euphemisms such as 'sources close to the prime minister' and 'sources at Westminster'. British journalists routinely supported the non-attribution system because, according to BBC political journalist Nicholas Jones, 'guidance which is off the record suits the press because it allows for a wider interpretation of the facts than is either possible or desirable in the tighter confines of broadcast journalism' (Jones, 1996: 87). Indeed, official lobby briefings went on-the-record under the New Labour administration in the late 1990s, not because of pressure from journalists, but because Press Secretary Alastair Campbell felt that 'it has got to the stage where the doorman at the hotel where the Prime Minister had lunch becomes a senior Government source' (in Penman, 1997).

What is very clear in the discussions of news management and spin, is that there is a difference of opinion between journalists (and academics) and the people who largely do the job of managing government communications – the 'spin doctors'. For the latter group, as indicated by the quote from the British government report earlier in this chapter, governments and their officials regard news management as a vital part of successful government. Richard Nixon argued rather candidly that in the US, presidents 'must try to master the art of manipulating the media not only to win in politics but in order to further the programs and causes they believe in; at the same time they must avoid at all costs the charge of trying to manipulate the media' (in Maltese, 1994: 238). Part of the reason for this is that because 'media stories concentrating on conflict and controversy within the ranks can make a president look weak and ineffective, control of what Jimmy Carter's advisors called the 'communications budget' is a vital aspect of presidential power' (ibid.: 215).

For critics, however, government news management is anathema to the concept of open, democratic government. A number of key concerns emerge (McNair, 1998b: 50). One is that government activities are increasingly concerned more with image and presentation that with substance and policy. Another is that efforts by government and their officials to manage the news restrict rather than enhance the information provided to the public, and thirdly that this is exacerbated by the increasing role of spin-doctors, professionally trained media relations specialists, often coming from the emergent new profession of the late twentieth century, public relations (see below).

In Britain and some other nations, these latter two concerns are compounded by the job of government information provision being traditionally a civil service role – in other words, a job done by non-political appointees who are supposed to provide information about the government to the public in a non-partisan manner. In this regard, concern in Britain has centred in recent years around the role of the prime minister's press secretary, and the highly partisan way in which some holders of that post are perceived to have operated, despite it being a civil servant post. The two most widely discussed individuals have been Bernard Ingham and Alastair Campbell. Ingham was press secretary to Margaret Thatcher throughout her period in office in the 1980s, and resigned when she was removed as party leader in 1990 (for discussion see Harris, 1990, and Ingham's own book, pithily entitled *Kill the Messenger*, 1991). Campbell, while press secretary for current PM Tony Blair, became the subject of much media coverage himself, including a major documentary about his role (*News From No. 10*, BBC, 2000). Campbell's profile remained high even after he became the government's Director of Communications, not unlike the US equivalent in the West Wing. In 2003, this culminated in his personal and very public involvement in a dispute between the government and the BBC over the case made for the war in Iraq, leading to a public inquiry after the apparent suicide of the BBC's source, Dr. David Kelly, an expert on weapons of mass destruction apparently unhappy with government spin over the Iraqi threat, and subsequently to Campbell's (allegedly unrelated) resignation. Both men were noted for being very close to their respective prime ministers, and therefore extremely important news sources, but also had reputations for exerting a lot of power over journalists, through aggressive and skilful control of their interactions with Westminster journalists. Indeed, the control exercised by these individuals and their staff, has led to accusations that politics in Britain has become 'packaged' for the media (Franklin, 1994), and even that there is a crisis in British political communication whereby 'the vital function of independent and critical political reporting is being progressively undermined to the ultimate benefit of those in power' (Barnett and Gaber, 2001: 1). This criticism has been made not only of the arcane procedures of Westminster but also of the devolved parliament in Scotland. After the Scottish people voted for a parliament in 1997, the parliament began operating supposedly according to a desire to avoid the kind of closed, secretive environment of politics at Westminster. Yet an extensive analysis of the first few years of the parliament's operation showed that far from being more open, Scotland's parliament appeared also to operate in ways that benefited the powerful, and in which local journalists were at least tacitly complicit in sustaining (see Schlesinger, Miller and Dinan, 2001).

In the US, where political communication strategies are generally seen more pragmatically, as an inevitable part of the free marketplace of ideas in a capitalist democracy (e.g. Jamieson-Hall, 1996), there is still criticism of the extent to which administrations' expertise in news management undermine journalists' capacity to act as a check on government. The Clinton administration was noted for its capacity for successfully manipulating, and even sidestepping, the White House Press Corp during the Monica Lewinsky scandal. In one famous incident, Clinton used a routine event, the White House prayer breakfast, to finally publicly acknowledge his 'sin' with Lewinsky in front of an audience of religious leaders (for a description of this see Helen Thomas's insider account (1999: 372)). This took the Press Corp by surprise, as Clinton and his press secretary Mike McCurry had been refusing to answer questions or make statements about this, either in the official on-the-record briefings, or even in 'the gaggle' (the early morning off-the-record briefings, so-dubbed because of the chaotic gaggle of journalists huddling around the press secretary's desk to find out what was on the President's agenda for the day (Kurtz, 1998: 2)). When the infamous Starr report into the matter was due to be published, the White House produced a refutation of the report's claims *before* it had been published, which was dubbed a 'pre-buttal'. Clinton's survival of the impeachment process is often seen as an indication of the skill of his administration's news management tactics.

Japan's Kisha Club System

In Japan the relationship between institutional sources and journalists operates at another level entirely. Like other nations, there are particular groups of journalists assigned the beat of reporting the government (known as *ban kisha*). But the organisation of government–journalist relations via the kisha club system is far more formalised and controlled than in many other democratic nations. Hamilton explains:

> Essentially a kisha club is a room attached to a government ministry or commercial organisation where reporters from the big media outlets spend their day attending briefings, processing news releases and cultivating official contacts. The 'pack' not only works but socialises together. There are estimated

to be 400–500 press clubs and the information generated within this closed system significantly influences the content of the news available to the public.

(Hamilton, 2000: 99)[3]

Initially designed to accommodate journalists' desire for access to the political elites in Japan, they have become a significant means of governmental influence over journalists. The level of access club journalists get to their respective political sources is remarkable, with journalists able to turn up to politicians homes and legitimately expect to be invited in for food, drink, and conversation. In such a close relationship, however, comes a real risk of going native, and such close personal ties mean that a lot of the information gathered by journalists is off-the-record information that isn't supposed to be published. One estimate suggested about 80 per cent of the information journalists in the kisha clubs receive is of this type (in Hamilton, 2000: 100). That is not to say that the information gained doesn't always come out in other forms, but clearly there's the risk that the dependency of the journalists on these club relationships can limit what journalists report. In 2000, for example, controversy arose over delays in information about the illness of Prime Minister Keizo Obuchi being released into the public domain. The kisha club system was seen as a root problem in such instances because of its 'fostering cosy relationships between journalists and news sources' (AP, 2000).

Another problem of the kisha club system is that it is almost exclusively for Japanese journalists, and then only those from organisations belonging to the Japanese News-papers Publishers and Editors Association. It wasn't until the 1990s that Western news agencies were able to get some access to clubs relating to the stock market and foreign affairs, and today access for foreign journalists remains very limited indeed (Chow, 2000). Even Japanese journalists have expressed criticism of the system, one journalist recently claiming that about 90 per cent of the information disseminated out of the clubs was little more than government press releases (ibid.).

COUNTER-SPIN: THE STRUGGLE FOR THE AGENDA

Despite the evidence of attempts by sections of the powerful to significantly influence their presentation in the news, the primary definition model has some flaws that are important to recognise in order to understand the complexity of source power. Schlesinger and Tumber in a later analysis of the media and crime offered a number of critiques of the primary definition model that are useful to explore (1994, 1999). At the core of their critique is the challenge to the presumption in Hall *et al.*'s model that 'the structure of access *necessarily* secures strategic advantages for "primary definers"' (original emphasis Schlesinger and Tumber, 1999: 258). They do not deny that accumu-lated evidence suggests that institutional sources generally dominate (ibid.: 260), but

---

[3] Chow suggests there may be as many as 1000 kisha clubs throughout Japan (2000).

question the stability of this general pattern. Hall *et al.*'s model appears to assume that institutional sources do not suffer from either intra-institutional or inter-institutional differences that might be very significant in source–journalist relations. An example of intra-institutional differences might be when members of a government disagree over a policy, as happened in Britain in the early 1990s, when the Conservative government was riven over party disagreements on attitudes towards British member-ship of the European Union. Examples of inter-institutional differences might include conflicts between government and military institutions in the USA over policy in the Vietnam War, or between government and the police over law and order policies. What potentially happens in such circumstances is that instead of a consensual, uniform 'primary' definition, sources compete for that defining role, offering differential definitions and interpretations of events.

Schlesinger and Tumber point not only to potential conflicts within and between institutional sources but also to questions of the stability of relationships within and between institutional sources in terms of news access (ibid.: 258–9). Britain in the 1970s, when Hall *et al.*'s study was written, was a very different country to that of the 1990s when Schlesinger and Tumber were writing. In the 1970s, the key players in terms of institutional players involved business associations like the Confederation of British Industry (CBI) and trade unions. But through the 1980s and early 1990s the landscape of British society was radically transformed by a new right Conservative gov-ernment, which engaged in a massive programme of privatisations of public utilities (such as gas, water, electricity, the railway system, the telecommunications system, and other areas), as well as a liberalisation of trade laws which massively undermined the power of unions in particular. So, the relationships between institutional sources change over time, with some groups moving away from axes of power and others moving closer to decision-making. Arguably levels of news media access may thus reflect these changing fortunes, indeed may even contribute to them through the news media's differential treatment of sources.

So, while it is reasonable to assert that institutional sources might occupy advanta-geous positions in terms of news access, these positions are not stable, as institutional authority changes over time. Add in the possibility there may be a range of competi-tors for the defining role themselves seeking news access, and primary definition becomes not a necessary outcome of institutional sources' relationship with journal-ists, but a continual competition, in which 'those seeking access to the media must engage in the active pursuit of definitional advantage' (ibid.: 264). Indeed, this explan-ation of the source–journalist relationship is arguably evidenced by the growth of resource expenditure by democratic governments on news management as indicated above – if they could guarantee primary definition without contestation then they would not need to spend the resources they do on news management.

Of course, official institutional sources are not the only groups and individuals trying to get access to the news. Whilst Hall *et al.* largely dismiss the efforts of those outside the institutional framework to achieve any significant level of news access, Schlesinger and Tumber's critique offers at least the potential for non-institutional sources to achieve access and perhaps definitional success. Success outside of institutional sources depends on a number of factors. A useful theoretical framework for evaluating the different kinds of sources comes from work on pressure groups. The term pressure group has many possible interpretations, and it's in the differences between groups that significance over the ability to be influential sources rests. A useful definition of a pressure group is:

> A pressure group is an organisation which seeks as one of its functions to influence the formulation and implementation of public policy, said public policy representing a set of authoritative decisions taken by the executive, the legislature and the judiciary.
>
> (Grant, 1995: 9)

Although this definition focuses on efforts to influence policy decisions, evidence strongly indicates that news media access is often seen as a primary means of achieving impacts on policy. Indeed, by far the most important method, apparent by what British pressure groups claim to spend time doing, is establishing and maintaining good media relations, as Table 4.1 (below) indicates.

One way in which pressure groups differ is in terms of their composition (i.e. membership) and their apparent goals. It is possible to see two broadly different groups – interest groups and cause groups, the former reflecting a sectional interest of a

Table 4.1   Contacts between pressure groups and decision-makers in Britain

Institution	% of groups in contact at least		
	Once a week	Once a month	Once a year
Media	81	94	98
MP	31	61	89
Junior minister	11	49	86
Junior civil servant	34	67	85
Peer*	18	50	84
Senior civil servant	19	50	82
Cabinet minister	8	37	81
Prime minister	1	11	53

Source: After Baggott, 1995: 93; * = member of the House of Lords. Used with permission.

particular group of people (e.g. a trade union, or corporate lobbyists), whilst the latter reflects groups with a society-wide agenda (e.g. CND – the Campaign for Nuclear Disarmament) (Baggott, 1995: 13). Another difference is in terms of organisation and resources, with some having highly organised hierarchies with extensive resources for trying to influence both policy-makers and the news (e.g. business organisations), whilst others have a far more fluid, even fractious membership and organisation (e.g. anti-globalisation protesters).

Since a key aim of pressure groups is to try and influence the policy process, either directly through interaction with policy-makers or indirectly through influencing public opinion, a useful way of differentiating between pressure groups is in their degree of access and influence on the policy making process. In terms of a group's proximity to policy-makers, this may have a strong parallel consequence for the group's potential level of news access. Grant offers a useful model regarding groups as essentially 'insider' or 'outsider' groups (Grant, 1995: 20).

Insiders ...

Insider groups are regarded as being more legitimate by the policy-makers and are regularly invited to participate in the policy formation process. There are three types of insider groups: *prisoner* groups who, because of reliance on governments for their existence and support, are essentially restricted in their ability to pursue goals that conflict with government goals (e.g. the military); *high profile insider* groups who have a high public profile through the deliberate use of the mass media to try and engender public support (e.g. trade unions and business organisations like the CBI); and *low profile insider* groups who rely more on behind the door lobbying than public campaigning (e.g. arms companies).

Insider groups have a distinct advantage in terms of access to the policy process, often through being directly involved by governments in consultation during policy formation. In terms of news access, insider groups are able to utilise significant resources towards news management. The primary means through which insider groups like corporations attempt to manage the news is through *public relations* (PR), a term originated by the nephew of Sigmund Freud and 'father of spin' (Tye, 1998), Edward Bernays, in America in the early years of the twentieth century. Public relations emerged as a discipline in part out of government information management strategies used in the two World Wars, and the perceived recognition by governments and major corporations (particularly in the USA) that management of public opinion for both governmental and corporate ends was increasingly necessary in modern mass societies, even in peacetime. PR has been increasingly seen as absolutely central to the transformation of a number of developed democracies through the course of the twentieth century (including Britain and the USA), in areas such as the rise of the consumer society, the decline of the political left, and the increasing ideological ties between capitalism and democracy.

Miller and Dinan's study of the growth of PR in Britain from 1979 to 1998, for example, argues that not only has the industry increased massively over that period, but that it played a central role in the reorganisation of British society (2000). In the 1960s there were fewer than 50 public relations firms in Britain, but by the early 1990s, there were over 2000 (Miller and Dinan, 2000: 10). Income of the largest PR firms in 1979 amounted to significantly less than £50 million, but by 1998 they generated nigh on £450 million in income (ibid.: 11). Miller and Dinan argue that the use of PR firms by corporations was instrumental in shaping the Conservative Party's policy agenda towards privatisation when they took power in 1979. Their programme of privatisation hadn't been a policy in the party's manifesto for the general election of that year, emerging out of successful corporate lobbying for such a programme (ibid.: 13). Miller and Dinan state further that the role of PR firms in promoting the sell-off of public utilities was crucial in acceptance of the programme by industry, the press and the public. They cite one commentator of the time writing about the sell-off of British Telecom, saying that 'the pervasive doubts' of the media were turned into headlines 'almost unanimous in their enthusiasm' (in ibid.: 18). Tens of millions of pounds of public money was given to PR firms to conduct these promotional campaigns for the privatisation programmes, with key firm Dewe Rogerson, for example, receiving £23 million for the campaign to promote the sell-off of British Petroleum (BP) in 1987 (ibid.: 21).

Public relations is a specialised occupation where persuasive communication techniques are utilised in order to try and influence what are dubbed 'target publics'. In political affairs, this often means government politicians who, through techniques such as lobbying, PR firms try to influence on behalf of their clients. One part of PR is media relations, where it is the news media (and through them public opinion) that are the targets, and PR professionals in this area are often nicknamed 'flacks' (to echo the pejorative nickname for journalists – 'hacks'). PR people working in this area often have prior experience as journalists (for example, this is true of Alastair Campbell), and the job involves sophisticated strategies designed to cater to the needs of news media in such a way as to generate news access. From the holding of press conferences and issuing of press releases (skilfully written in ways conducive to being published in the print media), to the more elaborate use of publicity stunts designed purely for the news media's benefit, PR firms try to access and shape the news for their clients interests. PR specialists often also act as a kind of buffer in times of institutional crises, using their media skills to cope with the difficult questions of investigating journalists more effectively than perhaps their clients would be able to. It is in this kind of role, often as corporate (or government) apologists, that PR practitioners are most heavily criticised both within and outside journalism. (See for example Stauber and Rampton's acerbically titled *Toxic Sludge is Good for You*, 1995.)

... and Outsiders

Whilst governments and corporations have the resources to employ such specialists in news management, many other groups do not. The other category offered by Grant's model to cover such groups is 'outsider' groups (Grant, 1995: 20). *Outsider* groups, in political terms, are groups generally not considered legitimate by policy-makers, and thus do not regularly contribute to the policy formation process – at least not by invitation. Again there are three categories: First are *potential insider* groups which, either by virtue of their interests or causes becoming more politically acceptable, or because their campaigning strategies become more acceptable, may achieve insider status from outsider origins. Good examples here would be many environmental groups, who from the 1950s to the early 1970s were largely very marginal groups of dedicated campaigners with small levels of support, but by the 1990s had in many cases become global organisations with massive public support and often significant access to policy-makers. Friends of the Earth, for example, had about 1000 British members in 1971, but by 1991 had about 111,000 in Britain alone (Baggott, 1995: 169). By the 1990s, members of Friends of the Earth had also managed to get close to policy makers, with senior member Jonathan Porritt advising heir to the throne Prince Charles, whilst other former activists were working as government advisers. The rise of environmentalism as a significant political force is a good example of how source power changes over time. Having said this, many environmental groups remain only 'potential insiders' at best because of the significant resources and strong institutional position of corporate interests in the area of environmental concerns, as can be seen by the current Bush administration in the USA listening more closely to domestic energy companies than to global pressures for environmentally friendly energy policies.

In order to fit news agendas, potential insider groups try to utilise the same kinds of strategies used by institutional sources. In order to operate within existing norms of news gathering, such groups hold press conferences, issue press releases, and even try to ensure that spokespeople fit the accepted faces for news. To give an example, the British HIV/AIDS group the Terrence Higgins Trust, have had to cater their organisation to suit media conventions. One spokesperson, Nick Partridge, felt he suited the news media saying:

> I'm not threatening in a way. I am 35, I'm middle class, I speak in BBC type English, I'm very acceptable. I am the kind of homosexual you'd want to take home to your mother and that is a great relief to them, especially the ones who are desperately trying to show their liberalism.
>
> (in Miller and Williams, 1993: 132)

The second type of outsider groups are *'by necessity' outsider* groups (Grant, 1995: 20). Activism at a local, grass roots level, initially at any rate, lacks the resources and expertise to engage in this kind of professional campaigning strategy. Often groups may begin in local communities made up of ordinary people with little knowledge or skill in either influencing news or policy-making. Examples might be Mothers Against Drink Driving in the US and the similarly titled Mothers Against Drugs in Glasgow, Scotland. As such groups evolve, and (if) they achieve success, their organisation, resources, and expertise increase to the point where they are able to engage in other forms of campaigning. Third, come *ideological outsider* groups (ibid.), those who wouldn't even attempt traditional pressure group strategies because they often believe that the system of government and policy-making is entirely illegitimate, and who may genuinely be excluded from contributing in any other way. An example here would be a group like the ANC during South Africa's apartheid era, when black South Africans were excluded from political decision-making and were also largely excluded from the mainstream news media.

The further away from the policy-process and 'insider' strategies of lobbying and public relations, the more varied the efforts to raise public awareness and influence policy decisions. If direct routes to influencing policy decisions are difficult or even impossible, then utilising the news media may be an alternative route. The media can be useful for raising the visibility of a group, providing information about key issues, raising public awareness (perhaps even influencing the climate of public opinion), offering a chance to respond to official definitions, and indeed influencing the media's own attitudes towards topics (Grant, 1995: 86–9). But generating media interest in an environment where governmental and insider sources are actively engaged in trying to shape definitions of issues and events is difficult. Many outsider groups cannot compete with insiders in terms of resources and expertise in news management, so their tactics in getting news access are quite frequently different to insider groups' use of PR, and other strategies.

As will be explored in more detail in the next chapter, those outside of the institutional hierarchies of society often have to do far more extreme things than the powerful to get into the news. Outsider groups often do exactly that. The most obvious tactic comes in the form of *protest*. Baggott says protests have three main purposes: First, to express concern about an issue; second, to act as a rallying point for those with grievances; and third to raise public awareness (1995: 177). This is a familiar tactic the world over, from the US Civil Rights marches of the 1960s, to present day anti-globalisation demonstrations at G8 and EU summit meetings.

An arguably more extreme strategy used by 'outsiders' is *direct action*. Direct action is often more ambitious, aiming either to disrupt the implementation of policy or to make a law unworkable, usually by non-compliance (Baggott, 1995: 177). A good example here from Britain would be anti-road protesters who, in the 1990s, dug tunnels and camped in trees on sites due to be cleared for road-building. Of course, protests and direct action, depending on the scale of or the disruption caused by the protest, often generate news media coverage, which serves in turn to enable greater public awareness of the issue at hand.

Sometimes direct action can be remarkably effective, as in the case of the Brent Spar incident in 1995. This was an oil storage platform in the North Sea which its owner, oil giant Shell, and the British government (whose waters the platform was in), agreed should be disposed of at sea. Greenpeace, objected in principle to dumping in the deep sea, and mounted a campaign to publicise this action and try to prevent it happening. Having once been a small, marginal environmental group, by the early 1990s Greenpeace was a global pressure group, with some 400,000 members in Britain alone (Baggott, 1995: 169). The revenue generated by this large membership coupled with the rise in environmentalism as an important issue, itself in part due to previous activities by Greenpeace, meant that Greenpeace was able to employ a wide range of tactics in conducting its campaign. Alongside a sophisticated news management strategy, involving holding press conferences, having media savvy spokespeople to appear on news programmes and issuing press releases, they also engaged in direct action. Filming themselves, and with invited news media on board one of their ships, Greenpeace activists landed on the oil platform, in the wake of water-cannon from Shell/UK government ships. It would later emerge that the scientific claims behind the Greenpeace campaign were highly suspect, but the images generated by the activists on the rig being blasted by water cannon had by that time helped make Shell and the government back down in light of growing public disapproval of their policy. This event stands as a very clear example of how, on occasion, non-institutional sources can wrestle the agenda from the control of institutional authorities and influence how events are depicted and defined by the news media (Bennie, 1998).

JOURNALISTS AS 'SECONDARY DEFINERS'?

Another key critique of Hall *et al.*'s model of primary definition offered by Schlesinger and Tumber concerns the assumption of journalists as passive reproducers of institutional sources' primary definitions (1999: 259). Schlesinger and Tumber argue that this ignores or marginalises the active role journalists often take in the articulation of issues and investigation of events that may have an impact on policy decisions and public perceptions of events (ibid.). An example of this would be the 'name and shame' campaign began in 2000 by the British Sunday newspaper, the *News of the World*, which called for the revelation of the names and location of convicted sex offenders and gave out names, general locations and photographs of dozens of registered sex offenders. Begun in the wake of a highly publicised murder of a young girl, the campaign generated significant public response, and much controversy also (see Chapter 6 for more on this case). Although the government refused to alter the existing policy, the definitional 'battleground' was initiated and shaped by the newspaper, and was successful in terms of the paper's readers, if not the wider public.

Aside from proactive journalists generating their own definitions of events and issues, there is another important problem in regarding journalists as secondary definers. This arises from differences between journalists and sources in their perceptions of journalists' role in the dissemination and interpretation of information. Journalists, even those on beats, operate in different professional environments to the sources they report on. Thus their responses to information gleaned from sources, whether politicians, public relations officers, or other source groups, are shaped by professional values and practices that may conflict with the values and practices of the sources. Hence reproduction of sources' agendas might not even be possible in some circumstances, as the motives and goals of journalists and sources differ.

Scientists and Journalists

To illustrate this problem, perhaps the best example comes in the area of science. As Hansen argues '... science is, in news terms, a slow process of small incremental developments; and rarely, if ever, does science happen in the form of a continuous series of significant or major developments synchronised to the 24-hour time-cycle of press reporting' (1994: 115). Science then, arguably, doesn't fit easily into news production processes, and questions of newsworthiness or news value, and its impact on the presentation of issues, events, and individuals will be discussed in more detail in the next chapter. Science, though, also has the added feature of being a highly specialised area of professional practice and knowledge quite different from that of journalism. It therefore represents a good indicator of how sources' and journalists' perceptions of information may be very different. Studies comparing the attitudes of scientists and journalists towards scientific news are revealing in this regard.

Studies in Germany (e.g. Peters, 1995) and Britain (e.g. Gunter, Kinderlerer, and Beyleveld, 1999) have compared attitudes of scientists and journalists towards the reporting of science in the news. Many scientists feel some antipathy to journalists, regarding journalists as people who, deliberately or otherwise, trivialise, sensationalise, and distort scientific information. Peters' survey suggested that scientists have a paternalistic attitude towards journalists, expecting them to generally support the goals of scientists in their presentation of science news, try and influence public opinion, and, as is the convention in the publication of scientific papers, give the scientists the chance to review articles before publication (Peters, 1995: 42). Journalists' views of scientists, on the other hand, include the opinions that they suffer from being 'long-winded, afflicted by jargon, difficult, and being hung up on detail and accuracy'

(Gunter *et al.*, 1999: 376). Peters indicates that these differences may 'indicate a struggle for control over the communication process' (Peters, 1995: 42), but note this refers to a struggle between scientists and journalists. Gunter *et al.*, offer:

> These differences partly can be explained by the influences of the respective professional cultures. Journalists consider scientists to be passive sources who are used by them to perform the media function of informing and entertaining the public and criticising elites. Scientists, in insisting that the mass media should operate similarly to scholarly journals, will inevitably get into disputes with journalists. Scientists and journalists do not work in the same way and according to the same rules or objectives.
>
> (Gunter et al., 1999: 377)

The consequences of these kind of professional differences are quite wide ranging in the area of science. A continual concern of many writers is the extent to which journalistic values in relation to the reporting of science have consequences for both news production and news presentation. Both the production and presentation of science news are shaped not only by source strategies but also by journalistic values as to what constitutes interesting, entertaining, and informative news. This makes the communication of science not a straightforward reporting of facts, but as much a site of contestation between scientific and journalistic goals. In cases where science becomes part of the political agenda, as for example in the public health scare around BSE ('mad cow disease') in Britain, the professional conflicts between scientists and journalists can be exacerbated by a range of other sources with vested interests in the representation of such issues – such as governments trying to assuage public fears about health risks or environmental pressure groups trying to mobilise public opinion against intensive farming techniques. Miller's analysis of the definitional struggles in Britain around the public health risk of BSE, for example, argues that to some extent 'risks are represented according to the outcome of promotional strategies and their negotiations with the media' (1999: 1252). In other words, news media representations are influenced more by those sources able to interact with journalists in ways conducive to the news media than by any simple relationship to 'reality' or the 'truth'. That scientists don't easily gel with journalists in terms of professional attitudes may contribute further to potential distortions of scientific information in the news media, and some books lay out in detail critiques of media misrepresentation of science in general, and risk in particular (e.g. Glassner's *The Culture of Fear*, 1999).

CONCLUSION

In trying to understand how news ends up the way it is examining sources is vital. But trying to pin down a stable model of the source–journalist relationship is difficult. Some theories are 'media centric' focusing on the journalists and how they operate in terms of their working on beats, and representing social issues. Others are more 'source centric' looking at the development of news management strategies utilised by a wide range of potential sources in competing for access and definitional control. Even looking at the relationship through source oriented approaches, the professional attitudes and practices of journalists become crucial to factor into the news production process. At the end of the day (subject to the whims of their paymasters), journalists are still the people who make the final decisions about who does or doesn't get access to the news on a routine, daily basis. Understanding success and failure in source access requires not only an understanding of the external strategies, organisation, and resources of potential sources, but also of the internal procedures of a news organisation – the *how* and *why* behind news selection decisions and news production processes. The next chapter explores processes of news selection, factors contributing to news selection decisions, including the professional attitudes towards newsworthiness, collectively dubbed news values.

Chapter Five

NEWS VALUES AND NEWS SELECTION

In late 1984 news of a major famine in the East African nation of Ethiopia hit Western headlines. An initial television news report, shot by Mohammed Amin of Visnews and reported by the BBC's Michael Burke, produced a significant response from both the public and other journalists who saw it. Tom Brokaw, lead anchor of NBC's primetime news programme, apparently insisted the report be screened on that night's news after seeing the footage, and the subsequent response in the USA was extensive (Dearing and Rogers, 1996: 70). The response of celebrities and the general public led to a series of massive charity-fundraising efforts that stretched across many parts of the world, culminating in the global rock concert Live Aid. Yet Western media audiences nearly didn't find out about the famine at all. Aid agencies had been warning of impending famine since 1982 but despite such warnings, and the presence of some reporters in the area, the story did not get off the ground until the later part of 1984. Joe Agnotti, at the time head of NBC's London bureau, explained why the story hadn't taken off:

> At the risk of sounding callous, when you say over the telephone that we have
> a story on the Ethiopian famine, there's nothing compelling about that in
> terms of rushing to get on the air – because everyone has seen the pictures
> and the swollen bellies before.
>
> (in Philo, 1993: 107–8)

Whilst the Ethiopian famine did, in the end, reach the news in the West, another famine occurring at the same time in Brazil largely did not. Some 6 million people were affected by the famine in Ethiopia, but some 24 million were affected by the worst drought in 200 years in Brazil, and aid agencies regarded both situations as equally important (Dearing and Rogers, 1996: 69). Dearing and Rogers cite similar reasons to those expressed by Agnotti above as to why the Brazilian situation failed to make the news:

> The nature of the Brazilian famine did not fit with 'good television':
> Government feeding stations were scattered over a vast territory, rather
> than being crowded together, as in Ethiopia, where dying children were
> concentrated in places that were convenient for television camera persons.
>
> (Dearing and Rogers 1996: 69)

It could also be argued that while famine in Africa had become, by the early 1980s, so 'typical' an occurrence that Western news media felt little incentive to report it, famine in Brazil, home of the Amazonian rain forest, didn't sit easily with Western news media pre-conceptions of the country.

Much of the literature that deals with issues of states, markets, and sources could often be regarded as implicitly suggesting that journalists have very little to do with what actually becomes news. Their attention to investigative journalism is distracted by the competition between sources vying for access, and some areas of investigations are constrained by economic and political considerations. Yet even within those restrictions, on a day-by-day basis journalists themselves are the ones making decisions about what becomes news and what doesn't. What the above example shows is how consequential those decisions may be for our perceptions of what's going in the world at any given time. How journalists make those decisions, and what possible implications for journalism lay in those decision-making processes, are the subjects of this chapter.

THE PROCESSES OF NEWS SELECTION

Much of the news we receive is determined by elements outside journalists' immediate control. The state can prescribe areas out of bounds for journalists' investigations, and the market can do this also, through conglomeration, advertising, and ownership controls. Professional competition may push journalists towards seeking easily accessible information in order to beat rival journalists (Tiffen, 1989: 59); and those eager to get news coverage, particularly those with the resources to actively seek news access, may exploit this competitive environment.

Even accepting all of this, there is still a role for editors and journalists in terms of narrowing down the millions of things that happen every day around the world into the comparatively few stories they actually present. With television news bulletins this is particularly evident, with one study of 8 European countries' bulletins showing an average of around 13 stories per bulletin, and an average report duration of one minute 49 seconds (Heinderyckx, 1993: 429). Even with the advent of 24-hour news channels, and the (in theory) limitless space of the Internet, it's simply not possible for journalists to report everything that happens. Obviously, then, there is a process of selecting and structuring issues and events as news. The external factors of state, market, and sources already direct the news selection process into certain areas before selection processes begin, so in effect editors and journalists probably have a narrower range of events they could potentially actually report on. As David Altheide comments, for example, journalists can only select stories they know about, and sources are actively engaged in both promoting and covering up stories (1974: 67). Exploring this selection process requires dealing with two related but distinct questions.

The first concerns the location of selection decisions in news organisations. The second question concerns how news selection decisions are made.

NEWS FLOW IN THE NEWSROOM

The newsroom is the centre of news production and, as a working environment, is also a potentially very stressful place to work (Herbert, 2000: 32). The newsroom has been a focal point for sociological studies of news production (e.g. the seminal studies of Altheide, 1974, and Schlesinger, 1978). In recent years the pressures of the newsroom have been offset in part by the arrival of new technologies that have made the editing and composition processes of news easier and more efficient. Against that, many newsrooms have seen their workloads increase massively, as newspapers have expanded their pages and sections, and broadcast journalists now have to produce for several bulletins a day, rather than one or two, or even continually for a 24-hour news channel. Online journalists, at least those within traditional journalism organisations, are also under constant pressure. The BBC's online news service (http://news.bbc.co.uk), for example, claims to be updated every minute of every day.

This increased number of deadlines is pressure enough during a routine news day, but when a major story breaks the pressures mount inordinately. The September 11 terrorist attacks, for example, were undoubtedly the most significant events this century so far, and one of the biggest in recent decades, so it was always going to be a major news story. In Britain, the timing of the attacks (beginning 2 P.M. UK time) meant that in order for news organisations to report the event the pressure of deadlines increased massively. Most of the broadcast news operations went open-ended, that is going out live on camera with no fixed length for the broadcast, effectively turning news teams used to working around fixed bulletins into a rolling news team. For some of the news presenters this was a particular challenge. Kirsty Young, for example, had to go open-ended whilst knowing that her husband was in Manhattan near to where the tragedy was unfolding (Brown, 2001). For British newspapers, the start of the attacks was only about 6 and a half hours before the printing deadline, and it was a couple of hours before some idea of the full extent of the attacks became known. That meant that British newspapers had some 4 hours or so to cover the most important event for many years, and they did so by including extra pages (12 at *The Times*, for example). On average, British nationals devoted about 30 pages each to the events of September 11 in their next day editions – 30 pages of newsprint all written in 4–6 hours (MacArthur, 2001b: 20–1).

On a less exceptional day, newsrooms still have to deal with a tremendous amount of potential news material, that has to be considered, selected, or rejected, written up, edited, formatted, and approved before finally going into print or on air. Selection decisions are thus crucial in this process, and it in fact occurs at many stages in the

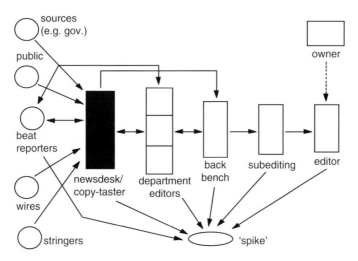

Figure 5.1 News flow in the newsroom.

news production process. If we consider newspapers first, the flow of news inside a typical newspaper newsroom looks something like that in Figure 5.1 above.

In newspapers the front line of news selection is the *news desk*, which filters all the incoming information, which includes everything from agency news coming in on the newswires, press releases from a wide range of active sources (e.g. politicians, celebrities, corporations etc.), stories from specialist correspondents (such as the political correspondent), staff reporters (general reporters covering all sorts of topics), and stringers. Stringers are freelance journalists usually paid on a story-by-story basis, rather than being permanently on the payroll. Newspapers often use stringers for covering events at distance from the organisation's headquarters, e.g. for regional or foreign news (see Chapter 10). The news desk could mean a single news editor, who is solely responsible for sifting through material, but in larger operations often means a team of people each with a responsibility for filtering news originating from different sources. The news editor is also often known as a copy-taster, a term that offers a pretty clear sense of what the job involves.

The news desk has several basic options when confronted with a story, depending on the particular news organisation. They can reject the story outright (known as 'spiking' in the trade), and indeed the majority of material received by the news desk suffers this fate (see below). Material deemed of potential interest/significance can be sent on to relevant departments, politics to the politics desk, for example, who in turn may send beat reporters to gather more material. Some material, such as that coming in from the news agencies over the newswires is already formatted as a news story, and members of the news desk can send material like this straight on to the back-bench or sub-editing stages of the production process. Some organisations use their news desk to conduct sub-editing work on material like this as well. In effect then, the news desk acts as a rigorous filtering system for incoming information. But selection decisions don't stop there.

Spiking can occur all the way through the organisation, from the news desk through individual departments, all the way up to the senior editorial meetings. The back-bench is effectively where the first draft of the newspaper is put together, with senior editorial staff having a first look at the potential content of that issue, and here too potential stories can be rejected. Sub-editing is something of an art in newspapers, as stories are virtually re-written, usually by a team each with different responsibilities, such as headline writing. Again, stories here can be rejected, but the motivations for including/rejecting stories relate here more to questions of layout and balance within the paper. Successfully subbed stories then also end up with the editorial board for approval. The editorial team can send stories back for further or initial subbing – if there is time for further editing before going to print, can reject stories or give approval. In each area there is a hierarchy with news editor, chief sub-editor, and the paper's editor all having a yes/no say over stories being considered for news. Depending on the nature of ownership within the organisation, owners may or may not have an influence on final editorial decisions (hence the dotted line). Depending on the nature of the story, editors' meetings also often include the newspaper's lawyer to comment on the legal ramifications of running a particular story (see Rosenberg, 2000). If there is uncertainty from lawyers, pressure from owners, or even if the editor is simply not completely convinced, the editor may throw the story back into the system or spike the story.

Events thus have to pass through a lot of hurdles before becoming news in a news-paper. In television the system is more or less the same, again we see the importance of the front line of news selection – here called the assignment editor, but this role is also referred to as the news desk (Altheide, 1974: 67). In television news, the assign-ment editor not only filters incoming events, but makes decisions about which events to assign to camera crews. So TV news is filtered first through the assignment editor and then through the assigned news crews. After the processing of the crews' film and commentary by scriptwriters and film editors (doing much the same job for TV that sub-editors do in the press (Schlesinger, 1978: 58)), the structure or running order of any particular bulletin is then organised by the news producer and the news director. So again, there are many phases of selection and structuring events as television news. New technologies have already had a significant impact on these traditional patterns of copy flow in both print and broadcast newsrooms and some of these effects are discussed in Chapter 10. At this point it is simply important to note that any potential news story has to go through many pairs of hands before making onto the page or onto the airwaves.

GATEKEEPING

Now with all of these phases of news selection, the question of how news is selected emerges. The first model to really attempt to assess how news is selected was White's 1950 study where sociologist Kurt Lewin's concept of 'gatekeeping' was applied to the news selection process (1997). The gatekeeping idea basically 'can be thought of as the process of reconstructing the essential framework of an event and turning it into news' (Shoemaker, 1991: 1). White's study explored this process at work in a provincial US newspaper. The subject of the study was an individual journalist, to keep him anonymous White called him 'Mr Gates', who worked as a wire editor on the news desk. In other words his job was to select stories solely from the newswires, but also included editing and providing headlines for them to fit into the newspaper. White wanted to know why Mr Gates selected some stories over others and what criteria were used to select stories as news, this basic model of testing gatekeeping theories in journalism has been adapted and re-applied in a number of different contexts (e.g. looking at female journalists, broadcast journalists, etc.). In the initial White study, Mr Gates was asked to keep all of the newswire stories he examined during one week and to write a reason on every piece he rejected as to why he had rejected it. The results were collated and categorised, as shown in Table 5.1.

The first point to note was that of the material received, Mr Gates used only a tenth of the available stories, rejecting an average of some 190 stories *per day*, so selection was very rigorous. According to White, selection was based on two factors: First, the newsworthiness of the piece; and second, selecting from multiple reports of the same event. As the table shows, in the first category 18 stories were rejected on the extremely scientific basis of being 'Bull Shit!'. Another 16 were rejected as being 'propaganda', with one story rejected because its protagonist was 'too red' in Mr Gates' view. White argued that this showed that 'many of the reasons which Mr Gates gives for the rejection of the stories fall into the category of highly subjective value-judgements' (1997: 66).

But this interpretation of the evidence focused more on the exceptions rather than the typical reasons offered by Mr Gates for rejecting stories. Out of 423 items rejected on the grounds of newsworthiness, around a quarter of stories were rejected as not being interesting, a further fifth for being dull or vague, and around 15 per cent because a lot had appeared about that topic already. Similarly, in terms of selecting from multiple reports of the same event, the amount of space available was by far the most important factor in Mr Gates' news selection decisions. As the day went on,

Table 5.1 Reasons for rejection of Press Association news given by Mr Gates during seven-day period

Reason	No. of times given
Rejecting incident as worthy of reporting	423
Not interesting (61); no interest here (43)	104
Dull writing (51); too vague (26); drags too much (3)	80
No good (31); slop (18); B.S. (18)	67
Too much already on subject (54); used up (4); passed – dragging out; too much of this; goes on all the time; dying out	62
Trivial (29); would ignore (21); no need for this; wasted space; not too important; not to hot; not too worthy	55
Never use this (16); never use (7)	23
Propaganda (16); he's too red; sour grapes	18
Wouldn't use (11); don't care for suicide stories; too suggestive; out of good taste	14
Selecting from reports of the same event	910
Would use if space (221); no space (168); good – if space (154); late-used up (61); too late – no space (34); no space – used other press service; would use partially if space	640
Passed for later story (61); waiting for later information (48); waiting on this (33); waiting for this to hatch (17); would let drop a day or two (11); outcome will be used – not this; waiting for alter day progress	172
Too far away (24); out of area (16)	40
Too regional (36)	36
Used another press service: Better story (11); shorter (6); this is late; lead more interesting; meatier	20
Bannered yesterday	1
I missed this one	1

Source: After White, 1950. Note reasons cited without following numbers were given only once. Used with kind permission from the Association for Education in Journalism and Mars Communication.

space was filled up by reports, so late appearing stories were less likely to get in. A further fifth of these kinds of reports were rejected in favour of waiting for later reports, which might have more complete detail. White noted how with some stories that if their content wasn't approved early in the day, Mr Gates might wait until later versions of the report before rejecting the story as not having arrived in time to include. White also noted Mr Gates' dislike of statistics and figures in reporting, which impacted on the news he selected.

White's over-riding interpretation was that the gatekeeper idea was extremely important in journalism, indicating how journalists on the news desk made significant selection decisions, rejecting large numbers of stories, often on the basis of personal opinions rather than overt professional conceptions of newsworthiness. He concludes:

> It begins to appear (if Mr Gates is a fair representative of his class) that in his position as 'gate keeper' the newspaper editor sees to it (even though he may never be consciously aware of it) that the community shall hear as a fact only those events which the newsman, as the representative of his culture, believes to be true.
>
> (White, 1997: 71)

Studies testing these conclusions in different context have made this conclusion problematic. Forty years on from the original study Bleske repeated the experiment, this time with a female wire editor, dubbed Ms Gates (1997). Despite the difference of gender and the changes in production technology and practices, the results of this study were remarkably similar. The top three subject categories selected by Ms Gates were the same as Mr Gates, for example: human interest, international politics, and national politics (Bleske, 1997: 75). Ms Gates rejected around 188 stories per day, also very similar to her male counterpart forty years earlier, although technology meant that the length of stories reviewed by Ms Gates was on average a lot longer (ibid.: 75–6). Also, the dominant reason for rejecting items was the same – a lack of space, and Bleske could find no evidence of an impact of gender on news selection decisions (ibid.). From such findings one might conclude that the role of the individual is perhaps not as significant as White suggested.

This has led some theorists to argue that news selection is not simply about the personal opinions of editors based on their life experiences, and may be due to other factors, like their organisational socialisation, and the kind of job they are doing, as Figure 5.2 suggests.

Evidence for this more complex set of contributions to selection processes has come from other tests of gatekeeping. Berkowitz's study from the late 1980s into gatekeeping in television news found that group decision-making was much in evidence in news selection decisions. Whilst the assignment editor rejected some three quarters of stories before the beginning of the news day, subsequent decision-making 'was a group process based on discussion that began with a morning story conference and continued in the newsroom throughout the day' (Berkowitz, 1997: 87). Although one of the journalists in the study stated that news selection decisions were done by 'committee', another did acknowledge that this process wasn't an egalitarian one, with the views of the senior figures, like the news director, carrying a lot of weight (ibid.: 87–8). Nonetheless, the point here is that decision-making processes are arguably institutional in nature, with individual gatekeepers making decisions based on pressures to

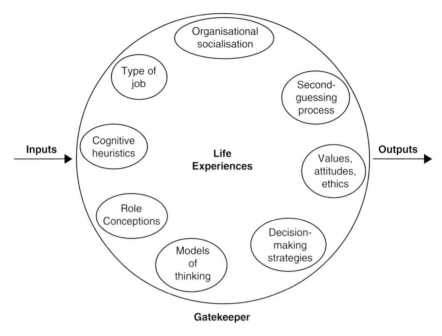

Gatekeeper

Figure 5.2   Intra-individual gatekeeping processes. Berkowitz, 1997. Reprinted by permission of Sage Publications, Inc.

conform to institutional requirements. As far back as the 1950s, Breed argued that journalists were socialised – often without deliberate instruction or guidance – into the requirements of that particular news organisation. As such the production of news is a product not so much of individual selection decisions, but of the organisational framework acting on members of the organisation (Breed, 1999). In this way, the patterns of similarity between studies looking at a wide range of different individual journalists, in terms of gender, medium, and time gap, become explainable as evidence of journalists reflecting professional and institutional norms of newsworthiness. This could be true even if, as is often the case, journalists are reluctant or unable to clearly articulate the criteria that go into their news selection decisions.

TOWARDS A FORMULA OF NEWS SELECTION

So if news selection is not just about personal opinions, other elements must influence the way journalists select news. Berkowitz's analysis of gatekeeping in television suggested that beyond individual attitudes, other key organisational criteria seemed to be at work: principally questions of resources, format, and audience.

Resource factors, such as the question of whether an event can be covered by a news crew efficiently, play a key part. Altheide suggests that because of problems of resources and time limits on getting news packaged (i.e. film, commentary etc.) for a bulletin, the assignment editor tends to rely upon regularly available and reliable sources such as press releases and the newswires. Only if information is reliable that an event is going to happen is it worth sending out a news crew to film it. Altheide says 'to this extent, planned and scheduled news is good news' (Altheide, 1974: 67). Broadcasters in Berkowitz's study acknowledged this view, one stating 'planned events are a lot easier to cover than enterprise stories ... we're more likely to cover them as opposed to trying to scrape up something on our own' (in Berkowitz, 1997: 89).

Format factors are also important, although they 'are usually taken for granted and so remain invisible' (Tiffen, 1989: 62). In other words, journalists will rarely refer to format overtly when judging an event's newsworthiness, but it is a vital factor. As with the limits of space in a newspaper that was a big influence on Mr Gates, the need to fit stories into a broadcast news bulletin's duration has been shown by several studies of TV news production. Schlesinger's study of BBC newsrooms declared that only one thing determined newsworthiness in BBC newsrooms, and that 'a story's duration in a news bulletin ... indicates its newsworthiness' (1978: 98). The need to fit reports into the tight restrictions of a new bulletin meant that, above all else, the length of a report was the most crucial element in its selection and construction. Schlesinger quotes a BBC news executive stating 'what we leave out is what in our judgement doesn't rank as news in the context of limited time and space' (Schlesinger, 1978: 99).

Alongside duration, topic balance was paramount in Berkowitz's study; you can't have 14 items on car accidents in one bulletin (a journalist in Berkowitz, 1997: 88). Herbert Gans quotes one US news producer in his study as saying '80 per cent of the show determines itself' (in Gans, 1979: 160). This suggests that stories are judged in relation to an overall balance within a bulletin or newspaper, and that the format is relatively fixed. In Rodney Tiffen's study of Australian news, a newspaper editor said:

> I watch very closely the mix of the paper. At the moment I watch, not censor, the amount of doom and gloom ... If you printed it all, you would produce something unreadable.
>
> (in Tiffen, 1989: 63).

In both newspapers and broadcast news, organisations operate within routine formats, even though these are flexible to allow for the variety of events that can occur. Such formats have a significant impact on the available space for different kinds of news, as indicated by the breakdown of a typical news bulletin shown in Table 5.2. The overall structure of bulletins has not changed much in recent years, and this sample running order looks not dissimilar to that offered by Altheide, over 20 years earlier in the US (Altheide, 1974: 67). In some broadcast newsrooms, operating within

Table 5.2   A typical news bulletin running order

No.	Title	Source	Writer	Dur.	Cum. Dur.	Chk.
001	TITLES/HEADS	VTS	JB	0:45		
002						
003						
004						
005	ELECTION/INTRO	CAM 1/INSET/STILL		0:45	01:30	AP
006	ELECTION/SCENES	VT/SUPERS	CR	1:03	02:33	AP
007	ELECTION/REACTIONS	CAM1/INSET		0:32	03:05	A
008	ELECTION/INTVWS	VT/SUPERS		1:30	04:35	
009						
010						
011						
012	ELECTION/REST	CAM 2/CU/CHARTS		0:48	05:13	
013	ELECTION/ROUNDUP	CAM 2/CU		0:18	05:21	A
014	ELECTION/POLITICAL	OB/SUPERS		2:15	07:46	
015	ECONOMY	VT/SUPERS		0:15	08:00	
016	ECONOMY/JONES	CAM 3/CHART	JL			
017	ECONOMY/WRAP	VT/SUPERS		2:53	10:54	AP
018						
019						
020						
021						
022	DAMAGES	CAM 2/INSET/MAP	RS	0:40	11:34	AP
023	DAMAGES/INTERVIEW	VT/SUPERS		1:00	12:34	
024	DAMAGES/2-WAY	OB/SUPERS		1:45	14:19	
025	DAMAGES/BACKGRD	VT/SUPERS		1:30	15:49	
026	DAMAGES/TRAIL	CAM 1/INSET	TC	0:15	16:04	AP
027						
028						
029						
030	HALFWAY	CAM 1/CU	TC		16:19	
031	FARMING	VT			16:34	
032	ORPHANS	VT			16:49	
033	RECORD	VT	RB		17:04	
034	CRIME FIGS	CAM 2/INSET	MR	0:50	17:54	A
035	CRIME/NW	VT/SUPERS		1:45	19:39	
036	CRIME/MET	CAM 2/INSET/CHARTS		0:30	20:09	
037	CRIME/CHIEF	STUDIO 1+1/SUPER	JS	2:15	22:24	
038	KIDS	CAM 1/CU	RA			
039	KIDS/SMITH	VT/CHARTS/SUPERS		2:21	24:45	AP
040	JOY RIDERS	CAM 2/MAP	FS	0:15	25:00	
041	JOY/MOTORWAY	VT/SUPERS		0:45	25:45	
042						
043	TOPFIELD	CAM 2/CU	MR	0:15		

(continued)

Table 5.2   (continued)

No.	Title	Source	Writer	Dur.	Cum. Dur.	Chk.
044	TOPFIELD/EUROPE	VT		0:30	26:30	
045	TOPFIELD/REPORT	VT/SUPERS		3:02	29.32	AP
046						
047	PICASSO	CAM 1/INSET		0:15		
048	CRICKET	CAM 2/INSET	JG	0:15	30:02	A
049	CRICKET/AUSSIE	VT		1:00	31:02	
050						
051						
052	ENDS HEADS	CAM 1/CU				
053	END/PIA	VTS/SUPERS		0:45	31:47	
054	CLOSE	CAM 3/END TITLES		0:30	32:17	AP

Source: After Yorke, 1995: 187. Reprinted as permission of Elsevier Ltd.

a formal running order format is neither possible nor desirable, but for others, particularly larger newsroom, it 'makes for speed and efficiency' (Yorke, 1995: 186).

From day to day, news editors produce a working draft of the running order some hours in advance of the bulletin's airtime, and whilst flexibility is important (to account for breaking stories, or potential problems with planned stories), a broad format emerges. In commercial news bulletins, time must be allocated for advertising slots, reducing yet further the amount of time available for stories. The table shows a hypothetical running order based upon typical television newsroom practices. The numbers refer to the script-page running order, and the gaps in this are designed to accommodate any changes to the order due to late occurring problems, or breaking news. The source column indicates the physical of the material, from studio-based camera work by the newsreaders, to videotape (VT) reports. A lot of contemporary television news includes extensive use of super-impositions ('supers') and graphical inserts (such as still photos, maps, and charts), and this is also evident in the table. The last column indicates the extent to which elements of the running order have been checked and approved ('A') by the news editor, and scripts printed ('P') and distributed to the production team. By airtime all of the items will have been approved and distributed to the whole team.

The duration columns indicate that there really is very little time in a TV news broad-cast to cover stories such that, in broadcasting terms, events need to be reducible to, on average, around 2 minutes of screen time otherwise they simply won't fit in the schedule. Even if an event can be represented in 2 minutes or less, there may be several items of that kind vying for space and not all of them can or will be carried. A broader point evident in this table is the general positioning of news items, with sports stories towards the end of the broadcast and political stories at the beginning. The intent to balance out different subject matter in this way is a central part of the news selection process, not only in broadcasting, but in newspaper and magazine journalism also. Different formats create a range of environments for events and issues, such that what might not get into a daily television news bulletin, may suit the format of a weekly news magazine.

The question of *audience interests* is also apparent in studies of journalists' selection decisions, particularly when weighing up stories that fit resource and format require- ments. As Yorke suggests, selection decisions when compiling a bulletin's running order carries significant weight:

> Being entirely responsible for what perhaps several million people will see on
> their television screens for a precious half hour or so is a thrilling and privileged
> proposition for those who care to think about it, so the editor will attempt to
> bear all this in mind when roughing out a first draft.
>
> (Yorke, 1995: 189)

A news director in Berkowitz's study declared that selection depended upon 'how interesting the story is, judged on how interesting I think the story is, or how inter- esting the viewer will think the story is' (Berkowitz, 1997: 90). Rodney Tiffen also found this to be a key criterion of news selection in the Australian news media, with one journalist saying 'it's got to be people news for people viewers' (in Tiffen, 1989: 59). This idea goes back a long way in journalism history, at least as far back as the First Royal Commission on the Press in Britain in 1949, which argued that 'to be news an event must first be interesting to the public' (in Hetherington, 1985: 2). Herbert Gans suggested that this kind of consideration involved two aspects; importance and interest (1979: 147). Putting this into sharp relief though, a key point about audience interests is that evidence suggests journalists mostly make their decisions based on *assumptions* about audiences, rather than rely on research or feedback about audi- ences (Tiffen, 1989: 54–5).

Of course, responding to audience interests is a central concern of the crisis in con- temporary journalism debate, with the criticism that news media are increasingly pan- dering to audience interests rather than audience needs. What is noteworthy about this, from an analytical point of view, is the relative lack of academic attention given to those news media outlets that appear to do this most overtly and indeed most successfully (in terms of audience reach). As Hogshire says of US supermarket tabloids, the six national titles (of which *The National Enquirer* is the biggest selling) sell more issues than the entire stable of Gannett newspapers (1997: 2–3). Despite this, they are largely dismissed in US journalism studies. In the context of relating perceptions of audience interests to news selection decisions, however, US supermarket tabloids offer a pretty clear example of how such perceptions can radically shape the topics presented by journalists. (More on supermarket tabloids appears in Chapter 9.)

So now we are beginning to home in on aspects that influence news selection for all journalists. All journalists have to think about resources and formats, which in turn influence selection in terms of space and duration, and questions of layout and composition. Somewhere in the equation come thoughts about questions of importance and interest to the audience as perceived by the journalists. But this is still some way from giving us a clear indication of why particular events are selected over others. Given two stories that a news organisation has the resources to cover, will fit into their space/time constraints, and will equally appeal to the audience, why is one picked over the other?

Those analysing story selection tend to argue that there are intrinsic elements of certain events that suit their becoming news. Altheide suggest there is something called the 'news perspective', which is 'the capacity to approach events from one dimension and then show their significance by constructing a narrative account with a beginning, middle, and end' (1974: 73). This suggests that events have to have certain characteristics in order to fit the format, style, and inherently narrative nature of news. Several authors have elaborated on this or similar ideas, producing formulas of what criteria are used to judge events for their newsworthiness, and these have collectively come to be referred to as *news values*. Golding and Elliott offer a simple definition of news values stating that they 'are qualities of events or of their journalistic construction, whose relative absence or presence recommends them for inclusion in the news product' (1999: 119; for full details see Golding and Elliot, 1979).

MODELS OF NEWS VALUES

Models of news values vary from the simple to the complex. According to the First Royal Commission of the Press in 1949, news must be 'interesting to the public' and must also be 'new', two simple criteria (in Hetherington, 1985: 2). It's worth pointing out before going any further that most news values studies view them as causally significant in journalist's news selection decisions. In other words, the values journalists assign to events determine which events get into the news (and the kind of coverage those events receive). There are those who contest this view, however, arguing that news values (or news 'factors') are at least as much a consequence of news selection decisions (Staab, 1990: 438). In this idea, news values become a way of making sense of, even legitimating, selection decisions in journalistic terms, as opposed to more pragmatic terms. So, for example, running an item on a shark attack might ultimately have been decided based upon the availability of a piece of footage of the attack, rather than the event having any inherent news value, but this still can be explained within the varied models of news values.

One of the key problems with news values research, which this point highlights, is the lack, usually, of organisational frameworks for judging the news value of events. Few news organisations write out their editorial conceptions of what constitutes news (Hetherington identifies the *Guardian* in Britain, unusually, doing this in the 1960s (1985: 8)), so it's not as if there's a professional checklist that all journalists explicitly and formally work to. Furthermore, individual journalists routinely disavow the idea that they use some model or other, preferring to see their selection decisions as based on their own professional judgement and situation-specific (i.e. what is major news one day may not be the following day) (Hetherington, 1985: 7). Academics, then, have tried to undertake systematic analysis of the values journalists use in judging events as news, and a number of varied models have emerged. Studies have developed models based on either analysis of news content, or on surveys and interviews with practising journalists. Some of these have proved more influential than others, notably the model of Galtung and Ruge (1973). Perhaps the best way to explore what news values may exist, or may be inferred from analysis of news production and output, is to compare a number of suggested models to find common elements. A summary of a number of models of news values is given in Table 5.3 below.

Table 5.3 Selected models of news values

Galtung and Ruge (1973)	Gans (1979)	Golding and Elliot (1979)*	Hetherington (1985)	Shoemaker et al. (1987)
Frequency	Importance	Drama	Significance	Timeliness
Threshold	Interest	Visual attractiveness	Drama	Proximity
Unambiguity	Novelty	Entertainment	Surprise	Importance, impact or consequence
Meaningfulness/ relevance	Quality	Importance	Personalities	Interest
Consonance	Balance	Proximity	Sex, scandal, crime	Conflict or controversy
Unexpectedness		Brevity	Numbers	Sensationalism
Continuity		Negativity	Proximity	Prominence
Composition		Recency	Pictures/ visual attractiveness	Novelty, oddity or the unusual
Elite nations		Elites		
Elite people		Personalities		
Personification				
Negativity				

(*An extracted summary of this model appears in Golding and Elliott, 1996).

The first big area of agreement seems to be that for an event to become news it must have significance, importance, or impact. Hetherington argues that in Britain:

> Most journalists in national newspapers or broadcasting are concerned with events or decisions which may affect the world's peace, the prosperity or welfare of people in Britain and abroad, and the environment in which we live.
>
> (Hetherington, 1985: 10)

As examples he says industrial disputes and government policy-making are these kinds of concerns. As seen in the last chapter, Gans argues that one way to judge a story's importance is where the main protagonists in the event come in institutional hierarchies – so the president's actions are more newsworthy than a bureaucrat in the White House (1979: 147). Galtung and Ruge argue that in Western news media at least, this also means that there is greater focus on elite nations and elite figures, so it's the economically and militarily powerful nations and their leaders that dominate the news, or at least foreign news (1973: 66). (There are other, structural, factors in the global dissemination of news that underlie such a situation – See Chapter 10). Interestingly, this often means covering events that journalists assume audiences won't be interested in, but that they have a responsibility to report in the social role. As such, topics can be covered that often 'are assumed to be of greater interest to journalists than to their audience' (Golding and Elliot, 1996: 407).

Another element Gans points to is the number of people affected by an event (1979: 151). Hetherington rates this element that he calls 'numbers' as very important (1985: 8). Put simply this concept is that the more people affected the more likely the event is to become news. This kind of thing is partly what is meant by Galtung and Ruge's term 'threshold' (1973: 64). This works in terms of the simple number of people involved but also in other ways. The more extreme or extensive an event the more likely it is to be news – which is why serial killers are covered so extensively as multiple murders are more newsworthy than one. This may also account for the relative reporting of things like transport accidents. Airline accidents routinely generate prominent news coverage, whilst accidents on the roads, despite occurring more frequently and resulting in more deaths each year, don't appear on the news with the same level of prominence (unless large numbers of vehicles are involved, and/or large loss of life/injury results).[4]

Related to the scale of the event is what several models refer to as the proximity of an event. Galtung & Ruge refer to this as the meaningfulness of event, which for them refers to the 'cultural proximity' of events (1973: 64). Put simply, if an event occurs close to the news media organisation's audience it may be more likely to become news

---

[4] Glassner points out, for example, that in the history of commercial aviation, between 1914 and 1999, fewer that 13,000 Americans have died in plane crashes, whilst three times that number lose their lives each year in car accidents (1999: 183).

than a similar event thousands of miles away. One news editor at the British national newspaper the *Independent* acknowledged that, on hearing of a natural disaster 'the first question you are always asked is: "Any Brits dead?" ' (in Crawshaw, 1999: 13). In general then there is parochialism evident in the news media in any given country (certainly in Britain, according to Hetherington, 1985: 10). With some kinds of event there seems to be a kind of sliding scale whereby small numbers of dead nationals, in a natural disaster say, warrant coverage, whereas even multiple deaths of non-nationals don't warrant coverage. A senior editor at the *Independent* in 1999 explained:

> There are rings and rings. Anything that happens in Europe and America registers high on the Richter scale ... The news editor is interpreting the resonance for the reader. It's perhaps not how it should be, but it's how it is.
>
> (in Crawshaw, 1999: 13)

In this sense, even large-scale events don't result in coverage unless there is some sense of proximity and relevance to the audience. Golding and Elliott add that literal geography is also 'distorted by the mechanics of news collection' (1996: 408). If news organisations have correspondents in place, or perhaps can access agency or local news material, then coverage may follow, but if such sources aren't available then coverage won't follow. Historically, before the days of portable satellite technology and video satellite phones (as used in Afghanistan in the war on terror), this was a major distorting factor in the representation of world events. Even if journalists can get to a location, beyond the physical distance of an event, cultural differences may limit events becoming news. The most obvious barrier is language. A rather blunt example of this comes from foreign correspondent Edward Behr, who entitled his autobiography *Anyone Here Been Raped and Speaks English?* a question apparently asked by a journalist during the civil war in the Congo in the 1960s. Other differences in practices and understanding may also limit the capacity to report events in a very different culture such as, say, western women journalists trying to report in an extremist Islamic country. (For more on global newsflow See Chapter 10.)

Another common element to many of these models is the focus on personalities. Golding and Elliot remark 'news is about people, and mostly about individuals' (1996: 410). Famous and important people, politicians and celebrities, for example, are also a major focus of news. Furthermore, famous people don't have to do extreme things to make the news, with celebrities like movie stars generating coverage just by walking down the street. Galtung and Ruge argue that this is because it is easier to construct a news story around individual people:

> Personification is more in agreement with modern techniques of news gathering and news presentation. Thus, it is easier to take a photo of a person

than of a 'structure' (the latter is better for movies – perhaps), and where one interview yields a necessary and sufficient basis for one person-centred news story, a structure-centred story will require many interviews, observation techniques, data-gathering, etc.

(Galtung and Ruge, 1973: 67)

Disputes between nations or groups, thus get represented as disputes between individuals, and normally the key institutional figures, rather than the individuals on the ground involved in events. In the recent resurgent conflict in Israel and Palestine, the focus of much reporting in the West has been on Palestinian leader Yassar Arafat and Israeli prime minister Ariel Sharon. The names of Palestinian suicide bombers, Israeli soldiers, and their respective victims are marginalised if mentioned at all. It is also easier to visualise stories in terms of personalities, i.e. get a photo or film of individuals rather than processes (e.g. European heads of state, rather than the complex decision-making procedures of the European Union). Human interest in events is perceived to be a core hook for audiences, and tying even complex social issues into the personal emotions of individuals is a primary news strategy. The case of Elian Gonzalez in the USA in 2000 is a good illustration of this. The relationship between Cuba and America is a complex one, particularly around the issue of those Cubans who seek entry to the USA. Elian's arrival in the US cost his mother her life in the treacherous 90-mile sea journey between Cuba and the Florida coast, and led to a major diplomatic struggle, as his father, happily living in Cuba, wanted him returned while Cuban-Americans wanted him to stay in the USA. Suddenly a major political issue was being articulated around the case of young boy by both the news media and the public. Although the issue was ostensibly a complex question of international relations, the human interest around the boy's fate became the central focus of the story. Nowhere was this more evident than when the US military finally went to take the boy back to his father. Alan Diaz's photograph of a crying Elian as a heavily armoured soldier grabbed him from a friend's arms appeared on front pages around the world (e.g. Campbell, 2000: 1), concretising the whole event in a simple and evocative image.

Ordinary people too can become news subject to their involvement in events. Disaster survivors become newsworthy, lovers of adulterous politicians can make the news, and as Gans points out people doing unusual things, or being unusual in some way often make the news (1979: 156). So stories about people who have lost 10 stone on a diet, or the classic urban myth 'Man Bites Dog' story, or the woman with the world's largest breasts (the late Lola Ferrari was a tabloid favourite in Britain) can all make the news. This often means news in the sense of interest rather than importance. Famous people are intrinsically more 'interesting' (in the news value sense) than ordinary people, who thus have to be or act more extreme to get into the news.

The next common element is the attribute of novelty or unusualness. In Galtung and Ruge's view 'events have to be unexpected or rare, or preferably both, to become good news' (1973: 65). Now this has significant consequences, because it arguably tends to result in negativity in news, as people focus on things that go wrong. Journalists report the occasional plane crash rather than the thousands of flights weekly that don't crash. They report conflicts over government policy rather than consensus, and conflicts between nations more than agreements. Galtung and Ruge also argue that negative events more easily fit into the harsh time/space limits that the news media have (1973: 67–8). It is easier, for example, to report a person's murder than the years it took to bring someone up as a responsible citizen. So negative events tend to fit their criterion called 'Frequency', which refers to the problems of space and time that were evident in the study of Mr. Gates (White, 1997), and in Schlesinger's study (1978). Some models explicitly include conflict as a distinct news value in its own right due to its ubiquity in news content (e.g. Shoemaker *et al.*, 1987). Some go even further arguing that the attention to conflict and negative events is inherent to journalism, reflecting its historical roots as a form of social surveillance and monitor of threats to the status quo (Golding and Elliot, 1996: 408).

A final common element is a focus on questions of style and composition. Some models emphasise drama, and core to this are emotive features. Golding and Elliot cite a veteran of NBC, Reuven Frank arguing that 'joy, sorrow, shock, fear, these are the stuff of news' (in ibid. 406). Galtung and Ruge argue that clarity, or unambiguity, is important since complex events with lots of possible interpretations are not favoured, again perhaps because of constraints of time and space which limit the chances of covering all the angles (1973: 64). Also there are the questions of aesthetic considerations, such as visual attractiveness and the importance of overall balance in the paper or bulletin mentioned in several models.

So to sum up we have news selection based on criteria like the importance of an event, based on the people involved, its scale, its proximity, its novelty, and stylistic considerations. Authors argue quite strongly that these criteria result in a certain kind of representation of events in the news. For Galtung and Ruge, their central concerns are about the domination of elites, personification, and negativity (1973). Altheide goes further stating that the end result of news selection decisions, his 'news perspective', 'fundamentally distorts most events it is presumed to illuminate' (1974: 73). Another similar idea that has resonated with news researchers in recent years is the idea of news 'frames', whereby the consequence of news selection and presentation practices is to represent events in particular ways that frame how events may be perceived by audiences (Allan, 1999: 63–4). Partly this relates to ideas discussed in the last chapter about source strategies and ideas like primary definition, but what is added to such ideas is the impact of intrinsic journalistic values that also contribute to how events are articulated through the news media.

LIMITATIONS OF THEORIES OF NEWS VALUES

These models might seem to go a long way to providing a way of assessing underlying features in news selection. There are, however, a number of limitations that must be put on to any assertions about just how accurate or valid any model of news values can be. As already mentioned, and an important point to remember, most actual practising journalists tend to reject any notion that they select news according to such news values, one journalist at *The Times* telling Hetherington that 'it's largely instinct' (1985: 9). Indeed, some might argue that the nature of the job compels them into routines of decision-making that lack the kind of individual value-judgements that analysts have been trying to explore for the decades since White's gatekeeping study (Tiffen, 1989: 66). Rodney Tiffen highlights four features of news values that limit claims about their veracity.

First, he argues that 'there is no elaborated universal formula' (ibid.: 67). In other words, journalists do not work to a concrete set of values that are universal to news production around the world. Instead, decision-making is relational, such that the same event might be news in one part of the world, but not in another, or considered news by one organisation but not another. Systematic comparisons between different countries is particularly difficult here. Most of the dominant models of news values have been developed in relation to Western news media, but it is evident that different countries often exhibit very different, culturally-specific attitudes towards events' news value. For journalists in authoritarian regimes, for example, a pro-social function is usually part of the job, promoting activities of the state rather than focusing more on a critical watchdog role. In countries like, say, China, perceptions of news value is shaped by this promotional function and can lead to a quite different style of news to that of the critical negativity identified by news values theorists as typifying Western news media (Chen, Zhu, and Wu, 1998). But even between politically similar nations there can be major differences in journalistic attitudes towards news value. In Britain and America, for example, the sex scandals of politicians are major news and seen as in the public interest, but in France (partly due to privacy legislation) there is no culture of investigating politicians' private lives. Indeed, when *Paris Match* published a picture of recently retired President Mitterand with his illegitimate daughter in 1996, the magazine was universally condemned by the French press for what was seen as an illicit intrusion into a public figure's private life.

Stemming from this, a second limitation of news values theory is that 'news values are not necessarily consistent' (Tiffen, 1989: 67). News values are highly context-sensitive, such that events that might become news at one time will not at another, depending in part upon what else is happening. The balance between commercial and economic pressures, i.e. between what might generate audiences against what might be costly to produce, often plays a major contextual part in news selection decisions. This occurs often over and above the perceived news value of an event by journalists. This depends very much on the particular news organisation and the politico-economic pressures that impact on an organisation. After CNN's ground-breaking coverage of the Gulf War in 1990–1, for example, the BBC felt that in order to compete as a global news provider it needed to invest large amounts of resources into its foreign news reporting, which it subsequently did during the Balkans conflict in the mid to late 1990s. Yet unlike CNN, who as a commercial news organisation had used innovative strategies designed to generate audience response, the BBC did this even though there were no direct rewards for it doing so. Whilst CNN could benefit financially from larger audiences, the BBC's licence-fee based funding is not related to audience size, and so covering the Balkans conflict, in financial terms, simply cost the organisations a lot of money. The justification behind this lay in the view that in order to retain its privileged status as Britain's publicly funded network, it had to be seen to offer the most comprehensive news service of any British broadcast news service. The point here is that factors other than any intrinsic elements of the events themselves contribute to news selection decisions in a manner that is not necessarily consistent. In both these cases it was institutional agendas within CNN and the BBC that shaped the news selection decisions in those respective conflicts.

A third qualification that needs to be recalled, according to Tiffen, is that 'news values are not necessarily universally held or adhered to' (ibid.). Not only do organisations disagree on the newsworthiness of events, but disagreement can also occur within organisations between the staff. Readers of the British national press would be able to identify the former easily enough between the serious broadsheets and the populist tabloids, which routinely offer vastly different topics on their front pages. Disagreements within the newsroom are not evident from content analysis studies (showing a flaw in the news values studies based on content analysis), and are more difficult to assess. Certainly there can be disagreements between reporters and editors over the value of stories. As already mentioned, in some organisations there can be collective decision-making, with senior figures having more of a say. In Chapter 3 the point was also made that professional competition may add to conformity in the newsroom in order to please the bosses. Nonetheless, the point here is not so much about the eventual outcome, but that different points of view will exist within any news organisation even after allowing for organisational pressures of socialisation and conformity.

Finally, Tiffen points out that 'news values are not necessarily realisable' (1989: 68). Even if there was a consistent, universal system of news values there is still the problem of supply. The zenith of political reporting in America might be the uncovering of a corrupt president *à la* the Watergate scandal, for example, but not all presidents are corrupt, or as bad as Nixon at covering it up. A more practical problem comes from being able to get access to locations to gather the material needed, particularly visual material for photojournalists and television news teams. Reporting the conflict in Afghanistan post-September 11 has undoubtedly been a major news story, but the difficult terrain, the antipathy of local radicals to news media (evident by the many journalists killed in the conflict), and the sheer costs of sustaining reporters in the area has been enormous. In the early weeks after September 11, CNN were spending around £500,000 a week, and the BBC around £1 million per week on covering events (Sherwin, 2001: 19). Such increased costs can't be sustained for a prolonged period, as BBC director of news Richard Sambrook acknowledged in October 2001 when he said 'clearly if we are still on a war footing in six months time we will have to decide how to cut our cloth' (in ibid.: 19). Tiffen agrees with Altheide's view that this kind of thing in itself contributes to the situation in television news that planned and pre-scheduled events dominate (1989: 68). Alternatively the quality of imagery can be compromised due to costs. The Afghan conflict has seen the widespread use of satellite videophones rather than the more typical truck-based satellite technology. Pioneered by CNN's Nic Roberston, the images are of a much poorer quality, but videophones only cost about £10,000 compared with the £250,000 for a satellite truck (ibid.). So, there are practical limitations on the realisation of events' and issues' news value. A final aspect to mention here, linking to the next chapter, is that it is possible that ethical considerations might also limit the potential for realising the news value of events.

CONCLUSION

The selection of news is perhaps the hub of the news production process. While many authors focus on genuinely important aspects such as politico-economic factors, or perhaps on source strategies, there can be a failure to really recognise the significance of the news production process, and selection decision-making within that process. Whether models of gatekeeping and news values offer real insight into this process or not, they at least highlight the ways in which journalists' decision-making could have a major impact on the construction and presentation of news. That so many journalists regard this process as an instinctive, creative skill rather than a product of subjective value-judgements or institutional socialisation, is of particular interest from a sociological point of view. Investigating the role of mainstream journalists in the news production process further can shed more light on this question of whether or not there are fundamental aspects of journalism regardless of who's doing the job and where they are doing it. The next chapter looks at another area of journalistic decision-making that equally highlights the importance of the choices made by journalists when gathering news, specifically the many situations where newsgathering practices raise ethical questions.

Chapter Six

☐ NEWS GATHERING AND PROFESSIONAL ETHICS

Herbert Altschull's critique of the role of journalists as 'agents of power' concludes with a list of what he regards as the seven laws of journalism, some of which have already been touched upon in this book. The last of these states that 'press practices always differ from press theory' (1995: 441). Although he meant something rather more polemical, in practical terms it serves as a pretty fair description of the relationship between theories of best practice, and what happens in journalism on a day-to-day basis. Just as many practicing journalists deny operating to some kind of set of news values, or at least those drawn up by scholars, the notion of what constitutes ethical newsgathering practice routinely tests the relationship between theory and practice. This is particularly true when journalists are confronted by situations involving difficult topics such as war, murder, rape, euthanasia etc. and those that generate tensions between the rights of individuals and the public interest. In this chapter some of the primary ethical dilemmas that emerge in newsgathering will be examined, along with a look at the attitudes of journalists around the world as to what constitutes ethical practice, and a consideration of professional codes of ethics in journalism.

ETHICAL QUESTIONS IN JOURNALISM

Distinguishing between morality and ethics is important when exploring such concepts in a particular profession like journalism. Some authors talk about morality in journalism (e.g. Klaidman and Beauchamp, 1992). Although this is a complex philosophical area, for the purposes of this book it's worth making a simple distinction regarding morality and ethics. Klaidman and Beauchamp define morality, for example, as a set of 'culturally transmitted rules of right and wrong conduct that establish the basic terms of social life' (1992: 39). Morality then, is about the fundamental values and beliefs about right and wrong in a given society. Within the terminology of the philosophy of ethics, questions of morality could be seen to correspond to what is sometimes referred to as normative ethics. News photographer Kenneth Kobre offers a good example of normative journalism ethics. Kobre argues that there are three main approaches to newsgathering ethics (1991: 292). The *utilitarian* approach takes the position that news provides information crucial to democracy, and as such no matter how terrible the events they must be reported (and photographed) in order to inform the public. The *absolutist* approach, on the other hand, is the position that news must take account of basic human rights, such as privacy, and no matter how important the event these rights should not be breached. Kobre offers a final possible approach, which he dubs the 'Golden Rule', in which journalists should put themselves in the position of the people involved, and ask themselves 'if it were you would you want journalists asking you questions or taking photographs?'.

Kobre's model suggests that there may be almost absolute rules of ethical conduct, which whilst they might vary from journalist to journalist, should in principle be applied consistently by every journalist. In the area of ethics known as applied ethics, however, the onus is on actions and behaviour in particular situations. Values and behaviour do not necessarily fit neatly together in certain situations. Applying absolute ethical rules in some situations creates conflicts, particularly within certain professions such as priests, doctors, and lawyers. As Daniel points out 'most journalists do not live and work in an environment of *ordinary* interaction and communication' (original emphasis, 1992: 51). We've seen through the course of this book so far persistent examples of normative claims about journalists – claims about what journalists *should* or *shouldn't* be doing. A distinct part of the climate of crisis evident in some nations relates strongly to normative perceptions of the journalists' ethical standards. In the USA, for example, surveys of public confidence in the news media have shown persistent declines in confidence about the press over the last 10 to 20 years (Cook et al., 2000). In Britain, a 1995 survey of Members of Parliament (MPs) showed that some 77% regarded journalists as having 'low' or 'very low' standards of honesty and ethics (Tunstall, 1996: 231). In order to assess the validity or otherwise of criticisms of journalists' ethics, a variety of ethically problematic situations in journalistic practice need to be explored. The next few sections of this chapter explore attitudes towards and examples of some of these situational dilemmas.

INTERVENTION

Many of the criticisms of contemporary journalism relate to normative ideas about what journalists should or shouldn't be doing. From a conceptual point of view this will be examined in some detail in the next chapter, but there is an ethical dimension to normative ideas about the role and function of journalists in this regard, to do with when, if ever, journalists should attempt to intervene in the events they are reporting on, either literally in the field, or editorially.

THE KOSANESE AMBUSH

Intervening in the field would seem to offer a prime example of the conflicts of interest an individual journalist may face between their requirements as a professional journalist and their human nature. Certainly the way some critics have attacked journalists' approach to possible intervention situations suggest that the 'correct' journalistic decision may not be the correct one for other points of view. James Fallows' famous attack on the US news media, *Breaking the News*, effectively begins with this kind of intervention dilemma (1996: 10–16). He cites a hypothetical example put to two well-known US broadcast journalists on a television discussion programme about ethics in wartime. The journalists were told they were covering a war between the USA and the 'North Kosanese' (a synthesis of Korea and Vietnam), and had been invited by the North Kosanese to accompany a troop on manoeuvres. Both journalists agreed they would do this, and it had been done in the past in real war situations. Whilst on patrol the North Kosanese troops come across an American unit and decide to lay an ambush for them. The journalists were then asked what they would do: Would they try to alert their fellow Americans of the danger, or remain quiet and just watch what happened?

Fallows' criticism of the journalists' responses had two elements. First was their assertion that their journalistic responsibility would prevent them from intervening and warning their fellow countrymen of the ambush (ibid.: 14). The other panellists (predominantly military people from combat soldiers to top brass) were critical to the point of contempt for this position, and Fallows clearly concurred with those sentiments. Second, was that when pushed for a justification of this position, neither journalist could offer a reason, and Fallows criticised the apparent lack of thinking through of the rationale and consequences of their (hypothetical) actions (ibid.: 15).

The incapacity of either journalist to offer a clear reason for their position is arguably indicative of the professional environment in which they operate. The pace of newsrooms is such that the values that inform journalists' practice are not necessarily spelt out or written down. In other words, as discussed in the previous chapter journalists are socialised into certain organisational practices, which they recognise and assert as appropriate to their profession, but have not necessarily thought through, or are able to articulate at any individual level. The same criticism could be placed at the feet of many professions, such as doctors, lawyers, or anyone else for that matter. Indeed, Fallows recounts another hypothetical situation considered on the programme, of the possible torture of a captured enemy soldier in order to find out the location of several captured US soldiers (ibid.: 10–12). The panellist confronted with this situation was a former field soldier and he said he would indeed torture the captive. Fallows makes no judgement about this decision other than to argue that the decision was clearly thought through, even though the senior military panellists criticised the soldier's decision as inappropriate behaviour. To some extent then, Fallows takes these particular journalists' lack of articulation and self-reflexivity and generalises their responses to all journalism whilst not doing the same for the responses from the military panellists.

There is a defence of non-intervention in such a situation that more articulate journalists might have offered. Assuming that the journalists by not intervening were able to escape the ambush unhurt and were allowed to return with their film intact, the potential for shifting public and political attitudes to the war may have been profound. Images of US soldiers being cut down in an ambush may harden public and political attitudes either for the war or against it. The net result may be changes in policy and strategy that may save many more lives than the journalists might have saved by intervening. No doubt there is a long chain of 'ifs and buts' in this defence, but there are precedents for this. Several famous violent images of Vietnam, for example, have been cited as influential in shifting public attitudes in the US against the war, such as the Pulitzer Prize-winning 1972 photograph, by Nick Ut, of Kim Phuc (then a young child, now a UN representative) running naked from the ruins of a US napalm attack. It's also possible that attempting to intervene in such situations might get the journalists killed, and therefore no-one would ever find out about what happened.

The problem is undoubtedly one of weighing up the relative value of the immediate circumstances and the wider socio-political impacts that reporting of events might have. Journalism, in the context of events like wars, is as much about trying to illustrate and articulate the causes and consequences of major events as it is about covering particular incidents. Arguably seeing that 'bigger picture', and thus reflecting and reporting the entire sweep of an event, may require non-intervention in any one particular incident. A rather stark example of this comes in the context of famines. The now deceased award-winning photographer Kevin Carter was renowned for his capacity to capture large-scale events in small-scale scenes. In one key photograph of a famine in Somalia, Carter captured an image of a small child, close to death, with a vulture in the background waiting patiently for the child to die. A colleague later discussed this Pulitzer Prize winning photograph with Carter:

> I asked the obvious question of the vulture photograph: 'What did you do with the baby?' He looked at me in bewilderment and said: 'Nothing, there were thousands of them'.
>
> (Beresford, 1994: 17)

One commentator condemned this kind of situation as a 'revolting orgy' of journalists in pursuit of awards in exchange for images of the sick and the dying (in ibid.). Yet, as Beresford points out, without people like Carter, the wider world would not know about such tragedies, and potentially not recognise the severity of such situations (ibid.). The responsibility of the journalist then could be seen as getting their images and information back to the wider world and not getting embroiled in the particulars of the situation however harrowing they may be.

NAMING AND SHAMING

Although the examples above may suggest that journalists' inaction can create serious
ethical dilemmas, intervening in an event may be just as problematic, especially when
a news organisation decides to campaign around a particular cause. A good example
of this would be the 'naming and shaming' campaign conducted by the British
Sunday tabloid newspaper the *News of the World* in the summer of 2000. The high profile child murder case, mentioned in Chapter 4 in relation to news stories contributing to policy debates, prompted the newspaper's editor, Rebekah Wade, to run a
series of stories in which photographs, names, and places of residence of a number of
convicted sex offenders were listed. The notional aim was to push for legislation similar to that of Meagan's Law in the USA, where communities are entitled to information
about convicted sex offenders resident amongst them (this law was itself a response to
a high profile child murder, where a young girl was killed by a convicted offender
living in her neighbourhood without other residents' knowledge). Critics argued that
Wade was merely jumping on the back of an emotive news story in order to try and
boost sales of her paper, pointing out that it would have taken the paper two or three
years of continuous publication to actually 'name and shame' the 110,000 or so convicted sex offenders (Holborow, 2000: 11).

The News of the World's campaign was widely criticised by the authorities, and many
of the criticisms of the campaign's possible effects were realised. With emotions over
the child's death running high in many communities, innocent people who looked
vaguely like, or shared the name of someone named on the list, were attacked and
had their families and homes attacked, sometimes by large mobs of people. A paedi-
atrician was even attacked – mistaken for a paedophile. Some offenders whose location had been known to the police went into hiding making it more difficult for the
authorities to track them. One of the named men, at the time facing a jail term for a
sex crime, even had his sentence suspended by the judge due to the adverse media
coverage. In all of this, including major criticism from the British broadsheet press,
Wade refused to publicly defend her campaign outside of her own editorial column,
invoking even more criticism from other journalists (Morgan, 2000: 2).

The British paper eventually halted the campaign in light of such criticism, the unin-
tended consequences of the coverage, and the government's refusal to change its
policy. But Britain isn't the only nation to have witnessed this kind of news media
campaign. Periodicals elsewhere in Europe have also conducted comparable campaigns in the face of crimes against children. In Belgium, the paedophilia crimes
of Marc Dutroux in 1997 shook the national consciousness, and magazines there
have also listed details of convicted sex offenders. In August 2000, two brutal child
murders led the right-wing Italian paper *Libero* to publish information about convicted offenders, although Italian privacy laws prevented the paper from giving the

kind of details possible in the British case (such as the towns where people lived) (Willey, 2000).

The central ethical dilemma in such cases rests on the consequences of media coverage. There is a real risk of media coverage of crime resulting in investigations and subsequent trials being affected and, paradoxically, criminals that news media might want to demonise through their coverage might get off (or innocent people may be jailed). The concern is that juries may be influenced by media coverage in a way that would prejudice a verdict making it unsound. The infamous O.J. Simpson trial of the mid-1990s was a classic example of this, where even finding enough jurors for a trial of a case that had received masses of media coverage was difficult enough. Once selected, jurors had to become virtual prisoners in hotels and be denied access to both print and broadcast media for the duration of the trial.

In Britain, the high profile trial of two football stars from Leeds United Football Club in 2001 was dramatically aborted at the last minute, when the *Sunday Mirror* published a story from the victim's father the day before the verdict. The two white sports stars were accused of grievous bodily harm on an Asian man, whose father claimed the attack was racially motivated. The judge decided that the story could have prejudiced the jury who weren't restricted in their access to news media during the trial, and ruled that the trial had to be re-conducted. The editor of the *Sunday Mirror*, Colin Myler, resigned over the incident though the organisation maintained that their own lawyers had amended and approved the story believing it to be unlikely to be prejudicial (MacArthur, 2001a: 22).

Even coverage after trials are over can be problematic for journalists. Different countries have different attitudes to interviewing participants in trials after they've finished. In America trial participants can talk to the media about their experiences but it is forbidden in Britain to interview jurors after a trial. In Australia a debate about this kind of restriction occurred after the prosecution of well-known radio presenter, John Laws, who in 1999 interviewed a juror in contravention of a 1997 law (Pink, 2000). He was convicted in 2000 and given a 15 month suspended sentence, adding to his notoriety (see below). In these and many other cases an evident tension emerges between merely reporting events and intervening in them in the sense of offering opinions and value judgements on events. Particularly in the area of crime reporting, ethical dilemmas are a routine hazard for journalists. The pros and cons of intervention, whether situational or editorial, is just one of them.

INTERACTION

Chapter 4 dealt with patterns of interaction between journalists and sources, but there are some particular aspects of the journalist–source relationship that raise ethical questions. These rest primarily in areas of confidentiality and money being paid to sources or vice versa.

CONFIDENTIALITY

The right to keep the identity of sources confidential is seen around the world as a fundamental principle of journalistic practice. Sources may be reluctant to go on the record for a range of reasons from the cynical to the serious. As discussed in Chapter 4, canny sources may use confidentiality for their own ends, such as politicians leaking possible policies only to officially deny them if the public response is negative. From the journalist's point of view this isn't a particularly helpful use of confidentiality, and risks accusations of complicity in source strategies, but there are other situations where confidentiality may be essential in order to cover a story. Institutional corruption, for example, whether it be in government, corporations, or any other kind of organisation would be very difficult to uncover without inside information, yet people risk their jobs and even their freedom if they give information illegally to the news media. 'Whistle-blowing', whether corporate or governmental, risks fines or even jail for those who commit it, or for the reporters who fail to disclose those who commit it. In 1984, for example, the *Guardian* newspaper published details of leaked government plans to manage public opinion over the arrival of US nuclear missiles in Britain. The paper was taken to court by the British government and the editor, Peter Preston, faced jail unless he revealed the source, which he did, and civil servant Sarah Tisdall was subsequently jailed (Burnet, 1992).[5]

Source confidentiality has become a central aspect of international human rights debates. A British case, for example, went all the way to the European Court of Human Rights (ECHR) in the 1990s. In *Goodwin vs. the UK* (1996), reporter William Goodwin received confidential material on a company called Tetra's financial difficulties, which took him to court to try and find out who had given him the documents and prevent publication of any material. Under British law, judges found that Goodwin had breached section 10 of the 1981 Contempt of Court Act, which states:

> No court may require a person to disclose, nor is a person guilty of contempt of court for refusing to disclose the source of information contained in the publication for which he is responsible, unless it be established to the satisfaction of the court that disclosure is necessary in the interests of justice or national security or for prevention of disorder or crime.

[5] Despite the public interest in Tisdall's disclosure, as a civil servant she was in breach of the Official Secrets Act. The Official Secrets Act was reformed in 1989, nominally to provide more open government, but in reality it retained, or even tightened restrictions on these kinds of leaks.

The ECHR judges, however, ruled that this judgement was in contravention of Article 10 of the European Convention on Human Rights, and as such an illegitimate restriction of freedom of expression (Moncrieff, 2002). The tensions between corporate privacy and reporting are a continuing problem for reporters in many nations.

Another firm reason for providing source confidentiality occurs in relation to crime reporting. Getting the perspective of criminals, or researching certain kinds of crimes, proves difficult without providing sources with confidentiality. Aside from the straightforward problem of either witnessing or being aware of criminal activity but not reporting it to the police, sometimes reporters can find themselves torn between maintaining source confidentiality and resolving a criminal case. In the USA, Nancy Phillips of *The Philadelphia Inquirer* became embroiled in a lengthy court case when a source she was using to investigate the murder of a Rabbi's wife admitted to having been hired by the Rabbi to commit the crime (Kaplan, 2000). Phillips regarded the information as confidential, and it was several months after confessing to the journalist before the hit man confessed to prosecutors (ibid.). The defence team argued that Phillips had, in effect, acted as a covert agent of the state in extracting the confession and unsuccessfully tried to get her story notes (Reporters Committee for Freedom of the Press, (RCFP) 2001). Vanessa Leggett was not so lucky, being jailed for several months in the USA in 2001 over refusing to hand over confidential material from an investigation of another murder case. She was denied reporters' privilege of confidentiality even though she was writing a book about the case and had already given some information over (Dias, 2001). The potential minefield of using sources in crime reporting has led some to even more ethically problematic behaviour (see below).

CHEQUEBOOK JOURNALISM

Whether on the record or not, another big concern of the press is the ethics of paying people for their stories. The most straightforward reason for paying for stories is that some people won't talk without being paid as a form of compensation against any consequences of their participation, but a more pervasive reason is to ensure that your newspaper or bulletin gets exclusive information. There are a number of particular issues arising out of chequebook journalism. Celebrities, in particular, can generate large amounts of money from granting exclusive media access, such as the wedding of England football captain David Beckham and Spice Girl Victoria Adams, photograph rights of which were sold to *OK!* Magazine for £1 million (McCann, 2000: 3–4). Sometimes, being in the right place at the right time can generate large amounts of money, such as Andras Kisgergely's photograph of Concorde on fire as it took off, moments before the fatal accident in 2000. Reuters snapped the picture up quickly, and British newspapers bid tens of thousands of pounds for exclusive use of the image (MacArthur, 2000: 22–3). The amounts of money involved in chequebook journalism, then, are often a cause for concern.

Perhaps the most controversial aspect, however, is the routine payment of those involved in notorious criminal cases. A key concern rests on the payment of witnesses in major court cases, something that the British government was considering outlawing (Greenslade, 2002), until the Press Complaints Commission (PCC) amended its code of practice to prohibit payments to witnesses during trials in 2003 (PCC, 2003). This practice had gone on for some decades in Britain at least, a nadir being reached in 1995 when large numbers of people involved with the trial of serial killer Rose West made deals with the news media (Greenslade, 2002). The practice is also widespread in America, with the case of female serial killer Aileen Wournos in 1991 prompting even police officers and lawyers involved in the case to seek news media deals (detailed in Nick Broomfield's documentary *Aileen Wournos: The Selling of a Serial Killer* (UK, 1992)).

Further distress has been generated through payments specifically to those convicted of crimes, whether it is for exclusive interviews, or access for documentary makers or book writers (for more on true crime see Chapter 8). Such concerns were expressed in a number of stories in Britain in 1998, where laws and guidelines limit payments to criminals for their stories until at least 6 years after their crimes. Three cases were put before the PCC involving the serialisation of a convicted IRA terrorist's book, payments to two nurses wrongfully convicted of murder in Saudi Arabia, and finally the serialisation of a book about infamous child killer Mary Bell (PCC, 1998). In all three cases the PCC ruled that the public interest defence was appropriate, stating 'these were all matters on which the public had a right to know and about which wide debate was legitimate. Furthermore, payment was in all probability necessary in the terms of the Code to secure the material' (PCC, 1998). Continuation of the practice since then has led to governmental consideration of extending the limit on payments to criminals from 6 years to life, not least because of public concern about some current prisoners' possible behaviour on release (Greenslade, 2002).

Another concern is that money might encourage people to engage in unethical or even dangerous behaviour. In Hong Kong in 1998, a woman killed her two children by throwing them out of a window and then killed herself the same way. A few days later, the *Apple Daily* newspaper and two TV stations produced sensational reports on the widower Chan Kin-hong's trip to Shenzen, where he was shown in bars with prostitutes whilst his family's funeral was being held back in Hong Kong. The widower said that he'd done that to get the media off his back, and it later transpired that the newspaper paid the widower after this trip, forcing an apology from the paper's founder *(Hong Kong Standard*, 1998), whilst the TV stations were fined for their exploitative coverage (Schloss, 1998). An equally harrowing case in 1996 in Britain involved Mandy Allwood, a woman whose fertility treatment had left her carrying eight foetuses. Doctors said that in order for any to survive, some of the foetuses would have to be selectively aborted, but Allwood refused to do this. All of the babies eventually died, and some criticised the influence of publicist Max Clifford and tabloid newspaper the *News of the World*, which reputedly offered Allwood money both for her story and for each baby delivered (Tomlinson, 1997: 70).

Bribery

Journalists paying sources for stories offers one set of problems, but a whole other can of worms is opened when sources offer financial inducements to journalists. There are many kinds of conflict of interest that can occur, some personal (see the end of this chapter), some organisational (increasing due to the conglomeration of media companies), but the most ethically problematic is when journalists accept money from outside sources. Depending on the context, and the openness with which journalists take money from external sources, different attitudes are taken. In early 2002, for example, the philosopher and writer Roger Scruton was sacked as a columnist by a number of newspapers including New York's *Wall Street Journal* and London's *Financial Times*, after it was discovered that he was paid by a Japanese tobacco company to write positive material about smoking in his articles (Allison, 2002).

In Australia, on the other hand, another case failed to produce a similar outcome. The radio broadcasters John Laws and Alan Jones were discovered to have accepted money from a range of organisations, including A$1 million from the Australian Bankers' Association, in exchange for favourable commentary, and cutting off critical phone comments from listeners. The Australian Broadcasting Authority's investigation found that their only wrongdoing was not to have publicly admitted their financial arrangements with any organisations they had deals with (Knightly, 2000: 19). Knightly earlier commented:

> Free trips for travel writers, extended loans of cars for motoring correspondents, lavish gifts for executives – all these ethical breaches, Laws's supporters say, are common in Australia – along with public relations retainers for reporters and 'advertorial' features where the line between advertising and editorial is blurred.
>
> (Knightly, Knightly 1999: 44)

Indeed, critical comment was not that extensive in Australia, partly because of the popularity of Laws, but partly because of the possible wide extent of this kind of practice. Australia is no exception here, in many other countries these kinds of practices go on, without wider public awareness of them (Knightly, 2000: 19).

INTRUSION

When sources or subjects are particularly unwilling participants in a newsworthy story the potential conflict between press freedom and the right to privacy arises. Both the right to free speech and the right to privacy are seen as intrinsic human rights, in documents like the US Bill of Rights, the European Convention on Human Rights, and the UN Declaration on Human Rights. In the context of the news media, these two basic rights are constantly in conflict. The aspect of this debate that gets most routinely aired, mainly as its victims have the financial means to challenge the press and put the issue on the agenda, is the relationship between the press and public figures. The privacy of 'ordinary' people, on the other hand, is treated very differently, and appears to be seen as a different kind of question altogether. Indeed, the differences in some ways highlight the complexity of the term 'privacy' in the first place. As Archard points out there are different ways of defining privacy, but his working definition serves very well for the purposes of this discussion (1998: 84). He states:

> What I take to be a paradigmatic invasion of privacy in my sense is the publication of the details of someone's personal circumstances: that someone is gay, is HIV positive, is having an extramarital affair, engages in a certain kind of sexual activity, has an illegitimate child, and so on.
>
> (Archard, 1998: 85)

As well as typifying the kinds of reporting that generate controversies over privacy this definition reveals the routine overlap between questions of privacy and other ethical concerns such as questions of confidentiality, taste and decency, and libel (see also Parent, 1992).

PRIVACY AND PUBLIC FIGURES

The definition given above also points to one reason why a distinction needs to be made about the privacy of public figures and private citizens. There are a number of reasons why public figures' private lives are routinely seen as fair game in many Western countries. There are different kinds of public figure and the arguments are slightly different for each group. The first group are elected public figures like politicians. For such people, their lives are regarded by the press in some countries as being essentially in the public interest, and thus fair game. It may be necessary, for example, to investigate the private life of a politician in order to uncover corruption, inefficiency, or dishonesty (Archard, 1998: 88). Outside of these kinds of investigations, however, the public interest defence becomes more clouded. The Monica Lewinsky scandal is a good example here. The sex scandal that led to the impeachment of President Clinton essentially rested on a question of infidelity and inappropriate sexual conduct with a White House intern. Although the case was a major story one might ask where the public interest was in Clinton's dalliance with Lewinsky. Clinton is not alone in having his sexual infidelities impact on his political life. In America, and in Britain also, there have been many scandals of this kind in recent decades suggesting a possible public interest defence.

There are arguably four ways in which such personal circumstances could be seen to meet the public interest (Archard, 1998: 89–90; see also Belsey, 1992). First comes the view that public figures should simply not behave immorally in their private lives. After a string of sex scandals in the 1990s, and other kinds of scandal, British political life has become very puritanical, with even the slightest question mark over a politician's (or their family's) actions likely to generate major news and force senior politicians out of office (which has happened on numerous occasions in the last decade or so). Second, public figures may be being hypocritical if their private lives do not reflect their public policies. A good recent example of this occurred in 2001 in Britain, regarding concerns about the safety of the measles, mumps, and rubella (MMR) vaccination and hypothetical links with autism. Government policy declared the vaccination safe and formally denied parents the right to have the alternative separate vaccinations. By chance the prime minister had a new baby of vaccination age but press efforts to find out whether the baby had the MMR jab were rebuked by the government as being a private matter. Yet, as critics pointed out, the public interest defence here seems strong if the PM did something different to what he was recommending to the public, and the impact on the baby would be minimal, even nonexistent (Liddle, 2001). Third is the idea that those who cheat and lie in their personal lives are likely to be lying and cheating in their public duties, and finally comes the idea that problems in someone's private life may distract them from their public duties (Archard, 1998: 89–90). Whatever the merit of these arguments, they have been used to defend and justify news media exposes of elected officials' private lives.

The second group of public figures are un-elected public figures who hold important social positions, such as senior members of the clergy, heads of non-government organisations, or royalty. Again, a key argument here is that these people's lives are in the public interest, and in some ways even more so than elected figures, as the press becomes the only means of ensuring the public accountability of these figures. On the other hand, the status of some non-elected public figures might make them more entitled to privacy. In terms of royalty, for example, different nations take idiosyncratic approaches to how they treat their royal figures. The deference to royalty evident in nations like Thailand mentioned in Chapter 2, used to be evident in many European nations also. In Britain, where the monarchy retains political authority (albeit in practice only symbolically), deference was the approach until only a few decades ago. Today, the British Royal Family have become a major target for scandalous stories in the tabloid press, whilst broadcasters have generally tried to remain more sacerdotal. In exchange for presumed deference, the Royal Family does not generally make formal complaints to either the regulatory body of the British press (the Press Complaints Commission) or through the courts (not suing for libel for example). In the 1990s and early part of the twenty first century, however, the British royals have become increasingly robust in their criticism of the press in light of ever more explicit coverage including: photographs of the Duchess of York indulging in intimate contact with a male friend; details of explicit phone conversations between the heir to the throne and his then mistress; numerous photographs and stories about Princess Diana, including the infamous car crash; topless photographs of the bride of Prince Edward, the Queen's youngest son; and more recently stories and photos of Princes William and Harry and their teenage encounters with drink, drugs, and girls.

The final group of public figures are celebrities from music, film, television, sport, and so on. With this group there is a kind of paradox, as the public interest defence is probably the weakest for this group, and yet it is with this group that you arguably find the greatest amount of interest from the public. One of the justifications used particularly for celebrities is that a diminishing of privacy is part of the price of fame. According to this view, in exchange for the wealth and comfort received through fame, celebrities should expect people to want to know details of their private lives, whether it is out of fan adulation, voyeuristic curiosity, or other reasons. It's quite clear, however, that most celebrities do not regard this as a legitimate defence. In 1998, under intensive lobbying from the Screen Actors' Guild, Hollywood movie stars managed to get the US state of California's privacy laws tightened up to limit the extent to which they could be followed, filmed, or photographed, even in public places (Langton, 1998). Many major stars welcomed the decision, having experienced what they consider to be effectively stalking by the paparazzi. Oscar winner Tom Hanks, for example, said:

> Ordinary family events such as shopping for shoes in the neighbourhood has often found our family being pursued by professional photographers who are specifically seeking a picture of myself with my children.
>
> (in Langton, 1998)

Whatever one's view is about public figures' rights to privacy, the specific concern dealt with in this ruling is over persistent pursuit of a public figure, amounting to what might be seen as harassment or stalking. Where investigation becomes harassment this might be justification for regarding a journalist's actions as an invasion of privacy (Archard, 1998: 83). The problem rests, however, on how one defines harassment, and indeed whether harassment means the same thing for public and private figures. One kind of newsgathering tactic along these lines to generate criticism has been dubbed 'honeytrap journalism', when attractive young journalists flirt with and flatter celebrities in an effort to try and entrap them into some kind of newsworthy behaviour or comment (Bennett, 1999: 5).

These kinds of celebrity complaints generate at least two points in defence of this kind of scrutiny of public figures (Archard, 1998: 87). First comes the cynical, but largely accurate, point that public figures routinely use the media for their own self-promotion.

The criticism here is that public figures *want* media coverage but only on *their* terms, and that is not what the press is for. Public figures to varying degrees rely on the media for their careers, in terms of exposure, and celebrities also benefit more directly through money received from endorsements and advertising. This highlights a second justification, with particular regard to celebrities, that they make a living from projecting particular images, and the public – who directly or indirectly pay their wages – have the right to know whether those images are real or not.

PRIVACY AND PRIVATE CITIZENS

However one views the rights of public figures to privacy, they at least have the means to protest, complain, and seek redress for what they perceive to be invasions of their privacy, something that ordinary people largely do not, although direct legal redress for privacy breaches is not available in some countries like Britain. Normally, the private lives of ordinary members of the general public are not newsworthy, but in those situations when ordinary people's lives do become newsworthy, they are often also in situations in which they're unable to exercise any control over how they are represented. A straightforward example of this would be in the event of a natural disaster, terrorist attack, or wartime event. The classic Vietnam War photograph of Kim Phuc running naked from a napalm attack mentioned earlier in this chapter is a good example of this. The young Vietnamese child was in no position to give consent for the taking of that photograph or, subsequently, for its dissemination around the world. This kind of image certainly contrasts starkly with the complaints of Hollywood stars over images of them in public places.

In France, which has a tradition of privacy laws, efforts have been made to address the question of the use of images of victims of crime, wars, disasters, and so on in the news. In 2000 a law was passed that included a section on news film and photography nominally limiting the publication 'of any image or photo that a court decides would hurt the dignity of the subject' (Conniff, 2000). This law also covers images of people in handcuffs having been arrested but not yet convicted. The courts test an image on the question of whether or not the subject's dignity is conserved or not. Politicians and sections of the public had been upset by news images from bomb attacks in Paris in 1995/6, and by photographs of the crash in which Princess Diana died in 1997, and the law was prompted by these events. The French news media are highly critical of the new law, seeing it as an infringement of their reporting rights. A test of this has already occurred when a magazine was fined after using a photograph of a former chief of national oil company Elf Aquitaine in jail. The court did not accept that his public status made the image in the public interest (RSF, 2002).

The combination of situations in which ordinary people become news and the lack of means of redress often means that ordinary people get a far rougher deal than any public figure, and without any of the trappings of public life that public figures enjoy. An example of this occurred in the wake of the bomb attack during the 1996 Atlanta Olympics in the USA. Richard Jewell, a security guard at the park where the bomb went off and the person who actually found the device, became a suspect and had his entire life splashed across the media, although he was never actually arrested or charged. Commenting on the case Woolner states:

> From the journalists' standpoint, everyone was just doing his job, and as a result, an innocent man's name and face were flashed around the world as those of a possible, indeed probable, terrorist, with every aspect of his career history and many aspects of his personal life given a negative spin. Yet given the enormity of that story, the feverish competition to report it, and the journalists' charge to report events of public interest, it's hard to imagine how it could have turned out substantially different – unless, of course, those involved had stepped back and considered the totality of what they were doing to this man.
>
> (Woolner, 2000: 3)

One of the problems in the reporting of private citizens' personal circumstances, as discussed in Chapter 5, is that the news media are often only interested when those circumstances are extreme, or relate to particularly extreme events. In some events, though, public interest responsibilities routinely outweigh private individuals' privacy, as in the US practice of journalists being present at executions as public representatives. In US states where executions are commonplace, some journalists, like Michael Graczyk of AP, based in Texas, have effectively become beat reporters on death row (Rumbelow, 2001).

Questions of Consent

An indication of just how far factual media may go in representing the personal circumstances of private citizens arises over the question of a person's consent. Confessional talk shows on TV have highlighted this problem. The USA's *The Jenny Jones Show* filmed a particularly notorious (and un-aired) edition where participants were introduced to their secret admirer. One participant, Jonathan Schmitz, willingly appeared on the show to discover that his admirer was a man, Scott Amedure, and not a woman as he felt he had been led to believe. Three days after the filming of the programme, Schmitz shot and killed Amedure, citing the programme's humiliation of him as the motive behind the killing. Schmitz was convicted for the killing and, in 1999, Amedure's family won damages of $25 million from the programme's producers. The problem rests on the question of whether or not private citizens are in a position to genuinely give *informed* consent over their participation/representation in factual media content (Belsey, 1992: 89).

One of the most remarkable cases of recent times to bring privacy and consent to the fore occurred in Florida in 1999. What began as an allegation of rape committed by a university fraternity member against Lisa Gier King, who had been hired as a stripper for a fraternity party, ended up with the broadcasting on television of a home video recording of the alleged assault. Initially the Florida police not only rejected the allegation but, based on their interpretation of the videotape, proceeded to try and charge King with making a false report of a crime. The case became a major political issue in Florida, accommodating a wide range of issues from sexism and class prejudice to the conduct of local law enforcement and politicians. The video became part of the complex court battle and, under Florida law, evidence used in court cases has to be made available for public access. Demand was so great that multiple copies of the video had to be made, and eventually was screened on television in the documentary *Raw Deal: A Question of Consent* (USA, 2000). What the documentary highlights is the evident ambiguity of the footage, chiefly an ambiguity in the question of consent given by King to what was being done to her. Yet there's another level of consent here – her consent to participate in the documentary that also uses key sequences of the video. When screened on British television, where victims of alleged rape are legally entitled to anonymity unless they choose otherwise,[6] commissioning editors published their reasons for showing the documentary, arguing that 'we believed it was essential to allow the viewer to be able to judge the footage against the conflicting testimonies of the witnesses' (Barker and Naik, 2002: 10). Regardless of the possible public interest value of the case, one could question what value the film serves for King when shown after the case is concluded and in a different country at that. That she consented to be in the film is not in question, but the case offers a concrete example of when journalism's desire to meet the public interest arguably conflicts with wider ethical values.

Taste and Decency

When the subjects of the news are the dead or dying, consent is not necessarily a possibility. There may also be the related question of taste and decency, which is treated quite differently from country to country. Unlike in France, depictions of victims of even highly gruesome crimes can end up in the news, or even on the front page. In December 1999, Thailand's largest newspaper *Thairath* published a crime scene photograph on its front page of a near-naked woman who had been raped and murdered, to widespread criticism (Cunningham, 2000). A few months later in mid–2000,

[6] Debate continues over this right in the UK, designed in part to try and encourage more victims of rape to pursue their attackers in court. Part of the concern arises because those accused of rape (and other sexual offences) do not share this anonymity, although at the time writing this is under review. Similar guidelines exist around cases involving children, although here they have been recently tightened so that children remain anonymous during a trial whether victim, accused, or witness.

Rasmei Kampuchea, the largest daily paper in Cambodia, printed front-page photographs of the corpses of an 8-year-old murder victim and a municipal official who had also been murdered (Neumann, 2000). In both cases the motive for publication seems to have been competition for readers.

If this rather cynical reason underpinned publication of such extreme images, in other countries even more serious motives may not see explicit material being released. The conflict in Sierra Leone in 1999 included many horrific incidents, including the use of child soldiers and indiscriminate violence by anti-government rebels. Sorious Samura risked his life to film the rebels' actions, in the process winning the high status Rory Peck Trust award. Yet, Samura was upset that the real aim of his film, to show the plight of the people of Sierra Leone, couldn't be realised as many broadcast news organisations in the West felt the footage to be too explicit to screen in its entirety (Owen, 1999). The concern of new organisations was not so much for the victims of the violence, however, as much as for the risk of offending and upsetting their domestic audiences.

The restraint with which the Sierra Leone conflict was treated by Western news media is problematic when placed against some other cases where guidelines on taste and decency seem to have been overtaken by public interest claims. A tragic example of this surrounds the murder of 6-year-old beauty queen JonBenét Ramsey in Colorado in 1996. Ambiguities over the circumstances of her murder in her home over Christmas of that year, led rapidly to media speculation fuelled by police informants that the parents, John and Patsy Ramsey, were the most likely suspects despite the presence of an apparent kidnapper's note in the home. In the years since the crime the story has become a virtual national obsession, and disputes between the Ramseys and investigators, and between investigators, have given the story legs. People involved with the case at all sorts of levels have contributed their views on events to the media, and competition from the supermarket tabloids and lifestyle magazines has meant that a lot of detail from the case, including crime scene photographs, have appeared in the news media (for a discussion of the case see Rosman, 2000). In 2001, close-ups of the girl's body even appeared in a television documentary, *Real Crime: Who Killed the Pageant Queen?* (UK, 2001), as part of investigator Lou Smit's presentation of evidence that an intruder might have been responsible for the crime, evidence others had tried to suppress. The case shows that if the public interest is deemed to be sufficiently great by journalists in a particular situations, then even photographs of a murdered 6-year-old girl can be shown in print or on television.

INVENTION

Perhaps the most apparently indefensible tactic of newsgathering is when an aspect of a story, such as a photograph or even an entire story, turns out to have been faked by the journalists. That this is even a possibility in contemporary news production is evidence for some of the depths to which journalism has sunk. Yet, like it or not, fabrication has played a major part in the production of news since its earliest days. In fact, in the early days of journalism, fabrication in one form or another was possibly more routine than genuine news and information. As mentioned in Chapter 1 a key problem for journalism up until the invention of the electric telegraph was supply of up-to-date information. News that arrived from foreign shores by boat, or distant parts of a country by horse, could be weeks after the events recounted. Early writers for newspapers were not specialist reporters, there was no such thing in the early years, so often newspapers consisted of letters offering accounts of events, and not always first-hand accounts either and often in a foreign language. There was a lot of potential for errors to occur, and indeed the early history of newspapers is dogged by criticism over invention and inaccuracy (Cranfield, 1978).

Although new technologies extend the reach of news organisations and their speed of gathering news, practical concerns have continued to put pressure on journalists to fabricate material. After the invention of cinema in 1896, film rapidly became a popular mass medium, and one of the uses made of film was for factual recording of events. Official newsreels didn't come into being until 1908, appearing first in France, but prior to that many film companies offered factual films recounting a range of incidents that were known as 'Actualities'. Some of these were genuine films shot on locations (e.g. of the inauguration of President McKinley in 1897), but others involved re-enactments, something not always evident to audiences. Edison's company filmed a number of re-enactments of events in the Spanish-American War,[7] for example, and Edison and others shot re-enactment films of the Boer War. One of the most famous fakes was the American Mutoscope and Biograph Company's film of the 1906 San Francisco earthquake, which in fact was filmed using a model in a New York Studio.

The main problem was that the early film cameras were relatively clumsy and immobile devices meaning that film-makers were rarely able to capture real events as they happened, or where that might have been possible, such as in war zones, the dangers to the cameramen (and it *was* a male preserve at that time) were immense. By the start of the First World War, actualities had been replaced by fully-fledged newsreels, several minutes in length and with a clear structure (Pronay and Wenham, 1976). Yet the practical problems of filming in a war zone remained. One of the most famous newsreels of all time encountered this problem. Geoffrey Malins' 1916 film *The Battle of the Somme* was seen by millions of cinemagoers, and generated mass public debate and comment in

---

[7] The Spanish-American War is notorious in US history for being a war allegedly generated by circulation competition between US press Barons Hearst and Putlizer. The ambiguous sinking of the US battleship *Maine* in Cuban waters that started off the war was interpreted by the US press as an act of sabotage by the Spanish. To this day the exact cause of the sinking of the *Maine* is not known.

Britain due to its explicitness. A particularly famous sequence depicts a unit of British troops going over the top of a trench to attack the opposing Germans as part of the Great Offensive, only for one of the soldiers to fall back into the trench shot dead. Another sequence shows soldiers advancing through a smoke-filled no-man's land. Although much of the film includes absolutely genuine footage of the battle and its aftermath, these emotive close-up images were faked (although this was not known until many years later). This was not necessarily because of deliberate attempts to be misleading, and is more likely because of the virtual impossibility of filming the battle at close quarters. *The Battle of the Somme* was by no means an exception, and even though some reconstructions were not uncovered, newsreels eventually developed a reputation for 'fakery, re-creation, manipulation, and staging' (Fielding, 1978: 5).

The practical difficulties of newsgathering combined with the perceived responsibilities of journalism cloud the distinction between fact and fabrication. It might be argued that there is a potential in journalism for what would be called noble cause corruption in other professions. Noble cause corruption is where people take inappropriate and unethical (even illegal) actions for what they believe to be the greater good. Examples might be police officers planting evidence on people they know committed crimes, or doctors committing euthanasia. In this chapter we've already seen the hypothetical example of a soldier willing to torture a prisoner to ensure the safe return of fellow soldiers.

One notorious case in 1980 might be a candidate for a noble cause corruption defence, when a Pulitzer Prize-winning story by Janet Cooke about a young child with heroin addiction turned out to have been faked. The story, entitled 'Jimmy's World' and appearing in *The Washington Post*, recounted a horrific tale of an 8-year-old heroin addict living in the inner city of Washington DC, routinely being injected by his mother's boyfriend. The mayor on reading the story set up a task force to find the boy, local communities offered to help, and a $10,000 reward was posted. The newspaper set up a team of 11 reporters to follow up the story, 6 of whom were sent to find other child addicts in the city in the common belief that child addicts were typical in inner cities. Six months later the story won the Pulitzer Prize, only to be taken away days later when Cooke admitted that she had made the whole story up. The newspaper only found out because of discrepancies in her claims about her background, such as language skills and college degrees that she didn't have. This prompted closer scrutiny of her story by the likes of Bob Woodward, a senior editor famous for having broken the Watergate story some years before. An internal inquiry put the failure of the newspaper to pick up on the fabrication down to a breakdown in the quality control procedures (Reinarman and Duskin, 1992: 11). Yet critics have pointed to the evident flaws in the stereotypical and inaccurate description of heroin addicts' behaviour. The story itself made inaccurate claims about the speed with which users become addicted to heroin, and also depicted users injecting heroin in front of the reporter, and an adult doing it to a child at that. The massive follow up investigation conducted by city authorities and the newspaper were, of course, never going to find the imaginary 'Jimmy', but they didn't find *any other* child addicts at all. At least part of the reason Cooke concocted the story was due to pressure from her immediate editor to follow a child addict angle when researching stories about Washington DC's drug problem (ibid.: 8). Instead of some kind of noble cause corruption being at work here, where serious social problems that are important but difficult to research pushed a journalist into faking a story, it could be argued that news media stereotypes of illegal drug use contributed to the production of a story that fitted in with those stereotypes, and that is why so many experienced senior journalists at the Post and on the Pulitzer jury were taken in (Reinarman and Duskin, 1992).

Whether noble cause corruption applies in this case or not, in others a more cynical interpretation is appropriate. Some news organisations around the world have suffered the ignominy of exposes of incidents of faking that would be difficult to interpret as in any way noble. The respected US news magazine the *New Republic* acknowledged in 1998 that up to two-thirds of the stories provided by a journalist named Stephen Glass had been fabricated. Glass had made up people and events, creating false documentation and claiming source anonymity to hide his fabrications (Helmore, 1998: 4–5). In Germany in 2000, it was revealed that celebrity interviews appearing in *Süddeutsche Zeitung* over several years had probably been faked by the Swiss interviewer Tom Kummer. Although his main employers were not happy at this revelation, others in the German media had a more cynical view, typified by this comment from the *Frankfurter Allegmeine Zeitung*:

> These days no one is offended any more by interviews that never were; they merely document the tragedy of the gossip columnist in a totally professionalised media world. If he writes down what the stars actually said and did, he's just making life even more tedious than it is. If he writes down what people really want to read, he has to tell lies.
>
> (in Boyes, 2000: 28)

A few years earlier in Germany, freelance documentary maker Thomas Born was jailed after it was revealed that he had fabricated a number of films he'd provided for prime time German television, including a film of supposed Ku Klux Klan members active in Germany. In fact they were friends of his wearing Klan outfits made by his mother (BBC, *The Truth About TV*, 1999). In 1999 in Britain, daytime TV talkshows *Trisha* and *The Vanessa Show* were criticised for, knowingly or otherwise, using fake guests. Some were allegedly hoaxers, but others claimed to be actors hired by the programmes to play roles such as feuding sisters (Bonsu, 1999: 41). Lying behind all of these examples and many other similar cases were motives including satisfying perceived audience demands and thus maintaining audience attention and share, and questions of internal newsgathering/researching procedures that may allow potential fabricated material into print or onto the airwaves.

LIBEL

Aside from the straightforward ethical breach of claiming something to be truthful and real that is actually a fabrication, there are potentially serious risks for news organisations that deliberately or otherwise end up presenting fabricated material. Faking a celebrity interview might not seem a heinous crime to anyone save the celebrity involved, but producing false information in more serious incidents is a different category of dilemma. In situations where the exact facts are unknown, journalists may find themselves, knowingly or otherwise, publishing/broadcasting claims that turn out to be false, or presenting information in a distorted way. The risk here is for an accusation of libel.

There are a number of kinds of libel that have created problems for the press. The earliest libel laws (which date back at least to the sixteenth century in England) were mainly concerned with heavily controlling criticism of public authorities, which is known as seditious libel. Although it is not an issue in most developed nations today, in the developing world, where many nascent democracies are unstable, several retain the threat of seditious libel (such as Zimbabwe). Blasphemous libel is another form of libel, concerning falsehoods about religious beliefs/practices. Again, this is rarely an issue in most developed nations, although there was a test of the English blasphemous libel law in the 1980s row over Salman Rushdie's controversial novel *The Satanic Verses*, but no prosecution was brought as the law was deemed to refer only to Christian faith and not to others. Seditious and blasphemous libel have had, and in some countries continue to have, quite strong forms of reprimand, including jail, for those convicted of committing the offence.

A much more common kind of libel in contemporary developed nations is that of defamatory libel. Defamation essentially involves comments about individuals and the impact of those comments on reputation, and those convicted face compensation payments to the victim of the defamation. Lord Atkin offered a famous summation of the test for whether or not a defamatory libel has been committed in the 1936 English trial *Sim vs. Stretch*:

> Would the words tend to lower the plaintiff in the estimation of right-thinking members of society generally?
>
> (in Irish Law Reform Commission, 1991: 31–2)

In other words defamatory libel is about the impact of content on reputation. Countries differ as to whether or not this needs to have been intended or not. The USA, for example, weighs libel claims against the First Amendment rights of the press. In the 1964 case *New York Times vs. Sullivan*, which involved a dispute over an advert in the paper criticising a local police commissioner, an eventual Supreme Court ruling set the precedent that public figures could not sue for defamatory libel over criticisms of their activities or person, unless they could prove 'actual malice' on the part of the critic (Hachten, 1998: 43).

In other countries though, it is the effects of rather than the intent behind content that is of concern. In England,[8] defamatory libel cases have been rather common. This is partly because of the prurient nature of the popular press in England, but also because of the lack, until recently, of human rights legislation protecting things like freedom of speech and privacy. For the most part it has been the rich and powerful who have used the English libel laws to try and defend their reputations, as the system of state support for legal cases, Legal Aid, does not apply to libel.[9] Normally news organisations are able to survive court cases, even though there has been a precedent in recent decades for high damages to be awarded (McNair, 1994: 148). Celebrities and politicians seem to be the prime candidates for English libel cases, and after a glut of cases in the 1980s and early 1990s the rate of high profile libel suits has dropped off somewhat. This has partly been due to the failure of some notorious cases, with the politicians involved being jailed for perjury (Jonathan Aitken and Jeffrey Archer, both senior figures in the Conservative Party). In the 1990s, the law of defamation was revised (in 1996), and there were also changes in the procedures for awarding damages, with the Court of Appeal now having the right to reduce an award if it is deemed to be excessive. This makes the cost of conducting a libel trial a risk even for wealthy public figures.

On some occasions smaller news organisations in England have had their very existence threatened by libel actions. One recent and unusual case involved a libel action between two news organisations: ITN, the supplier of television news to the three commercial terrestrial channels in Britain, and *LM* (Living Marxism) magazine, a small-scale, left-wing political magazine. The case was brought by ITN after the magazine claimed that ITN's coverage of the Bosnian war included misleading claims about Serb treatment of prisoners in a prisoner of war camp at Trnopolje. The key allegation was that an ITN film crew shot images implying that prisoners were kept behind barbed

---

[8] In Britain, Scotland has an independent legal system from that of England, Wales, and Northern Ireland. In areas like libel the laws are not profoundly different, but they are distinct nonetheless. Most of the high profile cases that are referred to in the literature, and mentioned in this chapter, occurred under English law, hence the distinction here. English libel law has also been a starting point for a number of nations, such as Ireland, Australia and Canada, although all these nations have subsequently updated and revised their laws since achieving independence from Britain.

[9] Unlike the USA, for instance, there is no fundamental statutory right to legal representation in England.

wire, when the film had actually been shot from inside an enclosure with the prisoners on the outside. This was not a small matter as the film was picked up by networks around the world and widely interpreted as an example of Serb brutality. The onus was put on *LM* to demonstrate misleading intent on the part of the film crew, yet the magazine had limited resources to pay the costs of potential witnesses, and some of their other witnesses, like BBC journalist John Simpson, were ruled out by the judge as offering only hearsay (Hartley-Brewer, 2000: 8). ITN won the case and was awarded £375,000 in damages, enough to put *LM* out of business (McLaughlin, 2002: 180). Regardless of the veracity of *LM*'s claims in this case, it indicates the severe potential risks news organisations face when presenting any kind of information and claiming it to be an accurate and truthful representation of people and events.

PROFESSIONAL CODES OF ETHICS

With all of these concerns and problems, it is no wonder that most countries have tried to provide some kinds of ground-rules for newsgathering practices, most often in the form of professional codes of practice, which lay down the rights and responsibilities of journalists. Codes tend to refer more explicitly to newspaper journalists than TV news journalists – because of the much tighter public service controls on many TV journalists – in Europe at least. Codes serve three basic functions (Laitila, 1995: 531). First, they outline the conditions of journalists' accountability to the state, the public, their employers, their sources, and to their profession. Second, most codes in Europe and the USA are voluntary so they also act as a way of making the press appear responsible. Finally, codes are important in protecting the freedom, integrity, and identity of journalists.

Harris argues that codes are beneficial to three groups (Harris, 1992: 66–7). Journalism audiences arguably benefit from clauses requiring truthfulness and accuracy, thus protecting the audience from manipulation. Sources benefit through the convention of confidentiality of sources, but also by clauses again to do with truthfulness and accuracy. Subjects benefit, as codes generally outline what is or isn't deemed acceptable, degrees of intrusion, and other guidelines on acceptable practice. Given the different situational responses to ethical issues from country to country, comparisons of codes are quite interesting. One study of 31 codes in 30 European countries identified a general pattern of shared values (Laitila, 1995). The ten most frequent principles identified in that study are shown in Table 6.1.

Nine out of ten codes suggest that news must be accurate and error-free, whereas only three-quarters contain clauses on freedom of speech. The general pattern is a balance between the rights and responsibilities of journalists broadly shared from Reykjavik to Istanbul, and from Moscow to Limerick. Yet, as the rest of the chapter

Table 6.1   Common principles in European ethical codes of conduct

Principle	Percentage of codes containing
Truthfulness, honesty, accuracy of information	90
Correction of errors	90
Prohibition of discrimination on the basis of race/ethnicity/religion	87
Respect for privacy	87
Prohibition of accepting bribes or other benefits	87
Fair means in gathering the information	84
Prohibition of allowing any outsider to have influence on the journalistic work	84
Prohibition of discrimination on the basis of sex/social class etc.	81
Freedom of expression, speech, comment, criticism	74
Professional secrecy	74
Base*	31

(* 31 codes from 30 European countries. Source: After Laitila, 1995: 538). Reprinted by Permission of Sage Publications, Ltd.)

should indicate, this relative consistency of ethical standards for journalists in formal codes jars against the varying attitudes and practices from country to country. There are a number of reasons for this disparity.

PROBLEMS WITH CODES

A key problem of most ethical codes is that they don't have legal force in the majority of countries, so they vary in their effectiveness, as mentioned in Chapter 1. The Swedish system has been a notable exception here, the voluntary code of conduct ensuring that in the mid-1980s, a suspect in the assassination of the Swedish Prime Minister Olof Palme, was not named by the Swedish press, lucky for him because he was released without charge, and a subsequent suspect wasn't named until they had been convicted in court (Weibull and Börjesson, 1992: 121–122). Compare that to the case of Richard Jewell mentioned earlier.

Journalists' personal and professional pride is fundamentally undermined by the imposition of ethical codes of conduct. Some journalists openly resent the idea that they need someone else telling them what is ethical behaviour as though they are incapable of making ethical decisions. Swain's 1970s study of journalism ethics in the USA revealed this concern, with one reporter telling his publisher 'I resent your playing God and telling me what my ethics are and dropping them on my head' (1978: 92). Following from this, a related concern is that codes often appear to apply only to journalists, and not to senior figures in news organisations, particularly owners. Whilst journalists are supposed to be truthful, non-discriminatory, and so on, owners

149

of private news media organisations can do what they like (and often do, as previous chapters have shown).

Another criticism evident in some countries, like Britain, is that codes don't seem to affect how journalists behave. There are two ways in which codes may seem to have no effect on journalists' behaviour. Ethical codes in some journalists' eyes 'just codif[y] what we were already doing' (in ibid.: 94). In other words, codes just put into writing the values journalists instinctively or routinely apply to newsgathering practice. The more cynical interpretation, arguably better supported by actual reporting (including many of the examples in this chapter), is that codes, particularly those without regulatory force, don't prevent journalists exceeding the content of codes when they deem it justifiable to do so.

A particularly interesting problem is the idea that codes may impinge on journalists' rights as private citizens. Conflicts of interest may occur between a journalist and other aspects of their life, from their personal relationships to their political beliefs, but should this limit a journalist's range of stories? In 1988, award-winning journalist A. Kent MacDougall announced in his memoirs that whilst working for the *Wall Street Journal*, a bastion of US capitalism, he wrote for radical left wing titles under a pseudonym, and selected stories at the *Journal* from his political perspective. This caused something of a storm within the *Journal* (if not more widely) despite MacDougall's defence that he was 'a journalist first and a radical second throughout my career ... I stuck to accepted standards of newsworthiness, accuracy and fairness' (in Reese, 1997: 431). While he was never directly accused of breaching an ethical code, his case raises the interesting problem of the compatibility between individual journalists' beliefs, values and interests, and professional ethical standards.

CONCLUSION: JOURNALISTS' ATTITUDES

Different situations may generate diverse decisions reflecting a range of attitudes towards the ethical issues underpinning those decisions. Showing video footage of an alleged rape, or crime scene photographs of a murdered child, or giving explicit details of the sexual misdemeanours of a head of state may, on occasion, be deemed to be justifiable by journalists. If these situations and examples do not strongly indicate that journalism ethics are far from the normative, moral questions as some writers and professional codes suggest, there is another way to test the nature of journalism ethics. It is clear from many of the above examples that responses to these situational dilemmas by journalists vary around the world. Another way to illustrate this comes from survey results when journalists are asked questions about what they regard as acceptable newsgathering practices (e.g. Delano and Henningham, 1995; Henningham, 1996; Weaver, 1998b). Table 6.2 shows a summary of Weaver's 1998 study comparing a range of countries.

Table 6.2 Reporting methods (percentage of journalists saying practices 'May Be Justified')

Region/country	Reveal confidential source	Pay for secret information	Claim to be somebody else	Badger/harass news sources	Use personal documents without permission	Use personal or government documents without permission	Get employed to gain inside information
Asia							
Hong Kong	6	51	38	84	26	77	45
Korea	9	27	59	17	27	50	37
Taiwan	10	28	44	38	13	26	40
Oceania							
Australia	4	31	13	55	39	79	46
Pacific Islands*	3	20	14	14	12	43	29
Europe							
Britain	9	65	47	59	49	86	80
Finland	39	62	53	43	39	72	68
France	4	36	40	82	12	69	56
Germany	10	41	45	12	11	54	54
North America							
Canada**	2	9	7	31	17	60	36
USA	5	20	22	49	48	82	63
Latin America							
Brazil	7	24	63	–	43	83	67
Chile	2	39	58	76	14	53	22
Mexico	5	38	36	21	13	64	45

Source: Adapted from Weaver, 1998a: 471–2.
* Percentage of those 'who approve'; ** Percentage saying practices are 'highly justified' or 'justifiable'.

Revealing a confidential source is one clear ethical boundary that the majority of journalists from the nations surveyed believe shouldn't be crossed, but other practices reveal a divergence of views, such as paying for secret information regarded as justifiable by almost two thirds of British journalists, compared to only one fifth of US journalists, and less than a tenth of Canadian journalists (Weaver, 1998a: 470). Some of the biggest disparities are seen in perceptions of justifiable harassing of news sources. In Hong Kong and France, both states where legal restrictions limit other kinds of access to official sources in particular, most journalists see harassment as legitimate, but barely one in ten German journalists regard this as justifiable.

Using personal documents without permission isn't seen as justifiable by a majority of journalists in any country, although just under half of British and US journalists feel it may be justified. Government documents, on the other hand, brings the almost opposite consensus that it is legitimate, with even three fifths of Canadian journalists, otherwise displaying tough attitudes towards acceptable practices, seeing this as justifiable. Weaver concludes that:

> Given these very large differences in the percentage of journalists who think that different reporting methods may be acceptable, it seems that there are strong national differences that override any universal professional norms or values of journalism around the world.
>
> (ibid.: 473)

The practices of newsgathering then, raise some important questions about the ethics of news production, and it is clear that despite attempts to codify what journalists should or shouldn't do, journalists around the world chiefly do not share the same attitudes about what is or isn't ethical behaviour. This finding, along with many of the examples discussed in this chapter, strongly suggest that many aspects of journalism ethics should be evaluated on a case-by-case basis and not in a more normative sense. That appears to be what happens in daily newsgathering practice, and perhaps it is this fluidity of ethical decision-making in journalism that underpins public discontent over journalistic standards in some contemporary Western news media.

Chapter Seven

OBJECTIVITY AND BIAS $\Box$

In the early days of the 1999 Kosovan War, under fierce aerial assault from Nato air attacks, the Serbian regime of Slobodan Milosevic attempted to remove Nato nations' journalists from Serbia. Whilst the likes of Reuters and CNN were harassed into leaving, the BBC's John Simpson decided to stay after hearing that an Australian journalist was going to stay (Australia not being a member of Nato), thus sharing the risk (Simpson, 1999: 3). His position in Belgrade provided him with a starkly different perspective to other journalists forced to report from the borders of the conflict, or from the seats of power in Nato and its member states. As a journalist for a British broadcasting organisation, Simpson was bound by the principle of due impartiality (see below) which requires journalists to provide balanced reports free from their own partisan views. Even though he was compromised in achieving this through being restricted by the Serbs in terms of where he could go and what he could report, Simpson made this clear to viewers in every televised report. His interviews with Belgrade citizens suggested growing popular support for Milosevic, the opposite of a key aim of the Nato attacks, and Simpson also wrote newspaper articles (where he was free to offer his own opinions) asserting this point explicitly. After Serb claims that Nato planes had attacked a refugee convoy, Simpson's report suggested that if the Serbs responded by taking foreign journalists to the site then it probably was a Nato attack. This they did, and indeed eventually Nato had to concede that US planes had mistakenly bombed a convoy of refugees despite warnings from British planes. All this was too much for the British government who decided to attack Simpson directly, accusing him of deliberate pro-Serbian reporting and a lack of objectivity. This attack drew both national and international criticism, and paradoxically helped Simpson's later reporting on the ground, as Belgrade citizens began to see him (wrongly) as on their side and allowed him greater freedom to report events during the war.

Whilst news values may vary from organisation to organisation, and ethical attitudes vary from nation to nation, in Western nations the principle of objectivity traditionally stands as a fundamental cornerstone of journalistic professionalism and integrity. To accuse a journalist of a lack of objectivity, as in the case of John Simpson, has been to challenge their core integrity and professionalism, akin to accusing police of framing innocent people for crimes, or doctors of failing to do all they can to treat patients. Yet, as with so many other aspects of contemporary journalism, the professional ideal of objectivity in journalism is under threat. Unlike ethical concerns, however, the threat to objectivity stems not only from apparent (or imagined) breaches of objectivity like the one Simpson was accused of, but also from conceptual challenges to the principle of objectivity itself. Many critics and journalists challenge both the viability and desirability of objectivity in journalism. What adds to the interest in this area are two factors. First, the concept of journalistic objectivity did not emerge with the arrival of journalism but much later, reflecting the developments and concerns of the mid- to late-nineteenth century. Second, contemporary challenges to objectivity reflect the concerns and developments of contemporary society particularly surrounding new media technologies. This chapter explores the principle of objectivity's origins, the philosophical debates surrounding objectivity, contemporary challenges to journalists' efforts to be objective, and some proposals and practices that offer alternatives to the convention of objectivity.

ORIGINS OF OBJECTIVITY

Objectivity has not always been seen as an intrinsic aspect of journalism. From the beginning of the seventeenth century through to at least the middle of the nineteenth century, newspapers had few of the trappings of contemporary journalism's claims to objectivity. That is not to say that newspapers were without their critics, with many complaining about inaccuracy, misinformation, sensationalism, and so on. Yet the restrictions of newspaper production, alongside the difficulties in gathering information about events, meant that newspapers were as much tools for political advocacy and partisanship, whether that be pro or anti-Royalist newsbooks in mid-seventeenth century England, or pro-revolutionary papers in France in the 1780s. Throughout this period, and on into the twentieth century in other parts of the world and indeed to this day in some countries, news media have often fallen into two clear camps, either as an accepted part of the political establishment representing the interests of the social and political elites, or in opposition to the interests of the elites. Opponents of the establishment were and are often ardently adversarial and opinionated. This was true of pro-independence American newspapers in the 1770s, of the radical press in Britain in the 1830s, and is equally true of NTV in contemporary Russia, or *The Standard* newspaper in contemporary Zimbabwe.[10]

DEMOCRACY AND ECONOMICS

The role of the news media has been seen as critical in many nations' political development, and the status and nature of state-run versus independent news outlets has

---

[10] *Standard* Journalists Mark Chavanduka and Ray Choto were arrested and tortured by the Zimbabwe regime in 1999, after publishing a story about a possible coup attempt felt by the regime to be 'false news likely to cause alarm and despondency' (in Bishop, 1999). Eventually the pair were released, and after a time in the USA and Europe speaking on press freedom, Chavanduka returned to Zimbabwe to continue to voice independent and oppositional journalism to the Mugabe regime, despite the risks.

largely reflected that. Anti-establishment partisanship and radicalism of many kinds (e.g. political, religious, etc.) has tended to be a key selling point for independent news media in emerging democracies, suggesting to audiences that despite (or even because of) the clear partisanship independent news is more credible than state-run or state-sanctioned news. However, as democracies develop and begin to stabilise the clear ground between state and independent news media begins to disappear. Partly this comes about as the issues of concern to independent news media are gradually addressed and thus the basis for radical partisanship diminishes. The British radical press of the 1830s, for example, reflected the concerns of the growing working class over issues such as the right to vote, workers' rights, and so on. As the nineteenth century progressed many of these concerns began to be addressed and thus the basis for the political radicalism of many newspapers began to diminish, although this is not to ignore the actions of the British state in attempting to suppress the radical press. Amongst the most significant changes of this kind in a democratising system is the change in attitude towards independent news media organisations themselves. Instead of being regarded as illicit operations run on ideological grounds for select groups within a society, independent news media organisations eventually become an established and accepted feature of democratic society. This changes the conditions in which radical independent news organisations can operate and, in conjunction with the transition of their concerns into mainstream attitudes, it enables them to in effect become part of the establishment news media. Some argue that the political liberalising of news media systems effectively forces once radical and independent news media to conform to establishment news production practices in order to compete with establishment organisations, which has de-radicalising effects through the greater susceptibility to commercial pressures such as advertisers' demands (e.g. Curran and Seaton, 1997). The only other outcome, particularly when concerns are not taken up by mainstream society, is for a radical news outlet to sit outside the mainstream news media, to become part of what is collectively referred to as the 'alternative' media (see Chapter 8).

Of concern in this chapter though is how the development of journalism as a commercial industry may also contribute to the emergence of objectivity as a professional ideal in journalism, as it arguably did in the USA. In the USA journalistic objectivity began to emerge, at least in part, as a selling point for news media organisations. USA newspapers in the mid-nineteenth century began to promote themselves as not only independent watchdogs of the state, but also as increasingly removed from close associations with particular political parties. From a commercial point of view this allowed newspapers to follow public trends of political support and thus maintain commercial credibility and viability. Mindich's analysis of the emergence of objectivity in US journalism cites the example of the founder of the explicitly non-partisan *New York Herald*, James Gordon Bennett, who said of his competitors in 1835 'none are "free as the mountain wind" … We are the fellows that tell the truth' (in Mindich, 1998: 45). The same basic principles Bennett espoused can still be seen in comments from contemporary US journalists such as ABC News' Sam Donaldson:

> Well, people on the right say we're too liberal and people on the left say we're in league with the status quo, which probably means we're right where we should be, right in the middle.
>
> (in Mindich, 1998: 40)

So, in the USA at least, objectivity emerged from the free market system as a marker of professional independence and thus a commercially valuable feature. Variability or attempted neutrality in politics, for example, benefited free market news organisations not only from the point of view of being able to follow audience trends, but also from the point of view of advertising revenue. Diminishing political partisanship, and indeed political coverage, makes a news outlet more attractive to potential advertisers, who continue to try and shape news outlets' editorial content in a manner favourable to the goods and services they're trying to sell to audiences (see Chapter 3). Since US journalism in all forms is subject to this conception of the free market-place of ideas, objectivity stands as a professional value across print, broadcast, and other kinds of US journalism.

In parts of Europe, however, the free market was not seen as offering any greater chance of a genuinely independent and non-partisan news media, for precisely this risk of pandering to commercial pressures and thus the interests of corporations rather than the public. Objectivity in many European nations emerged out of quite different routes such as the establishment of public service broadcasting systems and press subsidies (see Chapter 2). Requirements for features such as non-partisanship and political balance were often written into the regulatory requirements for public service broadcasters, as in the British regulatory principle known as 'due impartiality', and remain in place today in many countries. State regulation was an attempt to protect new broadcast media from commercial pressures seen to be potentially detrimental to society given their potential reach. Regulating for objectivity in broadcast news was also one of the ways nations attempted to protect journalistic independence within state-regulated and financed news organisations like the BBC. Interestingly, whilst many European nations took on similar approaches to broadcast journalism, regulating content in similar ways to Britain, there was also a parallel trend for maintaining legitimate partisanship and advocacy in other kinds of journalism, principally in print journalism (see below).

SOCIAL SCIENCE AND TECHNOLOGY

As this chapter will show, despite there being some widely divergent factors contributing to the emergence of objectivity from nation to nation, there is far more convergence on ideas about what objectivity means in practice. One possible reason for this, and the reason why the principle of objectivity took root so firmly when it did, is that many of the underlying assumptions about the *possibility* of journalism to be objective are linked to the application of a range of technologies in journalism, that in turn reflect wider changes in attitudes towards the interpretation of social phenomena.

In the developed world of the nineteenth century the hard certainties of the natural sciences were being problematised by the 'lesser certainties of experience and observation' (Winston, 1995: 132). Probabilistics began to emerge as an increasingly dominant strand in a range of scientific areas of study, with statistics also becoming central to the emerging social sciences. Researchers began to look at social phenomena, like disease, crime, poverty, and so on, in terms of statistical aggregations of large groups of people rather than individual anecdotes. Such an approach arguably contributed to the emergence of some of the dominant political philosophies of the time, such as Mill's utilitarianism and Marx's communism (Mindich, 1998: 106–7). Not surprisingly this new way of looking at social phenomena began to also appear in journalism of the time. Mindich offers the example of the way cholera epidemics in the USA in the early part of the nineteenth century tended to be treated by US newspapers in terms of questions of 'God and sin', i.e. in terms of morality and spirituality rather than medicine and science (ibid.: 111). By the 1860s, however, newspapers' approach to cholera outbreaks had shifted 'from God to outhouses', in other words from discussion of sin and morality to discussions of sanitation, disease prevention, and detailed discussions of effluence in language approaching that of scientific journals (ibid.). Winston offers the example of articles on the poor of London in the *Morning Chronicle* in 1849–50, written by Henry Mayhew and replete with statistical information, much of it gathered by Mayhew himself (Winston, 1995: 133). Winston comments that Mayhew's research methods 'are elements that elevate the work from the higher journalism into the realm of social science' (ibid.).

These changes from anecdotes to statistics in reporting weren't only a product of changing approaches in other areas of social investigation, but were heavily influenced by the emergence of, and attitude towards, a range of new technologies that became central to the journalistic enterprise. One of these, that has been mentioned before in this book, was the electric telegraph. As well as massively expanding the reporting scope for news organisations, it also brought limitations to extravagant and fabricated stories about distant people and places, as it afforded opportunities for checking stories (Mindich, 1998: 108). More significantly, perhaps, the commercial potential of the telegraph for the dissemination of news to an ever wider audience was to play a significant role in the emergence of objectivity as a professional value in journalism. The telegraph never really took off as a means of direct news delivery to the public, instead people in several nations realised there could be a significant market in acting as news content agencies supplying news organisations with material, thus saving those organisations from the costs of maintaining correspondents and offices all over the country (and latterly the world). Many of the major news agencies of today, like the Associated Press, Reuters, and others, have their origins in the mid-nineteenth century, closely tied to the emergence of the telegraph. What these agencies worked out was that in order to sell their material to a large and diffuse body of news organisations they could not afford to produce highly stylised and partisan reporting. As one representative of Associated Press said around that time:

> My business is merely to communicate facts. My instructions do not allow me to make any comments upon the facts which I communicate. My despatches are sent to papers of all manner of politics, and the editors say they are able to make their own comments upon the facts which are sent them ... I do not act as politician belonging to any school, but try to be truthful and impartial. My despatches are merely dry matters of fact and detail.
>
> (Gobright in Mindich, 1998: 109)

So, in this instance, a close relationship between new information technologies, commercial imperatives, and journalistic practices and values can be seen. An argument could be made for similar impacts of other early technologies such as the typewriter, or telephone, let alone developments in printing techniques. But perhaps another technology to impact very specifically on early conceptions of journalistic objectivity deserves a brief discussion.

When photography was first invented, in the 1830s, initial pronouncements on possible applications of the new technology were focused on scientific and evidential uses (Winston, 1995: 128). This was partly due to the growing recognition of the evidential value of certain kinds of imagery, such as maps and botanical illustrations, so images were increasingly thought of in terms of scientific rather than aesthetic applications (ibid.). Photography offered the additional potential for use as another new measurement/observation tool, to go along with things like the telescope and microscope. It is out of this idea of the photographic camera as a scientific instrument that the popular cliché 'the camera never lies' emerges, or as Winston puts it 'the camera lies no more than does the thermometer, the microscope, the hygrometer and so on' (1995: 130). An obvious example of this, still much in evidence today, is the use of photography in criminal cases that took off in the latter part of the nineteenth century (e.g. for mug-shots, photo-fits, and latterly also seen in the use of CCTV, and video-fits which extends this principle into moving and electronically-acquired images). The perception of photography, and later film, as evidential media detached from the interpretations and opinions inherent in written accounts of events also contributed to journalism's sense of the possibility of accurate, authoritative, and potentially objective reporting. Of course, as the last chapter showed, perceptions of the reliability of photographic and film images have never really been well founded, with fabrication, selective cropping (and editing), and of course subject selection all contributing to cameras offering the illusion of reality, but not reality itself. How use of camera in both news photography and television news can wittingly or otherwise contribute to the undermining of pretensions to objectivity, will be discussed later in the chapter.

The Technological Paradox

Whilst technologies like the telegraph and photography can be identified as having clear influences on the emergence of objectivity as a professional value, as the range of technologies available has continued to increase so ever more question marks over the relationship between technology and objectivity have arisen. Apart from the major developments of radio, television, and online journalism, a range of other technologies have dramatically changed reporting practices. As MacGregor states, we are in:

> a world where the 'flyaway' portable satellite dish, the 'sat phone', the fax, the laptop computer, the digital palmcorder, non-linear editing the edit suite in a suitcase, and the multi-skilled working practices they are bringing with them have changed the way in which news stories are reported ... It is a world where a certain news bias has developed, one which turns around technology.
>
> (MacGregor, 1997: 2)

These technologies aid reporters in the field to go places that were previously unreachable, allows rapid and immediate delivery of news material and the appearance of entirely new styles of news, such as 24-hour rolling news. Yet whilst these technologies all superficially appear to enhance journalistic capability there is the risk that the technology dictates not only how stories are covered, but what stories are covered. News that utilises images, for example, has a tendency to favour events and issues that offer a range of arresting and engaging images (whether photographic or filmic), which may distort what is produced compared to text or audio only news. These concerns will be discussed in the last chapter of this book in more detail, but to give one example here, the ease of use of satellite technology now allows television news programmes to have individual reports transmitted from locations, and indeed include live updates from the journalist at the scene. The perception audiences are presumably supposed to receive is one of both the genuine nature of the report, because the reporter can be seen at the scene of the event, and just how up-to-date the information they are getting is. But whilst this strategy has become a staple of television news, in Britain at least, not all British TV journalists see this as valuable

159

journalism. This is how *Channel 4 News* presenter Jon Snow critiqued the live link-up in a speech in 2000:

> How often have you seen a report in which Sue Bloggs signs off, We cut back to the studio, and the knowledgeable old newscaster says 'live now to Sue Bloggs' ... and in the midst of her succeeding answer to the newscaster's question, utters the words 'as I said in my report just then' or 'as you saw in my report.'? One great benefit of the techno revolution is that Sue's pre-recorded report will have contained material shot right up to a few minutes before transmission. Rare it is indeed that events are so 'live' that an update from her is immediately justified. Sue's live add on is cheap – using the same 'feed facility' as her report. It is also safe, no danger of some member of the public uttering information that fails to fit the pre-ordained structure of the news programme, either in content or length, the entire transmission has been kept safely within the broadcasting family.
>
> (Snow, 2000)

So, rooting the origins of objectivity in information and communication technologies has some merit, but with the move into the information age, technology in journalism appears to create problems for any simplistic understand of objectivity.

WHAT IS OBJECTIVITY?

If the possible origins of objectivity offer more questions than answers, the notion of what objectivity actually means needs exploring, particularly as it is a much disputed concept (Lichtenberg, 1991). There is a distinct body of criticism of the Western news media's attachment to objectivity, and objections tend to fit into three broad categories. First are those who decry objectivity on grounds of it being an impossible goal, such as Pavlik:

> Although objectivity is a laudable goal toward which to strive, much as the pursuit of truth is a worthy endeavour, in most cases it is impossible to obtain or least impossible to know whether we have achieved it.
>
> (Pavlik, 2001: 24–5)

Second, are those who regard objectivity as undesirable regardless of whether it can be achieved or not, reflected in the comments of former BBC war reporter Martin Bell who states:

> I am no longer sure what 'objective' means: I see nothing object-like in the relationship between the reporter and the event, but rather a human and dynamic interaction between them.
>
> (Bell, 1998: 18)

Third, and perhaps the most recent school of thought, are those who decry objectivity on the basis that technology has made the concept unnecessary and redundant. Objectivity in European broadcasting, for example, emerged in a context of limited or even monopolistic early broadcasting systems, but the arrival of multi-channel digital television and the Internet provide audiences with a multitude of alternative sites of information. Hall, for example, states:

> There must be a better, let us say less tendentious, way of documenting events. Perhaps the Internet will lead us to it. By taking information from as many, and as wide a range of sources as possible and perhaps even by abandoning an impossible objectivity for a reasoned subjectivity or reflexivity, readers will be able to make up their minds for themselves.
>
> (Hall, 2001: 46)

Contestation over the possibility, desirability, and necessity of objectivity in journalism rests on questions of facts and interpretation, consensus and contingency, and ideology and responsibility.

FACTS AND INTERPRETATION

The primary objection to objectivity being genuinely achievable actually rests on questions about truth and reality. A root issue is that of the role of what Mindich calls 'facticity' in journalism (Mindich, 1998). Schudson argues that the first proponents of objectivity in American journalism were primarily interested in the separation of facts from values. He states:

> They were, to the extent that they were interested in facts, naïve empiricists; they believed that facts are not human statements about the world but aspects of the world itself.
>
> (Schudson, 1999: 293)

'Facts', in this view, are things independent of individuals' perceptions, and arguably reflects 'a positivist view of the world' and 'an enduring commitment to the supremacy of observable and retrievable facts' (Glasser, 1992: 176). This is essentially a belief in the existence of a reality 'out there' beyond individuals' experience of reality, a reality that could be observed, analysed, assessed, and particularly in journalism's case, recorded. A number of factors contributed to this approach, including dominant ideological attitudes in science and politics in the nineteenth century, and also the evolution of media technologies, like photography, film, and later, radio and television, as mentioned above.

The counter-argument goes that there is no such thing as an objective reality, that the world can only be experienced through our own perceptions. This position argues that people individually and collectively *construct* their realities (Schudson, 1999: 293), and as such there are only *interpretations* of reality, it does not exist somewhere 'out there' (Edgar, 1992). In the journalistic context this is evident because what counts as truth and reality for journalists is what eventually appears in the news, and this, as has already been indicated in earlier chapters, excludes many events and individuals. Edgar explains:

> A given event occurs amid a plethora of other social events to which the journalist may or may not respond. The journalist's initial decision to attend to that event will rest upon the anticipation of the place of that event in a broader whole. The whole will in part be constituted as the journalist's perception of 'reality'.
>
> (Edgar, 1992: 117)

Certainly, the question of the role of the individual journalist's interpretation of events shaping the representation of those events has long been recognised as a flaw in the objectivity argument, with authors like Walter Lippmann identifying the problem as far back as the 1920s. Lippmann argued, for example, that journalists' pre-existing stereotypical attitudes would shape their interpretations of events (1992). Thinking in terms of the debates of the last couple of chapters, a clear link can be seen between questions of news values and newsgathering ethics being major contributory factors in journalists' interpretations of the significance of events in the first place, even before those events are presented as news. To give the clichéd example, this is an underlying explanation as to why 'Man Bites Dog' is a news story but 'Dog Bites Man' isn't (usually). For some this contributes to what is regarded as 'unwitting bias', a product of professional practices and attitudes, but not of ideology or malicious intent (McQuail, 1992: 193, see below). For others, selection processes are indicative of both overt and underlying ideological influences on journalistic practice, undermining any claims to objectivity (e.g. the criticisms of crime reporting in Britain by Hall *et al.*, 1978; see below).

For some analysts the construction of reality as it occurs through news production practices contributes to what has been dubbed *framing* (Kosicki, 1993, McCombs and Shaw, 1993). Put simply, framing is the process by which journalism directs 'attention toward certain attributes and away from others' in covering an issue or event (McCombs and Shaw, 1993: 62). Inherent to the concept is the assertion that 'journalists do not merely mirror reality but rather – through their work ways, norms, and rules of thumb – actively construct news out of the available raw materials' leading to what is dubbed the *news frame* (Kosicki, 1993: 112). Studies of framing in the news focus not just on the accuracy or otherwise of the factual content of news coverage, but also examine the manner of presentation of information. One study of the US Federal Budget Deficit in 1995/96, for example, found that public awareness and understanding was affected by how the budget deficit was 'framed' as a fight or conflict, so it was the nature of coverage rather than just the informational content that was significant (Jasperson *et al.* 1998: 219). Other studies, such as Iyengar's study of the framing of poverty in US media, have similarly highlighted the importance of framing. Iyengar concluded that public 'beliefs about who or what is responsible for poverty vary considerably, depending upon how poverty is framed' (1997: 281). Framing studies thus highlight the problem with asserting the objectivity of journalism based on facticity, given that 'facts' are both selected and filtered through newsgathering processes, and are also framed in particular representations that may influence the interpretation of those 'facts' by audiences.

This is a difficult problem for advocates of objectivity in journalism to resolve. Claiming objectivity in this conception is inherently flawed as it 'assumes the possibility of genuine neutrality, of *some* news medium being a clear undistorting window. And that can never be' (Fowler, 1991: 12, original emphasis). But, far from stopping at the contention that journalistic representations of the world are mere constructions of reality, critics deny 'that we can know what the world is like *intrinsically*, apart from a perspective' (Lichtenberg, 1991: 219, emphasis added). There are a range of major philosophical problems with this kind of reasoning. At one extreme lies scepticism and solipsism, that is the situation where knowledge beyond one's own viewpoint is impossible and therefore nothing can be trusted or known, moreover there's no point in trying to find anything out. Although these concepts exist in philosophy they aren't widely regarded as practically applicable to everyday life.

Another problem is relativism, particularly cultural relativism (Lichtenberg, 1991: 221). For relativists, if all claims to truth and reality are merely subjective interpretations then no one view is more valid than any other. As such, views that offer even radical interpretations of events are inherently as legitimate as any other, whether that be claims that the world is flat, world leaders are really 12-foot-tall alien lizard people (according to former BBC sports journalist turned conspiracy theorist, David Icke), or that the Holocaust never happened. Yet few people would argue in favour of accepting this position, and in practice some interpretations are favoured even though *absolute certainty* can't be achieved. Denial of the Holocaust, for example, apart from being a core factor in neo-nazi values, rests heavily on the absence of conclusive documentation of Hitler ordering the extermination of the Jews via the concentration camps. Yet the welter of other kinds of evidence indicating that the Holocaust not only happened but was a deliberate, planned strategy of the Nazi regime strongly points to that interpretation of events even though it cannot be demonstrated with absolute certainty. There was certainly enough evidence to persuade a British Libel trial in 2000 that the historian David Irving was indeed a Holocaust denier, who misrepresented and ignored evidence to support his pro-nazi viewpoint (Dodd, 2000). Nazi sympathisers see in cases like Irving's evidence only of a conspiracy intent on ensuring a particular interpretation of the Second World War is accepted, but it should be remembered that detailed investigation of events of the Holocaust has not only undermined the deniers. Proper research methods were also used to uncover the fraud in Binjamin Wilkomirski's *Fragments*, a celebrated memoir of a child survivor of concentration camps which turned out in 1998 to have been a total fabrication written by a Swiss citizen named Bruno Grosjean.

But relativism is not the preserve solely of political extremists, religious fundamentalists, or conspiracy theorists. Relativism is often a lay response to questions of value or quality but it has also been used to make academic and political points. One political usage has come from people attempting to protect indigenous cultural practices from the onslaught of cultural imperialism and globalisation. Yet, here too, campaigns are selective as *some* cultures are deemed worthy of protection, such as the indigenous tribes of the Amazonian rain forests, but others are not, such as the fundamentalist Islamic regime of the Taliban. Noted French academic Jean Baudrillard offered one of the best known applications of relativism when he famously stated that the Gulf War of 1991 did not happen (1995). Part of his point was that many people, particularly in the Western nations who participated in the war, did not witness the war first hand but only through the media, and that the media representation of that war was a 'hyperreal' construction. Lichtenberg points out that highlighting the social construction of reality does not in fact prevent criticism of media representations as being somehow flawed. She states that 'in showing us how, say, British news stories construct reality, critics of necessity depend upon the possibility of seeing and understanding alternative versions of the same events' (1991: 220). Baudrillard's claims about the Gulf War, for example, implicitly reflect a concern that 'those who see things in one way are missing something important, or getting only a partial view, or even getting things wrong' (Lichtenberg, 1991: 220). So, in fact, proponents of reality as socially constructed still criticise news media for failing to represent reality 'correctly', at the same time as rejecting the possibility of objectivity.

CONSENSUS AND CONTINGENCY

It may be possible to reach a pragmatic resolution between the extremes of reality as absolute facts or reality as entirely socially constructed. Two key elements are needed to do this. First, it is difficult to dispute pragmatically, if not philosophically, that there appear to be features of 'reality' over which there is a high degree of *consensus*. Lichtenberg uses the example of the president of the United States (1991: 223). Whilst there may be wide disparities in interpretations of the current president's ability, status and so on, it would seem ludicrous for anyone to deny that nominally at least George W. Bush is president of the USA (at the time of writing). Lichtenberg states it is important not to 'conflate the distinction between meaning and reference' (ibid.: 225). In other words news reporting routinely uses reference points that may be reasonably assumed to be consensually accepted as fact, such as who the political leaders happen to be at any given time, or general features of major events like the Holocaust or September 11. Through framing journalists play an active part in the ongoing construction of this consensus and the positioning of new events and issues within that ever-evolving consensus, as Pavlik explains:

> We can never know whether we have revealed it [the truth], and mostly we can only hope to approximate it through triangulation, like the best research in either the physical or social sciences. By offering different perspectives on what may or may not have occurred, journalism can facilitate the public's understanding of an event or process by revealing as many verifiable facts as possible.
>
> (Pavlik, 2001: 25)

Using consensus to legitimate a claim to objectivity is insufficient on its own, however, as consensus is not the same as 'tangible and monolithic' truth (Hall, 2001: 47). One limitation of reliance on consensus is that apparent consensual opinions may in fact be the views of a particular group who have merely succeeded in shaping interpretations of events and issues (as discussed in Chapter 4). In the wake of new evidence consensual opinion can also simply be wrong, and that is true whatever the source or scale of consensus may be. Take the anthrax attacks in late 2001 in the USA, assumed at the outset by politicians, the media, and the public to be undoubtedly directly related to the September 11 attacks, and thus the act of terrorists external to the US. Yet as the investigation into the attacks progressed it became more likely that the attacks were committed from within the US.

The other important conceptual element that is therefore needed, and which can also be drawn from the physical and social sciences, is the recognition of the *contingency* of facts. In effect this needs to be recognised in considerations of journalism by producers, audience members, and critics of news media content. A key problem in journalism is that unlike, say, the manner and style of scientific journals, reporting routines preclude constant assertions of the contingency of the information being presented. Sometimes this is done in weekly magazines, or in daily newspapers in elections when print deadlines are exceeded by final results, and reports may contain a disclaimer such as 'at the time of publication' to denote the absence of full information. Most of the time though, this kind of overtly explicit acknowledgement of the limitations of news reporting is absent, and there is also very little of the kind of qualification of points that is routinely seen in other forms of publication, like academic journals. It is perhaps in this implicit presentation of information as fact that the claim to factual objectivity in journalism is problematised. But acknowledging the contingency of facts also has implications for critics of journalism, because it points to the impossibility of a journalistic text being absolutely accurate, and therefore it can only be judged in relation to the availability of evidence to support or refute claims presented as fact. So, in the example of the US anthrax attacks, it serves little purpose to condemn the US news media for initially suggesting a foreign culprit purely on the grounds that later evidence suggested a domestic culprit.

IDEOLOGY AND RESPONSIBILITY

There may be another way to question claims to objectivity other than in terms of the presence or absence of factual accuracy, which relates to questions of the concept's desirability. Another claim of the principle of objectivity, according to Herbert Gans, is that it involves the exclusion of ideology (1979: 190). He claims that US journalists 'do not formulate conscious and consistent political viewpoints; they are not ideologists' (ibid.), unlike journalists in state run or state regulated news media. He goes further, saying that journalists 'believe ideology to be an obstacle to story selection and production' (ibid.: 191). Yet such statements conflict with two other aspects of professional ideology as identified by Gans. First, Gans acknowledges a feature of US journalism that is still broadly true today, that journalists are dominated by a particular socio-demographic group (ibid.: 209; see also Butterworth, 2000). Journalists in the USA (and indeed in many other Western countries) tend to be highly educated, are from middle and upper class families, and are dominated by white males. Second, as if to acknowledge the impact such a particular group of individuals might have on professional values, Gans refers to what he calls 'the enduring values' of journalists (Gans, ibid.: 204).

What is remarkable is the lack of association by Gans of what he sees as collective values held by US journalists, and a claimed absence of ideology. In one sense ideology is precisely a set of shared values within a particular group, nation, or profession. In contrast to Gans, Theodore Glasser goes to the other extreme, arguing that journalistic objectivity is intrinsically ideologically-biased in three respects (1992: 176). He argues first that objectivity as a practice biases against a fourth estate function of the press, instead making journalists 'biased in favour of the status quo' through their reliance on official sources (ibid.). To go back to the anthrax example, in this context assumptions of a foreign culprit by the US news media can be legitimately criticised as an example of US new media organisations' tendency to accept the institutional agenda of the political authorities in the US.

Second, by requiring a separation between journalists' opinions and the 'facts', Glasser claims objectivity biases against journalistic independence. He states:

> Objective reporting has stripped reporters of their creativity and their imagination; it has robbed journalists of their passion and their perspective. Objective reporting has transformed journalism into something more technical than intellectual; it has turned the art of story-telling into the technique of

report writing. And most unfortunate of all, objective reporting has denied journalists their citizenship; as disinterested observers, as impartial reporters, journalists are expected to be morally disengaged and politically inactive.

(Glasser, 1992: 181)

It is this last point that is also of particular concern to advocates of public journalism and Bell's journalism of attachment, both to be discussed later in this chapter.

Glasser's final assertion about the ideological nature of objectivity is that it biases against notions of journalistic responsibility (ibid.: 176). He argues that what 'objectivity has brought about, in short, is a disregard for the consequences of newsmaking' (ibid.: 183). Yet, for some authors this is not only acknowledged but lauded as a positive attribute of journalistic objectivity. Herbert Gans, to draw the comparison again, declares that:

> Because objectivity is defined as a matter of intent, it includes the freedom to disregard the implications of the news. Indeed, objectivity could not long exist without this freedom, for the moment journalists are required to consider the effects of news on sources and others, they would have to begin assessing their own intent and to relinquish their detachment, especially if they wanted to prevent injury to someone. .
>
> (Gans, 1979: 188).

Yet Glasser contends that responsible reporting means 'a willingness on the part of the reporter to be accountable for what is reported. Objectivity requires only that reporters be accountable for *how* they report, not what they report' (original emphasis, 1992: 180). Consequently here lies a vital question mark over the desirability and possibility of objectivity, resting on two elements. First, is the question of whether objectivity frees journalists from ideological baggage, or is in itself an indicator of ideology. Second, in the presumed benefits of being 'free' from ideology comes the freedom from responsibility for what is produced and thus whether this is desirable.

WHAT IS BIAS?

Whilst objectivity might be mired in definitional problems, it might be possible to examine this area by exploring the related concept of bias (McQuail, 1992: 191). There is an undoubted lengthy history of allegations of bias in journalism in many countries, so perhaps an examination of bias might be a more profitable route into understanding what journalistic objectivity might refer to in practice. Given the problems in the conceptualisation of objectivity, bias can't simply be defined as the absence of objectivity. Accusations of bias are typically *relational*, in other words features of society are examined in terms of their representation in the news media and how that relates to features as they genuinely exist in society, or how they appear in other kinds of representation such as official statistics. Notable examples in the litera-ture might be the previously mentioned study by Hall *et al.* into the representation of crime (1978), or the Glasgow University Media Group's series of seminal works on the British news media (1976, 1980, 1982, 1985). This kind of work highlights how media representations distort phenomena in a range of ways, such as through presenting events more (or less) frequently than they actually occur (e.g. strike action, stranger rape, child abduction, and murder), focusing on atypical examples of phenomena (e.g. deaths due to illegal, rather than legal, drug use), or relying on the official inter-pretations of phenomena by privileging official sources (as discussed in Chapter 4).

Examining journalistic output for evidence of such bias means evaluating content according to some clear ideas about what is acceptable practice. Kieran's qualified approach to the evaluation of news content, for example, states that:

> The standards by which we assess the value of a news report concerns adequacy to the facts and the cognitive virtues of rational coherence, plausibility and explanatory value.
>
> (Kieran, 1998: 31)

If Kieran's test is combined with Pavlik's idea of a degree of investigative triangulation mentioned earlier, then evidence that the news media have, and arguably continue to, offer representations of events and issues that fall short of these expectations and thus may be called biased, becomes compelling. This is because even if objectivity is seen as impossible there is still a recognisable gap between reports that offer coherent, plausible explanations of events based on sound newsgathering methods and those that don't. In this conception bias can basically be thought of as 'the *absence* of good journalistic practice' (McQuail, 1992: 192, original emphasis).

A clear example of this comes from French writer Thierry Meyssan's book on the September 11 attacks, *L'Effroyable Imposture* ('The Horrifying Fraud', 2002). He claims that rather than being a terrorist act carried out by al-Qaida operatives, in fact the US military-industrial complex orchestrated the attacks, using remote-controlled planes to destroy the World Trade Center in New York and a missile rather than a passenger plane to attack the Pentagon. Although the books sold well in France, Meyssan's claims do not stand up to detailed scrutiny. In researching his books he conducted no original inter-views and did not travel to the sites of the attacks. Instead he relied upon pre-existing accounts in the news media, such as interviews with eyewitnesses, and publicly released photographic and video images of the attacks. When asked to explain the disappearance of the people on the plane that hit the Pentagon, he has no alternative explanation. Despite multiple witnesses to the plane hitting the Pentagon (many were people stuck in traffic on their way to work) he rejects their statements outright. His claims are partly based on photographs from the scene of the Pentagon attack which show no obvious evidence of a plane and show the main wall of the Pentagon appearing to have remained structurally intact. Experts have pointed out how the plane would have crumpled and disintegrated in the combination of the impact with the very strongly constructed walls of the Pentagon and the intense heat of the explosion on impact. In other words, in the terms suggested earlier, Meyssan presents no substantive evidence to offer a plausible challenge to the consensus opinion and current body of evidence as to what happened on that day, and his investigative process has been far short of what would be expected in order for his account to have real journalistic credibility.

In such cases where an account claiming journalistic merit falls short under critical analysis, and therefore may be regarded as biased, the question then becomes one of the reasons behind the bias of the account. Reasons for bias may relate simply to differing political (or other) allegiances, or can be multi-faceted and complex, being products not of deliberate intent, but of the newsgathering process. For the purposes here a distinction can be made between bias as deliberate advocacy or as an unwitting or systematic product of journalistic routines.

ADVOCACY: DELIBERATE, OVERT BIAS

The identification of bias in news output is often seen as deliberate – the conscious intent of journalists to produce an account which strongly favours a particular interpretation of an issue or event and promotes this interpretation through selective use of information and other methods. Before objectivity appeared as a professional ideal, the notion of advocacy journalism was widespread with newspapers explicitly following particular political and social agendas. In fact, the suppression or removal of advocacy and partisanship is chiefly particular to the US model of objectivity (and arguably hides a more systematic degree of bias anyway, see below). Indeed, in many parts of the world, particularly in relation to print journalism, advocacy has remained a legitimate and persistent feature. In some regions, such as post-Soviet states in the last decade or so, partisanship and advocacy has been favoured over US-style objectivity (Heibert, 1999: 81). Part of this undoubtedly has to do with the perception of journalists in such states as finally having achieved freedom of speech, and thus voluntarily subsuming this under some kind of professional standard seems undesirable. Certainly a lot of the problems of Russian news media, like the very partisan treatment of the reactionary presidential candidate Gennady Zyuganov discussed in Chapter 2, can be seen as a reflection of Russian journalists' desperation to hang on to their newly won political freedoms over and above any pretensions to objectivity.

Even in more established and stable systems where objectivity does exist as a professional value partisanship and advocacy persist also. In Britain, for example, to offer overtly partisan coverage of political affairs continues to be a core value of the newspaper industry, most noticeable in individual newspapers' support for particular political parties. For much of the post-Second World War period such partisanship has drawn concern from critics of British national newspapers as there has been a persistent over-representation of newspapers supporting the right wing Conservative Party (see Seymour-Ure, 1995). Support for the Labour Party has fluctuated, and since the mid-1990s has enjoyed something of a resurgence reflecting the party's political fortunes with their regaining power in 1997. The third major party in British politics, the Liberal Democrats, have not had any explicit newspaper support since the early 1960s, and other parties trying to break into the political mainstream, like the Green Party for example, have found little space in the national press. British newspapers have also campaigned on single non-party issues, including in recent years things like tougher penalties for sex offenders, stronger asylum laws, or at the other end of the political spectrum, the decriminalisation of cannabis. This stands in stark contrast to British broadcast journalists bound by regulation to be non-partisan in political affairs.

In systems where advocacy is a recognised part of journalism sitting alongside objectivity, any potential tension between these two attributes is nominally avoided by the principle of the clear separation of fact from opinion (McQuail, 1992: 184). In this sense only news reports, and not opinion pieces or editorials, may genuinely offer the possibility of objectivity, and therefore it's only in these areas that critiques of journalism on grounds of objectivity are legitimate (Gauthier, 1993). In such mixed systems problems can occur as a direct result of this supposed clear distinction, as in the case of John Simpson that opened the chapter where criticism of his television reporting, bound by 'due impartiality' regulation, was prompted by his expressing of personal opinions in a newspaper column, which were not required to be impartial.

UNWITTING OR SYSTEMATIC BIAS?

There are other kinds of bias that can be identified in news media coverage that may be less deliberate or conscious. One area infrequently considered by analysts of the news is bias in the visual representation of individuals and events in photography or TV footage. The ethics of cropping, editing, and digitally manipulating photographs remains an overt issue in journalism debates, but there hasn't been much discussion of news photography per se in terms of objectivity, and arguably even less in terms of television footage. Part of the reason for this stems from the presumption that conventional practice amongst news camera-people (both still and film) is essentially about simply getting the clearest, most representative images of people and events in order to accompany the associated reports. Aesthetic considerations beyond this are not thought to be relevant to the enterprise of the news camera-person, and textbooks on news construction keep their descriptions of visual style and composition brief (e.g. Herbert, 2000: 216–17). Yet none of this prevents the possibility of different choices of camera position, angle, framing etc. having a potential impact on the subject in the camera lens. Stuart Hall, in a 1973 analysis of newspaper photographs, explains:

> News photos operate under a hidden sign marked 'this really happened, see for yourself'. Of course, the choice of this moment of an event as against that, of this person rather than that, of this angle rather than any other, indeed, the selection of this photographed incident to represent a whole complex chain of events and meanings, is a highly ideological procedure. But, by appearing literally to reproduce the event as it really happened, news photos suppress their selective/interpretive/ideological function ... At this level, news photos not only support the credibility of the newspaper as an accurate medium. They also guarantee and underwrite its objectivity (that is, they neutralise its ideological function).
>
> (Hall, 1973: 188, original emphasis)

A good example of what Hall is talking about is the photo of Elian Gonzalez mentioned in Chapter 5. That frozen moment of fear in the little boy's eyes as an armed soldier in full body armour grabs him from a relative is an evocative image, but to what extent and in what ways can that moment be seen as genuinely reflective of that particular case, let alone the complexities of Cuban-American political relations?

Although Hall talks here about the ideological function of news photographs, there is a sense in which the ideological connotations of particular choices of image in the news are not necessarily down to the selection decisions of camera-people or picture editors. An obvious example here would be the various images of the plane impacts on the World Trade Center towers, many of which come from tourists' camcorders who didn't understand what they were filming. Some images then, particularly of unanticipated events like terrorist attacks, major accidents, or natural disasters, may therefore involve the use of images that may have unwitting ideological connotations and consequences. This problem might be exacerbated by the increasing primacy of live coverage of events by global TV news providers (see Chapter 10).

For the planned events that take up a significant part of news production routines, particularly for television news (as suggested in Chapter 5), choices about how individuals and events are visually represented may play a greater role. One study of candidates in the German general election of 1976, for example, concluded that despite apparent balance in the verbal aspect of reporting, 'with the aid of optical means, the television journalists presented – deliberately or unconsciously – the two candidates as they actually saw them' (Kepplinger, 1982: 445). A later study of British television news coverage of the 1994 European election campaign found that although individual politicians were treated relatively consistently, the predominance of domestic politicians in domestic locations in what was supposed to be a *European* campaign, may have contributed to the framing of the election by television news programmes (Campbell, 1999).

Routines of practice may amount to unwitting bias, as ideological connotations of patterns of content that result may not be the product of any conscious or deliberate intent of the journalists. However, it is in the very routines of practice that some critics argue that journalism is inherently and systematically biased. Gaye Tuchman's analyses of news practices in the 1970s offer some seminal insights into production processes, and in one study notions of journalistic objectivity are associated with what is referred to as a 'strategic ritual' (1999). In this sense, the routine practices of journalists in attempting to ensure 'objectivity' constitute a set of ritualistic procedures that have come to be identified by journalists as providing objectivity. Tuchman identifies four procedures including the ordering of information in terms of importance (in other words the so-called inverted pyramid format), the clear use of direct quotation (in print through quote marks, in broadcasting through sound-bites), and the use of supporting evidence (ibid.).

The other aspect identified by Tuchman is the 'presentation of conflicting possibilities' (ibid.: 299). This is an important idea because it highlights a systematic bias in news for the presentation of issues and events as conflicts, and one that actually emerges out of efforts to be objective. Tuchman suggest that journalists' response to reporting something like, say, a claim by a politician is to try and find an alternative politician's conflicting viewpoint, thus presenting ' " both sides of the story" without favouring either man or political party' (ibid.). One possible consequence of this is that in the pursuit of balance and objectivity, the efforts to present issues and events in terms of conflicting viewpoints produce the systematic dominance of negativity in much news output (as suggested in Chapter 5). This occurs simply because it is far easier to find conflicting viewpoints in areas of literal conflict, disagreement, or problem, than it is in areas where there is widespread consensus and agreement. It could be argued that in contemporary Western nations the narrowing of political choice since the end of the Cold War has lessened the opportunities for political journalists to find policy conflicts between parties, and as such more trivial matters of personal behaviour have become the focus of political journalism and political controversy, whether that be the sex life of Bill Clinton, the hair colour of Gerhard Schroeder, or the personal affairs of almost countless British MPs.

Another possible consequence of the attention to conflicting viewpoints is that it potentially gives an advantage to whichever of the parties involved is better able to present their viewpoint. Going back to the themes of Chapter 4, this is a clear site through which resource-rich sources skilled in the construction and presentation of messages can succeed in getting their interpretations of issues and events across more effectively, even if their opponents are nominally given the same amount of space/time. Indeed, part of the problem in attempts at objectivity through equal presentation of conflicting viewpoints is the differing abilities of vested interests to be able to actually fill that space. In addition the willingness or otherwise of particular groups to offer their viewpoints also complicates the efforts of journalists to achieve objectivity through presenting all sides of the story.

The systematic response of journalists to this kind of situation is to use 'experts' on subjects effectively as proxies for those groups unwilling or unable to participate. A good example is the use of military advisors or retired officers to comment on possible military strategies in times of conflict, or people from charities or pressure groups as representative of the views of marginalised or disenfranchised groups. Soley's analysis of the kinds of people used by news organisations in this capacity suggests that far from ensuring a balanced and objective treatment of issues, organisations tend to favour sources from the same socio-demographic groups as themselves (1992: 22). So, figures from official and 'legitimated' institutional bodies are favoured over representatives from more radical, anti-institutional sources (ibid.: 23–4). So the requirements of some pressure groups to use particular types of people to front their campaigns, as discussed in Chapter 4, can be seen here as a direct, systematic result of genuine efforts at objectivity. It is in this kind of practice that the likes of Glasser, Hall, and others would assert that the underlying ideological consequences of the principle of objectivity are revealed.

ALTERNATIVES TO OBJECTIVITY

As discussed in Chapter 2, journalism exists within a wide range of social and political systems including those where objectivity is neither an ideal or goal, such as the party journalism systems of countries like North Korea. In many developing nations, news media are still in a stage of uneasy relations between state-sanctioned 'official' outlets and independent often radical outlets, and in such nations objectivity might be a principle journalists have heard of, but find unrealisable or undesirable in their particular socio-political circumstances. Even in developed democracies academic, conceptual criticism of objectivity has begun to be paralleled by practising journalists offering their own critiques and alternative approaches to conventional notions of journalistic objectivity. One example of each of these alternative approaches to objectivity is discussed below.

THE JOURNALISM OF OPINION

Advocacy, as mentioned earlier, has persisted in many parts of the world as a legitimate part of journalistic practice. It is evident in parts of Europe, both West and East, but perhaps has seen its most overt realisation in South America. In South American nations what has been dubbed the 'journalism of opinion' (Waisbord, 2000: 8) was the dominant model for much of the history of the press in that region, although it is less prevalent today than in the past. Essentially, the journalism of opinion involved the perception that 'the mission of the press was conceived to be the promotion of party dogmas, the propagation of policies, and the support of candidates rather than turning a profit or delivering "objective" news' (ibid.). South American newspapers have routinely represented the interests of political parties, trade unions, as well as other organisations and interest groups, often being owned and run by these vested interests. This reflects the ideas of journalism 'as a political tribune rather than an impartial chronicler of facts, and for the journalist as an activist for specific causes rather than a "neutral witness to history"' (ibid.).

This is not to suggest that questions of truth, realism, accuracy, and so on have not arisen in South American journalism, only that there has not appeared the kind of consensus around the social scientific, evidential model of journalism that developed in the USA (ibid.: 123). For South American journalists 'reporting has long been attached to literary ambitions and political endeavours' rather than a professional end in its own right (ibid.: 121). Despite the impact of technology, external working practices, and increasingly commercial environments, this aspect of journalism in South America has persisted. Waisbord suggests this is at least partly because South American nations have rarely achieved or enjoyed political consensus (ibid.: 125), in the way that, say, Western European nations have since the end of the Second World War. Turbulent swings between right wing dictatorships, liberal democracies, and left wing socialist states has typified South America through much of the twentieth century, and continues to do so. Debatably, journalism in the region has reflected this lack of political consensus, with journalism seen as playing a necessarily active part in the political struggles in South American nations, rather than as some kind of detached, non-partisan observer of events (ibid.).

Waisbord does note a transition in more recent South American journalism towards a greater fact-based reporting of issues, but he states that 'in the mind of South American journalists, facticity and objectivity are not identical' (ibid.: 140). Indeed, comments from a range of South American journalists cited by Waisbord indicate an overt rejection of objectivity, such as the blunt comment of Brazilian journalist Jose Hamilton Ribeiro 'that business of objectivity is a disgraceful stupidity. What is important is an honest report of reality' (in ibid.: 147). Similarly, Peruvian journalist Cesar Hildebrandt sums up the situation South American journalism has developed that impacts on attitudes towards objectivity, stating 'I am against objectivity. Without constitutional tribunal and with disappearances, torturers and uncertainty about the country, there is no alternative but journalism in the trenches. Neutrality is not possible' (in ibid.).

THE JOURNALISM OF ATTACHMENT

The 'journalism of opinion', and other similar approaches to news, might be seen as a result of the political and economic realities of developing nations. One recent alternative to conventional notions of impartiality in the more established British broadcast journalism was suggested by the highly experienced BBC war correspondent Martin Bell. His experiences in the war in former Yugoslavia in the early 1990s, and the increasing pressures on broadcast journalists in a competitive market driven by global satellite networks like CNN, shaped his thinking on how journalism should be conducted. He argued for what he calls the 'journalism of attachment'. He explains:

> By this I mean a journalism that cares as well as knows; that is aware of its responsibilities; that will not stand neutrally between good and evil, right and wrong, the victim and the oppressor ... This is not to back one side or faction or people against another. It is to make the point that we in the press, and especially in television, which is its most powerful division, do not stand apart from the world. We are a part of it. We exercise a certain influence, and we have to know that.

> (Bell, 1998: 16)

So, unlike Herbert Gans' notion that objectivity is a necessary marker of journalistic distance from the consequences of reporting, Bell regards such assumptions as unrealistic. He regards journalism based upon this kind of attitude as often little more than 'bystander journalism' (ibid.: 15). Some might say that this sounds like crusading journalism – the pursuit of truth for virtuous ends – but Bell claims a key difference with the crusading journalism of the likes of Woodward and Bernstein or John Pilger, in that he regards crusading journalism as political and polemical, tending to be blind to inconvenient evidence that undermines that crusade (ibid.: 16).

The Sniper Story

Bell offers an anecdotal example, a story told to him by another journalist to demonstrate why journalists are a part of what they report and thus bear some level of responsibility for those events (ibid.: 16–17). Basically the story goes that a war reporter wanted to get a story about a sniper. Having arranged it, the reporter meets up with a sniper in his position. Suddenly, two people move into the sniper's line of fire, and the sniper asks the journalist which one he should kill. The journalist, realising he's made a terrible mistake and has compromised his desire to remain isolated from the events he reports on, refuses to answer and turns to leave. Two shots ring out, and the sniper says, 'That was a pity ... you could have saved one of their lives' (ibid.: 17).

Echoing the discussion mentioned by James Fallows (and discussed in the last chapter), about a reporter witnessing an ambush of troops from his home country, Bell's point is that the mere presence of the reporter in such a situation changes the nature of that situation. The presence of the reporter, however neutral and dispassionate that reporter is, has consequences for the events they are reporting upon. In many ways such a view echoes that of critics of 'reality' television, where the presence of cameras being known to the subjects of the programme consciously or otherwise has an effect on their behaviour (see Chapter 9). It also highlights how for individual journalists, the principle of objectivity may not be right in certain situations. Tumber comments that 'the values which may serve journalism well in peacetime or amidst someone else's war do not necessarily serve the individual journalist well in the middle of his or her own conflict. The values of impartiality and objectivity look wrong' (Tumber, 1997: 4). Recalling research into journalists in the Falklands War (as discussed in the section on 'going native' in Chapter 4), Tumber makes a clear link between questions of the relationship between reporters and the subjects of their reports, and the possible limitations of the principle of objectivity in circumstances where that relationship is particularly strong. He concludes that 'the problems for the participant journalists … wedded to the events around them, is how to respond when events force a choice between professional commitment and participatory loyalties' (ibid.: 7). In the specific case of Martin Bell it led to him leaving reporting after some 30 years or so in the profession, and then to a single term as an independent MP in Westminster, before returning to journalism.

CONCLUSION

Despite the challenges of theory, technology, and changing attitudes, objectivity retains a forceful presence at least in Western discourses about what is good journalistic practice. If the analytical deconstruction of objectivity suggests it has become a rather empty term, this hasn't stopped it being used as a means of defence by journalists, and a means of condemnation by journalism's critics in the on-going debates over the 'crisis' in contemporary journalism.

One of the interesting things about debates about objectivity, ethics, news values, and the relationship between sources and journalists discussed over the last few chapters is that the majority of the dominant theoretical ideas about these topics have occurred in relation to a rather narrow section of journalistic output. Sometimes explicitly, but often merely assumed to be self-evident, the concern of much journalism studies research has been mainstream journalism genres such as social affairs, politics, crime, and industrial affairs. Of course it is quite appropriate to examine these areas, particularly given their apparent importance in mass mediated democracy. Two things make a broader analysis of journalistic output necessary though. First, many of the analyses of these narrow areas of journalistic content reveal significant distortions, misrepresentations, and omissions of important social issues which have often appeared in other parts of factual media content. A simple example would be the once familiar trend of newspapers separating and marginalising gender issues to 'women's pages', always positioned some way away from the front of newspapers, i.e. away from the 'real' news. These alternative sites of otherwise marginalised material have often been equally marginalised by journalism studies researchers.

Second, related to this, part of the supposed crisis in contemporary journalism is the alleged increasing tabloidization of news media. Yet, again, the emergence of different forms of factual media content has been noted, derided, and then often ignored by many journalism scholars, even though they are identified as areas of journalism that are expanding in terms of both the proportion of journalistic material produced and in terms of audience preferences. So, in order to effectively explore the status and nature of journalism in the information age, some analysis of features of these emerging alternative and parallel forms of journalism is necessary. Over the next few chapters particular examples of genres of factual media will be examined in the context of how these genres relate to debates about contemporary journalism.

Chapter Eight

☐ ALTERNATIVE JOURNALISMS I:

ATTITUDES, AUDIENCES AND AESTHETICS

> It was so quiet, one of the killers would later say, you could almost hear the sound of ice rattling in cocktail shakers in the homes way down the canyon.
>
> (Bugliosi and Gentry, 1974: 3)

So far, this book has examined journalism concepts and practices mostly within what we could call the established mainstream of journalism practice. Yet criticism of contemporary journalism in many nations often relates as much to forms of factual media output that the harshest critics regard as anything but journalism and as such not worthy of much more than contempt and derision. As pointed out earlier in the book, there is something of a paradox in terms of critics' attitudes and audience trends towards very different kinds of factual media output, and rather than simply dismissing these as undermining conventional journalism, or even as antithetical to journalism, these forms of factual media need to be examined to see exactly how they relate to core concerns of journalism. In this chapter and the next a range of these alternative sites will be examined with this goal in mind.

POSITIONING 'ALTERNATIVE' JOURNALISMS

Before discussing some of the emergent areas of alternatives to mainstream journalism, it is necessary to try and position a number of questions about alternative journalisms into a coherent theoretical and explanatory framework. Note that the term 'journalisms' is being used here, for two reasons. First, this chapter and the next are concerned with both forms of journalism that are devised as challenges to mainstream journalism conventions, but also with genres of journalism that aren't considered within the theoretical literature as having much if anything to do with the goals and functions of serious journalism. Second, within both of these categories a diverse range of strategies have emerged that offer no simple, coherent notion of a singular 'alternative journalism'. Although terms like the 'alternative press' are often used, they are really broad-brush collective terms for a disparate body of practices.

THE PUBLIC SPHERE: THE FAILURE OF MAINSTREAM MEDIA?

Amongst the questions that arise relating to alternatives to conventional journalism, one of the most fundamental addresses why alternatives to mainstream news media appear at all. The concept of the 'public sphere' has become part of contemporary academic and journalistic rhetoric around the social impact of news media, and may provide a theoretical basis for alternative journalisms. It stems from an important, if problematic, critical theoretical analysis of the relationship between democratic society and the media from German sociologist Jürgen Habermas (1989). As with the 'four theories' model discussed at length in Chapter 2, the theory of the public sphere has become both a very central theoretical framework for assessing the relationship between the media and democracy, and also the subject of extensive and very detailed analysis and criticism. Habermas starts with the assertion that democracies only operate effectively when decisions are made visibly in public. In classical democracy, such as that of ancient Athens, this was very literal, with the citizens meeting in the market place (the agora) and all discussions open and face to face. Until the re-emergence of democratic ideas in Europe, decisions were not made in this way but in the secret decision-making processes of monarchical courts. Habermas argues that social forces in seventeenth and eighteenth century Europe (and North America) provided the context for the emergence of what he calls the 'bourgeois public sphere' (Habermas, 1989: 221). This was an arena in which the emerging bourgeoisie, whose wealth and influence was increasing through developments like industrialisation and colonialism, began to debate and discuss a wide range of subjects. Fostered by the new media forms of newspapers and journals, absorbed and debated in the new trend of coffee houses, frequented by the emerging bourgeoisie, the notion of open, rational debate of social problems began to emerge reflected in the attitudes and philosophies of some of the great thinkers of the time. Immanuel Kant, for example, argued in 1784 that:

> The public use of man's reason must always be free, and it alone can bring about enlightenment among men ... by the public use of one's own reason I mean that use which anyone may make of it as a man of learning addressing the entire reading public.
>
> (Kant, 1784/1991: 55)

The Federalist letters of Franklin, Washington, and others, that represent the key discussions underpinning the drafting of the American Constitution provide another excellent example of this bourgeois public sphere. The public relaying of letters on matters of political and constitutional importance between 'men of learning', as Kant describes such people, typifies this idealising of rational debate. For Habermas, however, the potential for the continued expansion of the public sphere, and thus more openness and greater public debate, was stifled by what he calls the 'refeudalisation' of the public sphere in the twentieth century (Habermas, 1989: 221).

179

Amongst other factors, a vital component in this process was the commercialisation of the mass media. With mass media being subsumed into the capitalist system, the press ceased to be an independent and critical arena for discussion, and instead became a tool of the evolving capitalist state. Instead of rational, open debate, decision-making once again became controlled by the political elite, with decisions being 'introduced with consummate propagandistic skill as publicity vehicles into a public sphere manufactured for show' (ibid.). In a sense then Habermas collates the trends and problems identified in earlier chapters in this book (particularly Chapter 3 on the impact of market forces on the news media, and Chapter 4 on the impact of sources strategies), and suggests that they combine to, in effect, leave the mainstream news media failing in its central fourth estate role in modern democratic society. This model has been widely critiqued from a range of different perspectives (e.g. Garnham, 1986; Downing, 1988; McLaughlin, 1993; Thompson, 1995; Verstraeten, 1996; Hesmondhalgh, 2000), and some of those specific criticisms will be highlighted later on in this chapter and the next as they relate to particular questions of certain kinds of alternative journalism. Criticisms aside though, what Habermas's model offers for the purposes of this book is a possible explanatory framework for the presence and nature of alternative journalisms, in the simple sense that if conventional journalism was perceived to be fulfilling its function as a conduit for the public sphere, then no-one would feel any need to offer alternatives to conventional journalism.

CATEGORISING 'ALTERNATIVE' JOURNALISMS

Some of the established definitions of alternative journalism can be situated in the context of Habermasian notions of the public sphere. Atton's review of the alternative press in Britain, for example, cites a number of definitions of alternative journalism that highlight the perceived limitations of the structures underlying the mainstream press, such as the view that alternative journalism 'is not the established order; it is not the capitalist system; it is not the mainstream view of a subject ... or it is simply not the conventional way of doing something' (Comedia in Atton, 1999: 51). In other words the system of production and modes of newsgathering and presentation are, of necessity and by design, distinct from the conventional practices of the news media. Atton regards the alternative press as also having another element in which the members of society normally marginalised by mainstream media (for reasons discussed in Chapter 4) are foregrounded in content, and are even directly active in the production of content (ibid.: 52).

One problem with these formulations is that they place ideological restrictions on what constitutes 'alternative' journalism and what doesn't. The growth of free newspapers (as mentioned in Chapter 1), for example, is not generally regarded by writers on the alternative press as relevant to their discussions. Distributing newspapers to readers for free is undoubtedly an alternative to the conventional system of selling newspapers, and there have been some very interesting developments in free newspapers, such as the (originally) Scandinavian *Metro* newspaper, versions of which are distributed freely via metropolitan public transportation systems (buses, trains, trams etc.), in 15 countries (Burnett and Marshall, 2003: 170). What prevents free newspapers being discussed by alternative press scholars is the fact that despite their differences from conventional newspapers, they are still subject to the pressures and practices of conventional commercial news media, so cannot offer genuine alternatives to traditional news media.

A similar problem occurs in relation to the content and audience for alternative journalisms. Some definitions, such as that of the third British Royal Commission on the Press in 1977, include the notion that 'an alternative publication deals with the opinions of small minorities' (in Atton, 1999: 51). As Atton points out, for one thing the classification of a group as a minority over-simplifies and in some cases under-estimates the presence and importance of particular social groups (ibid.: 52). On the other hand, taking the other defining aspects into account, when news media outlets appear to conform to all other attributes of conventional news media, the extent of their 'alternative-ness' is uncertain. In Britain, for example, there are small circulation newspapers for religious and ethnic communities (e.g. *The Catholic Herald, The Jewish Chronicle, The Voice*) that, aside from their content and target audiences, are structured, run and financed in largely conventional ways. Instead of offering fundamental alternatives to conventional journalism such outlets arguably reflect the targeting of particular niches in the market, not really any different than mainstream newspapers reflecting allegiances to particular political parties, only more distinct in their allegiances.

Fully-fledged 'alternative' media then, in some authors' proscriptions, involve a more fundamental ideological separation from conventional news media. Such media outlets utilise different strategies to mainstream commercial (or public service) media at every stage of the news production process, from finance to organisation, content to distribution. Central to such definitions is the designation of 'the nature of the alternative media conceived as methods of achieving social and political action' rather than being 'merely information resources' (Atton, 1999: 73). Certainly in the historical sense, alternative news media in developed nations have involved overt activism in relation to the politically disenfranchised, such as the Black press in apartheid South Africa, or the working classes in 1830's Britain addressed by the unlicensed 'pauper' press (see Chapter 3). More recently, though, it has been, to use the terminology of Chapter 4, 'ideological outsider' groups that have contributed to the presence of a distinct alternative press in many developed nations. Particularly with the advancement of liberal capitalism and the retreat of socialism and communism in many developed nations, accelerating with the collapse of the Soviet Union in 1991, it has been the radical left whose agenda has been most consistently represented in the alternative press. Alongside the political left have emerged new issue-oriented social movements, such as the massive growth of the environmental movement since the 1960s (as discussed in Chapter 4), or those concerned with social problems like homelessness. What such groups broadly share is an antithetical position regarding the practices and processes of commercial news media. In particular there is often a deliberate intent to avoid adopting or utilising commercial strategies of production, such as using advertising to generate revenue or including content with mainstream appeal to widen audience reach, which often leaves alternative news outlets financially very vulnerable and in a marginal 'ghetto' (Comedia in Atton, 1999: 53). In addition, these ideological alternative media outlets often attempt alternative organisational practices that are based on collective management and collaboration rather than hierarchies (Hesmondhalgh, 2000: 111–13), and eschew traditional conceptions of copyright and intellectual property (Atton, 1999: 66–7).

Atton argues for seeing such media as parts of an 'alternative public sphere' that 'provides opportunities and outlets for the production and consumption of the alternative press, at the same time as the press itself provides material that sustains the sphere's function as a place for the formulation, discussion and debate of radical and dissenting ideas' (1999: 71). A particularly notable and problematic example of this is *The Big Issue*. *The Big Issue* is a weekly news magazine, founded by a former homeless person in Britain in 1991 as an outlet aiming to 'help the homeless help themselves' (in Atton, 1999: 58). It has been a major success story in part because of an innovative distribution strategy which sees the magazine sold on the street by homeless people themselves, who get a proportion of the cover price as a wage to help them get back on their feet. The content, although explicitly including material about homelessness and by homeless people, also includes much more conventional material for a news magazine, such as music reviews. Like earlier alternative titles that managed to breach the mainstream media environment (e.g. the radical left-wing magazine *Marxism Today* in the midst of the right-wing political climate of 1980s Britain (see Pimlott, 2000)), its very success has arguably comprised *The Big Issue*'s designation as an alternative news outlet. The choice it seems is a stark one between existing in a kind of economic and political isolation from the mainstream, or being subsumed into the mainstream public sphere, but only by conforming to mainstream practices – in *The Big Issue*'s case in terms of a de-radicalising of content.

This rather narrow categorisation of alternative journalism, in relation to radical politics and activism, fails to note alternatives to conventional practices operating both outside of radical political and social movements, and, on occasion at least, *within* conventional media organisations apparently dealing with mainstream audiences and mainstream concerns. Instead, then, of a cataloguing and analysis of specific localised alternative news outlets, this chapter is concerned with this analytical gap regarding the trends and initiatives within factual media outlets that problematise the assumptions of conventional journalism without necessarily fitting the narrow criteria offered by scholars for defining 'alternative' journalism. By doing this it is possible to examine forms of factual media output that do not sit easily either within conventional notions of journalism or within definitions of alternative journalism, but need to be addressed, rather than marginalised, by journalism scholars. It is in this sense also that the notion of a narrowly defined 'alternative journalism' can, and perhaps should, be replaced by the notion of alternative *journalisms*.

ALTERNATIVE ATTITUDES: ALTERNATIVE POLITICAL JOURNALISM

Aside from the journalism produced by groups on the margins of mainstream politics discussed above, there are also more complex interrogations of mainstream news media treatment of political and social affairs. As discussed in the last chapter, the dominant Western notion of objectivity has been conceptually and practically challenged as an appropriate manner in which to present issues of social and political importance. Not least of the criticisms, and often stemming primarily from practising journalists themselves, is that the distanced, supposedly objective style of reporting social issues fails to address those issues in a sufficiently engaged and investigative manner. In the specific area of political news, alternatives have emerged from within mainstream media organisations ranging from attempts to offer constructive contributions to civic society, through aggressive scrutiny of political actors and institutions, to satirical deconstructions of contemporary issues and events.

MUCKRAKING

In Chapter 7 the emergence of objectivity as a professional value of journalism was discussed in relation to the notion that the increasingly commercial nature of journalism production may contribute to the de-politicisation of the news, or at least the de-radicalising of political news, as some argue occurred in Britain in the mid- to late-nineteenth century (e.g. Curran and Seaton, 1997). Such views are certainly consonant with the Habermasian model of a public sphere undermined by the increasing control and management of the media by the political and commercial elites, and also the marginalizing of radical viewpoints into alternative media ghettos. Yet, neither the theory of the public sphere, nor the conventional definitions of alternative journalism, are able to easily accommodate some moments in journalism history that managed to maintain political radicalism within the emerging commercialised media landscape. Such a 'moment' occurred in the late nineteenth and early twentieth centuries in the USA with the movement of politically active journalism dubbed in 1904, by no less than US President Theodore Roosevelt, 'muckraking'. Although the original American movement lasted for barely a couple of decades, the term has remained as a description of politically engaged reporting directed at the close scrutiny of political officialdom that retains relevance today, especially as an indicator of the potential for alternatives within mainstream journalism.

Muckraking journalism emerged during the USA's 'progressive' era when a welter of political and social reforms were introduced to a country that had been expanding at an extraordinary rate. Increases in population from immigration, the opening up of the US continent through technologies like the railroad and the telegraph, alongside the rapid industrialisation and exploitation of the USA's resources was seeing the country rapidly modernising. A number of writers, most politically motivated, began to examine in close detail all kinds of aspects of US society as it became increasingly clear, to some at least, that the USA's political system was not keeping pace with the rate of change. Roosevelt's description of these investigative journalists as 'muckrakers' (making an analogy to a line from *Pilgrim's Progress*) was something of a U-turn. Having once been a champion of investigative journalism that highlighted political concerns he shared and tried to deal with via new legislation, once Roosevelt became president he found his own administration increasingly becoming a target for journalistic scrutiny, and that he did not like.

Three factors differentiated muckraking journalists from mainstream journalists of their time. First, was the extensive investigation that these writers routinely undertook. For example, probably the seminal work of muckraking was the investigation of John D. Rockefeller's Standard Oil Company conducted by Ida Tarbell between 1902 and 1904. The results of her research, published monthly in prominent muckraking outlet *McClure's Magazine*, was collated into a two-volume book stretching to over 500 pages of main text, and a further 200 plus pages in appendices (Tarbell, 1966: xxi). Second, the muckrakers were overtly politically partisan, and seeking political change and political action with regard to particular social problems. Writers like Ray S. Baker, and Lincoln Steffens engaged in lengthy investigations of issues such as the nefarious practices of the railroad companies, the problems of the African-American community, and municipal corruption. Third, some of the muckrakers utilised fiction as well as journalism to convey their concerns over social deprivation. Perhaps the best example would be the socialist writer Upton Sinclair, whose novel *The Jungle* (1906), was based on research into the meatpacking industry in Chicago. Muckraking investigations and writings were popular with the reading public and are regarded as having directly contributed to a range of changes in state and federal laws (Regier, 1932).

After muckraking journalism had begun to decline, partly due to the change in position of Roosevelt and the political establishment towards such writers and partly due to the ever-increasing commercialism of the US press, Sinclair would later offer a scathing critique of the mainstream press in *The Brass Check* (1929). This analysis offered arguments about the excessive influence of commercialism and conglomer-ation in the US press, not dissimilar to much more recent critiques of the modern day US press (for a discussion see McChesney and Scott, 2002). Despite the diminishing of the muckraking movement, some writers have continued to utilise their investiga-tive tactics, sometimes with significant impact, such as Jessica Mitford, whose 1963 book *The American Way of Death* presented a scathing picture of the US funeral industry and typified her muckraking style.

INVESTIGATIVE SATIRE

Another part of mainstream news media that has long historical roots is political satire, which stretches back as far as the earliest newspapers and is often typified in satirical cartoons which also have a lengthy history. In the contemporary era, complaints about the undermining of journalism's goals, through appeals to entertainment commercial news organisations are forced to make, are complicated by the emergence of what might be called investigative satire. With investigate satire, the satirists don't only sit on the sidelines making acerbic and cynical jokes at the expense of politicians and the like, but actively engage in investigation and interrogation of their subjects. Print titles like *Le Canard Enchaîné* in France, *The Onion* in the USA, and *Private Eye* in Britain (Lockyer, 2001) have become established outlets of a combination of satire and investigative jour-nalism, but recently investigative satire has become even more high profile. In the USA perhaps the leading example of this is the film-maker Michael Moore. Moore began his ascent to prominence with the film *Roger and Me* (USA, 1989), an account of his attempts to interview the head of the Ford motor company about their decision to close a plant in Moore's home-town of Flint, Michigan, thus overnight putting tens of thou-sands of people out of work and ripping the heart out of the community. Moore's mix-ture of pathos, comedy, and confrontation in addressing the USA's most contentious political subjects (such as racism, gun ownership, religious fundamentalism, and corpor-ate greed), has proved remarkably popular with audiences in the USA and abroad (his most recent book *Stupid White Men* (2001), for example, has topped best-seller lists and won awards in the UK). He has struggled to get access to US television, however, with his series *TV Nation* and *The Awful Truth* largely being produced by and for British television, whilst being censored or marginalised to cable television in the US. Similarly, there was a struggle to get *Stupid White Men* released in the US, as it was due to launch around September 11 and the Murdoch-owned HarperCollins felt that the book's critical exam-ination of the US was inappropriate in the wake of the terrorist attacks. The most recent demonstration of his thorny relationship with the US mainstream media came with the boos he garnered for criticising the war on Iraq in his acceptance speech for winning the best documentary Oscar for his latest film *Bowling for Columbine* (USA, 2003).

Moore's appeal beyond the US has undoubtedly inspired similar approaches to com-bining serious political investigation with satirical comedy. In Britain, comedian Mark

Thomas has found notoriety for a very similar style of socially conscious, campaigning comedy, with his *Mark Thomas Product*. Thomas's investigations into things like human rights violations around the world (including posing as a PR consultant offering services to dictatorial regimes, and getting senior military figures to admit to human rights abuses, such as torture, on camera) and the failure of major corporations to protect workers and consumers in the developing world, has seen him invited to major conferences organised by the big news organisations.

Like the muckrakers, these contemporary satirists offer a much more impassioned and involved treatment of political and social issues than mainstream news media are perceived to offer. Yet satire can be a risky approach to address issues that mainstream media ignore or misrepresent. A good example of this came with the widespread controversy over a satirical programme on paedophilia broadcast in Britain in the summer of 2001. *Brass Eye* was a series created by Chris Morris satirising contemporary broadcast news and documentary styles, and the willingness of celebrities to jump on public campaigns without any knowledge of what they were campaigning about. When a new programme was broadcast satirising the media's treatment of paedophilia it drew complaints from some 2,000 or more people and criticisms from government ministers (only one of whom appeared to have actually watched the programme). The controversy over the programme made front-page news in several national newspapers and was headline news on television news bulletins. Such coverage merely sharpened the very point of the programme, which was an identification of the tendency towards media hysteria produced when issues of paedophilia occur, with salacious audience-grabbing hiding behind public interest reporting, as evidenced by the 'name and shame' campaign discussed in Chapter 6.

PUBLIC JOURNALISM

As mentioned in Chapter 1, part of the 'crisis' in contemporary journalism in the developed world relates to declining audiences and concerns about the impact of this on civic society. In the USA, where no real tradition of European-style public service media exists (outside of the atypical PBS), these concerns about the civic role of journalism have led to the emergence of a distinct journalistic movement known as *public journalism*, or *civic journalism*. By the early 1990s the perception amongst some academics and journalists was that the fundamental goals of journalism were being undermined by trends in the media and in wider US society. Two of the key proponents of the new movement, academic Jay Rosen, and editor of the *Wichita Eagle* Buzz Merritt, summed up the problems facing US journalists in the 1990s:

> Threatened on one side by declining readership and new economic pressures in the media industry, they face a different kind of threat from the fraying of community ties, the rising disgust with politics, and a spreading sense of

impotence and hopelessness among Americans frustrated by the failures of
their democratic system.

(Rosen and Merritt in Rosen, 1999: 73)

The role of journalists in providing a free marketplace of ideas and a key component
of the public sphere was threatened not only by perceived trends in the media but
crucially, by trends amongst the US public and their relationship to politics. As well as
Habermasian ideas (an important theory in the evolution of the movement, Rosen,
1999: 62–4), a formative concept in this movement was the notion of 'social capital'
(Putnam, 1993). Putnam defined social capital in the following terms:

By analogy with notions of physical capital and human capital – tools and
training that enhance individual productivity – 'social capital' refers to
features of social organization, such as networks, norms, and trust, that
facilitate coordination and cooperation for mutual benefit.

(Putnam, 1993: 35)

This adds to the public sphere theory the notion of public engagement and participation, and means that the public engaging and participating is vital to effective
democratic society. In other words, rather than merely being about the news media's
role in the public sphere, as forums for public discussion, debates about journalism's
civic function need to address trends in public attitudes and behaviour. By the 1990s
Putnam, and subsequently subscribers to public journalism, argued that there had been
a decline in social capital in the USA. Declines in mainstream news media audiences
were just part of apparent declines of involvement in both formal civic activities like
parent-teacher association membership, attending public meetings, and voting, as well
as informal social networks like bowling leagues, church choirs, or scout groups (Rosen,
1999: 25; see also Hoyt, 1995).

This idea of declining social capital is not straightforward, as it has to be put into
the context of other trends suggesting a shift to new kinds of social network, rather
than a decline, like the growth of new social groupings such as the environment movement (mentioned in Chapter 4), or the more recent anti-globalisation movement.
Yet, other trends indicate more qualitative attitudinal features bolstering the public
journalism movement's position. A 1997 study, for example, found that some 79 per
cent of respondents viewed a journalist's job to be 'to cover bad news', and some
65 per cent that journalists also 'unfairly dwell upon conflict and failure' (in Benesh,
1998). So, rather than get bogged down in the quantitative debates over the levels of civic
participation or social capital, public journalism is as much about addressing audience
attitudes suggesting dissatisfaction with the news. These attitudes are interpreted as

187

resulting from a disconnection of journalism from the public, in terms of its respon-sibilities to the public as a democratic forum (e.g. Fallows, 1996). In this sense public journalism can be seen as 'an attempt to connect the media with the public' (ibid.: 247). A more detailed definition of the goals and aims of public journalism, here referred to as civic journalism, is offered by some of its key proponents:

> Civic journalism is about making connections between journalists and the communities they cover, and between journalism and citizenship. It is first of all a set of practices in which journalists attempted to reconnect with citizens, improve public discussion, and strengthen civic culture.
>
> Second, it is an ongoing conversation about the ultimate aims of journalism. Public journalists are people who believe that the press should take a far more assertive role in trying to make democracy work than they have in the past.
>
> (Friedland, Rosen and Austin, 1994)

A number of US news organisations have initiated public journalism programmes. In the 1996 US Presidential election, for example, a number of newspaper, radio, and television news outlets in North Carolina joined forces in a project called 'Your Voice, Your Vote' (Buckner, 1997). The project involved some collaborative investigation of campaign issues across the whole state, but importantly, the identification of key issues to focus on was made via two state-wide public opinion surveys (ibid.). Other public jour-nalism initiatives similarly structure at least some of their reporting on evidence from surveys, focus groups, and citizens' forums, such as those run since 1992 in Madison, Wisconsin with the help of local newspaper *The State Journal* (Hoyt, 1995). In essence public journalism involves techniques of newsgathering and news selection that rely far more heavily and systematically on public concerns, rather than the agendas of journalists and politicians, and also involves news organisations being more pro-active in attempting to provide additional outlets, like organising public meetings in their communities, for audiences to re-connect with social issues and political processes, or as Buckner, editor of *The Charlotte Observer*, suggests 'to provide the information they need to function as citizens' (1997).

Public journalism has generated significant debate in the US and some strident criti-cism. Rosen summarises some of the key criticisms of public journalism:

> Nothing new. A gimmick that draws attention away from cutbacks that have led to poor coverage and a dissatisfied public. A marketing ploy by an industry desperate to retain market share. A misplaced longing among editors who want to be loved. A invitation to go soft. An assault on the profession's

prerogative to judge what's important. A call for advocacy journalism, which would usurp the political process and further erode public trust. A distraction from the basic task of covering the news, difficult enough without adding the duty to repair society. An arrogant and preachy movement that pretends to have all the answers. A recipe for dumbing down the newspaper and backing away from courageous stands that defy popular opinion.

(Rosen, 1999: 182)

Picking through these, there appear to be a few common elements to critiques of public journalism. Amongst the elite of US journalism, the likes of the *New York Times* and *Washington Post*, scepticism and opposition to public journalism was the primary response (Hoyt, 1995; Rosen, 1999: 211). In these outlets, nominally not subject to the immense commercial pressures of much of local journalism in the USA, public journalism is a conceit hiding shortcomings in funds and journalistic ability. The problem with this as a criticism is that it directly acknowledges the problems of journalism functioning in its democratic capacity in a free market media environment. If local news outlets are having to resort to public journalism, even if it is merely a 'gimmick', then the free marketplace of ideas model of US journalism is fundamentally flawed. This is, of course, precisely what critics of mainstream US journalism are arguing and also confirms the Habermasian model of the undermining of the public sphere. This set of criticisms then is rather hollow as at the very least it acknowledges the fundamental problem that public journalism is trying to address.

Two other aspects of criticism of public journalism are perhaps of more interest. First, there are explicit concerns that public journalism practices undermine the gatekeeping function of journalists. Gartner, for example, suggests that public journalists 'cede editorial judgement to pollsters or, worse, to readers or viewers in focus groups who have no particular knowledge of a state, of politics or of politicians' (1997). Basing news decisions on the views of audience members who lack sufficient knowledge is one thing, but there is also the concern that audiences shy away from difficult and controversial topics. *Newsday* editor Anthony Marro, for example, produced a series of stories in the early 1990s that proved highly controversial amongst readers, and such stories might not have been run under a public journalism mandate as, he states, 'a lot of time people don't want to talk about the most important stories' (in Hoyt, 1995). Such criticisms do raise important points about the competence and willingness of audiences to understand and address issues of social importance. They also point to a criticism of the Habermasian model which, as Garnham comments, assumes 'that all participants possess complete information and engage in all debates' (1986: 44). The discussion of differences in the resources of potential news sources in Chapter 4 can be applied here at the level of individual citizens, who will undoubtedly differ in their knowledge and competences and thus their ability to contribute to the goals of public journalism.

189

The criticisms of Gartner and Marro, however, also imply a degree of professional superiority and distance, i.e. that journalists are in a better position to judge issues' news value, that seem to be dismissive of public views. From such positions, unpopular or controversial stories are perceived as audiences merely lacking sufficient awareness of those issues importance, and there's a sense in which journalists' superiority in issue recognition is simply assumed, rather than demonstrated.

Second, and relating to this comes the anxiety that news organisations may go 'soft', not only failing to address controversial or unpopular issues, but also start to concentrate on apparently positive issues and events so as to suggest the successes rather than the failures of public journalism initiatives (Hoyt, 1995). As Benesh argues, however, journalists 'often write about a social problem, then let other institutions, like government, worry about the solutions' (1998). Although Benesh distinguishes between public journalism and what she calls 'solutions' journalism, which is simply the effort to report situations where programmes to address social problems have had some success (ibid.), the wider issue of negativity in the presentation of social problems as opposed to pro-active efforts to address those problems with advocacy of public participation in addressing those problems, is relevant to public journalism. Rather like Martin Bell's commitment to the journalism of attachment discussed in the last chapter, this is a kind of pro-social advocacy that challenges conventions of journalistic objectivity. In addition, it offers a distinct alternative to traditional treatment of political and social affairs, and the potential for revitalising the public sphere, primarily through trying to achieve the greater involvement and participation of the public in the construction of news.

ALTERNATIVE AUDIENCES: PARTICIPATORY JOURNALISM?

Part of the context of public journalism debates relate to evidence of declining political participation, of which declining audiences for news media (discussed in Chapter 1) are merely one part. Membership of political parties, participation in conventional political campaigning (i.e. linked to political parties and focused around election campaigns), and most problematic of all, voting itself, have been declining in some nations, particularly the USA (Peer, 2000: 304), and Britain (McNair, Hibberd, and Schlesinger, 2002: 407). At first glance such declines in conventional political participation might seem to offer support to Habermasian notions of a decline in the effectiveness of the public sphere, or what Gitlin refers to as the 'hollowing public sphere' dominated by soundbites and spin (1991: 133). Public journalism essentially offers largely an indirect forum for political participation through the use of surveys, forums and the like which are then used to construct news coverage. In stark contrast to declines in conventional methods of participation, however, opportunities for more direct participation in *mediated* politics have increased in recent decades (McNair, Hibberd, and Schlesinger, 2002: 407). Of particular note here are the phenomena of political access programmes and talk radio.

POLITICAL ACCESS PROGRAMMES

Garnham's critique of the public sphere relates the theory to the concept of public service broadcasting (see Chapter 2), pointing out that the whole ethos of public service broadcasting (however problematic in and of itself) is geared towards the maintenance of 'a set of social relations which are distinctly political rather than economic' (1986: 45). Through financial and regulatory organisation public service broadcasting outlets are, at the very least, intended to provide a public service protected from the impact of both the state and the market, the two key factors that for Habermas limit the potential of news media to act as an effective public sphere. One important example of how public service broadcasting organisations might be able to provide something approaching a Habermasian public sphere is through political access programmes.

One of the criticisms of Habermas's model discussed at the beginning of this chapter is that it idealises the forms of communication in the public sphere. In societies of many millions, the kind of face-to-face or direct communication which Habermas prefers simply isn't possible (although new information and communication technologies may be changing that, see Chapter 10). However, the mass media do offer alternatives that provide, in their own ways, much greater opportunities for wide dissemination of issues. Brian McNair argues, for example, that the amount of contact with citizens provided by broadcasting outlets like Britain's political discussion programme *Question Time* far outweighs what could be achieved by door-to-door campaigning or public speeches (McNair, 1996: 50). What is distinct in political access programmes in public service broadcasting systems is that they are deliberately designed to try and address the issue of public participation in a mediated democracy. McNair, Hibberd, and Schlesinger suggest that in Britain political access programmes have the normative aspirations to achieve *representation, interrogation,* and *mobilisation* (2002: 409). In terms of representation, the aim of public service access programmes is to try and ensure some kind of representative sample of the body politic gets access to the programme. Programme researchers try to recruit audience participants for television discussion programmes from broad social backgrounds, whilst phone-in programmes use computer software to try and ensure a demographic cross-section of the public contributes (ibid.: 410–11). However, as with other kinds of political media coverage, such programmes tend to be dominated by those predisposed to following political news and participating in the political process, which in Britain tends to mean people who are 'male, middle class, middle aged, and white' (ibid.: 410).

Even given the limitations of access, in part due to the nature of the wider political culture, the interrogative aspect of political access programmes offers a distinction from conventional political journalism. Although political journalists' attitudes towards politicians has changed over the years in Britain, from sacerdotal to more critical and aggressive (see Jones, 1992), the growth of political access programmes offers an arena in which politicians can be placed under direct pressure from members of the public (McNair, Hibberd, and Schlesinger, 2002: 412). This pressure can come from the tone of questions offered by audience members for whom it may be their one and only opportunity to engage with a senior political figure in their lives, unlike political journalists who have to work with politicians on a daily basis. Coupled to the intensity of also being in the media glare, which members of the public aren't used to, political access programmes can be a 'rather robust forum' for politicians to appear within 'because if 150 people think you're talking nonsense they let it show' (Dimbleby in ibid.). British Prime Minister Tony Blair is, unusually, quite fond of appearing on such programmes, and appeared on several in the build-up to the Iraq war in 2003 as he tried to garner public support for the war. Whilst negotiations in the UN were faltering, a significant proportion of the British public were against the war and Blair's media offensive was not that effective, with one political access programme he appeared on closing with a slow hand-clap rather than the typical polite applause.

The biggest problem in terms of mobilisation comes with seeing political access programmes as somehow providing the basis for a mass mediated public sphere. Despite all of Blair's access programme appearances in the build-up to the Iraq war, neither public opinion nor the government's position changed. Whether or not such programmes influence the political process is certainly debatable, and even the normative goal to 'widen the appeal of the political process' (Dimbleby in ibid.) could be questioned. McNair, Hibberd, and Schlesinger argue that the problem for political access programmes, even within public service broadcasting networks, is that they still have to generate audiences and that 'in their efforts to mobilise audiences the makers ... have moved to what is a form of political *infotainment*' (original emphasis, ibid.: 413). In other words, to try and engage an audience beyond the already politically active and knowledgeable, who dominate the consumption of political media output, including political access programmes, programme-makers have had to try and ensure that programmes are entertaining and speak to the concerns, interests, and register of those parts of the audience who aren't routinely engaged in politics. This tension between mobilising the public and representing political affairs in 'appropriate' ways is evident in political access programmes in Britain where public service broadcasting requirements sit uneasily with the competitive environment of contemporary British broadcasting. Journalists hosting such programmes in Britain, appear to regard such programmes as still very much an environment for public access delimited by the competitive concerns of a news organisation, as summed up very clearly in this comment from David Dimbleby, host of the BBC's *Question Time*:

> The audience are not free to decide the questions or the order of the
> questions, or who I pick to talk about them. Our daily bread is earned not by
> providing an opportunity for our studio audience to do what they want; it's

about providing them with the opportunity to do what they want in a programme which is at the same time attractive to two and a half million people.

(in ibid.: 413)

'TALK SHOW DEMOCRACY'

The phenomenon of talk radio raises similar questions to political access programmes in public service broadcasting systems, although its roots and nature are very different. Talk radio in the USA began to grow in the 1980s as a result of deregulation and technological innovation (Peer, 2000: 301). In terms of deregulation, US radio's requirements under the 'fairness doctrine' of political balance were removed, and radio outlets 'turned to the more dramatic and provocative – and, therefore, more marketable – style' (ibid.). In terms of technology, satellite and digital telephony enable radio broadcasters to reach vast audiences, and receive input from across the nation and beyond in a very manageable way (ibid.). By the 1990s, the most successful talk radio hosts were reaching massive audiences, for example Rush Limbaugh, a staunch and fierce right-wing commentator, was reaching an audience of 18 to 20 million people by the mid-1990s (ibid.).

Unlike the highly moderated environment of political access programmes in the UK, US talk radio is fostered on the primacy of the first amendment and the extent to which vociferous and extreme viewpoints are good for generating and maintaining audiences. For Peer, US talk radio's format of mediated discussion and conversation places it close to the Habermasian idealised form of communication in the public sphere (2000: 307). In part this stems from talk radio's more inclusive structure:

in that ordinary citizens, unlike professional communicators, can call and voice their opinion with neither special training nor financial compensation. Thus, there is more opportunity for open, unrestricted, and unrehearsed conversation between host and ordinary citizens and among ordinary citizens.

(ibid.: 311)

Compared to television political access programmes, there is also a greater degree of anonymity for participants which frees them from social constraints on how and what they say, and more time for discussions to develop, with talk radio shows often lasting several hours (ibid.: 311–12). Arguably, this makes US talk radio more influential in terms of political processes than political access programmes in Britain, although whether that influence is positive or negative, or legitimate or not is a contentious issue. Certainly, the perceived influence of talk radio on political decision making has led to descriptions of broadcasters as 'governors on the airwaves' (Peer, 2000: 315),

193

and talk of 'talk show democracy' (Brokaw *et al.*, 1997). Two factors problematise the perception of talk radio having a positive, or at least neutral impact on the political process in the USA. First, the genre has been dominated by the political right in terms of programme hosts, skewing the nature and tone of political discussion on talk radio shows towards the interests and concerns of the notorious likes of Oliver North (of the Iran-Contra scandal) and G. Gordon Liddy (of the Watergate scandal). Like concerns about the skewed politics of the British press (see Chapter 7) the dominance of right-wing hosts combined with large audience reach for these hosts undermines claims about the virtue of such programmes as informational sources.

A second concern about these programmes' influence on democracy relates to questions of the legitimacy and effect of the more open environment for expression of political opinions. Some examples of talk radio shows, particularly at the local level, have developed into environments of extremist opinion-expression, such as the disaffected militia groups that are ardently and aggressively against the federal government in the USA. The 1995 bombing of a federal building in Oklahoma City by a lone bomber sympathetic to the militia cause, was linked by President Bill Clinton directly to talk radio giving a space to what he, and others, dubbed hate radio:

> In the days and weeks following the Oklahoma City bombing, Clinton and his surrogates launched an air raid, calling talk hosts 'purveyors of hatred and division'. He told the *Detroit Free Press*, 'I cannot defend some of the things some of these more extreme talk-show hosts have said, even more extreme than that in these little short-wave programs that plainly are encouraging violence'.
>
> (Paige, 1998)

Talk radio host and commentator Michael Harrison stopped short of endorsing Clinton's description of hate radio, suggesting that 'there are hateful things said on radio because talk radio is the arena of free speech and free speech is not tidy' (Paige, 1998). What this points to is the notion that 'acceptable' discourse about political issues, and 'acceptable' behaviour on the part of citizens remains highly circumscribed and delimited. That talk radio, in offering a more open space for citizens to engage in political discussion and expression, is perceived of as potentially dangerous by mainstream politicians, could be seen as indicative of the desire of political elites to manage the public sphere.

ALTERNATIVE AESTHETICS: LITERARY JOURNALISM

Progressive-era muckraking journalists have not been the only writers to address contemporary issues in lengthier pieces of factual writing. Over the course of the twentieth century a number of noted writers, some famous novelists others from traditional journalism backgrounds, have produced a loose body of work that has come to be dubbed 'literary' journalism (Sims and Kramer, 1995; Kerrane and Yagoda, 1997). Sometimes individual works are marked out as exceptional pieces of non-fiction writing, like John Hersey's 1946 book *Hiroshima*, which recounts in detail the experiences of six different people present at the first atomic bomb dropped in combat at the end of the Second World War. On other occasions it is a body of non-fiction, journalistic work from a writer that attracts attention, such as the work of George Orwell who, alongside his celebrated fictional works like *1984* (1948), is noted for his factual, journalistic works, such as his examinations of poverty including *Down and Out in Paris and London* (1933).

Literary journalism can be distinguished from conventional journalism in both superficial and more complex ways. Literary journalism generally occupies more space than traditional news reporting, or even conventional feature journalism, and thus is usually the preserve of news magazines and books rather than newspapers. Literary journalists Tracey Kidder highlights another key difference between literary journalism and conventional journalism, declaring 'our reporting takes months, and you're sent to get a story and write it up in three hours, and do two more before leaving work. A privileged journalist might get a few weeks for a feature' (in Kramer, 1995: 22). Rather than simply being conventional journalism in all but length and investigation time, though, such works additionally raise questions about the form, style, and structure of the recording and retelling of factual events. In other words, literary journalism and its related genres, such as true crime writing, offer *aesthetic* alternatives to conventional journalism.

WOLFE'S 'NEW' JOURNALISM

There have been previous eras of change in journalism where the term 'new journalism' has been used before in both positive and negative senses. The 'new' journalism emerging out of the telecommunications revolutions ushered in by the telegraph in the mid-nineteenth century, for example, was lauded by its supporters. Later with the commercialisation of the press, 'new' journalism took on a more derogatory meaning in its application to the trends for populist tabloid journalism (e.g. the 'yellow' press in the USA). In the 1960s and 1970s yet another conception of 'new' journalism emerged, only this time the source wasn't industry insiders but figures from literature and fiction writing, increasingly turning their hands to factual writing. There was not a deliberate, co-ordinated strategy behind the emergence of this new journalism, and it wasn't until 1973 that the novelist and non-fiction writer Tom Wolfe actually codified what aesthetically new journalism was about, in a collection of writing produced with E.W. Johnson called *The New Journalism* (1973). Kerrane suggests that part of the reason Wolfe's new journalism appeared when it did was the massive social and political upheaval going on in the USA at the time, including race riots, assassinations, Vietnam protests, and the rise of counter-cultural movements which meant that 'the "genteel voice" of traditional reportage was no longer sufficient to articulate public reality' (1997: 18).

Wolfe offered a useful model focusing on four 'devices' used by the 'new' journalists to capture what he calls the 'unique power' of realism (1973: 46). These four devices consist of 'scene-by-scene construction', recording 'the dialogue in full', use of the 'third-person point of view', and the recording of the 'symbolic details' of a scene (ibid.: 46–7). Wolfe's first three devices are essentially questions of structure and composition, but rather than representing a coherent position of all literary journalists, there are in fact diverging opinions amongst literary journalists as to how to treat aspects of construction, dialogue, and point of view. Some writers treat the recording of dialogue, for example, very systematically in order to try and capture as much as they can as accurately as possible. Truman Capote said of his preparations for writing the seminal *In Cold Blood* (of which more later):

> I began to train myself, for the purpose of this sort of book, to transcribe conversation without using a tape-recorder. I did it by having a friend read passages from a book, and then later I'd write them down to see how close I could come to the original. I had a natural faculty for it, but after doing these exercises for a year and a half, for a couple of hours a day, I could get within 95 per cent of absolute accuracy, which is as close as you need.
>
> (in Read, 1981: 101–2)

Some, like John McPhee, argue for a strict journalistic take on dialogue. He states that:

> [T]he non-fiction writer is communicating with the reader about real people in real places. So if those people talk, you say what those people said. You don't say what the writer decides they said ... you don't make up dialogue. You don't make a composite character. Where I come from, a composite character was a fiction.
>
> (McPhee in Othitis, 1998)

On the other hand, for other non-fiction writers this is seen as crucial to sustain the narrative's coherence and to explain aspects of character perceived by the author but not necessarily articulated by any of the subjects. A recent and notorious example of this is the biography of former US President Ronald Reagan written by Edmund Morris, called *Dutch: A Memoir of Ronald Reagan* (1999). In this book, Morris not only invents characters but also imagines himself as a character in Reagan's early career in a time before he was even born, in order to try and elucidate aspects of Reagan's life and character.

The justification for this kind of literary device in such writing comes from the notion that the need to engage readers is far more like fiction, in that the narrative itself, rather than what it necessarily contains, engages and then sustains reader involvement. One literary journalist suggested that:

> You want to take the reader to the last sentence ... That's the whole point of the story. I don't want to take him there just by fact. I want to take the reader there by going through an experience that I had that was revealing.
>
> (original emphasis, Mitchell in Sims, 1995: 11)

Another literary journalist concurs with this importance of narrative coherence and style, stating 'I want people who wouldn't read a book about Mexican immigrants to read my book because they see me as a tour guide they can trust or believe' (Conover in Sims, 1995: 14). Part of the basis for these stylistic concerns stems from two further distinct features of literary journalism. First, the final of Wolfe's devices involves the recording of 'symbolic details' (1973: 47). These are the tiny details that encapsulate 'the entire pattern of behaviour and possessions through which people express their position in the world or what they think it is or what they hope it to be' (ibid.). As examples, Wolfe offers aspects like 'everyday gestures, habits, manners, customs, styles of furniture, clothing decoration, styles of travelling, eating, keeping house' and so on (ibid.). Walt Harrington, author of *Intimate Journalism*, gives a clear example of the attention to incidental detail that literary journalists pursue:

> To say in passing that someone has a vase of Vivaldi roses in his apartment, you will spend an hour on the phone interviewing rose experts. You will go back to the scene of the crime the next day and walk off distances and check heights and angles. You will check maps to determine north, south, east and west. You will check decades-old weather reports to be sure it actually rained on the day someone says it rained.
>
> (in Reagan, 2000)

Of course this is the kind of detail that reporters working to a daily news cycle cannot gather, but then there is also the question of redundancy of information or information overload. Some conventional journalists warn that extra detail has to be relevant to be worth putting in. DeSilva cites an example of an award-winning story about a sea rescue, where a survivor is seen and then lost by a helicopter rescuer in a split second, and says of the author:

> He doesn't tell you what colour the helicopter is painted. Who cares? That's not all that important. But the look in the eyes of the man clinging to the

197

bottom of the basket before he fell – now there's a detail that matters in the telling of a story.

(in Reagan, 2000)

Second, and a feature that Wolfe does not address but has since become key to designations of non-fiction work as literary journalism, is the immersion of the literary journalist in the ordinary, everyday lives of their subjects. This is not just to grasp a sense of the 'symbolic details' of the subject's lives, but the aim is also, as Harrington states:

to understand other people's worlds from the inside out, to portray people as they understand themselves. Not the way they say they understand themselves, but the way they really understand themselves. The way, as a subject once told me, you understand yourself 'when you say your prayers in a quiet room'.

(in Weinberg, 1998)

Understanding people in this way involves not just paying attention to the details of a person's life, or spending a lot of time with them, but paying attention to the everyday routines of people's lives (Kramer, 1995: 27). Kramer argues that 'routine needn't mean humdrum. Most anyone's life, discovered in depth and from a compassionate perspective, is interesting' (ibid.). McPhee agrees with the comment 'I go off and look at people who are not making news and find in their stories something a great deal more interesting to me than the fact that somebody was murdered on the street' (in Sims, 1995: 17). It is in this sense that literary journalism is of more interest than simply in terms of aesthetics. Sims states:

At a time when journalism seems crowded with celebrities, literary journalism pays respect to ordinary lives. Literary journalists write narratives focused on everyday events that bring out the hidden patterns of community life as tellingly as the spectacular stories that make newspaper headlines ... Stories about wandering, work, and family – about the things that happen all the time – can reveal the structures and strains of real life. They say more about citizens' lives than do stories of singular disasters or quirky celebrities.

(Sims, 1995: 3)

In some senses then, literary journalism can be thought of as conveying distinct social benefits that mainstream journalism does not. It could be seen as addressing fundamental questions in social history such as 'how did it feel to live and act in a particular period of human history?' (Connery in Sims, 1995: 4). A parallel can be drawn here with the project of many documentary-makers to do the same thing, to capture aspects of human behaviour and attitudes that can't be recorded in any other way, such as the BBC's major documentary serial in the late 1990s called *People's Century* that covered the key events in the twentieth century largely through interviews with ordinary people who participated in those events. As well as arguably capturing public-centred material, as opposed to elite-centred conventional news, Kramer claims further that 'there is something intrinsically political – and strongly democratic – about literary journalism, something pluralistic, pro-individual, anti-cant, and anti-elite' (1995: 34). This capacity for alternative journalisms to provide sites for representation of and access to otherwise marginalised, or un-represented groups and individuals recurs in other distinct forms of factual media to be discussed further in the next chapter.

TRUE CRIME WRITING

The opening line of Vincent Bugliosi's book *Helter Skelter* at the beginning of this chapter, sounds in tone like classic hard-boiled crime fiction, but in content reflects the thoughts of a real killer, a member of the Manson 'family' on the night they committed their infamous murders. Furthermore, Bugliosi was no novelist but the prosecuting attorney in the trial of the Manson gang. Bugliosi's book is one of the most successful examples of a particular form of literary journalism, true crime writing. The obsession with crime that some may feel is a particularly modern phenomenon, has been one of the staples of journalism from its earliest days. The sixteenth-century pamphlet precursors of newspapers were often full of criminal cases, with graphic descriptions of the crimes and the punishments meted out. Witch trials, for example, were a popular topic of both the pamphlets and newspapers throughout the sixteenth and seventeenth centuries. In Britain, crime stories were popular enough to be collated into books by the 1730s, and towards the end of the eighteenth-century titles like the *Newgate Calendar* (Newgate was a famous London jail) began to fill in the gaps of crime stories, with details of the social milieu of criminals and their crimes (Byrnes, 1997: 3). By the first half of the nineteenth century, the notorious 'penny dreadfuls', such as the *Terrific Register*, were devoted to the gruesome retelling of crimes, with accompanying illustrations, and by the early decades of the twentieth century, Americans had become enamoured with true crime writing widely available in pulp magazines (ibid.: 6).

Although there had been collections of true crime writing and the occasional true crime book, extended works of true crime writing were rare until novelist Truman Capote wrote *In Cold Blood* in 1966. The massive popular and critical success of that book, an exposition of a multiple murder in Kansas in 1959, both in the USA and abroad, gave true crime writing a new prominence and respectability that it had never previously enjoyed. Capote helped legitimate true crime writing in both journalistic and literary terms, taking it beyond the pulp magazine and tabloid market. Since then, the market for true crime writing has massively expanded, with currently well over a thousand titles available in the USA alone, for example, and some writers becoming associated solely with this kind of writing, such as former policewoman Ann Rule (author of books like *Small Sacrifices* (1987)), or Brian Masters (author of *Killing for Company* (1985)). Other literary giants have also written true crime works, such as Gabriel Garcia Marquez's *News of a Kidnapping* (1996) about a series of kidnappings in the era of Columbia's notorious drugs crime-lord Pablo Escobar.

New techniques of criminal investigation have also added to the media appeal of crime. Developments in forensic science such as genetic fingerprinting, as well as the rise of criminal psychology such as the 'profiling' of serial criminals, have become staples of not just factual media, but also drama in popular TV programmes like the US series *CSI: Crime Scene Investigation.* The line between fact and fiction has also blurred most overtly in relation to crime, one trend to have emerged is high profile crime dramatisations, with well-known actors playing against type as the criminals. Notable examples include: Mark Harmon playing serial killer Ted Bundy in *The Deliberate Stranger* (US, 1986); Gary Cole (playing Jeff MacDonald, a decorated US Army surgeon convicted of killing his wife and two small daughters) in *Fatal Vision* (US, 1984); and Farrah Fawcet (playing Diane Downs a mother who tried to kill her three children) in *Small Sacrifices* (US, 1989).

Some of the leading lights of US true crime writing, figures such as Ann Rule and Jack Olsen, have lamented the explosion of true crime in the media, feeling that quality writing in the genre has been undermined by commercially successful works that are more fiction than fact (Hood, 1998). Also the combination of highly successful works, and high profile crime cases can lead to extremely rapid publication of 'instant books' (ibid.) and non-professional writers joining the ranks of those documenting the notorious crimes of the day. A couple of examples should clearly illustrate this. Perhaps the most prolific serial killer of all time, certainly of recent decades, stood trial in Britain in 1999. Dr Harold Shipman, a local community doctor in the North West of England, was convicted of over a dozen murders of elderly women via lethal injections. Even without television access to courtrooms, this was an extremely high profile case and not surprisingly it generated news media interest, not to mention the attention of true crime writers. Within a month of his conviction and sentencing, in January 2000, two books about the case were published in Britain (Whittle and Ritchie, 2000; Sitford and Panter, 2000). In 2002, a controversial televised dramatisa-tion of the investigation of Shipman was screened, again featuring a well known actor (James Bolam) playing the killer, only a short time before a public inquiry into the case announced that Shipman was responsible for over 200 deaths.

In the USA, where TV access to court cases is quite widely available, one might expect extensive TV coverage to undermine the possibility of book length accounts of high profile cases. This isn't necessarily the case, however, and in what was probably the highest profile trial of all time, the trial of O.J. Simpson, the spate of books has been remarkable. Making the Shipman authors look sluggish, Simpson himself had penned a book, *I Want To Tell You*, even *before* his trial began. In the wake of the now infamous not guilty verdict, literally dozens of books by academics and professional writers have been published about the case (including one by Bugliosi). Moreover, plenty of people involved with the case to varying degrees have chipped in with their versions of events including Simpson's niece Terri Baker, his former girlfriend Paula Barbieri, Nicole Brown Simpson's friend Faye Resnick, and William and Marilyn Hoffer, family to the other victim, Ron Goldman. Prosecution lawyers Hank Goldberg, Christopher Darden, and Marcia Clark all penned books, as did Daniel Petrocelli, who represented the Goldman family in the civil case against Simpson, whilst from the defence team, Robert Shapiro, Alan Dershowitz, and Johnnie Cochran weighed in on O.J.'s side. As if that wasn't enough, there have also been books from the police that investigated the crime, including Mark Fuhrman (the officer accused of racism by the defence team) and detectives Tom Lange and Philip Vannatter, and even jurors Tracey Kennedy and Michael Knox have given versions of their experiences (something that would be illegal in Britain).

One of the issues that such cases raise most overtly is the problematic relationship between the writers of true crime and the subjects being written about. Questions of objectivity are certainly compromised by authors who were key participants in the crimes being described. Even for authors detached from direct involvement in the crimes, though, the issue of journalistic distance from those involved is problematic. Capote, for all his claimed systematic research mentioned above, admittedly became emotionally attached to the people involved, crying at the execution of the murderers, and describing them as 'the two people he knew most intimately in the world' (in Read, 1981: 103). He argued, however, that:

> emotionality makes me lose writing control: I have to exhaust the emotion before I feel clinical enough to analyze and project it, and as far as I'm concerned that's one of the laws of achieving true technique.
>
> (in ibid.: 95)

Just as with wider literary journalism the concern of critics is that the demands of narrative can overtake the requirements for factual accuracy and detachment. Certainly a lack of factual accuracy is not a hindrance for 'true' crime writing success, as in the case of Lorenzo Carcaterra's 1996 book *Sleepers*, whose largely fabricated content did not prevent it being a bestseller, nor it being turned into a major Hollywood film (Byrnes, 1997; Hood, 1998). A prominent true crime editor seems to support the concerns about the regression in the genre towards commercial appeal:

> Quite frankly, if *In Cold Blood* came across my desk tomorrow I don't know if I would publish it. It's not intense enough, bloody enough, or lurid enough to

> meet the public's demand. People are looking for something over the top and, particularly in the paperback market the literary approach has been passed by the public's demand for blood.
>
> (Dinas in Byrnes, 1997: 254–5)

So, just as with conventional journalism, more aesthetically-minded factual writing can be subject to commercial imperatives and the pressure of audience trends. What is often missing from laments about these pressures, however, is any conception of the reasons behind audience trends.

CONCLUSION

The generic breakdown of journalism as a relatively uniform practice, evidenced by the many different ways one can think of alternatives to the traditional organisation and practices of journalism, arguably brings a wide range of media content into contact with some of the issues that pertain to journalism. The examples discussed in this chapter, for the most part, at least relate to the traditional concerns of mainstream journalism. In their efforts at attempting to address topics otherwise marginalised by mainstream media, to try to give access to otherwise marginalised groups, or simply through challenging the presumptions of conventional styles of journalism, these alternative journalisms are potentially significant in their impact on a deeper understanding of what journalism means. Some other alternative journalisms, however, are about as far removed as possible from what traditional journalists conceive of as journalism, but in the interests of thinking about what journalism does and does not do – particularly in terms of audience tastes – they require discussion, and that is what the next chapter attempts to do.

Chapter Nine

ALTERNATIVE JOURNALISMS II: □

ENTERTAINMENT, SPORT, AND LIFESTYLE

If the wide-ranging factual media forms discussed in the last chapter can be linked, however tenuously, to concerns of mainstream journalism through their focus on issues of social consequence, another set of topics covered by both mainstream and 'alternative' factual media forms arguably doesn't have that defence. When it comes to those aspects of factual media dealing with the concerns of the citizens of affluent societies and their lifestyle habits and interests, efforts to accommodate such material within the established definitions of journalism might be problematic beyond resolution. That such material exists, and is attractive to audiences, is very evident from analyses of both content and audience response. Tunstall, for example, collates a range of surveys from the 1960s, 1970s, and 1990s of British newspaper readers' preferred subjects that show consistent evidence for greater or equivalent attention to not only subjects like entertainment and sport, but also to things like TV listings, cartoons, and lifestyle material (e.g. fashion, travel, gardening, motoring, and so on), as to politics, social and international affairs (1996: 216–18). Rather than addressing these audience choices in the context of concepts about journalism, though, Tunstall describes them as 'not really part of journalism as traditionally understood' (ibid.: 217). Yet, again, news organisations provision of such material, indeed their expansion of sport, entertainment and lifestyle content over the last few decades (e.g. McLachlan and Golding, 2000; Rooney, 2000), demands an examination of how such material sits within and offers alternatives to traditional conceptualisations of journalism.

One suggestion, for example, is that rather than serving a unitary function, contemporary journalism is transforming into clearly differentiated kinds (Bardoel, 1996). The traditional model of journalism has an orientating function treating audiences as a public of citizens and providing 'background, commentary' and 'explanation' about political and social events and issues (Bardoel, 1996: 296). Alongside this though, emerging partly out of new technology (see Chapter 10), is 'instrumental journalism' which is 'geared to providing information (functional, specialistic) to interested customers' (ibid.). 'Instrumental' journalism addresses audiences not as citizens as part of the body politic in the public sphere, but as private individuals with a range of personal concerns that factual media can address. This disjuncture between the public and private seems not only to exist in terms of the dominant theory of the public sphere, but in many journalism scholars' treatments of these areas which are dismissed or ignored rather than analysed. By examining some of these areas, namely entertainment, sports, and lifestyle journalism, this gap in much journalism studies research can at least be addressed.

ENTERTAINMENT-ORIENTED JOURNALISM

One of the many criticisms of the theory of the public sphere (outlined in the last chapter) is its implicitly derogatory view of entertainment 'as merely a *distraction*, a diversion from what [is seen] as the most desirable goal of mass communication: the activism of the concerned, rational, participatory citizen' (original emphasis, Hesmondhalgh, 2000: 108). One problem with this, as Hesmondhalgh notes, is that people in many nations 'are bombarded by the images, sounds and words of the entertainment industries every day of their lives … Only by understanding the enormously powerful affective role of such texts can we grasp the politics of contemporary culture' (ibid.: 108–9). This applies far beyond the confines of factual media, but given the concerns outlined at several points in this book about the apparent growth of entertainment-oriented journalism (that is both journalism about the entertainment industries and journalism that is designed to be entertaining as much as, even more than, it is informative) it seems particularly relevant to the analysis of such forms of journalism. After all, as Gripsrud comments, 'a relative expansion of certain forms of popular journalism affects cultural, political, and public life in general, not just a set of journalistic formats' (2000: 288).

The related problem of merely regarding entertainment-oriented journalism as a distraction, or not 'real' journalism is a failure to address the significant issue of how audiences respond to such material. Normative theories of the relationship between the media and the public often presume that the nature of entertainment-oriented news is a distortion of issues and events with presumed negative consequences for audiences. Franklin, for example, offers some of the core accusations that such news 'exploits personal tragedy for public spectacle', appeals to 'morbid curiosity' and utilises 'scandal and sensationalism' (1997: 3). As Bird notes, though, 'what is often lacking in the 'lament' about news is any real understanding of why scandalous or sensational news is appealing' (1997: 100). Instead, critics side-step audience responses in favour of presuming detrimental affects on the audience to suggest, for example, that 'news which is highly personalized in its representations of reality makes it that much more difficult for readers to identify means of articulating their resistance to these power relations' (Allan, 1999: 112). In other words the focus of these kinds of illegitimate news fail to provide the informative functions necessary for audiences to be able to actively participate in the public sphere, by obfuscating important social issues with their emphasis on celebrity, scandal, and sensationalism. Such criticisms falter, not only in the straightforward sense that they are presumptive (and often not based on research evidence) but also because they ignore a crucial factor in news consumption. The theory of the public sphere also fails in this sense, which lies in the designation of the audience as being 'relatively passive consumers who are enthralled by the spectacle and easily manipulated by media techniques' (Thompson, 1995: 74). Such assumptions can be contested in at least two ways. First, as evident in the discussion of political access programmes and talk radio in the last chapter, and confessional talk shows discussed later in this chapter, there are opportunities for audiences to be active participants in media output, with concomitant consequences for the kinds of output that result.

Second, and of more concern in this section, is the possibility of active consumption of media output whereby audience members are perceived as actively engaged in constructing meaning from media texts. The dominant theoretical model dealing with how audiences make meaning from media texts is currently the 'encoding/decoding' model developed by Stuart Hall (Allan, 1999: 118–9; for a fuller treatment of the model see Morley, 1992). In this model, responses from audience members to media texts are not treated as straightforward and simplistic. In the case of journalism the simplistic perception is that people accept what they read, see, and hear to be the complete and total truth about an event or issue. The idea of framing in the news, discussed in Chapter 5, offers a slightly more sophisticated idea that acknowledges that audience members don't uniformly accept what they are exposed to as correct and truthful, but still presumes that news coverage shapes audience perceptions of issues and events. This occurs through journalists' construction of news frames, or in the terminology of the encoding/decoding model, the 'encoded' interpretations evident from the way in which journalists construct their coverage. In the encoding/decoding model, though, socio-demographic and other factors inherently contribute to members of the audience responding differently to media content. To give a simplistic example, however much BBC news reporting might work within its regulatory requirements for balance in its coverage of an event like the war in Iraq, the responses to, or 'decoding' of, that coverage might be very different between, say, an anti-war protestor, a refugee of Saddam Hussein's Iraqi regime, the spouse of a combat soldier, and so on.

In the specific context of attempting to address the appeal of entertainment-oriented journalism with audiences, account must be taken of the position of audiences in their decoding of such journalism. Critics seem to assume that the attitude of audiences is the same for entertainment-oriented journalism as it is for more conventional news. The perception is that audiences treat conventional news as largely factual and truthful accounts of issues and events, and thus the concern is that the same attitude applies to entertainment-oriented journalism. As Bird states, such views 'tend to have the effect of neuroticizing the audience, suggesting that there is something sick or abnormal about being attracted to unwholesome news' (1997: 100). Some writers question this presumption, however, arguing that audiences interact differently with entertainment-oriented journalism and conventional journalism. Fiske, for example, argues that entertainment-oriented journalism could be seen as offering a characteristic 'tone of voice [which] is that of a sceptical laughter which offers the pleasures of disbelief, the pleasures of not being taken in' (in Allan, 1999: 113). In this sense audiences for entertainment-oriented news are not brain-washed drones focusing on spectacle rather than substance, but critically aware consumers instrumentally appropriating a range of media output for their own ends. Whether this perception alters the widespread assumptions of the negative affects of problematic forms of journalism like entertainment-oriented journalism, requires closer examination.

SUPERMARKET TABLOIDS

An excellent test of both the negative connotations and positive possibilities of entertainment-oriented journalism comes with an examination of the USA's 'supermarket tabloids', like the *National Enquirer* and the *Weekly World News*. For a start, supermarket tabloids have been dubbed a 'disgrace to journalism' (Buckley in Bird, 1990: 377), and even some 'tabloid writers support the contention that their publications bear no relationship to journalism' (Bird, 1990: 377). These weekly papers are distributed mostly through supermarkets, hence the name, and by the late 1990s were reaching as many as 50 million Americans each week, with actual circulation figures of the leading six titles at around 10 million (some way ahead of leading conventional newspaper chain Gannett's entire stable of paper, Hogshire, 1997: 2–3). Hogshire defines the supermarket tabloid as 'a sensationalistic newspaper full of sex, "gore" and bizarre tales of human behaviour' (ibid.: 7). The broad roots of supermarket tabloids go back at least to the earliest days of printed news, when fantastical tales from over the seas were common subjects of broadsides and early newspapers (ibid.: 7–12; see also Cranfield, 1978; Byrnes, 1997). More specifically though, US supermarket tabloids owe a debt to *Confidential* magazine in the 1950s. This magazine, and its imitators, specialised in investigating the more sordid aspects of celebrities' lives, and 'was the first magazine to employ long-range lenses, hidden microphones and tape recorders', not to mention 'doctored photos' (Hogshire, 1997: 15). Persistent litigation eventually saw *Confidential* close, but its legacy of celebrity scandals and sensationalism was picked up by the emerging tabloids like the *National Enquirer*, still the market leader of the supermarket tabloids.

The content of these papers is highly formulaic, sensationalised, and often overtly fabricated, explicitly raising the issue of how audience relate to them. Hogshire suggests that 'as transmitters of gossip, tabloids are bound up with issues of social control' (1997: 7). Like the catholic priest with access to the private foibles of his parishioners, Hogshire is suggesting that for the mostly working class audience (ibid.: 76) these papers offer a suggestion of insider knowledge, and bringing down of those in superior positions within the social hierarchy. Scandal stories, for example, 'stress the imperfections and failures of famous or powerful figures, caused by hubris or debauchery' (Hogshire, 1997: 37). In this sense, supporting Fiske's contention mentioned earlier of a kind of sceptical enjoyment, Hogshire suggests that some supermarket tabloid readers 'often read tabs as a kind of inside joke with themselves' (1997: 80). However, Hogshire also suggests that at least parts of the audience for these tabloids do regard them as factual and truthful sources of information, but the reasons behind this are beyond his comprehension 'either [the magazines'] readers are some of the most gullible people on Earth, or there is something else going on' (ibid.).

Whether the audience for supermarket tabloids is critically active in interpreting their content or not, it could be argued that supermarket tabloids serve another function, particularly with their attention to scandal. Scandal stories are important as they can be seen to overtly dramatise and interrogate morality (Bird, 1997: 106–7; see also Chapter 3). It is in this sense of interrogating the moral norms of society in supermarket tabloids, and other forms of entertainment journalism, that the explanation for the appeal of such material may lie, and also a defence of such forms as having pro-social, and progressive effects. Bird, for example, suggests that 'through these media morality tales, people come to terms with their own moral codes and values' (1997: 119; see also Tomlinson, 1997). The problem is that rather than offering a simple site for Fiske's notion of anti-establishment scepticism and even subversion stemming through unconventional themes and styles, the moral position offered by the supermarket tabloids is not in itself subversive or oppositional. Hogshire indicates that the supermarket tabloids are 'full of moralistic stories designed to reinforce values that foster social control ... Despite their reckless and libellous image, tabloids never challenge the status quo' (Bird, 1997: 47). Given this limitation, Bird also argues that of the widespread use of scandal stories in contemporary journalism 'one would be hard pressed to conclude that highly popular news stories, whether scandals or not, have ever had any major subversive or liberatory outcome for "the people"' (ibid.: 118).

CELEBRITY AND PHOTOJOURNALISM

The dispute over the potential for some kind of subversive or liberating impact of the tabloid style of America's supermarket tabloids rests on the interaction between their audience and the highly judgemental content typical of tabloid journalism. Another area of entertainment journalism offers a more benign environment for journalism about celebrities and entertainment. In the days of *Confidential* magazine, photojournalism was a major feature of many developed nations' media environments. News magazines that centred their coverage around photojournalism, such as *Life* magazine in the US, and *Picture Post* in Britain were very important visual news outlets for audiences, especially in the years before television came to prominence, and arguably played a role in the recognition of photography as an art form (Becker, 1992: 138). Even for some time after television took off with audiences, the general news magazines of this type remained important, but by the 1960s the ubiquity of television was the death-knell for such titles. Developments in newspaper publishing were seeing the photojournalism magazines' approach being incorporated into weekend newspaper colour supplements, like the *New York Times Sunday Magazine*, and in Europe in the broader trend for weekly news magazines like *Paris Match* in France, or *Der Spiegel* in Germany. At the same time the emphasis of photojournalism in the West was beginning to turn away from attention to 'hard' news, and towards the burgeoning entertainment industries, of cinema, television, fashion, and popular music. It was at this time that the term 'paparazzi' was used to describe celebrity-chasing photographers in the Federico Fellini film *La Dolce Vita*, a term which has stuck and garnered increasingly negative connotations, the nadir being the car crash death of Diana, Princess of Wales in 1996, while trying to escape from photojournalists. The photojournalism magazines, like *Life*, treated the news photograph as an 'idealised' or 'decisive moment' encapsulating events in a manner that was both valid and accurate in its informational content and also satisfied formal aesthetic conceptions of 'good' photographs (Becker, 1992: 139). The paparazzi, on the other hand, and the rising tabloid photojournalism in various parts of the world, was focused more on opportunism and candid photography attempting to capture unofficial images, having little thought of composition or style.

The 1980s and 1990s saw the rise of a new kind of photojournalism magazine centred not on general news, but on social elites and celebrities. Titles such as *¡Hola!* in Spain, and its later companions *Hello!* Magazine in Britain, and *Oh La!* in France, record the social events and lifestyles of European royalty and aristocracy, as well as celebrities from other areas of society for millions of readers. Sacerdotal articles dominated with portraiture photography, celebrated the weddings, births, christenings, and general success of the great and the good, akin to the US television programme *Lifestyles of the Rich and Famous*. In Britain the market for such output has grown steadily in the last decade to become a highly competitive environment. The once unique title *Hello!* initially came under fierce competition from *OK! Magazine*, which used same general format, but focused more on figures from film, television, pop music, and sport. Its phenomenal success, rapidly reaching audiences in the hundreds of thousands, not only prompted changes at *Hello!* but the launching of a range of similar titles, such as *Heat*, *Star*, *Now*, and *New!* with varying degrees of success. These magazines, and others like them around the world, compete heavily for exclusive rights to major celebrity events, particularly celebrity marriages such as those of movie star Brad Pitt and *Friends* star Jennifer Anniston in the US, or former Spice Girl Victoria Adams and English football star David Beckham in Britain, and most recently between movie stars Michael Douglas and Catherine Zeta-Jones. Despite this onus on celebrity and public figures, such titles overtly claim a journalistic role and function as documents of record. Editor of *Hello!* Maggie Kuomi claims:

> *Hello!* is a news magazine. I mean we've given more coverage – visually, the impactive [sic] photos – our Gulf War coverage, things like that. We cover all the news. We're in fact a modern day *Picture Post.* The news pictures are all there, whether it be a state funeral, a big celebrity funeral, whoever's died, whoever's been born – major events in history ... Whatever the critics say, it's a history of our life and times.
>
> (*Cutting Edge: Hello!,* Channel 4, 1998)

Becker's position regarding tabloid photojournalism can be applied to celebrity photo journalism and the tension between photojournalism as a legitimate tool of historical documentation, and as an entertainment tool, in that they appear 'to both support and contradict the institutional standards of journalistic practice' (1992: 150). In the contractually arranged photo-shoots that dominate celebrity magazines, aspects of formal style and composition as well as negotiated access to those celebrities, suggest an accordance of such titles with conventions of acceptable journalistic practices. With increasing competition, however, there is also the trend for breaches of negoti-ated access, and deliberate attempts (through long-lens photography for example) to engage in the more candid, revelatory kind of photography. Like the sensation and scandal of supermarket tabloids, this kind of photojournalism implicitly claims authority through 'the higher truth of the stolen image' (Sekula in Becker, 1992: 142). Again, whether or not the enjoyment of having access to the private moments and practices of society's elite figures through celebrity photojournalism serves a signifi-cant function beyond entertainment, such as contributing to citizens' 'social capital', for example, remains debatable.

In entertainment-oriented journalism audience enjoyment of the revelatory insights (real or imagined) into the world of the elite, and the possible empowering *feeling* of control 'is very different from actually *having* control' (emphasis added, Allan, 1999: 115). Yet, as Thompson points out, there are aspects of entertainment-oriented jour-nalism content that can directly impact on the relative status of members of the elite (1997). The media are important sites for what can be called 'symbolic capital' (ibid.: 47), such as the construction of an image or reputation that benefits the individual in their particular goals (such as the politician depicted with their family, the rock and roll star shown trashing a hotel room, or a movie star looking dazzling at an awards ceremony). Just as media outlets offer opportunities for celebrities to exercise this 'symbolic power' (ibid.), so too can the media undermine and even destroy the basis for a celebrity's social status. The emphasis on status and celebrity also relates to evident themes of aspiration in entertainment-oriented and, more overtly, in lifestyle journalism where the emphasis is on audience members (see later in the chapter), and so-called 'reality' television.

'REALITY' TELEVISION

Another recent trend in broadcasting highlights a possible shift from an emphasis in providing the public with social capital, e.g. through political access programmes, to an emphasis on providing with opportunities for garnering symbolic capital, through becoming pseudo-celebrities via 'reality' television shows. The first phase of reality television occurred in the early 1990s and was fostered by the convergence of a number of industry trends. Technological advances making camera, sound, and lighting equipment more compact, more mobile, and of better quality than previous equipment saw an increasing use of the documentary technique of 'fly-on-the-wall' filming, where the intent is to film people behaving 'normally' as if the camera wasn't there. The increasing use of video by certain agencies, such as the emergency services in recording accident scenes, also offered readily available footage and ready-made narrative structures attractive to commercially minded programme makers subject to heightened competition and cost-cutting in news and documentary production, itself leading to smaller film crews, requiring journalists to multi-task (e.g. record their own sound). In Britain this resulted in a spate of programmes, subsequently dubbed 'docu-soaps', that proved very popular with audiences.

The reason this term has been adopted comes from the formulaic structure of such programmes. Nominally, such programmes are focused around a straightforward documentary, and thus journalistic, goal of representing a behind-the-scenes account of an unusual or socially important institution. Popular subjects for such programmes have included, for example, the police (e.g. the US show *Cops*) and hospitals (e.g. the British show *Children's Hospital*). In Britain, programmes in this vein have covered areas as diverse as airports, shopping malls, traffic wardens, sanitation departments, holiday cruise ships, and student vets. In some cases, the 'ordinary' people featured in these programmes have become minor celebrities in their own right, some moving into television presenting themselves. As such the soap-like, rather than documentary-like, features of this sub-genre come to the fore as the particular 'characters' and their personalities and private lives become of greater interest than the original reason the people were on camera in the first place. Docu-soaps thus highlight the apparent tension between conventional journalistic goals and the particular category of human interest factual material.

In the late-1990s reality TV took another leap when the fly-on-the-wall programming was taken a stage further into full surveillance-as-entertainment. In 1999, large sections of the Dutch television audience became hooked on a programme called *Big Brother*, in which a group of people lived for 10 weeks in a specially constructed house where there were cameras *everywhere* (even in the toilets and showers). Those viewers with Internet access could view proceedings as the cameras rolled 24 hours a day, whilst those reliant on conventional television were given regular edited highlights programmes. The idea was that each week the people in the house would nominate at least two people and the audience (via Internet or phone) would then vote for the person they wanted to leave. The last person left in the house after the other nine had all been voted out won a cash prize. The ratings success of this programme prompted versions in Germany, Spain, the USA, Britain, France, Portugal, and elsewhere, generally capturing large audiences in 2000 and 2001.

Interestingly the behaviour of the house occupants was very different in each nation. In Holland and Germany, for example, romantic relationships developed on screen even to the point of sex acts being performed (under the bed covers, mind you). In Spain, the housemates rebelled against the system of voting, and each week voted in such a way that it was always all of the housemates that were up for eviction. In Britain, contestants have achieved notoriety in a number of ways from 'Nasty' Nick Bateman, who was kicked off the show for cheating, to Jade Goodey who was rather cruelly lampooned in the tabloid press over her appearance, naivety, and lack of general knowledge. The initial British version was so successful for the channel that ran the programme, that since it first aired there have been three further series featuring members of the general public, and two week-long charity editions featuring celebrities.

Variations and extensions of the format have been produced in a number of countries, including a pornographic version (Spain), a series based on teams running competing bars (Sweden and Britain), and a series where one of the contestants was secretly working for the programme producers (an award winning Belgian programme, also produced in Britain as *The Mole*). Other countries, however, treated reality TV with more caution. In Portugal regulators expressed concern about the screening of information from the *Big Brother* house about a contestant's family, whilst the French version, known as *Loft Story*, provoked criticism over dumbing down, and concerns about protecting the contestants after their exposure on the programme.

The US version of *Big Brother* was relatively unpopular in comparison to the other nations, partly because another reality TV show was also being screened, which captured the US public's imagination in a way that *Big Brother* didn't. That programme,

Survivor, placed contestants on an island, and fellow castaways voted for whomever they wanted removed, with 40 million people watching the last programme to see who would win the $1 million prize. The problematic relationship between such programmes and journalism was very overt in the US, as CBS, the channel running both *Survivor* and *Big Brother*, used up space in its news programmes and used a high profile news anchor as the voice of Big Brother. When Britain's main commercial terrestrial channel, ITV, ran its version of *Survivor* in 2001, it too used a news reporter as the taskmaster for the castaways, although it was not a ratings success. Variations on the *Survivor* theme included versions that focused on sex (*Temptation Island*), teenagers (*Shipwrecked*), and celebrities (*I'm a Celebrity, Get Me Out of Here!*), and at the loftiest extreme, the BBC's *Castaway*, a *year*-long project with some 30 people living on a Scottish island in a 'sociological' experiment, than included its fair share of controversy (one 'castaway' left the island after offering to sell his story to the tabloids).

The widely different audience responses to such programmes from country to country reflect not only the cultural differences of countries, but possibly also the different relationships of countries' news media towards entertainment. Comparing the different responses to *Big Brother* in Britain and the USA, for example, highlights the different nature of news media's treatment of entertainment-oriented journalism. In Britain, the extensive tabloid newspaper coverage of *Big Brother*, during the normally slow summer news period, devoting front pages to the housemates campaigning for particular individuals to be voted out, gave the programme a much wider profile than it might otherwise have got. Dragging up sleazy stories about the housemates from opportunist friends was right in the British tabloids' area of expertise, and perhaps the lack of a co-ordinated national press engagement with the series in the US was a factor in its relative lack of success there.

Whilst it could be said that these kinds of programmes have little to do with genuine factual television, let alone journalism, they evidently do; whether it be through TV news reporters as hosts, extensive popular press coverage, or even simply through offering a space for the self articulation and representation of otherwise disenfranchised groups. Such programmes overtly blur the boundaries between news narratives, supposedly positioned in relation to reality and truth, and fictional entertainment narratives, focused more on questions of plots and characters. Moreover, it is precisely this tendency, so evident in trends like the docu-soap and reality TV, that critics mean when they talk of the transformation of news into infotainment (e.g. Franklin, 1997). The anxiety is not just that these entertainment forms are appropriating journalistic techniques, or making appeals to journalistic credibility through their claims to the real, but that traditional journalism is in turn being traduced through the commercial success of such programmes, being pressured to become more like the 'factual entertainment' that garners audiences.

SPORTS JOURNALISM

In Britain sports journalism is both literally and figuratively on the back pages in discussions on journalism. There are still outlets of hard news that eschew sports reporting altogether, and even those that have acknowledged the wide audience appeal of sport have tended to place sport low on the news agenda. The highly-rated *Channel 4 News*, for example, only started covering sports systematically in the last couple of years, and then only in weekend editions. In the print media, sports reporting has traditionally been positioned on the back pages, although in recent years British newspapers have begun to lavish space on sports, most now offering sports supplements on a regular basis. In other parts of the world, however, sportswriting has not been regarded with such implicit disdain, and specialist sports periodicals like *L'Equipe* in France, *La Gazzetta Della Sport* in Italy, *Marca* in Spain, and *Sports Illustrated* in the USA command significant audiences and critical acceptance. Some of the national differences in the treatment of sportswriting rest on the different status of sport, both in general, and in terms of some particular sports, within different national cultures. What is more universal though, is the close relationship between sport and the media.

THE SYMBIOSIS BETWEEN SPORT AND THE MEDIA

Sportswriting is not one of the oldest forms of journalism, partly since in the earliest days of the press most sports lacked formal organisation like competitions, leagues, and even rules. Organised sport didn't really being to appear until the mid-eighteenth century, with the establishment for example of the Jockey Club, which to this day governs horseracing in Britain. The press in fact played a key role in the establishment and reinforcement of organised sport. The British Jockey Club's *Racing Calendar* gradually became the official calendar of recognised races, as well as a means of informing the public of upcoming races, and this informational role of the press was pivotal in the institutionalisation of other sports such as football and cricket. It was also pivotal in the nineteenth-century growth of new patterns of leisure activity amongst the working class who, with standards of living increasing rapidly, had more disposable income, and for whom sports were very much a part of other leisure pursuits such as gambling and drinking (Haynes, 1995: 21–2). As well as providing listings, the press could make money through employing tipsters and betting experts, the demand for which in horseracing saw *The Sporting Life* being the only specialist sports newspaper in Britain to survive into and through the twentieth century, only closing in 1998. The development of organised and commercialised sport occurred in parallel to the development of organised and commercialised news production, and other forms of mass production. The mass media was growing alongside the growth of mass spectator sports like football and cricket, and the combination of servicing a distinct community, through association with local teams or clubs, and garnering advertising from local breweries and other local businesses, saw sportswriting become a staple feature of journalism (ibid.: 22).

In time, the media came to have a significant impact on the shape and direction of many sports' evolution. The legacy of media impacts on sport can be seen in a number of areas, such as the changes to American Football since the 1960s to make it more television friendly, or changes to the format of European football's premier club competition from a knockout cup competition, to the more lucrative Champions League in the 1990s. Global sporting events like the Olympic Games, or the football World Cup generate vast television audiences, and thus major revenue for broadcasters. Sports events have been central to the generation and maintenance of audiences for satellite, cable, and digital television services, allowing multinational conglomerates like News Corporation to expand. Media organisations and senior political figures have had high profile relationships with sports teams, from Disney's ownership of the current World Series Baseball champions the Anaheim Angels, to Italian Prime Minister Silvio Berlusconi's ownership of football team A.C. Milan.

SPORTS WRITING NEWS VALUES, OBJECTIVITY, AND ETHICS

In terms of news values, sports are something of a paradox. On the one hand they are very suitable for the requirements of news organisations, offering planned routines (e.g. a league season), regular events (e.g. championship finals), simple networks of key actors (e.g. players, coaches, owners, fans), and neat conclusions (e.g. winners and losers). Within this framework, there is potential for newsworthy material such as conflict (e.g. local or national rivalries), controversy (e.g. in refereeing/umpiring decisions, or cheating through drug-taking or other nefarious actions), and the unusual and spectacular (e.g. and perhaps most noticeably the exploits of exceptional sports people like single season home-run record holder Barry Bonds, or women's marathon world record holder Paula Radcliffe).

Yet, on the other hand, this very routine nature of sports, the repetition of events, and the relative simplicity of those events (in comparison to say, a war or election), has left sportswriting with a less important status than other forms of journalism. Some sportswriters have even used pseudonyms to protect their identities and presumably their professional standing. Some, like cricket writer Neville Cardus, managed to establish a reputation based on extensive knowledge of their particular specialist sport. Yet even here, sportswriters have a struggle to legitimate their work. Umberto Eco has written of how sportswriting has proliferated to the point where reporting of sports events has turned into 'sports chatter' (1986), sportswriting and commentary about sportswriting and commentary. Such views reflect overt concern, and disdain, for the devotion of broadcast time, and print media space to discussion of sport as though sport were an insignificant, or unworthy topic for journalists to spend their time engaging with.

Expert knowledge of particular sports also fails to rid the sportswriter of the image of them as little more than fans with typewriters 'cheering for the home team' (Garrison and Salwen in Rowe, 1992: 98). This view may have some degree of validity but it seems to eschew the possibility of good quality journalism emerging from enthusiasm for the subject matter. Over the years a wide range of novelists, for example, have turned their attention to sports of various kinds, such as Ernest Hemingway, Norman Mailer, Joyce Carol Oates, V.S. Naipaul, and Martin Amis (see Coleman and Hornby, 1996). In Britain in the 1990s, a hybrid of sportswriting and literary journalism emerged with the success of Nick Hornby's *Fever Pitch* (1995) that has seen many authors come out of the woodwork as sports fans. As television coverage of sports has increased, so has the presence of former athletes as pundits, commentators and presenters, and the apparent ease of transition for some athletes into journalistic roles causes many professional journalists to bristle with irritation. When former Wimbledon champions John McEnroe, Pat Cash, and Boris Becker, for example, demonstrate themselves to be as able commentators as they were players, they have extra kudos with audiences from having been successful tennis players. For the professional sports journalists, who've honed the craft of commentary (Haynes, 1999: 149), this both undermines their claims to professional expertise, and gives superficial weight to the claims of their colleagues from more 'serious' genres of news as to the lack of professional skill in their roles. So whether it be famous writers addressing their sporting interests, or retired famous athletes turning their hands to media commentary, neither of these groups seem to satisfy critics of sportswriting.

Beyond the question of sportswriters being fans of the sports they cover, and thus concerns about their potential partiality regarding events in that sport, come wider issues of partisanship in relation to local and national interests. Yet the perception of sports journalists as highly partisan spokespeople for their preferred sports (and teams or athletes) makes an unfounded presumption of a requirement for objectivity. Given the problems outlined in Chapter 7 about objectivity in areas where it arguably matters a great deal, it is not clear in the simple terms of reporting sports events why objectivity would be an essential requirement, and indeed sportswriting often reflects partisan, subjective accounts aimed firmly at the partisanship of the audience (e.g. in national reporting of World Cup football matches, or Olympic Games events) (see Rowe, McKay and Miller, 1998).

Some critics offer even more strident condemnations of sports journalists, such as noted fantasy novelist and former journalist, Terry Pratchett, who stated that he'd never want to be a sportswriter 'because even vultures will throw up on something' (in

Rowe, 1992: 98). The extremity of such criticisms may have to do with other aspects of sportswriters' closeness to the sports they cover. Partisanship on local or national grounds may have some degree of legitimacy in terms of a outlet's audience, but the role of sportswriters becomes much more problematic when a sport experiences a period of fundamental crisis or controversy. An obvious example would be the controversies surrounding many sports over athletes' use of drugs, such as in track and field athletics, weightlifting, and cycling (seen most overtly in the problems of the Tour de France where teams and former winners in recent years have tested positive for drugs). Another problematic area has been the financial and political arrangements behind certain sports, from bribes from cities bidding for the Olympics, to insider deals in footballers' moves between clubs, to match-fixing such as the recent cricket scandal involving South African Hansie Cronje and others. The chief criticism in such topics is that sportswriters are firstly too close to the figures and institutions involved. Through their regular contacts with the key figures as part of their news beats and through their (presumed) inherent bias towards the sport and its representatives, they are deemed to not be in a suitable position to investigate such issues effectively. Secondly since their routine work involves mainly reporting sporting events, the sportswriter's ability to cover wider issues like financial mismanagement, corruption, drug use, and other difficult issues in sport (such as racism, and hooliganism) is again deemed to be inadequate. In such areas sportswriting 'may often be partisanship of an unenlightened and unenlightening kind' (ibid.: 105), in which political concerns are subsumed by commitment to the sport above and beyond wider ramifications. This can be seen most overtly around issues of sporting boycotts over political issues, and the desire of sports organisations and sportswriters to separate sport from politics. Moreover, since there is a tendency for sportswriters to treat events in partisan terms, when they do address such issues they use what has been dubbed an 'orthodox rhetoric' in which comments 'are calculated to stimulate debate in a manner that shadows physical contest between sportspeople and partisan conflict between supporters' (Rowe, 1992: 104).

Following from this, another set of features that marks sportswriting out as distinct from other genres of journalism, concerns news language and newsgathering. Some researchers suggest that persistent problems in sport and wider society, such as the hooliganism and violence that plagues football in Britain, Italy, Argentina, and other countries could be unintentionally exacerbated simply through the routines of language use in much sportswriting. Sport is about competition, conflict, winning and losing, and according to a New Zealand study, the language of sportswriting is often dominated by violent imagery in excess of its use in other genres (Holt, 2000: 90). Whether or not this contributes to audiences' perceptions about the wider social legitimacy of violence or not is something of a moot point (Holt, 2000: 102). There is certainly the tendency for the utilisation of particular athletes, willingly or otherwise, as heroes, villains, victims, and scapegoats, and the impact of this on the athletes themselves has been little researched (McNeill, 1998: 104). Whilst relations between, say, politicians and political journalists may be close, and the paparazzi may do their best to get close to celebrities, the routines of sports journalists' access to athletes are in a different territory altogether. In the US, for example, Diana Luciani recounts her disquiet at accompanying some sportswriters into a basketball team's locker-room, for post-game interviews, only to be confronted by a multitude of half-naked men (1997). The post-match interview is rarely revelatory, but does indicate the degree to which professional sportswriters feel entitled, even obliged, to invade the space of the athletes. McNeill highlights, for example, the disparity between the requirement for athletes selected to compete in the Olympic Games to abide by the Olympic charter, which has many rules and regulations for competitors, and the lack of similar rules and regulations for journalists covering the Olympics (1998). The Olympic Charter's comments on the media regard them as vital parts of the Olympic 'family', and the differing standards and practices of news media around the world would be difficult to accommodate in a uniform code or set of guidelines. This thus exposes athletes to potentially the worst excesses of press intrusion, interrogation, and investigation, disempowering them in regard to the press (McNeill, 1998: 101). So, rather than dismissing it as the 'toy department of the news media' (in Rowe, 1992: 98), examining sportswriting reveals a range of issues pertinent to discussions of alternative journalisms.

LIFESTYLE JOURNALISM

Critiques of contemporary journalism are sometimes attitudinal, sometimes empirical, and amongst the most persistent criticism evident in both kinds of analysis is the lamenting of public affairs journalism being replaced with what could collectively be called 'lifestyle' journalism. Lifestyle journalism, exemplified by lifestyle magazines of which more below, addresses audiences not in their role as public citizens concerned with the social and political issues of the day, but in their role as private individuals whose personal fears, aspirations, attitudes, and emotional experiences become the subject material. Like entertainment and sports journalism, lifestyle journalism is seen as a trend in journalism content antithetical to traditional conceptions of what journalism is *supposed* to be for. Most critiques on these grounds do little more than dismiss such content out of hand. Yet to do so on the grounds that 'it's not journalism', misses the reality of such output's apparent appeal to audiences, the clear self-perception of lifestyle outlets' producers that they are journalists engaged in journalism, and elides areas of social life touched on by such media that mainstream 'hard' news is criticised for marginalising. One area where these critical tensions arise most overtly is in relation to gender and factual media, which is a dominant aspect of lifestyle journalism.

217

FEMINIST CRITIQUES OF NEWS MEDIA

The exclusionary nature of the bourgeois public sphere has been highlighted by feminist critiques above all others who challenge some of the fundamental distinctions that the concept rests upon (Pateman, 1989; Fraser, 1992; McLaughlin, 1993). In the original Habermasian model the public sphere is seen as 'encompassing all social life *apart from* domestic life' (emphasis added, Pateman, 1989: 121). Historically this was very overt with women excluded from voting in even the otherwise most democratic nations until the early part of the twentieth century, and struggling for other political and legal rights. Whilst such overt limitations no longer exist in developed nations, as Peer contests, 'informal exclusions – such as particular rules of deliberation or dominant cultural values – still tend to privilege dominant groups over minority and oppressed groups' (2000: 310). As mentioned in Chapter 7, for example, the demographic composition of news media in many countries tends to reflect the highly patriarchal nature of news media organisations. Estimates put male domination of senior positions in news organisations anywhere from something like two-thirds in the US to four-fifths in Britain (in Allan, 1999: 136, 139). US columnist Barbara Reynolds suggested in 1995 that something like '95 per cent of all the decisions made in the media are made by white males' (in Altschull, 1995: 185). Not surprisingly, perhaps, this domination by men in news organisations does see a consonant marginalising of gendered issues in mainstream news, these issues instead being 'dealt with through the popular, less 'respectable' genres such as talk shows, docudramas, and even soap operas' (Rapping, 2000: 229). It is this perception, both within the journalism industry and amongst traditional journalism scholarship, of these alternative sites as being less respectable, non-journalistic, and so on that has left them also marginalised as a subject for critical scrutiny within the theoretical boundaries of journalism studies (as opposed to feminist media research which does address these genres extensively). In relation to the themes of journalism studies examined in this book, two useful genres to examine in more detail are 'confessional' TV talk shows and lifestyle magazines.

CONFESSIONAL TV TALK SHOWS

One of the problems of separating out supposedly 'public' and 'private' topics is that it massively over-simplifies the inherently political nature of much that goes on in the so-called 'private sphere'. One of the dominant slogans of the second wave of feminism that arose in the 1960s and 1970s was the concept that 'the personal is the political' (Pateman, 1989: 131). Essentially the point here was that issues in the domestic, private, personal space were inherently political in a number of different ways, for example re-positioning domestic life 'at the heart of civil society rather than apart or separate from it' (ibid.: 132–3). The consequences of this kind of view, and its eloquent and vociferous articulation by a range of prominent feminist campaigners (such as Betty Freidan, Gloria Steinem, and Germaine Greer amongst others), meant that for the first time issues such as domestic violence and rape (previously seen as issues of domestic life and thus not up for debate) began to be discussed within mainstream media and politics, albeit in quite marginalised ways (such as in the inclusion of 'women's pages' in newspapers).

Whilst the mainstream news media dragged their feet somewhat, other genres became focal points for the explicit articulation and discussion of these previously taboo topics. One of the most notable outlets have been the daytime television talk-shows, sometimes dubbed 'confessional' talk shows. Originating in US television in the late 1960s, with the *Phil Donahue Show*, and addressing a daytime television audience presumed to be dominated by housewives, the genre has spread around the globe to become a significant feature of many nations' daily television output. The key difference between the confessional talk shows and the political access and talk radio shows discussed in the last chapter comes from their focus on these gendered, 'private sphere' issues, not fully addressed by mainstream news media. As Rapping suggests 'it is on these daytime shows that one is most likely to hear about, and see discussions of charged issues such as rape, homosexuality and bisexuality, domestic violence, prostitution, family and marital strife, and so on' (2000: 230).

Associated with these thematic concerns, the confessional element of the programmes is particularly important. Rather than invited guests and audience members discussing issues of public policy or political opinion, these shows often concentrate on people's actual personal experiences, so a programme about marital infidelity, for example, would probably include people who have committed or have been victims of marital infidelity. The general format of these shows, pioneered by Phil Donahue, involves a mobile host moving amongst the audience, rather than sat behind a desk, and addressing guests sat facing the audience, or even eschews a separate panel altogether. In the British confessional talk show *Kilroy*, for example, the host (Robert Kilroy-Silk) moves around a semi-circular set in which the audience sits, and he simply moves from one row to another, often sitting directly next to an audience member, encouraging them to offer their opinion or personal experience. Rapping suggests that such formats indicate that they are 'specifically oriented toward feminine audiences and issues' (2000: 237). Grindstaff highlights why this is so important stating that such programmes:

> make public issues of personal experience, and they do so by privileging
> emotion, confession, and conflict among 'ordinary' people over rational
> debate among experts or the pleasant chatter of celebrities. Daytime talk
> thus challenges conventional boundaries separating public from private,

> reason from emotion, news from entertainment, fact from fiction, and expert
> knowledge from common opinion[.]
>
> (Grindstaff, 1997: 165)

It is in this way that such programmes might be regarded as at least 'marginally progressive' in their engagement with the gendered issues so marginalised by mainstream news media (Rapping, 2000: 234). This approach also offers a dynamically different approach to the conventions of journalistic treatment of social affairs, turning some of the assumptions of journalistic objectivity and newsgathering practice on their head (for more on feminist critiques of conventions of news practice see Allan 1999: 132–5).

As the genre evolved, and a multitude of similar shows began to compete for viewers, the progressive possibilities of the genre have arguably been undermined. Whilst the likes of Phil Donahue or Oprah Winfrey, say, created largely supportive environments for discussion of sensitive issues, even offering expert help to participants, in other programmes the confessional dimension began to be accompanied by an interrogative dimension. Unlike the interrogation of public officials and politicians, as with political access shows or the views of the host in talk radio, the participants in confessional talkshows come under the direct interrogation of the audience, as well as of the host and other participants. Sometimes programmes dressed their interrogative dimensions up as 'tough love' as, for example, teenage criminals or drug-users are confronted by hostile, and confrontational audiences, experiences ameliorated by the offer of places on rehabilitation and support programmes for participants.

As some shows evolved further, the progressive value of the genre has been called ever more into question, as interrogation of participants has segued into excoriation, most evidently in the nadir (or zenith depending on your opinion) of the genre *The Jerry Springer Show*. An astute and articulate former politician, Springer has made robust defences of his programme's sensationalised style, the programme, for example, regularly descends into physical confrontations and fights between participants. Critics suggest that Springer's show, and those like it, essentially are merely 'turning the experiences of ordinary people into a circus sideshow' (Grindstaff, 1997: 196). The defence, offered by Springer and others, is that regarding the words and actions of participants on such programmes as 'undignified or debased' (ibid.) merely echoes the prejudices of conventional news media that keep such people off the screen in the first place. As Grindstaff contends 'the so-called respectable media must also be taken to task for rendering these people so completely invisible in the first place that daytime talk is their best or only option for public exposure' (ibid.). Rapping also points out that 'it is not surprising that people who do not have the incomes or even the information to seek help privately chose, desperately, to go on television and get it from members of the live and electronic "community" of viewers' (2000: 235). So, even given the problems evident in the more entertainment oriented versions of this genre, the central issue highlighted by confessional TV talk shows remains the perceived failure of mainstream news to offer sufficient space and freedom for the articulation of views from all sections of society, and the continued popularity of such programmes suggests that audiences too see interest and value in confessional TV talk shows.

LIFESTYLE MAGAZINES

Magazine journalism has a long history, stemming back to long before the muckraking magazines of the late nineteenth/early twentieth centuries. The term 'lifestyle magazine' began to overtly appear in the 1960s and 1970s, but in many ways 'the concept is as old as magazines themselves. The very nature of magazine editorial is to associate itself with lifestyle, or the mode of living of the sort of reader it seeks to attract' (Braithwaite, 1998: 106). Indeed, magazines dedicated to particular interests, or intended for particular audiences, have a long history, for example one of the first dedicated women's magazines in the USA, simply titled *Ladies' Magazine*, was founded by Sara Josepha Hale in 1828 (Johnson, 1993: 134), whilst the first women's magazine in Britain was *The Ladies' Mercury* published in 1693 (Braithwaite, 1998: 106). Yet from the 1950s onwards the rise of television, as well as affecting other media forms like cinema and newspapers, had a significant impact on magazines. As already mentioned the general news photo-magazines, like *Life*, were undermined by television somewhat, and general interest magazines were hit hard. In the USA, and in Western Europe, a lot of magazine producers responded by aiming for the widest possible audience reach, with titles like *Time*. The other response seen in the West, and seen more overtly in Britain where there essentially are no equivalents of *Time* or *Der Spiegel* and the like, was the growth of special interest magazines. This created a panoply of titles covering an ever-growing range topics. One rather broad category to emerge has been lifestyle magazines. These are important in relation to questions about alternatives to journalism that address the issues of gender that are marginalised or ignored by conventional journalism theory and practice. In the way they represent and articulate issues around lifestyle they arguably offer an important journalistic site in which the otherwise marginalised private sphere is addressed.

Global Niches

One of the important features of lifestyle magazines that makes them worthy of discussion is the rather paradoxical trend over the last few decades for an ever-increasing range of niche markets, at the same time as some titles have become global brands in a way newspapers never have. Lifestyle magazines such as *Vogue* or *Cosmopolitan* are now known through much of the world. *Cosmopolitan* (a US magazine founded in the

41 editions, in 25 languages, across 46 countries worldwide

Figure 9.1   Cosmopolitan, 1999: a global magazine.

1880s), for example, has over forty editions around the world and is continuing to expand (see Figure 9.1).

Other titles like French *Marie Claire* and German *Prima* have also been exported to international markets. As with most other parts of the media industries the global markets are dominated by a few companies, including German outlet Gruhner and Jahr, Anglo-Dutch Reed-Elsevier, and American Condé-Nast. This global expansion of magazine titles is built in part on large domestic audiences for magazines, although these audiences have declined in the television era. By the late 1990s, for example, weekly women's magazines were selling upwards of 5 million copies per week in the Britain, from a peak of over 9 million sales in the late 1950s (Winship, 1991: 132). In America, by the early 1990s some 164 million people were reading magazines each month, and more than half of that audience were women (Johnson, 1993: 135).

The other trend has been for a diversification of magazines within a particular country, which has led to a problem in defining and categorising magazines (ibid.). There is also a rather high level of churn in magazine markets. Unlike newspaper markets, which tend to be highly stable in mature media environments, the magazine market is much more volatile with magazines launching and closing on a regular basis. These two factors combine to make it difficult to easily gauge the magazine market in any one country, but the key point is that there are a wide range of magazines available at any one time. Braithwhaite's overview in 1998 suggests over 5000 titles in Britain, some 3000 or so in France, and over 5000 in Germany (1998: 97, 99), whilst Biagi's 1999 overview of the USA suggests as many as 11,000 there (1999: 70). Efforts to simply categorise all these varied titles achieve little consensus, however, with different authors offering different categories (Johnson, 1993: 136; Braithwaite, 1998: 97; Biagi, 1999: 75).

Lifestyle magazines, as a broad category of magazines, have become distinct both in terms of their general content, but also in terms of their producers and audience. Women, from quite early on, have been far more involved in the production of lifestyle magazines at the editorial level than in other journalistic outlets, and to an extent this continues to be true (Johnson, 1993: 134). Similarly, the audience for lifestyle magazines, until quite recently, has been dominated by women, such that lifestyle and gender, specifically women, have become very closely associated. Braithwaite comments:

> Down through the ages women's magazines have classified their potential
> readerships into such broad categories as domestic, the working woman, the
> sportswoman, the socialite, the fashion conscious, the political, the flighty, the
> serious or the light-hearted. The very nature of magazine publishing is to
> exploit those cultural differences.
>
> (Braithwaite, 1998: 106)

So, even in the simple terms of the global appeal of some titles, and the diversification of local markets into ever more narrow niches, lifestyle magazines offer a journalism geared towards the specific rather than the general, and the private rather than the public.

Constructing the 'Lifestyle'

Social science research focusing on women's magazines has tended to regard lifestyle magazines as being important in terms of their discourses around gender. In other words, given the presumed audience of women interested in reading things of relevance and value to them, research focuses on how those presumed interests are addressed and represented. This is important also for considering sites of factual media content that address the domestic and personal spheres, left out or marginalised by the mainstream media in the 'public' sphere. Despite the wide range of titles aimed at different categories of reader, researchers have found some consistent aspects of lifestyle magazines for women that offer some problematic representations and articulations of gender and social roles.

One recurring feature of lifestyle magazines is a focus on aspiration. Ballaster *et al.*, contend that magazines present women as 'wholly preoccupied with aspirations or achievements in the realm of the personal' (1991: 154). This is important because in addition to this the magazines are profoundly apolitical (ibid.: 156). The emphasis is on domestic and leisure activities, not professional or overtly political concerns. Lifestyles for women are thus defined by these magazines as being related to domesticity, (food, home, and garden), and personal appearance (clothes, physical). Ferguson offers a similar perspective, interpreting magazines as being 'how to' guides, offering solutions to the day to day problems of womanhood (Ferguson, 1983: 8).

This focus on personal development, but in a non-political sense, has been evident in women's magazines for some time. Iris Burton, editorial director of *Prima* and *Best* in the late 1980s, demonstrates this focus on the relationship between personal development and the domestic sphere:

> Shared by you and me, by your mother, my sister, the lady down the road, the girl in the office next door. It doesn't matter what you are doing by way of a career or lifestyle ... there are very few women, whether they are living on their own or have huge families or working or not, who don't maintain a home and who don't have the interest in it to want it to be lovely, who want to be creative with their homes.
>
> (Burton in Winship, 1991: 135)

This emphasis recurs again and again, even in new titles launched in the last few years. Sally O'Sullivan, former editor of *Good Housekeeping*, persists with this kind of rhetoric when talking about the launch of a British magazine in 1999 called *Good Health*. She says:

> It works from the basic lifestyle premise that most modern women understand that there is no one better to chart their pathway in life than themselves and the more information, direction and energy they have the better. Therefore, the magazine will cover every aspect of their lives from the point of view of personal well-being and happiness.
>
> (O'Sullivan, 1999: 12)

One of the limitations of the aspiration-centred content is the viability of readers ever actually achieving those aspirations. Iris Burton acknowledges that a title like *Prima* is not necessarily presenting realistic goals, stating that 'the magazine is a kind of wish-fulfillment thing' (Burton in Winship, 1991: 146). Aspirations of readers are clearly differentiated from title to title. Aspirations for 'personal well-being and happiness' may include an independent career, with a great sex life and designer clothes for readers of *Cosmopolitan*, but in *Woman's Own* aspirations might mean being able to cook, clean, look after the kids, and still look great and have a social life (see discussion in Ballaster *et al.*, 1991: 137–61). Winship notes that lifestyle magazine content often reflects a tension between these aspirations and women's actual 'real life' roles. She says 'at one and the same time there is a desire for a more leisured life with time and space to allow pursuit of these activities, *and* a defiance about "independence", which currently means doing it all: child and husband care, paid work' (original emphasis, Winship, 1991: 148). Some magazines are founded on exactly this tension, such as the US magazine *Working Mother*. It's CEO claims it 'is the only magazine that helps women integrate their professional lives, their family lives and their inner lives. A must-read source for new ideas, inspiration and strategies, *Working Mother* is the smart guide for a whole life – because that's what women want' (Evans, 2003). Another good example, from 1990 to 1996 *She* magazine carried the catch-line 'for women who juggle their lives' under its title (Brown, 1996: 13). In magazines like *Working Mother* and *She* this tension is explicit on the front page, but it is also often explicit in the articles such magazines regularly carry.

Winship calls this kind of tension evidence of 'the impossibilities of womanhood' (1991: 134). These stem from the contradictory tensions of women's lives, and the lack of realism in the aspirations and claims of the magazines. The one area where the tensions between aspirations and reality are most overtly articulated, and where those aspirations are heavily delimited, is in terms of relationships. Whilst lifestyle magazines for gay men and lesbians do exist, the issue of sexuality in mainstream magazines is very clearly restricted to heterosexual relationships, but in a way that simply takes for granted that the readership is uniformly heterosexual. This is reflected in the discourse of women's magazines through a predominant focus on the problems of relationships with men (Ballaster *et al.*, 1991: 137). Relationships are a staple feature of women's magazines, and relationships that are tension-filled are commonplace. Ballaster *et al.*, argue that 'women's magazines are about being female, and the problems of being female, their almost exclusive emphasis on heterosexual relationships positions women wholly in relation to men' (ibid.). Again, examples abound of articles indicative of this locating women is relation to men, such as the 1999 *New Woman* articles entitled 'Improve Your Bloke in Bed', and 'Your Handcuff-free Guide to Getting 100 per cent Commitment' (May issue, 1999).

One coda to the academic rhetoric surrounding the treatment of gender, more specifically women, by lifestyle magazines, comes in the content and style of the emergent men's magazines of the last decade or so. Men's magazines have been so successful in Britain, and distinct from their US counterparts, that some British titles have been exported to the USA (e.g. *Maxim*) (Turner, 1999). Originating largely in the 1980s phenomenon of the 'new' man (Nixon, 1993: 469), which in itself was a response to the advances of the feminist movement of the 1970s, men's lifestyle magazines have rapidly become a significant part of the magazine environment. UK men's magazines have become noted for a 'laddish' mentality, with an emphasis on humour, non-seriousness, and an attention to the female form verging on the pornographic (enough to get the US supermarket chain Wal-Mart to ban some of the titles from their shelves in 2003 (Usborne, 2003: 11)). Women's magazines, in contrast, are often regarded as serious to the point of being po-faced at times (some titles, like *Ms*, and others, have been vociferous campaigners for women's rights, and a commitment to serious journalism is evident in many titles). Other than the more humour-focused style, however, many of the tropes of women's magazines are present in men's magazines also (Featherstone, 1998). Men's magazines are equally heterosexual in their presentation, for example, and whilst they possibly focus on relationships less, when they do again they're talking in purely heterosexual terms, and in terms of possible tensions, such as in the 1998 *FHM* article 'How to have a pain-free wedding' (June issue, 1998).

Another perception of women's magazines is that they articulate women's desires through representing women as consumers. Ballaster *et al.*, argue that 'female leisure is inextricably bound up with (commodity) consumption' (Ballaster *et al.*, 1991: 149). Fashion, cookery, home and garden articles are another staple feature of women's magazines. Yet, again, men's magazines in recent years have contained large amounts of consumer content, and not merely the stereotypical kinds of 'male' commodities, such as electronic or motoring goods. Men's magazines like *GQ*, contain as much fashion content – clothes, accessories, and cosmetics – as many women's magazines. It might be better said, then, than it is lifestyle magazines (rather than just women's magazines) that construct and represent readers' aspirations and their means to achieve those aspirations, in terms of commodity consumption. In wider debates about contemporary society and the rise of consumer culture, lifestyle magazines are just another part of that process, but given their relationship to journalism, they also highlight a final issue, which is the relationship between journalistic and advertising goals.

Journalism-Centred or Advertising-Centred?

In Chapter 3, the importance and influence of advertisers in the magazine sector was discussed in terms of the influence of the market on journalism. Whilst concerns about advertising's impact on newspaper and broadcast journalism are overt, in the magazine sector producers are more equivocal about the influence of advertisers in relation to their journalistic goals. Some are overt in their recognition of the commercial imperatives of a magazine. James Brown, former editor of *Loaded* and *GQ* in Britain, for example, asserts that 'a good magazine is a commercial magazine' (in Edwards, 1997: 16). 'Good' means magazines that attract the desired audience of the publisher, and that audience can be very narrowly defined. Amongst the first men's magazines to launch in Britain in the mid 1980s, for example, *GQ* was set up to fulfil very specific goals as outlined by its first editor Paul Keers:

> [T]he men's magazine I and others would like to see would be aimed specifically at this yuppie male audience ... By isolating the interests of this specific, large, wealthy and image-conscious demographic bulge in the male market, a UK men's magazine could succeed.
>
> (in Nixon, 1993: 482)

A little over a decade later the market for men's magazines in Britain was established enough to attempt even narrower demographic appeal. Andrew Harrison edited a short-lived men's magazine *Deluxe*, which was aimed at the audience between magazines like *Loaded* and *GQ*. He said:

> First, in *Esquire* and *GQ*, there was the idea of the metropolitan sophisticate ... We were all supposed to to move to Docklands. Then came the lad mags, and we were only supposed to be interested in getting pissed up, coked up and larging it.
>
> (in Dugdale, 1998: 4)

Whilst *Deluxe* has not lasted, other titles have succeeded, but whether that's due to effective definition of an audience niche, because of good journalism, or both is unclear. In the men's sector, for example, *Esquire* represents good journalism to editor Peter Howarth, who claimed in an editorial that the magazine has a 'good name and reputation for journalistic integrity' (Howarth, 1998: 16). *Esquire*'s publisher, Chris Hughes, however, says that the magazine delivers 'a high quality audience to advertisers' (in *Media Week*, 1998: 32). Other magazines to launch in recent years also seem keen to identify important niche audiences. Promotional material for *Red* magazine described its ideal reader, for example, as someone who does things like 'rent *Toy Story* as well as *Trainspotting*'. Its editor Kathryn Brown goes further, claiming 'there is a whole new generation of women in their thirties who still have a very youthful attitude but broad interests like gardening and food' (in O'Rorke, 1997: 4). A key determinant of the possible nature of new lifestyle magazines is certainly advertising-centred, rather than journalism-centred, as indicated by a comment from a US ad agency about trends in the US magazine market for increasing specialisation in titles:

> This is a reflection of advertisers going for more targeted media placement. The people who really have the money are a very small segment of the population so you have to look more carefully at the affluent marketplace.
>
> (Muller in Biagi, 1999: 65)

Still, delivering audiences to advertisers can still require journalistic pedigree. The glossy magazines, amidst the pages and pages of advertising and consumer-oriented articles, often include lengthy pieces of journalism and non-fiction writing from established names in other fields of journalism and fiction, such as novelist Martin Amis, or the BBC's John Simpson, and some titles produce award-winning piece of journalism, such as *Marie Claire*'s Marina Cantacuzino's 1998 work on women with HIV. In Britain and other European nations, the glossy monthly magazines are joined in the market by much cheaper weekly magazines, aimed much more at working-class audiences. Experienced tabloid journalists, like Bridget Rowe and Richard Barber, have helped shape weekly magazine style (Winship, 1991: 139). Winship comments on their journalistic style involving the 'profuse use of exclamation marks, and a vocabulary of excess emphasizing fun, entertainment, pleasure on the one hand, melodrama and tragedy on the other – partly a matter of ... reliance on scoop stories and on royalty and television as the shared reference points for readers.' (ibid.: 139–40). Winship also describes the woman's weeklies of the late 1980s as having a distinctly 'newsy' style: 'There is also a firm strand of utilitarianism, the notion of a useful and practical knowledge, with much informative reporting, little discursive writing' (Winship, 1991, 141). Once having contained a lot of fiction in the form of short stories, many of these weekly magazines now routinely include readers' own true stories, perhaps reflecting the popularity of confessional television talk shows, and covering much the same kinds of themes.

CONCLUSION

This chapter has only been able to skim the surface of the wide range of factual media material that exists around the world today. Even so, alongside the material discussed in the previous chapter, it highlights how even within supposedly mainstream media outlets, alternatives to conventional print and broadcast journalism exist. Whether these examples collectively represent a fundamental fragmentation of journalism into different forms or not depends heavily on how journalism is defined, but however one defines it, there's little doubt that these examples raise questions about the definitional boundaries of journalism. Moreover, they raise important questions about the limitations of grand unifying theories of journalism, such as the four theories model, or the theory of the public sphere. Yet there is still one set of features of contemporary journalism to address in this overview of journalism in the information age. These features relate to questions of patterns in global journalism, and trends in new information and communication technologies, and these are the subject of the final chapter of this book.

Chapter Ten

GLOBAL JOURNALISM IN THE ⬜ INFORMATION AGE

The September 11 attacks on the USA in 2001 were an epochal moment in many different ways. Shattering American illusions about their safety from international terrorism and audacious attacks on their homeland, and subsequently changing the whole direction of global politics and international relations, these attacks are likely to be amongst the most significant events for years to come. Against such consequences, the impact of 9/11 on journalism might seem to be only a tangential issue, and yet the impact on both journalism practice and perceptions of journalism in the information age might also resonate through the coming decades. Amidst the rhetoric of crisis that has been a constant contextual frame for the discussions in this book, the journalistic response to 9/11 in some cases is equally shattering to some of the widespread presumptions about the state of contemporary journalism, not only within the USA and the West, but also in other parts of the world. Events subsequent to 9/11, particularly the war in Afghanistan, have also added new dimensions to possible directions for journalism in the future, highlighting the current topography of global news networks and audiences and channels of evolution through a combination of new technologies and emerging journalism traditions. In this last chapter, the current dominant patterns of global news will be explored, as will the challenges presented to these patterns by new technologies.

GLOBAL NEWS FLOW

Some of the earliest journalism was international in scope, with seventeenth-century newsbooks in Britain, for example, giving accounts of events in mainland Europe like battles and witch trials (Cranfield, 1978), but it wasn't until the development of technologies such as the telegraph and broadcasting that the notion of global news really emerged. Up to the emergence of the Internet and online journalism (see later in the chapter), global news was essentially disseminated through four main routes (leaving out the now defunct newsreel): news organisations' own foreign correspondents, news agencies, shortwave radio stations, and satellite television. In examining the primary routes of global news dissemination, it is not surprising then that the politically and economically powerful nations of the last century or so dominate global news flow, producing what has been identified as an east-west-east flow across the northern hemisphere (Hachten, 1998: 121), as depicted in Figure 10.1.

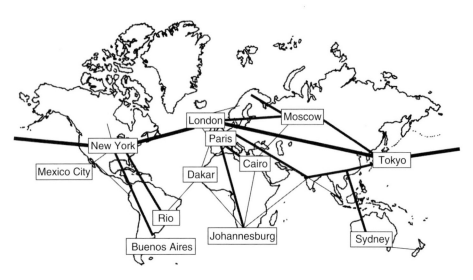

Figure 10.1   Global news flow.

Through a combination of industrial development and colonialism, countries like Britain and France were able to establish global communication networks: first through the trade routes with their respective colonies, then later through the telegraph by the latter half of the nineteenth century. The pace of economic development in Western Europe and North America led to large domestic audiences for newspapers in some of those countries and this in turn allowed Western newspapers the luxury of expanding their newsgathering internationally. Newspapers never really developed into international titles, however, for a number of reasons. First, even today, it remains difficult to regularly produce and distribute a newspaper with content synchronised across countries (indeed across continents). Second, and a much larger problem, is that of language barriers limiting possible audience reach and therefore commercial viability, and this is true even for widely spoken languages like English. Third, and making this even more problematic, literacy rates in much of the world have been very low in comparison to the developed West, and remain a major barrier to expanding access to information in many parts of the developing world (Randall, 1993: 627; Sreberny-Mohammadi, 1996: 195).

The Rise (and Fall?) of the Foreign Correspondent

The absence of a distinct international press, aside from a few newspapers with international editions, has meant that for print news the role of the foreign correspondent has been particularly important, with relatively high levels of prestige and autonomy for individuals in that role (Tunstall, 1996: 349; Hachten, 1998: 122). Maintaining a foreign correspondent is an expensive business, however, and is vulnerable both to fluctuations in the financial position of news organisations, as well as the ebb and flow of world affairs. Even in nations with strong domestic newspaper markets, the maintenance of fully contracted correspondents overseas is a cost few organisations are willing to bear in the current climate. To give an example from the British press, by the early 1990s only the national broadsheet newspapers (and one mid-market tabloid) had foreign correspondents on staff, and amongst that select few there was only one staff correspondent for the whole of Africa – one in the entire national press of Britain (Tunstall, 1996: 347). The cheaper option, increasingly employed by news organisations (both print and broadcast) is to have correspondents based domestically who, when needed, travel to wherever the events are occurring. This has changed the nature of foreign correspondents' reporting who, instead of being immersed in a particular local environment thus having the opportunity to develop a deeper understanding of events in that location, now engage in what has been dubbed 'parachute journalism' (Hachten, 1998: 124). The US version of this trend is described by *Newsweek* reporter Larry Martz:

> Our remaining correspondents fly from earthquake to famine, from insurrection to massacre. They land running, as we were all taught to do ... [But] we miss anticipation, thought, and meaning. Our global coverage has become a comic book: ZAP! POW! BANG-BANG!
>
> (in Fallows, 1996: 137)

Opportunities for journalists being able to understand and interpret complex local events and thus report them to audiences are diminishing. This shrinking of the number of foreign correspondents is not uniform, with some parts of the world appearing to justify locally-based correspondents more than others, particularly places like Washington and New York, and for member-states of the European Union, Brussels. Yet even in such places, only the most highbrow of news organisations bother to invest the resources to maintain correspondents there, and for other organisations and most other parts of the world, a significant proportion of news in print (and also audio and video) comes from stringers (see Chapter 5). Also, much global news provision has shifted from domestic news organisations' own specialist journalists, to global news agencies and global television news networks.

Shortwave Radio

Another factor limiting the rise of global printed news outlets, arriving at what was arguably the peak of newspaper power in the West in the 1920s and 1930s, was the radio. Radio's clear advantages over print, alongside global events necessitating its use, saw it become a genuine medium for global news. One technological advantage of radio is that when broadcast at high frequencies (shortwave) it can be 'bounced' off the Earth's ionosphere and therefore travel thousands of miles without significant loss of sound quality, and this can be done relatively cheaply (Hester, 1991: 41). Of course this has both pros and cons. Shortwave radio signals aren't easy to block, so they can be vital sources of information for people in oppressive regimes, but this also means that governments can use shortwave radio effectively for propaganda purposes. Indeed, the importance of radio during the Second World War as a propaganda tool for all sides in the conflict, has left a legacy for the shape of global radio news broadcasting today, with dominant players including the highly regarded BBC World Service and also the US Voice of America (amongst others) regularly reaching hundreds of millions of listeners daily.

Such networks wouldn't work without an audience, and an economic advantage of radio is that it is relatively cheap to access even in terms of the developing world, unlike television or the Internet which both require expensive equipment and consume a lot of electricity when running. In the early 1990s Trevor Bayliss made radio even more accessible through his invention of the clockwork radio. Even before then radio had already become a dominant means of reaching the wider populations of developing nations, especially in Africa (Randall, 1993: 627). Relating to this, a social advantage of radio is that illiteracy is not a barrier, so it has become very important in nations with low literacy rates. Radio's impact hasn't been entirely benign as it has also been implicated in some of the worst atrocities in recent times, being the principal route through which the genocide in Rwanda in 1994 was orchestrated, for example, although that was a largely internal event.

GLOBAL NEWS AGENCIES

The dominance of a few Western news agencies is a product of the historical dominance of these nations as modern mass communications appeared. The biggest agencies are all western companies, including the likes of British-based Reuters, US-based Associated Press (AP), and France-based Agence France-Presse (AFP). These agencies dominate partly through their location in the economically dominant nations of the West, but also because of their longevity. The Associated Press, for example, began in the 1840s as an agreement between US newspapers to pool resources in gathering news from overseas. The roots of a number of important news agencies grew out of Frenchman Charles Havas' agency begun in 1825 (itself to transform into AFP after the Second World War) and where the likes of Paul Reuter worked before later establishing his own agency in Britain in the 1850s, by this time utilising the ever-growing telegraph network to collect and distribute news. The telegraph was key to these agencies long term success, and utilising material coming from the agencies over the telegraph – the newswires – rapidly became a routine part of news production (as the studies of gatekeeping discussed in Chapter 5 demonstrate). So, some of the biggest agencies have long historical traditions reinforcing their position in global news flow. Now these news providers are by no means the only ones of course, there are many news agencies, but these particular Western agencies have a tremendous advantage in

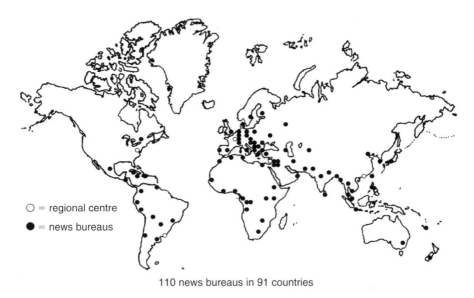

○ = regional centre
● = news bureaus

110 news bureaus in 91 countries

Figure 10.2   AFP – a worldwide news agency.

terms of the extent of newsgathering resources that they have at their disposal as a result of this. As Hester points out 'the global news agencies still maintain the most complete transmission networks and capacity for widespread, rapid coverage' of world affairs (1991: 35). Currently, for example, Reuters has some 184 news bureaus in 163 countries around the world, providing articles in print, video reports, video and still images, and news graphics (http://www.reuters.com). Agence-France-Presse similarly has a major global reach, as shown in Figure 10.2 (above).

AP has some 242 bureaus worldwide, producing 20 million words and 1,000 photographs each day, reaching a daily audience of some 1 billion people, leading to the organisation's self-description as 'the backbone of the world's information system' (http://www.ap.org). Essentially then, 'a few thousand journalists, photographers, and technicians are responsible for gathering and conveying news involving the lives of the more than [6] billion persons who live on the earth' (Hester, 1991: 35).

Even from the earliest days of the news agencies the impact of co-operative newsgathering, as at AP, on news formats and style were significant. Two consequences can potentially be seen through the dual developments of the news agencies and their use of the telegraph. First, pooling resources between often very disparate news organisations in a satisfactory manner requires the development of a style of reporting that ensures it can appeal to very different audiences. Newspapers at that time largely produced news in highly idiosyncratic ways, and reports tended to be written in a personalised style with events presented chronologically. Part of popular mythology routinely trotted out in the US, is that the dominant style to emerge from AP (and others') practices was heavily influenced by the vagaries of the telegraph, particularly during the American Civil War of the 1860s. Many US historians of journalism point to the Civil War in general, and some to the reporting of the assassination of Abraham Lincoln specifically, as the point at which the 'summary news lead', or the 'inverted pyramid' form of news reporting was born (Mindich, 1998: 67).

The reason it emerged at this point in time, such authors claim, is that the Civil War made the telegraph network very unreliable, often being disrupted by battles or sabotage. Reporting events in the war, particularly at long distance, could therefore be really problematic if done in the personalised and chronological style that was the standard at the time, as reporters might get cut off before the important information in their account had been imparted. The result was the development of the 'inverted pyramid' format, whereby the most important and significant information was given first, in the headline and lead paragraph, with details following according to their perceived importance. That way the core of a story could be conveyed even over the potentially unreliable telegraph network. Systematic analyses of US newspapers of the time, however, find little evidence of the inverted pyramid being used during the US Civil War, and suggest it is little more than a modern myth (Mindich, 1998: 68). Nonetheless, after the US Civil War it is clear that the news agencies and their 'telegraphic journalism', as it was dubbed by some at the time, undoubtedly impacted on the development of the inverted pyramid style of news which subsequently became a dominant form of reportage in Western journalism (Allan, 1999: 19).

Second, as mentioned in Chapter 7, and related to this stylistic development, it was in the news agencies that questions of objectivity became in effect a commercial imperative. Again, in serving a wide range of potential clients news agencies could not afford the high levels of partisanship and opinionated reporting that typified most newspaper reporting when the agencies first appeared. In response to these imperatives, in terms of news presentation, news agencies developed highly proscriptive reporting practices. Agency news, for example, does not generally carry information about the journalist who has produced a report. From a practical point of view, this makes it that much easier for the material to be reproduced, edited and so on in whatever way the client news organisation chooses, with no journalistic ego to assuage. From a conceptual point of view, it indicates to clients a focus on 'communicating the essential facts of "hard" or "spot" news free from the distorting influences of personal opinion' (ibid.: 20). This approach was carried into broadcast news material once agencies in the post-Second World War period began to offer audio-visual material as well as print and photographs. To give an example, a spokesman for VisNews, an agency that provided television news material that since the early 1990s has been part of Reuters (as Reuters TV), once said:

> If the PLO bomb a bus load of kids in Tel Aviv, VisNews would not describe that as an atrocity; we would not describe the PLO as terrorists, nor would we describe them as freedom fighters ... The reason is quite simple. To many of our subscribers, the PLO blowing up a busload of children anywhere might be a victory for the oppressed people of Palestine. There are no militarists in VisNews; there are no freedom fighters. We have to choose this very precise middle path.
>
> (in Gurevitch, 1996: 210)

The key then, is the production of material that attempts to avoid 'all potentially controversial terminology' through an adherence to 'a minimalist language' (ibid.). At least two problems emerge from this approach. The first is that constructing material in this kind of way may make material more attractive to clients, but it arguably also makes it easier for client organisations to manipulate that material in whatever way they choose (ibid.: 211). In other words, by refusing to place particular terminology on events, client organisations are free to do so themselves, merely displacing the issue of bias onto the client organisations.

As discussed earlier in the book, aside from questions of presentation a second problem lies in the initial selection of issues and events as news. News selection decisions by agencies may reflect cultural biases as to what constitutes news in the first place. In this example, the focusing on a bomb blast would be seen by some researchers as reflecting the Western news value of focusing on negative events (see Chapter 5). The Western rhetoric of agency news producers can be quite explicit in this regard, as evidenced in the comments of one AP spokesperson:

> Keep in mind that our news-gathering system is no public service ... Forget the rhetoric: The news business sells a product that is blended and packaged, and the competition is cutthroat.
>
> (in Hannerz, 1996: 114)

So, the possible consequences for commercially-driven competitive journalism discussed in Chapter 3, applies at least as much with regard to global news agencies as it does to local news media markets. Beyond the questions of what kind of news these dominant agencies provide, and the attitudinal approach of news producers inside the global agencies, though, there is also the question of news access in terms of the audience for global news.

GLOBAL NEWS AUDIENCES: INFORMATION RICH AND POOR

The dominance of Western organisations and Western conceptions of news values and objectivity, is exacerbated by the economic disadvantages of much of the developing world, leading to an imbalance in peoples' access to both news production and reception. Concerns about this divide between the 'information rich' and 'information poor' became a key feature of debates about the developing world in the 1960s, focusing on the infrastructure of global news flow and the role of journalism and communication in the political, social, and economic development of the Third World (Sreberny-Mohammadi, 1996: 178–79). A focus for these debates has been the United Nations Educational, Scientific, and Cultural Organisation (UNESCO). Developing nations' concerns about the imbalance in access to information flows were expressed through the Movement of Non-Aligned Countries, made up mainly of poor, developing nations outside the loop of the economically and politically dominant nations within the UN. Their views were focused into calls in the 1970s for the establishment of a 'New World Information and Communication Order' (NWICO) (Picard, 1999: 358–59). The key concept in NWICO is the belief that:

> [U]nless communication capabilities are significantly improved, less
> developed nations cannot accomplish meaningful economic, political and
> social development that will improve the standard of living of their citizens.
>
> (Picard, 1999: 359)

This principle, outlined in a declaration in 1978 and then concretised in the McBride Commission report of 1980, arguably indicates an implicit precursor to notions of the information age, where the roots of human progress and development are explicitly associated with access to information flows. What was key about NWICO was its depiction of the state of global information flows, with the Western news media as dominant, as being detrimental to global development.

Whether or not new technologies are capable of disrupting this imbalance or merely perpetuate it remains a key question today, since the crucial factor is access to technologies of information and communication. The methods of measuring nations' differing access to information flows vary depending on which organisation is collating the information. For example, UNESCO as a key player in NWICO debates has annually assessed access to information outlets, such as daily newspaper consumption, in its continuing monitoring of levels of education, literacy, and so on. The UNESCO figures are also used by the World Bank in its data archives (see http://www.worldbank.org) despite acknowledgement that the method of measuring newspaper distribution varies from country to country, and varies in the accuracy of the figures generated. The Human Development section of the UN, however, has recently switched from measuring access to information outlets (like newspapers and radio) to measuring

Table 10.1   Global media consumption (1995)

Region	TVs Per 1000 people	Radios Per 1000 people	Daily Newspapers Per 1000 people	PCs Per 1000 people	Internet users Per 1000 people
North America	763.2	1989.9	212.8	314.6	38.3
OECD*	543.0	1089.2	260.3	169.1	19.8
European Union	521.8	879.9	243	137.6	17.1
Industrial countries	523.6	1005.2	234.7	156.3	17.9
All developing countries	145.3	185.1	49.7	6.5	0.5
Least developed countries	32.4	113.2	7.5**	...	...
World	228.4	364.2	114.8	43.6	4.8

Sources: United Nations Human Development Report 1998, and UNESCO Statistical Yearbook 1999;
* Member states of the Organisation for Economic Co-operation and Development; ** figure from
World Bank

access to information and communication technologies (like internet hosts and mobile phone ownership). Despite these differences, a composite examination of access to information flows in the latter years of the twentieth century show clear disparities around the world, as shown in Table 10.1 (above).

The table demonstrates the dramatic gap between the extent of access to information and communication technologies in the developed and developing worlds. In some regards developed nations have a surfeit of ICTs, particularly radio. What the table can't show is the rapid increases in access to new ICTs, which again are occurring chiefly in the developed world. Since these figures were produced, for example, the proportion of Internet users in the developed world has continued to increase dramatically to the point where significant proportions of some developed nations' populations (around 40 per cent in Britain, for instance) now have access to the Internet.

In terms of more traditional media forms the pattern of access to news for people around the world becomes clearer on closer analysis. Looking first at daily newspaper readership, the top twenty nations in this regard reflects quite clearly the dominance of the Western world, particularly Europe, as shown in Figure 10.3.

The countries that dominate here have affluent, highly literate populations, combined with well-established transportation networks, allowing for easy distribution even in harsh climates like those of Scandinavia. Europe dominates the leading press nations in terms of audience reach, with a few outliers that also share largely affluent

237

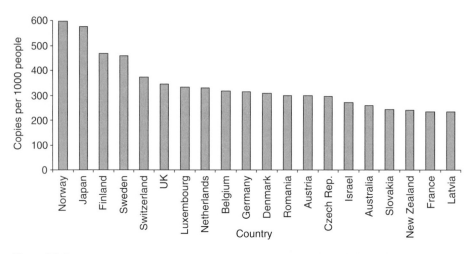

Figure 10.3 Top 20 nations for daily newspaper consumption (1995). From *Human Development Report* 1998 by United Nations Development Program. Used by permission of Oxford University Press, Inc.

and literate populations. Interestingly, the USA (scoring 218 copies per 1000 people) doesn't make this table (coming just behind Latvia), illustrating the problems for recent newspaper journalism in the USA (see Chapter 1). For global news providers, like the news agencies, it is these mostly Western markets that offer the best potential clients, and thus other parts of the world with few newspaper readers are still effectively out of the loop.

In terms of access to television, the top 20 nations according to the UN throw up some arguably surprising results (Figure 10.4). Again, mostly Western nations dominate, but small nations can also provide widespread access to television, particularly some of the oil-rich states around the world, such as the small Gulf state of Qatar (of which more later). The different nature of broadcasting, both television and radio, allow for far greater reach in nations with lower literacy levels – as long as there are resources for transmission and citizens have resources for receiving broadcasting, which, of course, the poorest nations do not tend to have.

Patterns of the widest access to media, occurring primarily in the wealthiest nations, persist across a wide range of different ICTs. What such indicators make clear is that whilst access to communications has undoubtedly increased in the latter half of the twentieth century, even within the least developed countries, the most developed nations have maintained significantly better resources and have expanded most rapidly in new communications technologies. Compounding the historical dominance of global news production and dissemination by the West, the audience for global news is similarly skewed to those countries where people can afford to buy

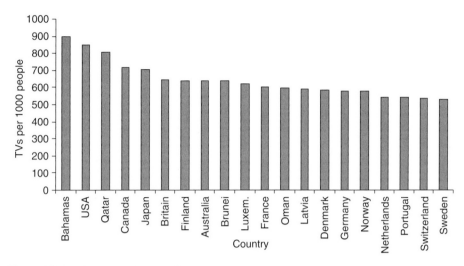

Figure 10.4   Top 20 nations for TV consumption (1998).

newspapers, radios and televisions, obtain access to the Internet, and so on. A generation on from the UNESCO declaration and the McBride Commission report on NWICO, there is little evidence of significant change in the global patterns of access to information flows, even though there have been dramatic developments in the technologies of global news provision, not least satellite television news.

GLOBAL TELEVISION NEWS: POWER AND RESISTANCE

Whilst patterns of global print and radio journalism have been around for most of this century in a relatively consistent shape, global television has only really emerged in the last few decades. In 1965 there were only 192 million television receivers in the entire world, most of those concentrated in the developed world, but this had grown to some 873 million by 1992 (Sreberny-Mohammadi, 1996: 181). By this time in the early 1990s, satellite technology was beginning to give some television news organisations a significant role in global events, not just in terms of disseminating information about them to global audiences, but also in terms of framing events and arguably shaping political and public responses to events across the globe.

'Until the End of the World'[11]: CNNization

By far the most significant player in global television news so far has been CNN, Cable Network News, a US organisation began in 1980 by Ted Turner, and now a part of the

---

[11] When CNN launched, owner Ted Turner proclaimed 'We're gonna go on air June 1, and we're gonna stay on until the end of the world. When that time comes, we'll cover it, play "Nearer My God to Thee" and sign off' (in Schechter, 2000).

largest media conglomerate in the world, AOL Time Warner. Initially a local US news channel using new satellite technology and new strategies for producing television news, CNN set a precedent for news organisations in the late twentieth century. Initially, however, they were ridiculed by the big US networks, being dubbed the Chicken Noodle Network, a cheap and cheerful network, rather than the gourmet, in depth, well written news of the major networks (MacGregor, 1997; Küng-Shankleman, 2000; Schechter, 2000). But by the early 1990s, CNN was clearly a dominant global player having gained in importance through fortuitous consequences of their innovative style of news presentation, a 24-hour, mostly live, 'as it happens', and open-ended rolling news format news. Being solely a news channel, as opposed to a general broadcasting channel, the network had plenty of airtime to fill, frequently with live feeds of events around the US and latterly around the globe. One of CNN's first coups as a result of this strategy was that it was the only channel that broadcast the explosion of the space shuttle Challenger live in 1986, since the routine nature of shuttle launches by that time meant that the major networks hadn't bothered to disrupt programming schedules for the launch. While other would-be global TV news providers were still filing reports over land, air, and sea, sometimes based at distance from the events they were reporting on, CNN routinely produced live broadcasts from the centre of events, such as in China's Tiananmen Square in 1989, and most noticeably their being the only Western TV organisation in Baghdad at the outset of the Gulf War in 1991.

Such events highlighted the advantages, in terms of journalistic exclusives if nothing else, of the immediacy offered by CNN's rolling news format. Moreover, by the time of the Gulf War of 1990–91 the immediacy of rolling news had effectively turned television news into a direct player in the events being depicted. MacGregor explains and illustrates this with an example from the Gulf War:

> Foreign correspondents who once packaged up their work and despatched it to the nearest airport and rarely saw the finished story can now see their own work literally come back on them.
>
> George Bush ended a presidential press conference saying that he had to leave and call the President of Turkey. In Ankara, Turgut Ozal turned off CNN, walked into his office, picked up the ringing phone and said 'Hello, Mr President'.
>
> (MacGregor, 1997: 4)

Through a combination of the immediacy and reach of global TV news networks, notions of journalistic detachment from the events they report on seems ever more problematic. As Gurevitch points out, global TV in effect creates a channel of communication between countries, politicians, and indeed citizens around the world (1996: 216–17). It is this role of global television networks as a possible player in international relations, as much as the impact of CNN on global TV news practices, that led to the term 'CNNization' being used (MacGregor, 1997: 5). One of the most inter-esting and socially significant developments in this regard has been the idea that awareness of international witnessing of events has sustained popular protest, from events like Tiananmen square, the fall of the Soviet Union in 1991 (where opponents of the coup occupied the TV station in Moscow), up to and including the organised mass public protests against a second war on Iraq in early 2003 (for a critique of such claims, in relation to the Vietnam War see Williams, 1993). Whether or not such asser-tions about the influence of television news on public behaviour are accurate or exag-gerations isn't really of concern here. The point is that television news in the age of global satellite transmission has possibly undergone what could be called a phase transition, where its potential social significance and role has fundamentally changed, akin to the impact printing had on the written word, due to the impact of techno-logical developments (see Buchanan, 2002: 157–58).

Part of the evidence for this rather grand claim lies in the consequences of the rolling news format on the form and content of television news. One of these is that through favouring the immediacy of live images, contemporary television news 'presents real-ity as *self-revelatory*, i.e. it makes it appear *as* reality rather than as a construction' (Gurevitch, 1996: 214, original emphasis). Another expression of this idea is that 'CNN redefined news from something that *has* happened to something that *is* happening' (Küng-Shankleman, 2000: 79, original emphasis). As has been pointed out at several points in this book, however journalists present what is in front of the camera, the choices of which direction to point the camera, what to film and what not to film, neces-sarily involve construction. As discussed in Chapter 7, by giving primacy to the live nature of reporting, to the point where virtually every report is accompanied by a live location link-up, the basis of journalistic credibility shifts. Instead of being about the validity and accuracy of what's being reported, the emphasis shifts to simply giving the *impression* of validity and accuracy through a demonstration of presence, i.e. that what-ever the reporter is saying it must be true because they are 'live at the scene'. This is most obviously problematic in those events that occur in multiple places at once, where the journalist can only be in one place at a time and may in fact be some way from where key incidents are occurring, and this was a key problem for reporting of the war in Afghanistan in 2001. In the remote parts of Afghanistan, broadcast journalists were reduced to filing reports via videophone (see Chapter 5), often miles from where the US attacks were occurring. In such circumstances, journalists based further away from the events, but closer to official channels of communication might have access to more accurate information about what's going on, but then they aren't 'live at the scene'.

The primacy of live-ness and immediacy raises another significant problem with rolling news. With rolling news journalists have to be constantly providing material for the screen, expected to comment on events as they happen, leading to a tendency for speculation over knowledge, and in one recurrent criticism 'immediacy without understanding' (in Eldridge, 1993: 11). Former British national newspaper editor, and former war reporter, Max Hastings expresses the concern that:

> Images are being transmitted much quicker than any reporter, however brilliant, can possibly sensibly interpret them. In other words viewers are in danger of being given the idea that they're being told what is going on whereas actually they're being given a wildly misleading impression of what's going on.
>
> (in MacGregor, 1997: 10)

Perhaps the best example of this problem comes from CNN's presence in Baghdad at the outset of the Gulf War. When the war started, CNN had only managed to establish its sound link, so the first live reporting of the war came from CNN journalists, and its feed was relayed live by a wide range of services around the world, including, for example, BBC World Service radio. On hearing of the beginning of the US air assault in the middle of the night, CNN cut live to its Baghdad-based reporter Bernard Shaw who (much to his declared subsequent regret) opined 'something is happening outside' (in MacGregor, 1997: 6). Later in the conflict, Jerusalem-based CNN reporter Larry Register and colleagues delivered some reports in gas masks uncertain about what was going on, and as Eldridge comments, 'became their own story as we witnessed their confusion and uncertainty' (1993: 11). Eldridge asks rhetorically 'what kind of knowledge is this?' (ibid.). False alarms, unfounded rumours, and inaccurate claims have a tendency to dog rolling news, but the pressure to use this format simply because the technology allows it, and the likes of CNN will do it, sees many events reported in this kind of way, including the September 11 attacks.

Another consequence is the potential relationship to questions of perspective and objectivity. There are two aspects to this. First, in live coverage the degree of journalistic interpretation and explaining of events for audiences reduces dramatically the role of the journalist (Gurevitch, 1996: 214). On the one hand this might seem a positive thing for audiences, able to construct their own interpretations of events without the efforts of journalists trying to frame audience responses. On the other, however, it highlights the problem of witnessing events without explanatory context, and also the risk of events being interpreted by audiences as if they have been presented in an un-mediated manner, which as stated above isn't the case (see also the discussion of unwitting bias in Chapter 7).

Second, with much more airtime to fill and a global audience to attract and serve, questions of perspective and opinion in global TV news are possibly even more pertinent than for the global news agencies. CNN executives claim 'we don't have an agenda – we are not exporting an American viewpoint' (in Schechter, 2000). One example of CNN output offered by supporters that appears to sustain this claim is *World Report*, a daily programme on CNN International, with the mission:

> To provide television viewers around the world with the opportunity to see other countries as they see themselves. *CNN World Report* gives the world's broadcasters a global forum from which to report the news 'as they see it' to the rest of the world.
>
> (www.cnn.com)

Ted Turner was apparently influenced by international debates about the imbalance of information flows around the globe (CNN launched only a few months before the McBride Commission Report was published) stating that:

> That was where I came up with the idea that in the *World Report* we would have a regular place where everybody in the world could be heard, where, for the first time, everybody in the world has the opportunity to speak to everybody else on a regular basis.
>
> (in Flournoy, 1992: 19)

With *World Report* the idea was to circumvent accusations of Western bias through allowing many voices to speak. Yet within this approach comes the explicit acknowledgment of potential conflict in different communities' interpretations and representation of issues and events. Flournoy explains 'it proceeds on the rather startling assumption that all viewpoints are valid components of reality, whether they are objective or not' (ibid.: 17). Unlike the news agencies who try to avoid language their potential clients might regard as propagandistic, a former producer of *World Report* claimed:

> The idea is that we've created a forum or marketplace for ideas. And what is propaganda to one person is valid news to another, depending upon your point of view. It's not propaganda if you have several points of view expressed.
>
> (in Flournoy, 1992: 22)

Yet despite these overt efforts to change the nature of broadcast news, CNN remains a fundamentally US company, in terms of organisation, production practices, content, and crucially audience. Although access to global television has expanded massively in the decade or so since the Gulf War, the dominant audience for global TV news remains a North American and Western European audience. Besides, regardless of its internal efforts to address issues of perspective its dramatic journalistic successes have seen television news networks around the world attempt to reproduce the styles and formats of news inherent to CNN. One particular broadcaster to have come to prominence very recently is worth discussing in this regard.

Al-Jazeera: An Island of Resistance?

In the aftermath of the Gulf War, the impact on television news in the Middle East was dramatic. The role of CNN in disseminating events during the Gulf War, largely from a US perspective, exemplified the potential power of satellite television broadcasting for presenting the viewpoints of particular countries and regions. Several nations in the Middle East launched satellite news channels in the years after war, and their relationship to Western news media is intriguing. One of the first was the Middle East Broadcasting Centre (MBC), begun by a brother-in-law of King Fahd of Saudi Arabia. Head of news at the outset, Stephen Marney, was apparently told 'Steve, we want CNN in Arabic' (in Friedland, 1992: 35). MBC bought the former US news agency United Press International in the 1990s, and has its headquarters in London, England, indicators of Western influence on MBC's organisations and operations. Yet, the domestic censorship that typifies journalism in the Middle East also applies to satellite channels like MBC, in a way that it does not for CNN and other Western global news providers. Although it reaches millions of Arab-speaking people across the region, there has been concern within the region over the Saudi-oriented nature of news output (Franklin, 1996: 49).

An example of the stringent Saudi controls on broadcast news occurred in 1996. The BBC World Service Arabic Radio network was attracting some 14 million listeners by 1994, and the BBC had the view that this could be converted into a television audience with appropriate funding from one of the dominant Saudi media organisations. However, the service was halted over a dispute between the BBC journalists and the Saudi paymasters over editorial independence and coverage of Saudi Arabia in particular. Fortunately for the journalistic staff, the Qatari government had agreed to subsidise a satellite news network and its executives employed virtually all the journalists from the old service. What is key here is that these journalists, from a variety of Arab nations, had been trained in BBC news production practices and as such the new network, called Al-Jazeera (meaning 'the island' or 'the peninsula'), 'inherited not only most of the staff of the former BBC network but also its editorial spirit, freedom, and style' (El-Nawawy and Iskandar, 2002: 31).

By 2001, with this core group of BBC-trained journalists shaping the network's news production, Al-Jazeera was employing some 350 journalists, with 50 foreign correspondents based in 31 countries around the world, and reaching an audience in the region of 35 million viewers (ibid.: 34). A significant key to the network's success is its location in Qatar, a small nation of less than a million people, atypical for the region for having a liberal monarchy that has abolished the kinds of media censorship habitual to many of its neighbours (ibid.: 37). This has allowed the network to gain notoriety in the region for its critical and analytical reporting, modelled on the critical scrutiny and political independence exemplified by the BBC.

Already a major regional player then, in the wake of September 11 Al-Jazeera has now become a major player in the global TV news environment. Its regional links have given the channel far greater access to events in the region, including the war in Afghanistan and, most controversially, the views of Al Qaida and Osama bin Laden. Just as the Gulf War raised CNN's global profile 'Al-Jazeera is in a way the CNN of the war in Afghanistan' (ibid.: 41). The airing of video and audio messages of bin Laden provoked outrage from the US administration who tried to put pressure on both Al-Jazeera and the Qatari authorities. The irony of the situation was that a news organisation run on Western journalistic principles of balanced and objective reporting, was inducing US calls for censorship of that network. A further irony comes from the polite but firm resistance of Qatar and Al-Jazeera to US demands, whilst US authorities were far more successful in getting the major US television news networks to agree to significantly limit any footage of bin Laden (acquired via Al-Jazeera) in the belief that his messages might contain coded instructions to terrorist cells (ibid.: 178).

Apart from having good local access, of particular relevance in current global political environment, Al-Jazeera's BBC-based ethos gave the network a degree of journalistic credibility with Western news organisations that allowed its material to be disseminated far more widely to Western news audiences. The problem with this is that Western journalistic practices, as this book has shown, are far from being problem-free, and it suggests that breaking the global dominance of Western television news organisations like CNN (or the BBC) may only be possible by conforming to Western notions of acceptable journalistic practices. For those news organisations without the markers of 'legitimate' journalism like political independence the opportunities for getting wider dissemination seem limited. Just as news coming from the official Soviet news agency TASS was treated as unreliable by Western news organisations, television news produced within authoritarian constraints has little chance of streaming into the dominant global television news flows.

NEW TECHNOLOGY AND NEWSGATHERING

Journalism has always been a profession whose basic capacities and functions are rooted in technology. As discussed in Chapter 7, even fundamental principles of journalism are closely related to the application of technology to journalistic practices. Printing was the midwife of journalism, and what journalism means has evolved alongside the emergence of new information and communication technologies. The last 25 years or so, though, have arguably seen a rapid acceleration, not just in the sense of new transmission technologies of satellite and digital broadcasting, but also in a wide range of technologies with actual and potential long term consequences for news in the information age. As suggested in Chapter 7, the application of technology, whilst apparently offering an expansion of journalistic capabilities, also appears to paradoxically problematise the nature of the journalistic enterprise.

DIGITAL NEWSGATHERING: THE VIRTUAL NEWSROOM

The development of new technologies is producing more systematic influences on news production processes, alongside the more specific influence of particular technologies like the camcorder. Journalism is one of the primary areas of media production where the concept of *convergence* applies very overtly (Hall, 2001: 6). Convergence essentially refers to 'the coming together of once-separate media in a digital, networked environment' (Pavlik, 2001: 38). While this may sound superficially like little more than a technological change, convergence arguably effects journalism in all kinds of ways from the organisational level to that of individual journalists and audience members.

Four Kinds of Convergence in Journalism

The organisational consequences of convergence can be seen in the conglomeration of media firms discussed in Chapter 3. The increasing synergy in the major media conglomerates has, in part, been fostered by the convergence of news production technologies that has begun to make once very discreet types of news production, i.e. print and broadcast, become much closer. As outlined in Chapter 3, the key problems here are the subsuming of journalistic practices within the overall corporate goals of the organisation. But more fundamentally, the incorporation of news outlets into massive media organisations places news production within predominantly entertainment-oriented commercial organisations, creating internal pressures on journalists that many argue are in conflict with the traditional principles of journalism, and which have contributed to the trends for the kinds of journalism discussed in the last chapter.

A second kind of consequence of convergence is that 'converging computing and telecommunications technologies are rapidly rewriting the traditional assumptions of newsroom organization and structure' (Pavlik, 2001: 108). Thinking back to the discussion of news flow in the newsroom in Chapter 5, the application of new technologies is changing such patterns of production. The key to these changes is the development of *non-linear editing*. The switch to computer-based composition and the development of network-based computing have created a very different environment for news production in both print and broadcasting. Whereas traditional newsrooms operated a largely linear process from the news desk to the print room or live broadcast, the computer-based newsroom can be more flexible in two ways. First, because the tools of composition are digital (in the form of computer software) more people can contribute to the composition process. So, for example, in broadcast news, bulletin scripts can be edited by producers, directors, and also by the reporters and presenters, all from their own desktop computers (or indeed, remotely by reporters on location). What makes this work is that the systems used allow changes to a report by any individual, and automatically updates all copies of the report, also indicating who has made what changes. Indeed, so rapid is this capacity that in broadcast news changes can be made to scripts whilst live on air – editing of a script in a newsroom will be relayed to the news presenter's computer, and indeed to their autocue. Second, digital composition allows the flexible composition of reports, such that text, audio, graphics, or video can be integrated into a report in any order (Pavlik, 2001: 107). So, for example, a newspaper page can be laid out and rearranged multiple times, with elements like reports, headlines, photographs, and adverts being able to be repositioned, resized, and edited at any time in the production process. It also allows journalist teams on location to play a direct role in the editing and composition of their material, by having portable versions of the editing equipment and software and using that before transmitting fully edited reports via satellite. This is some way from trying to a get a roll of film or video/audio-tape onto a vehicle to be physically transported back to the news outlet's offices before broadcast/publication.

The role of the individual journalist is also being changed by convergence. Non-linear editing has had a clear impact on notions of deadlines for journalists. Since the technology allows editors to wait until literally the last few minutes before the cameras or the presses roll, journalists are now not only able to work closer to deadline (Pavlik, 2001: 108), but arguably are increasingly expected to do this. Although superficially more apparent in television journalism with rolling news, print journalism too has seen the practicality of close-to-deadline working increase. For photojournalists, for example, deadlines have become tighter due to the capacity to transmit digitally-captured images down telephone lines and thus slot photos into a paper only minutes before printing. Non-linear editing also raises questions about the distinctions between reporting and editing roles and the autonomy of journalists. In some ways the availability of portable editing equipment, for example, undoubtedly empowers journalists giving them more control over the editing of their material. However, since non-linear editing gives wider access to material, there is also more scope for external editing of journalists' work. For photojournalists this a very significant issue, as the switch from film to digital cameras has brought the possibility of digital manipulation of images, which can in principle be done by anyone with access to the editing system of the news organisation (Pavlik, 2001: 86–7). Editorial cropping of news photographs has been done for many years, but the problem with digital images is that no original negatives exist with which to counter claims of manipulation and distortion, and digital images can be manipulated much more seamlessly than conventional photographs. More than manipulation per se, however, photojournalists have expressed concern about the control over picture composition and editing shifting from the photojournalists to photo-editors and computer-operators in the newsroom (e.g. Becker, 1991: 388).

Changes in role demarcation due to access to technology goes beyond the newsroom, as non-journalistic organisations, as well as members of the general public, get access to some of the tools of the journalistic trade. Some of the most striking images of recent journalism and current affairs came from eyewitnesses who just happened to be in those locations with camera in hand, for example, the images of the firemen carrying children from the ruins of the Oklahoma City bomb in 1995 (MacGregor, 1997: 39), or of Concorde in flames moments before its fatal crash in 1999 (MacArthur, 2000: 22). As well as amateur eyewitnesses, sometimes footage used by news organisations can come from the systematic recording of events in photographs and on video by a wide range of organisations, from official institutions like the military and emergency services to pressure groups. Whether from private citizens or formal organisations, the common problem is the dislocation of depictions of events from contextual understanding of those events. The importance of this can be seen in the now notorious US military involvement in Somalia in 1992, beginning with media fanfares and ending in a dead GI being dragged through the streets of Mogadishu. Those images arguably were key in the subsequent US withdrawal, but in fact they were not from a journalist, most of whom had by that stage left the country after some were killed, but from a Somali amateur who was given a camcorder and briefly shown how to use it by staff from Reuters TV (MacGregor, 1997: 34). So, whilst images of the dead GI and his treatment by the Somalis reached TV screens in the US, details of what happened, how and why, did not, because journalists were not there to verify those details. Indeed, footage from non-journalistic sources, whether private citizens or public institutions, can and are treated in very different ways, for example, the differences in footage of US police beating of suspects when captured by amateurs with camcorders, such as the infamous Rodney King beating, and those captured by police video, as seen in programmes like *World's Scariest Police Chases*.

Another impact of convergence on journalists has been the increasing requirement for multiskilling. Having the means to edit and format material is only really of use if journalists have the necessary skills, both in terms of editing and using the equipment, particularly computers. Moreover, with news outlets being integrated into media conglomerates, journalists are being expected to demonstrate skills outside of one particular mode of journalism, be it print, audio, or television journalism. With the rise of online journalism this is even more the case as online journalism can combine text, audio, graphics, and video, so that the clear demarcation between, say, a print journalist and a broadcast journalist, is rapidly being consigned to the past. When technologies are put together the capacity of individual journalists to produce news suitable for multiple formats is potentially very great, making multiskilling even more desirable for news organisations. An illustration of this need for technological competence on the part of information age journalists is the range of prototypes for the 'Mobile Journalist Workstation' (Pavlik, 2001: 54–5). This would possibly consist of a device (or suite of devices) capable of digital audio and video capture, Internet access, and voice and handwriting recognition. Pavlik offers some hypothetical situations to indicate how such a system might work (ibid.: 57–8). Consider a political candidate giving a speech, being captured in audio and video by the workstation-equipped journalist (and being converted to text by the voice recognition software, whilst the journalist's own handwritten notes are also being converted to printed text). The candidate makes a particular claim that the journalist checks by accessing public records via the Internet connection of the workstation, and by the time the candidate asks for questions, the journalist is able to ask a precise question based on the data received, without having moved from the spot. No such integrated system is yet in actual professional use, but in principle all the key technologies are already available and some are already impacting on newsgathering practices, such as mobile phones (Hall, 2002).

Familiarity and expertise in using computers is important for contemporary journalists in other ways also. As more and more information is put on the Internet, from the Human Genome Project to the FBI's UFO files, journalists are encountering a whole new form of newsgathering. But access to raw data is not the only benefit of the computer for journalists. Computer tools have allowed journalists to make the 'invisible visible' (Johnson, 2000: 58). In the early 1990s, the *Miami Herald*'s Steve Doig was central to a Pulitzer Prize-winning investigation into the effects of Hurricane Andrew on Florida in the US. Using a geographical informations system (GIS), Doig was able to map the track of the hurricane against the damage recorded by tax assessors. The analysis showed that there was a widespread inefficiency in the assessment of storm damage by public officials, adding significantly to the overall public costs of the hurricane (ibid.: 58–9). So, paralleling the development of journalistic objectivity in relation to the emergence of social science in the nineteenth century outlined in Chapter 7, there is possibly a growing association between patterns of journalistic investigation and application of computer modelling and databases in other fields. This pertains not only to external sources of information, but also to the digitisation of news outlets' own archives of news output. This has made it much easier for journalists to search their own organisations' archives for related material to their investigations (Pavlik, 2001: 50–1). Whether or not this encourages journalists to conduct their investigations from their desk rather than in the field, and what might be lost in reporting based on computer archive and database analysis rather than location reporting and interviewing, remain moot points at this time.

A final kind of consequence of convergence lies in the impact on the nature of audience consumption of journalism. Convergent media technologies are not only appearing inside the media industries, with audiences (primarily in the developed world) also getting access to new ICTs. Access to digital interactive television, for example, is giving audiences a degree of interactivity with television news output. Some limited options to supplement viewing of news reports are offered, such as additional text-based information linked to particular reports, and many broadcasters now invite audience contributions through e-mail and make those contributions a part of bulletins. But whilst these developments have so far represented a meagre augmentation of conventional television news, news on the Internet possibly represents the most dramatic transformation of news, particularly in its different relationship to audiences.

ONLINE JOURNALISM

The Internet began as a system for information transmission between scientific and computer researchers, with the underlying innovations and technology being born of Cold War concerns about maintaining military and governmental lines of communication in the event of nuclear war (Naughton, 1999). Early parts of the Internet (short for Inter-network) were mainly file-sharing networks, sending and receiving blocks of data between academic research teams, and their text messages and discussions relating to that data (e.g. through File Transfer Protocol or FTP). The Internet alone was not a particularly profitable medium for news production, and it wasn't until the emergence of the World Wide Web in the early 1990s that online journalism was really viable. The World Wide Web is part of the Internet, but a part that has become particularly dominant amongst users for two reasons. First, the Web offers a relatively simple means through which to access material on all the various networks that make up the Internet through the application of protocols for the location (through the designation of an 'address' for all connections to the Internet, the Uniform Resource Locator, or URL) and transfer of information (through the hypertext transfer protocol or http). The 'killer app' of the Web, however, is its use of *hypertext*. Hypertext has the characteristic of being able to act as both a meaningful text (or image for that matter) and also an electronic link to another part of that text, or as a link to any part of the Internet.

Second, as the Web has developed as a public arena, the layout and design of web-pages has become ever more sophisticated, incorporating graphics, animation, audio and video, as well as text (e.g. the virtual newsreader Ananova (Bold, 2000)). Furthermore, whilst early web-page construction required knowledge of the hyper-text mark-up language (HTML) that underlies the Web, today software packages like Dreamweaver, allow users to construct web-pages in a similar way to using word processing packages. Not surprisingly then, the use of the Internet for journalism, both by individual journalists and news organisations, has accelerated since the arrival of the World Wide Web. But a key question around online journalism is whether or not it entails an entirely new form of journalism, or is simply a new way to distribute news, a 'new delivery system' (Pavlik, 1997: 30).

FROM PYRAMID TO MATRIX?

The earliest forms of online journalism essentially involved little more than the simple repackaging of existing content for the Web (Pavlik, 1997: 36). Material from a traditional outlet, like a newspaper, is simply represented on a web-page with little change, save perhaps there being less content to ensure that sales of the newspaper aren't undermined. This is reminiscent of newspapers' attitude towards radio in the 1920s, concerned about losing an audience to the new medium, but it also reflects the lack of computer skills of news organisations in the early days of the Web (Hall, 2001: 29). This approach, derogatively dubbed by some 'shovelware', is still evident in parts of the Web (ibid.), and essentially retains the separation of forms of content seen in traditional media. There is little augmentation of reports, with text and graphics static, and presented pretty much as they appeared in print editions. Access to archives of previously printed material is a useful feature of shovelware for audiences, although many organisations restrict access to archives through requirements for users to subscribe and often pay for material.

Gradually, news organisations began to see ways of exploiting the Web, particularly the potential journalistic applications of hypertext in their routine presentation of news. One approach has been the application of *layering* (Hall, 2001: 71; Burnett and Marshall, 2003: 158). Layering essentially involves offering a structure:

> In which a top layer provides the traditional who, what, when, where and why.
> The next layer offers a historical context. Additional layers provide analysis,
> expert commentary, and reader discussion and feedback.
>
> (Burnett and Marshall, 2003: 158)

When laid out with hyperlinks to archives of previous reporting and links to relevant web-pages from external bodies, the web-user can engage in what Pavlik calls 'immersive storytelling' (1997: 36). Consumers of web-based news are thus able to navigate through an issue or event in their own way, which means that 'online news stories are not so easily shoehorned into the inverted pyramid shape' and could be viewed as being more like 'a net or matrix' (Hall, 2001: 70). In composing the various elements of the news 'matrix' around an issue or event, each part needs to be comprehensible on its own terms to have value to the user and to allow them to construct the new account in whatever way they choose. Significantly, this undermines the capacity of journalists to determine the news frame (see Chapter 7) of a particular story through their organisation and presentation of information. The user constructs the organisation of information from what they pay attention to and what they ignore, in this sense their literal consumption of a story may be 'far removed from the journalist's intention or understanding' (ibid.: 71).

THE END OF GATEKEEPING?

One problem of shovelware is that attracting audiences on the Web is not the same as for conventional media. Bold headlines and sensational images may help attract audiences' attention at the newsstand, or whilst channel-hopping through the few channels available on TV, but the Web had thousands of pages even it its early days and today has hundreds of millions of pages. News organisations have approached this problem in two ways, by developing what have been dubbed 'push' and 'pull' strategies. Push strategies are essentially the traditional strategies of regularly providing news content in convenient packages, attempting to 'push' the audience member into consuming that news product. Daily newspaper production, television news bulletins at the same time every day, and advertising of these in between, are traditional examples of push media. On the Internet (and with new mobile phones) news organisations offer services such as news delivered to you individually by e-mail (or other methods) tailored to your particular interests (Burnett and Marshall, 2003: 157). Reflecting Bardoel's 'instrumental' journalism, as Hall comments, push strategies are good for simple factual information like sports results, weather forecasts, and market reports (2001: 82). At the moment these kinds of automated services aren't so good for transmitting more detailed and lengthy reporting, although the take-up of ultra-fast broadband Internet connections may change this. The other strategy is the 'pull' strategy. Here web-based providers of news do not necessarily attempt to push their own content at audience members, but instead offer aggregation services, i.e. an audience member may request news on a particular issue, and pull media will search a range of news outlets for relevant information, collate it and send the results to the audience member.

In connection to the concept of the online news matrix this raises the question of whether the process of news selection, the process which arguably gives journalists power and authority, is being taken out of the hands of journalists. Singer argues, for example, that:

> Online delivery of vast amounts of information creates an even greater need for someone to make sense of it all – someone skilled not only in selecting information but, more importantly, in evaluating it.
>
> (Singer, 1997: 77)

So, in this sense the role of the journalist is still about the filtering and organising of information to help audiences makes sense of that information, therefore retaining a gatekeeping function of sorts. Singer quotes a US journalist arguing that:

> You need someone who can provide you with a condensed version of everything important that happened in your world that you can trust ... [which] is something that's clearly lacking in a lot of the online world.
>
> (in Singer, 1997: 87)

This presents online journalists' role as a kind of quality controller, providing a check on Internet information, as a necessary, reliable, and trustworthy social functionary. But part of the problem lies outside of the journalists' control, due to audiences' capacity for non-linear navigation through news content, made possible by hypertext.

It is in this power of the web-user that 'this 'You News' kind of journalism could thus become a force for atomisation, for further civic decay' (Pavlik, 1997: 30), reflecting the concerns outlined towards the end of Chapter 1. Audience members on the Web are no longer obliged to pay attention only to conventional journalistic framing of issues and events and, ironically perhaps, are actively encouraged to move away from conventional journalism through the provision of the layered news matrix. It is precisely because of this capacity for self-selection of content that 'as a form' the Web 'can actually *reduce* the content of what is read and viewed' (Burnett and Marshall, 2003: 167, original emphasis). This can occur as a web-user's selection of content 'can be progressively more and more narrow and so the news elements of the Web no longer serve the objectives of providing a generally informed citizenry and an active public sphere across the diverse domains of a culture' (ibid.: see Chapter 8 for more on the public sphere). Instead of the presumed shared attention of millions of listeners or viewers of broadcast output, or readers of newspapers, the Web theoretically allows for an entirely atomised audience, each individual looking at different content, with little possibility of a collective audience paying attention to the same material, in the same way, at the same time. And, consciously or otherwise, users' selectivity denudes their awareness of issues and events through their selection and rejection of topics to engage with.

Online News From Non-Journalistic Sources

Concern about civic decay comes not just from journalists' professional egos about this threat to their social status as gatekeepers of knowledge for the public (although that is clearly a part). It also comes from issues arising out of the use of the Web for information gathering and presentation outside of established news organisations whose impact might be increased due to web-audiences' potential for selectivity and avoidance, deliberate or otherwise, of established news organisations. A proliferation of both institutional and individual sources of information now exist on the Web, that offer alternatives to journalistic gatekeeping. Governments and official institutions, as well as private corporations and pressure groups, for example, routinely maintain their own websites offering access to a range of information, including things like press releases, to an extent side-stepping that struggle for news media access discussed in Chapter 4. The resource issues for news sources outlined in Chapter 4 continue to apply to an extent, as government institutions and corporations generally have more resources to dedicate to website design and maintenance, however, it is a more level playing field than getting access to conventional news media, and crucially the Web is a medium that has allowed the development of entirely non-institutional forms of information provision. Two of the most notable forms are newsgroups and weblogs.

Newsgroups originated on electronic communication networks before both the Web and the Internet entered the public consciousness, but have grown since then.

Essentially involving discussions between individuals with a shared area of interest, they typically take the form of an extended text-based 'conversation' between multiple individuals (Burnett and Marshall, 2003: 156). The software behind newsgroups automatically organises contributions in 'threads' linked by things like date posted, topic, and in terms of responses to previous posts. Instead of a hierarchy with clear designation of roles, newsgroups are generally very egalitarian in composition, the only hierarchical role being that of the moderator whose role is essentially to see that discussions stay on topic and remain as civil as possible. The advantage of this is that, potentially, a multitude of voices can contribute to discussions (as in the International War and Peace Reporting discussion forum, mentioned in Chapter 1). The disadvantages are that generally moderators are not authoritarian, and newsgroups are known for tendencies for topic drift, participants' discussions ending up way off the original topic, and for 'flaming' and 'trolling', essentially bouts of deliberately abusive and disruptive contributions. Nonetheless, for people searching for first-hand information about events, newsgroups have provided a very rich environment for audiences, that mainstream news media can do little about (except provide their own forums within their own websites, which many now do).

Weblogs (also known as 'blogs') are a more individualised form of information presentation. Essentially the equivalent of an online diary, the weblog has the additional features of being able to include hyperlinks to material the author finds interesting/important, and of being open to public scrutiny in a way that a conventional diary is not. Over time, a regularly updated weblog can offer a welter of thematically linked material, offering yet another means of navigating the Web for audience members looking for specific material. Of course, the content is entirely at the whim of the author, but some journalists and news media organisations (such as the British newspaper *The Guardian*) now maintain their own weblogs around particular issues, so the potential value of such a form of information gathering and presentation has been identified by some within mainstream journalism.

With all these alternatives to conventional journalism fundamental issues of objectivity, ethics, law and regulation were initially placed in limbo by the emergence of online alternatives to conventional news. Not bound by traditional laws governing print and broadcast content, and with the ease of producing material beyond the geographical boundaries of a particular nation, and thus not subject to that country's laws, much online content has breached conventions and laws of taste and decency, defamation and libel, and intellectual property and copyright. Countries are belatedly getting around to producing legislation specific to online content attempting to close these loopholes, such as the 1998 Digital Millennium Copyright Act in the US (Burnett and Marshall, 2003: 144). Even given these measures though, conventions of journalistic practice in any one nation can still be influenced by perfectly legal use of the Web for information dissemination. For example, injunctions sought against domestic news media to prevent publication of information in one country, not only don't apply to news media in other nations, but now can easily be accessed through web-versions of those nations' newspapers.

Even within a country, conventions of news media practice can be subverted by online news providers. Perhaps the archetypal example of this was the Bill Clinton/Monica Lewinsky scandal of 1998, where a freelance journalists and web author, Matt Drudge, published information about this case on his website (Hall, 2001: 129). He came across a story about a semen-stained dress, that *Newseek* magazine had spiked partly due to uncertainty about its accuracy, but also partly because of the story's sordid nature. An Internet author ran a story, therefore, that a traditional news organisation wouldn't run, and this smoking gun contributed not only to the impeachment of Clinton, but to the later lack of prudishness of US news media's reporting of the Starr Report's equally sordid details of Clinton and Lewinsky's sexual liaisons. Drudge later faced a libel accusation for a similar running of a story dropped by mainstream news outlets, prompting his lawyer, to defend him:

> I call Matt Drudge the Thomas Paine of the Internet ... He's in the tradition of the early American leafleteer who used to circulate material that was critical of the government.
>
> (in Shepard, 1998)

Hall describes Drudge as an agent provocateur who represents the role maverick online information and news providers play in accelerating the news process to the point where journalists are forced to run with stories that are little more than rumour, the justification for publication being that it has already been published somewhere else (2001: 130–31).

CONCLUSION: 'IT'S ALWAYS PRIME TIME SOMEWHERE'[12]

As technology enables ever faster, ever more automated forms of information transmission and communication, journalists in the most technologically developed nations face ever more pressures on their working practices. Deadlines have been tightening to the point where some news outlets operate permanent news delivery, from rolling television news channels to always on, always updated news websites. At the time of writing, the major news organisations have committed major resources and personnel (as many as 5,000 people, several hundred of them 'embedded' in US and British military units (Milmo: 2003)), reorganised network schedules, and employed new technologies like satellite videophones equipped with night vision lenses, all aimed at ensuring that the war on Iraq in 2003 will have been, in some ways, the most heavily

---

[12] Will King of CNN (in Hall, 2001: 81).

televised war ever. Whether this represents the increasing (technologically-enabled) capacity of contemporary news organisations to meet their public service functions more fully than ever before or, more cynically, merely the increasing intensity of competition in global news provision may only become clear in the months that follow. Either way, news coverage of the 2003 war in Iraq offers a potentially striking example of the often paradoxical and ambiguous status and nature of contemporary global journalism.

Pronouncing the trends in journalism in the developed world as either very positive or very negative seem premature, and over-simplistic, and attempting to apply these concerns about 'journalism in crisis' across the world as a whole is similarly misplaced. The crises of journalism in many parts of the developing world are significantly more overt and pressing, as journalists literally risk their lives attempting to live up to the crucial social functions of journalism. Sometimes they do this sharing Western notions of what those social functions of journalism are, and sometimes they appear to function without even beginning to address Western preconceptions about journalism's social role. As different attitudes, traditions, and practices in journalism begin to interact as ICTs open up new channels of news dissemination, sweeping pronouncements about journalism, what it is, what is does, and what it should or shouldn't do, seem ever more problematic and inappropriate. The only thing that can tentatively be said is that journalism, in its multiplicity of meanings, is absolutely central to the emergence of the information age.

BIBLIOGRAPHY ☐

Allan, S. (1999) *News Culture*, Buckingham: Open University Press.

Allison, R. (2002) 'Wall Street Journal drops Scruton over tobacco cash', *Guardian*, 5/02/02, at [http://www.guardian.co.uk] accessed 5/02/02.

Altheide, D.L. (1974) *Creating Reality: How TV News Distorts Events*, London: Sage.

Altschull, J.H. (1995) *Agents of Power: The Media and Public Policy*, 2nd edition, London: Longman.

Altschull, J.H. (1997) 'Boundaries of Journalistic Autonomy', in Berkowitz, D. (ed.) *Social Meanings of News*, London: Sage, pp. 259–68.

Anderson, A. (1991) 'Source strategies and the communication of environmental affairs', *Media, Culture and Society*, 13(4): 459–76.

APC (Australian Press Council) (2001) 'Complaints Statistics 1999–2000', 1/11/00, at [http://www.presscouncil.org.au/pcsite/complaints/stats00.html#complaints] accessed 31/07/01.

Archard, D. (1998) 'Privacy, the public interest and a prurient public', in Kieran, M. (ed.) *Media Ethics*, London: Routledge, pp. 82–96.

Armour, D. (1993) 'The Russian press in the struggle for power', *British Journalism Review*, 4(2): 27–32.

Armstrong, S. (1996) 'How Max made a name for himself', *Guardian*, 13/5/96, G2: 10–11.

Associated Press (2000) 'Japanese officials criticized for withholding news of prime minister's stroke', Freedom Forum Online, 4/4/00, at [http://www.freedomforum.org/international/] accessed 16/06/00.

Associated Press (2000) 'Journalist sentenced for "hate radio" broadcasts', Freedom Forum Online, 2/6/00, at [http://www.freedomforum.org/news].

Atton, C. (1999) 'A reassessment of the alternative press', *Media, Culture and Society*, 1(1): 51–76.

Aumente, J., Gross, P., Hiebert, R., Johnson, O.V. and Mills, D. (1999) *Eastern European Journalism*, Cresskill, NJ: Hampton Press.

Bagdikian, B. (2001) 'Excerpt from The Media Monopoly', Frontline: The Merchants of Cool, PBS, at [http://www.pbs.org/wgbh/pages/frontline/shows/cool/etc/Bagdikian.html] accessed 16/7/2001.

Baggott, R. (1995) *Pressure Groups Today*, Manchester: Manchester University Press.

Baker, R. (1997) 'The Squeeze', *Columbia Journalism Review*, September/October.

Columbia Journalism Review (1997) 'The Real Dangers of Conglomerate Control', March/April, pp. 46–51.

Ballaster, R., Beetham, M., Fraser, E. and Hebron, S. (1991) *Women's Worlds: Ideology, Femininity and The Woman's Magazine*, London: Macmillan.

Bantz, C.R., McCorkle, S. and Baade, R.C. (1997) 'The news factory', in Berkowitz, D. (ed.) (1997) *Social Meanings Of News*, London: Sage, pp. 269–85.

Bardoel, J. (1996) 'Beyond journalism: a profession between information society and civil society', *European Journal Of Communication*, 11(3): 283–302.

Barker, A. and Naik, P. (2002) 'A Question of Consent', *The Guardian*, 28/1/02, G2: 10.

Barnett, S. and Gaber, I. (2001) *Westminster Tales: The Twenty-first-century Crisis in Political Journalism*, London: Continuum.

Barron, J.A. (2000) 'Structural regulation of the media and the diversity rationale', *Federal Communications Law Journal*, 52(3): 555–60.

Baudrillard, J. (1995) *The Gulf War Did Not Take Place*, Sydney: Power Publications.

Baynes, K. (1994) 'Communicative ethics, the public sphere and communication media', *Critical Studies in Mass Communication*, 11(4): 315–26.

Becker, K.E. (1991) 'To control our image: photojournalists and new technology', *Media, Culture and Society*, 13(3): 381–97.

Becker, K.E. (1992) 'Photojournalism and the Tabloid Press', in Dahlgren, P. and Sparks, C. (eds) *Journalism and Popular Culture*, London: Sage, pp. 130–53.

Behr, E. (1982) *Anyone Here been Raped and Speaks English?*, London: New English Library.

Bell, M. (1997) 'TV news: how far should we go?', *British Journalism Review*, 8(1): 7–16.

Bell, M. (1998) 'The journalism of attachment' in Kieran, M. (ed.) *Media Ethics*, London: Routledge, pp. 15–22.

Belsey, A. (1992) 'Privacy, publicity and politics', in Belsey, A. and Chadwick, R. (eds) *Ethical Issues in Journalism and the Media*, London: Routledge, pp. 77–92.

Belsey, A. and Chadwick, R. (eds) (1992) *Ethical Issues in Journalism and the Media*, London: Routledge.

Benesh, S. (1998) 'The rise of solutions journalism', *Columbia Journalism Review*, March/April, at [http://www.cjr.org] accessed 23/06/98.

Bennett, C. (1999) 'Like bees to the honeytrap', *Guardian*, 27/5/99, G2: 5.

Bennie, L.G. (1998) 'Brent Spar, Atlantic oil and Greenpeace', *Parliamentary Affairs*, 51(3): 397–410.

Beresford, D. (1994) 'Dogged by haunting images', *Guardian*, 22/8/94, G2: 17.

Berkowitz, D. (1997) 'Refining the gatekeeper metaphor for local television news, in Berkowitz, D. (ed.) (1997) *Social Meanings of News*, London: Sage, pp. 81–94.

Berkowitz, D. (ed.) (1997) *Social Meanings of News*, London: Sage.

Biagi, S. (1999) *Media/Impact: An Introduction to Mass Media*, Belmont, CA: Wadsworth.

Bishop, C. (1999) 'Journalists tortured by Zimbabwe military', *Electronic Telegraph*, 22/01/99, at [http://www.telegraph.co.uk] accessed 25/02/99.

Bird, S.E. (1990) 'Storytelling on the far side: journalism and the weekly tabloid', *Critical Studies in Mass Communication*, 7(4): 377–89.

Bird, S.E. (1997) 'What a story! Understanding the audience for scandal', in Lull, J. and Hinerman, S. (eds) *Media Scandals*, Cambridge: Polity Press, pp. 99–121.

Bird, S.E. (2000) 'Audience demands in a murderous market: tabloidization in US television news', in Sparks, C. and Tulloch, J. (eds) *Tabloid Tales: Global Debates Over Media Standards*, Oxford: Rowman and Littlefield, pp. 213–28.

Bivens, M. (2000) 'Back to the USSR', *Brill's Content*, August 2000, at [http://www.brillscontent.com] accessed 30/08/00.

Blain, N. and Boyle, R. (1994) 'Battling along the boundaries: the making of Scottish identity in sports journalism', in Jarvie, G. and Walker, G. (eds) *Scottish Sport in The Making of The Nation: Ninety Minute Patriots?*, Leicester: Leicester University Press, pp. 125–41.

Bleske, G.L. (1997) 'Ms. Gates takes over: an updated version of a 1949 case study', in Berkowitz, D. (ed.) (1997) *Social Meanings of News*, London: Sage, pp. 72–80.

Bold, B. (2000) 'Giving news on the Net a friendly face', *PR Week*, 21/4/00, p. 13.

Bonsu, H. (1999) 'Get me a Yemeni chief on the phone', *The Times*, 12/3/99, S2: 41.

Bourdieu, P. (1998) *On Television and Journalism*, London: Pluto Press.

Boyes, R. (2000) 'The man who made up interviews', *The Times*, 19/5/00, S2: 28.

Bradberry, G. (2001) 'Limousines and goody bags', *The Times*, 8/6/01, S2: 21.

Braithwaite, B. (1995) *Women's Magazines: The First 300 Years*, London: Peter Owen.

Braithwaite, B. (1998) 'Magazines: the bulging bookstalls', in Briggs, A. and Cobley, P. (eds) *The Media: An Introduction*, London: Longman.

Breed, W. (1999) 'Social control in the newsroom: a functional analysis', in Tumber, H. (ed.) *News: A Reader*, Oxford: OUP, pp. 79–84.

Broadcasting Research Unit (BRU) (1985) *The Public Service Idea in British Broadcasting*, London: BRU.

Brokaw, T. *et al.* (1997) 'Talk Show Democracy '96', *Press/Politics*, 2(1): 4–12.

Brown, J. (1996) 'Rosie's aces', *Guardian*, 5/2/96, pp. B10–11.

Brown, M. (1996) 'How *She* tired of juggling', *Guardian*, 15/1/96, p. B13.

Brown, M. (2000) 'Unveiling anonymous sources', *Thunderbird: UBC Journalism Review*, December, at [http://www.journalism.ubc.ca/thunderbird] accessed 20/10/00.

Brown, M. (2001) 'Terror, tears, talk', *Guardian*, 17/11/01, S3: 2.

Buchanan, M. (2002) *Nexus*, New York: WW Norton and Co.

Buckner, J. (1997) 'Public journalism – giving voters a voice', *Media Studies Journal*, Winter, at [http://www.mediastudies.org/cov96/buckner.html] accessed 24/06/98.

Bugliosi, V. and Gentry, C. (1974) *Helter Skelter: The True Story of the Manson Murders*, New York: Bantam Books.

Burnet, D. (1992) 'Freedom of speech, the media and the law', in Belsey, A. and Chadwick, R. (eds) *Ethical Issues in Journalism and the Media*, London: Routledge, pp. 49–61.

Burnett, R. and Marshall, P.D. (2003) *Web Theory: An Introduction*, London: Routledge.

Butterworth, T. (2000) 'Study: journalists aren't like ordinary americans', *NewsWatch*, Centre for Media and Public Affairs, 31/03/00, at [http://www.newswatch.org] accessed 5/07/00.

Byrnes, T. (1997) *Writing Bestselling True Crime and Suspense*, Rocklin, CA.: Prima Publishing.

Campagna, J. (2000) 'Iran: The Press on Trial', CPJ Press Briefings, May, at [http://www.cpj.org] accessed 25/08/00.

Campbell, M. (2000) 'Give me the boy or I'll shoot', *The Sunday Times*, 23/4/00, p. 1.

Campbell, V.P. (1999) 'Frenzied apathy: British media agendas in the 1994 European election campaign', unpublished Doctoral Thesis, University of Sheffield.

Capote, T. (1965) *In Cold Blood*, London: Penguin.

Caruso, D. (1998) 'The law and the Internet: beware', *Columbia Journalism Review*, May/June, at [http://www.cjr.org].

Çatalbas, D. (2000) 'Broadcasting deregulation in Turkey: uniformity within diversity', in Curran, J. (ed.) *Media Organisations in Society*, London: Arnold, pp. 126–48.

Chalkley, A. (1975) 'Development journalism is NOT "government-say-so journalism"', *Media*, May, p. 27.

Chen, C., Zhu, J.H. and Wu, W. (1998) 'The Chinese Journalist', in Weaver, D.H. (ed.) *The Global Journalist: News People Around the World*, Creskill, NJ: Hampton Press.

Chomsky, D. (1999) 'The Mechanisms of Management Control at the *New York Times*', *Media, Culture and Society*, 21(5): 579–99.

Chow, C. (2000) 'Japan's self-regulating reporters' clubs withstand periodic changes', Freedom Forum Online, 8/02/00, at [http://www.freedomforum.org/international] accessed 16/06/00.

Clayton, A., Hancock-Beaulieu, M. and Meadows, J. (1993) 'Change and continuity in the reporting of science and technology: a study of *The Times* and the *Guardian*', *Public Understanding of Science*, 2(3): 225–34.

Cohen, E. (1997) 'Hong Kong: the future of press freedom', *Columbia Journalism Review*, May/June, at [http://www.cjr.org].

Cohen, E.D. (ed.) (1992) *Philosophical Issues in Journalism*, Oxford: Oxford University Press.

Cohen, N. (1998) 'The death of news', *New Statesman*, 22 May 1998, pp. 18–20.

Coleman, N. and Hornby, N. (eds) (1996) *The Picador Book of Sportswriting*, London: Picador.

Coleridge, N. (1993) *Paper Tigers*, London: Mandarin.

Collins, R. and Murroni, C. (1996) *New Media, New Policies: Media and Communications Strategies for the Future*, Cambridge: Polity Press.

Columbia Journalism Review (1997) 'The real dangers of conglomerate control', March/April at [http://www.cjr.org].

Conniff, K. (2000) 'France says "Non!" to certain photos', *Brill's Content*, August 2000 at [http://www.brillscontent.com] accessed 30/08/00.

Cook, T.E., Gronke, P. and Rattliff, J. (2000) 'Disdaining the media: the American public's changing attitudes towards the news', unpublished paper given to the 2000 meeting of the ISPP, July 2000.

Cooper-Chen, A. (1997) *Mass Communication in Japan*, Ames: Iowa State University Press.

Cozens, C. (2001) 'Government ad spend triples to £192 m', *Guardian*, 25/07/01, at [http://www.guardian.co.uk] accessed 26/03/02.

Cranfield, G.A. (1978) *The Press and Society: From Caxton to Northcliffe*, Harlow: Longman.

Crawshaw, S. (1999) 'Sad but true: dead Britons make better headlines', *Independent*, 16/2/99, p. 13.

Cribb, R. (2002) 'Journalist's association wants diversity of opinions protected in the wake of CanWest's editorial decisions', Canada.com News, 7/2/02, at [http://www.canada.com] accessed 21/02/02.

Cunningham, P. (2000) 'Thai paper's lapse directs fresh attention to Asian news coverage of sex, crime', Freedom Forum Online, 25/1/00, at [http://www.freedomforum.org/international] accessed 16/06/00.

Curran, J. (1991) 'Rethinking the media as a public sphere', in Dahlgren, P. and Sparks, C. (eds) *Communication and Citizenship: Journalism and the Public Sphere*, London: Routledge, pp. 27–57.

Curran, J. and Seaton, J. (1997) *Power without Responsibility: the Press and Broadcasting in Britain*, 5th Edition, London: Routledge.

Daniel, S.H. (1992) 'Some conflicting assumptions of journalistic ethics', in Cohen, E.D. (ed.) *Philosophical Issues in Journalism*, Oxford: Oxford University Press, pp. 50–57.

Darewicz, K. (2000) 'A Black Chapter', in Williams and Rich (eds) *Losing Control: Freedom of the Press in Asia*, Canberra: Asia Pacific Press, pp. 138–46.

Dearing, J.W. and Rogers, E.M. (1996) *Agenda Setting*, London: Sage.

Delano, A. (1997) 'Prepare for do-it-yourself news', *British Journalism Review*, 8(1): 53–6.

Delano, A. and Henningham, J. (1995) *The News Breed: British Journalists in the 1990s*, London: London Institute.

Dempsey, K. (1998) 'Thirties: the lost decade?', *Media Week*, 16/1/98, p. 8.

Department of Journalism and Mass Communication (1997) *EthicNet: Databank For European Codes of Journalism Ethics*, Tampere: University Of Tampere, at [http://www.uta.fi/ethicnet/].

Dias, M. (2001) 'Caged on principle', *The News Media and The Law*, 25(4): 25.

Dodd, V. (2000) 'Irving: consigned to history as a racist liar', *Guardian*, 12/04/00, p. 1.

Dolay, N. (1997) 'Press machinations', *Le Monde Diplomatique*, July, trans. Kristianasen, W., at [http://www.en.monde-diplomatique.fr/1997/07/turkeypress] accessed 11/02/02.

Downing, J. (1988) 'The alternative public realm: the organisation of the 1980s anti-nuclear press in West Germany and Britain', *Media, Culture and Society*, 10(2): 163–81.

Dugdale, J. (1996) 'Love, lies and loopholes', *Guardian*, 29/4/96, G2: 13.

Dugdale, J. (1998) 'Middle man', *Guardian*, 30/3/98, pp. B4-5.

Eco, U. (1986) *Travels In Hyperreality*, London: Picador.

Edgar, A. (1992) 'Objectivity, bias and truth', in Belsey, A. and Chadwick, R. (eds), *Ethical Issues in Journalism and the Media*, London: Routledge, pp. 112–29.

Edwards, M. (1997) 'On the record: James Brown', *Media Week*, 26/9/97, pp. 16–17.

Ehrlich, M.C. (1997) 'The competitive ethos in television newswork', in Berkowitz, D. (ed.) *Social Meanings Of News*, London: Sage, pp. 301–17.

Eide, M. (1997) 'A new kind of newspaper? Understanding a popularization process', *Media, Culture and Society*, 19(2): 173–82.

Eldridge, J. (ed.) (1993) *Getting the Message: News, Truth and Power*, London: Routledge.

Eldridge, J. (1993) 'News, truth and power' in Eldridge, J. (ed.) *Getting the Message: News, Truth and Power*, London: Routledge, pp. 3–33.

Eldridge, J., Kitzinger, J. and Williams, K. (1997) *The Mass Media and Power in Modern Britain*, Oxford: Oxford University Press.

Elliot, P. (1986) 'Intellectuals, the "information society" and the disappearance of the public sphere', in Collins, R. *et al.* (eds) *Media, Culture and Society: A Critical Reader*, London: Sage, pp. 105–15.

El-Nawawy and Iskandar, A. (2002) *Al-Jazeera: How the Free Arab News Network Scooped the World and Changed the Middle East*, Cambridge, MA: Westview Press.

Ericson, R.V., Baranek, P.M. and Chan, J.B.L. (1987) *Visualising Deviance: A Study of News Organisation*, Milton Keynes: Open University Press.

Ericson, R.V., Baranek, P.M. and Chan, J.B.L. (1989) *Negotiating Control: A Study of News Sources*, Milton Keynes: Open University Press.

Errico, M. (1997) 'The Evolution of the Summary News Lead', *Media History Monographs*, 1(1) at [http://www.Scripps.ohiou.edu/mediahistory/mhmjour.htm].

Esser, F. (1998) 'Editorial structures and work principles in british and german news-rooms', *European Journal of Communication*, 13(3): 375–405.

Esser, F. (1999) ' "Tabloidization' " of news: a comparative analysis of Anglo-American and German press journalism', *European Journal of Communication*, 14(3): 291–324.

Evans, C. (2003) 'Media Kit', *Working Mother*, at [http://www.workingmother.com/media7.shtml] accessed 7/05/03.

Evans, H. (1984) *Good Times, Bad Times*, London: Coronet.

FAIR (Fairness and Accuracy in Reporting) (2000a) *Fear and Favour 2000: How Power Shapes the News*, at [http://www.fair.org/ff2000.html#advertisers] accessed 11/02/02.

FAIR (2000b) 'Action alert: in the soup at the view: ABC allows corporate sponsor to buy talkshow content', 20/11/00, at [http://www.fair.org] accessed 25/02/02.

Fallows, J. (1996) *Breaking the News: How the Media Undermine American Democracy*, New York: Vintage.

Fang, I.E. (1972) *Television News*, 2nd Edition, New York: Hastings House.

Farivar, M. (1999) 'Dateline Afghanistan: journalism under the Taliban', CPJ Briefings, December 1999, at [http://www.cpj.org] accessed 25/08/00.

Feather, J. (1998) *The Information Society: A Study of Continuity and Change*, 2nd Edition, London: Library Association Publishing.

Featherstone, L. (1998) 'Boys will be girls', *Columbia Journalism Review*, May/June, at [http://www.cjr.org] accessed 23/06/98.

Ferguson, M. (1983) *Forever Feminine: Women's Magazines and The Cult of Femininity*, London: Heinemann.

Fielding, R. (1978) *The March of Time, 1935–1951*, New York: Oxford University Press.

Filler, L. (1976) *Appointment at Armageddon: Muckraking and Progressivism in the American Tradition*, London: Greenwood Press.

Fiske, J. (1989) *Understanding Popular Culture*, London: Unwin.

Flournoy, D.M. (1992) *CNN World Report: Ted Turner's International News Coup*, London: John Libbey.

Fowler, R. (1991) *Language in The News*, London: Routledge.

Franklin, B. (1994) *Packaging Politics*, London: Arnold.

Franklin, B. (1997) *Newszak and News Media*, London: Arnold.

Franklin, S. (1996) 'The kingdom and the power', *Columbia Journalism Review*, Nov/Dec, pp. 49–51.

Fraser, N. (1992) 'Rethinking the public sphere: a contribution to the critique of actually existing democracy', in Calhoun, C. (ed.) *Habermas and the Public Sphere*, Cambridge, MA: MIT Press, pp. 109–42.

Fraser, N. (1994) 'A polite press', *Guardian*, 7/11/94, p. B13.

Freedom Forum (2000a) 'Zimbabwean court ruling clearing journalists a victory for "concept of justice and true democracy"' Freedom Forum Online, 26/5/00, at [http://www. freedomforum.org/news].

Freedom Forum (2000b) *Press, Power and Politics: Asia*, Freedom Forum, 16–17 November, at [http://www.freedonforum.org].

Friedland, L., Rosen, J. and Austin, L. (1994) 'Civic Journalism: A New Approach To Citizenship', Waltham, MA: Civic Practices Network, at [http://www.cpn.org/topics/communication/civicjourn_new.html] accessed 23/04/03.

Friedland, L.A. (1992) *Covering the World: International Television News Services*, New York: Twentieth Century Fund Press.

Fulton, K. (1996) 'A tour of our uncertain future', *Columbia Journalism Review*, March/April, pp. 19–26.

Galtung, J. and Ruge, M. (1973) 'Structuring and selecting news', in Cohen, S. and Young, J. (eds) *The Manufacture of News: Deviance, Social Problems and the Mass Media*, London: Constable, pp. 62–72.

Galtung, J. and Vincent, R.C. (1992) *Global Glasnost: Toward a New World Information and Communication Order?*, Cresskill, NJ: Hampton.

Gans, H.J. (1979) *Deciding what's news*, London: Constable.

Garnham, N. (1986) 'The media and the public sphere', in Golding, P., Murdock, G. and Schlesinger, P. (eds) *Communicating Politics: Mass Communications and the Political Process*, Leicester: Leicester University Press, pp. 37–53.

Gartner, M. (1997) 'Public journalism – seeing through the gimmicks', *Media Studies Journal*, Winter, at [http://www.mediastudies.org/cov96/gartner.html] accessed 24/06/98.

Gauthier, G. (1993) 'In defence of a supposedly outdated notion: the range of application of journalistic objectivity', *Canadian Journal of Communication*, 18(4), at [http://hoshi.cic.sfu.ca/calj/cjc/Backissues/18.4/gauthier.html] accessed 2/07/98.

Gilbert, P. (1992) 'The oxygen of publicity: terrorism and reporting restrictions', in Belsey, A. and Chadwick, R. (eds) *Ethical Issues in Journalism and the Media*, London: Routledge, pp. 137–53

Gitlin, T. (1991) 'Bites and blips: chunk news, savvy talk and the bifurcation of American politics', in Dahlgren, P. and Sparks, C. (eds) *Communication and Citizenship: Journalism and the Public Sphere*, London: Routledge, pp. 119–36.

Glaser, J. (1998) 'Coming distractions: ABC News Goes to the movies', *Columbia Journalism Review*, September/October, at [http://www.cjr.org] accessed 25/02/02.

Glasgow University Media Group (1976) *Bad News*, London: Routledge.

Glasgow University Media Group (1980) *More Bad News*, London: Routledge.

Glasgow University Media Group (1982) *Really Bad News*, London: Writers and Readers.

Glasgow University Media Group (1985) *War and Peace News*, Milton Keynes: Open University Press.

Glasser, T.L. (1992) 'Objectivity and news bias', in Cohen, E.D. (ed.) *Philosophical Issues in Journalism*, Oxford: Oxford University Press, pp. 176–83.

Glassner, B. (1999) *The Culture of Fear*, New York: Basic Books.

Golding, P. and Elliot, P. (1979) *Making the News*, London: Longman.

Golding, P. and Elliot, P. (1999) 'Making the news', in Tumber, H. (ed.) *News: A Reader*, Oxford: Oxford University Press, pp. 112–20.

Goldlust, J. (1987) *Playing for Keeps: Sport, the Media and Society*, Melbourne: Longman.

Grant, W. (1995) *Pressure Groups, Politics and Democracy 1995 in Britain*, 2nd edition, London: Phillip Allan.

Greenslade, R. (1995) 'Turning on the heat', *Guardian*, 14/8/95, p. 15.

Greenslade, R. (1999) 'Niche work if you can get it', *Guardian*, 22/03/99, p. 10.

Greenslade, R. (2000) 'Do you want to go large?, *Guardian*, 22/05/00, Media, p. 6.

Greenslade, R. (2002) 'A storm in a chequebook', *Guardian*, 11/3/02, at [http://www.mediaguardian.co.uk].

Grindstaff, L. (1997) 'Producing trash, class, and the money shot: A behind-the-scenes account of daytime TV talk shows', in Lull, J. and Hinerman, S. (eds) *Media Scandals*, Cambridge: Polity Press, pp. 164–202.

Golding, P. and Elliot, P. (1996) 'News values and news production', in Marris, P. and Thornham, S. (eds) *Media Studies: A Reader*, 1st edition, Edinburgh: Edinburgh University Press, pp. 405–11.

Gripsrud, J. (2000) 'Tabloidization, popular journalism, and democracy', in Sparks, C. and Tulloch, J. (eds) *Tabloid Tales: Global Debates Over Media Standards*, Oxford: Rowman and Littlefield, pp. 285–300.

Gulyás, Á. (2000) 'The development of the tabloid press in Hungary', in Sparks, C. and Tulloch, J. (eds) *Tabloid Tales: Global Debates Over Media Standards*, Oxford: Rowman and Littlefield, pp. 111–27.

Gunaratne, S.A. (1998) 'Old wine in a new bottle: public journalism, development journalism, and social responsibility', in Roloff, M.E. (ed.) *Communication Yearbook 21*, Beverly Hills, CA: Sage, pp. 277–321.

Gunter, B., Kinderlerer, J. and Beyleveld, D. (1999) 'The media and public under-standing of biotechnology', *Scientific Communication*, 20(4): 373–94.

Gurevitch, M. (1996) 'The globalization of electronic journalism', in Curran, J. and Gurevitch, M. (eds) *Mass Media and Society*, 2nd Edition, London: Arnold, pp. 204–24.

Habermas, J. (1989) *The Structural Transformation of the Public Sphere*, Cambridge: Polity Press.

Habermas, J. (1996) 'The public sphere', in Marris, P. and Thornham, S. (eds) *Media Studies: A Reader*, 1st Edition, Edinburgh: Edinburgh University Press, pp. 55–9.

Hachten, W.A. (1992) *The World News Prism: Changing Media of International Communication*, 3rd edition, Ames: Iowa State University Press.

Hachten, W.A. (1998) *The Troubles of Journalism: A Critical Look at What's Right and Wrong With the Press*, Mawah, NJ: Lawrence Erlbaum Associates.

Hall, J. (2001) *Online Journalism*, London: Pluto.

Hall, J. (2002) 'Mobile reporting: peer-to-peer news', *The Feature* 20/02/02, at [http://www. thefeature.com] accessed 17/03/03.

Hall, S. (1973) 'The determination of news photographs', in Cohen, S. and Young, J. (eds) *The Manufacture of News: Deviance, Social Problems and the Mass Media*, London: Constable, pp. 176–90.

Hall, S., Critcher, C., Jefferson, T., Clarke, J. and Roberts, B. (1978) *Policing the Crisis: Mugging, the State, and Law and Order*, London: Macmillan.

Hallin, D.C. (2000) '*La Nota Roja*: popular journalism and the transition to dem-ocracy in Mexico', in Sparks, C. and Tulloch, J. (eds) *Tabloid Tales: Global Debates over Media Standards*, Oxford: Rowman and Littlefield, pp. 267–84.

Hamilton, W. (2000) 'The warmth of the herd', in Williams and Rich (eds) *Losing Control: Freedom of the Press in Asia*, Canberra: Asia Pacific Press, pp. 93–114.

Hannerz, U. (1996) *Transnational Connections: Culture, People, Places*, London: Routledge.

Hansen, A. (1994) 'Journalistic practices and science reporting in the British press', *Public Understanding of Science*, 3(2): 111–34.

Harrington, W. (1997) *Intimate Journalism: The Art and Craft of Reporting Everyday Life*, New York: Sage.

Harris, N.G.E. (1992) 'Codes of conduct for journalists', in Belsey, A. and Chadwick, R. (eds) *Ethical Issues in Journalism and the Media*, London: Routledge, pp. 62–76.

Harris, R. (1991) *Good and Faithful Servant*, London: Faber.

Hartley, J. (2000) 'The domain of journalism studies around the globe', *Journalism*, 1(1): 55–9.

Hartley-Brewer, J. (2000) 'High stakes in battle over Serbian guilt', *Guardian*, 15/3/00, p. 8.

Hayashi, K. (2000) 'The "Home and Family" section in the Japanese newspaper', in Sparks, C. and Tulloch, J. (eds) date *Tabloid Tales: Global Debates over Media Standards*, Oxford: Rowman and Littlefield, pp. 147–62.

Haynes, R (1995) *The Football Imagination: The Rise of Football Fanzine Culture*, Aldershot: Arena.

Haynes, R .(1999) 'There's many a slip 'twixt the eye and the lip': an exploratory history of football broadcasts and running commentaries on BBC radio, 1927–1939', *International Review for the Sociology of Sport*, 34(2): 143–56.

Heibert, R. (1999) 'Transition from the end of the old regime to 1996', in Aumente, J., Gross, P., Hiebert, R., Johnson, O.V. and Mills, D. *Eastern European Journalism*, Cresskill, NJ: Hampton Press, pp. 79–122.

Heinderyckx, (1993) 'Television-news programmes in Western Europe – a comparative study', *European Journal of Communication*, 8(4): 425–50.

Helmore, E. (1998) 'Woodward and Bernstein it ain't', *Guardian*, 22/6/98, G2: 4–5.

Henningham, J. (1996) 'Australian journalists' professional and ethical values', *Journalism and Mass Communication Quarterly*, 73(1): 206–18.

Herbert, J. (2000) *Journalism in the Digital Age: Theory and Practice for Broadcast, Print and On-line Media*, Oxford: Focal Press.

Herman, E.S. and Chomsky, N. (1988) *Manufacturing Consent: The Political Economy of the Mass Media*, London: Vintage.

Herman, E.S. and Chomsky, N. (1999) 'Manufacturing consent' in Tumber, H. (ed.) (1999) *News: A Reader*, Oxford: Oxford University Press, pp. 166–79.

Hermes, J. (1995) *Reading Women's Magazines*, Cambridge: Polity Press.

Hersey, J. (1985) *Hiroshima*, London: Penguin.

Hesmondhalgh, D. (2000) 'Alternative media, alternative texts? rethinking democratisation in the cultural industries', in Curran, J. (ed.) *Media Organisations in Society*, London: Arnold, pp. 107–25.

Hester, A. (1991) 'The collection and flow of world news', in Merrill, J.C. (ed.) *Global Journalism: Survey of International Communication*, 2nd edition, London: Longman, pp. 29–50.

Hetherington, A. (1985) *News, Newspapers and Television*, London: Macmillan.

Hilsum, L. (1997) 'Crossing the line to commitment', *British Journalism Review*, 8(1): 29–33.

Hirose, H. (1990) 'The development of discussions on journalism in postwar Japan', *Media, Culture and Society*, 12(4): 465–76.

Hogshire, J. (1997) *Grossed-Out Surgeon Vomits Inside Patient! An Insider's Look at Supermarket Tabloids*, Venice, CA: Feral House.

Holborow, J. (2000) 'Where is Thy victory?', *UK Press Gazette*, 11/8/00, p. 11.

Holt, R. (2000) 'The discourse ethics of sports print journalism', *Culture, Sport, Society*, 3(3): 88–103.

Honigsbaum, M. (1998) 'A case of trial and error?', *Guardian*, 9/3/98, G2: 2–3.

Hong Kong Standard (1998) 'Lai in front-page apology for Apple's juicy widower stories', 11/11/98, p. 1.

Hood, M. (1998) 'True crime doesn't pay: a conversation with Jack Olsen', *Point No Point*, Winter 1998/99, at [http://www.jackolsen.com/point.htm] accessed 11/07/00.

Hornby, N. (1995) *Fever Pitch: A Fan's Life*, London: Gollancz.

Howarth, P. (1998) 'From the Editor', *Esquire*, April 1998, p. 16.

271

Hoyt, M. (1995) 'Are you now, or will you ever be, a civic journalist?', *Columbia Journalism Review*, September/October, at [http://www.cjr.org] accessed 11/05/98.

Hoyt, M. (1996) 'Can James Fallows practice what he preaches?', *Columbia Journalism Review*, November/December, at [http://www.cjr.org] accessed 11/05/98.

Hume, E. (1996) 'Something's rotten', *Columbia Journalism Review*, March/April, at [http://www.cjr.org].

Humphreys, P.J. (1994) *Media and Media Policy in Germany: The Press and Broadcasting Since 1945*, 2nd edition, Oxford: Berg.

Humphreys, P.J. (1996) *Mass Media and Media Policy in Western Europe*, Manchester: Manchester University Press.

Illouz, E. (1991) 'Reason without passion: love in women's magazines', *Critical Studies In Mass Communication*, 8(3): 231–48.

Ingham, B. (1991) *Kill The Messenger*, London: Fontana.

Irish Law Reform Commission (1991) *Consultation Paper on the Crime of Libel*, available at [http://www.lawreform.ie/publications/data/volume10/lrc_65.html].

Iyengar, S. (1997) 'Framing responsibility for political issues: the case of poverty' in Iyenger, S. and Reeves, R. (eds) *Do the Media Govern?* Politiciaus, Voters and Reporters in America, London: Sage, pp. 276–82.

Jakobson, L. (1990) 'Lies in ink, truth in blood: the role and impact of the Chinese media during the Beijing Spring of '89', Harvard University, August 1990, at [http://www.nmis.org/gate/links/liesink.html] accessed 28/10/98.

Jakubowicz, K. (1992) 'From party propaganda to corporate speech? Polish journalism in search of a new identity', *Journal Of Communication*, 42(3): 64–73.

Jamieson-Hall, K. (1996) *Packaging The Presidency*, 3rd Edition, Oxford: Oxford University Press.

Jasperson, A.E., Shah, D.V., Watts, M., Faber, R.J. and Fan, D.P. (1998) 'Framing and the public agenda: media effects on the importance of the federal budget deficit', *Political Communication*, 15(2): 205–24.

Johnson, O.V. (1999) 'The roots of journalism' in Aumente *et al.*, *Eastern European Journalism*, Cresskill, NJ: Hampton Press, pp. 5–40.

Johnson, S. (1993) 'Magazines: women's employment and status in the magazine industry', in Creedon, P.J. (ed.) *Women in Mass Communication*, 2nd Edition, London: Sage, pp. 134–153.

Johnson, J.T. (2000) 'Wind of change', *Guardian*, 3/7/00, pp. B58–9.

Jones, B. (1992) 'Broadcasters, politicians and the political interview', in Jones, B. and Robins, L. (eds) *Two Decades in British Politics*, Manchester: Manchester University Press, pp. 53–78.

Jones, N. (1986) *Strikes and the Media*, Oxford: Blackwell.

Jones, N. (1996) *Soundbites and Spindoctors*, London: Indigo.

Jones, N. (1997) *Campaign 1997*, London: Indigo.

Kant, I. (1991) *Political Writings*, trans. Hans Reiss, Cambridge: Cambridge University Press.

Kaplan, A. (2000) 'Murder, off the record', *Brill's Content*, August 2000 at [http://www.brillscontent.com] accessed 30/08/00.

Katz, I. (1995) 'In mourning for the mastheads', *Guardian*, 24/7/95, p. B15.

Kees, B. (ed.) (1996) *Privacy and News Sources*, Oakland: Freedom Forum Pacific Coast Centre [http://www.freedomforum.org/FreedomForum/oakland/privacy1.html].

Kepplinger, H.M. (1982) 'Visual biases in television campaign coverage', *Communication Research*, 9(3): 432–46.

Kerbel, M.R. (2000) *If it Bleeds, it Leads: An Anatomy of Television News*, Boulder: Westview Press.

Kerrane, K. (1997) 'Making Facts Dance', in Kerrane, K. and Yagoda, B. (eds) *The Art of Fact: A Historical Anthology of Literary Journalism*, New York: Touchstone, pp. 17–20.

Kerrane, K. and Yagoda, B. (eds) (1997) *The Art of Fact: A Historical Anthology of Literary Journalism*, New York: Touchstone.

Kieran, M. (ed.) (1998) *Media Ethics*, London: Routledge.

Kimball, P. (1999) 'Downsizing the news: network cutbacks in the nation's capital', in Tumber, H. (ed.) (1999) *News: A Reader*, Oxford: Oxford University Press, pp. 209–12.

Kirkborn, M.J. (1990) 'The virtuous journalist', *British Journalism Review*, 1(4): 6–24.

Klaidman, S. and Beauchamp, T.L. (1992) 'The virtuous journalist: morality in journalism', in Cohen, E.D. (ed.) *Philosophical Issues in Journalism*, Oxford: Oxford University Press, pp. 39–49.

Knightly, P. (1999) 'Media on the ethics rack', *The Times*, 30/7/99, S2: 44.

Knightly, P. (2000) 'A journalist in the back pocket', *The Times*, 31/3/00, S2: 19.

Kobre, K. (1991) *Photojournalism: The Professional's Approach*, Boston: Focal Press.

Köcher, R. (1986) 'Bloodhounds or missionaries: role definitions of German and British journalists', *European Journal of Communication*, 1(1): 43–64.

Kosicki, G.M. (1993) 'Problems and opportunities in agenda-setting research', *Journal of Communication*, 43(2): 100–27.

Koss, S. (1981) *The Rise and Fall of the Political Press in Britain Vol 1*, London: Hamish Hamilton.

Koss, S. (1984) *The Rise and Fall of the Political Press in Britain Vol 2*, London: Hamish Hamilton.

Kramer, M. (1995) 'Breakable rules for literary journalists', in Sims, N. and Kramer, M. (eds) *Literary Journalism*, New York: Ballantine, pp. 21–34.

Küng-Shankleman, L. (2000) *Inside the BBC and CNN: Managing Media Organisations*, London: Routledge.

Kurtz, H. (1998) *Spin Cycle: Inside the Clinton Propaganda Machine*, New York: Free Press.

Laitila, T. (1995) 'Journalistic codes of ethics in Europe', *European Journal of Communication*, 10(4): 527–44.

Langton, J. (1998) 'Hollywood wins fight to tame paparazzi', *Electronic Telegraph*, 18/10/98.

Lanson, G. and Mitchell, S. (1994) *Writing and Reporting The News*, Fort Worth: Holt, Rinehart and Winston Inc.

Lewis, B. (1996) 'Self-censorship by French scribblers', *British Journalism Review*, 7(3): 36–41.

Lewis, B. (1997) 'India grapples with the Murdoch phenomenon', *British Journalism Review*, 8(3): 40–45.

Li, X. (1996) '"Asian values" and the universality of human rights', China Rights Forum, Fall 1996, at [http://www.igc.org/hric/crf/English/96fall/e11.html].

Lichtenberg, J. (1991) 'In defence of objectivity', in Curran, J. and Gurevitch, M. (eds) *Mass Media and Society*, London: Edward Arnold, pp. 216–31.

Liddle, R. (2001) 'Invasion of Privacy? Or Just Hiding the Truth?', *Observer*, 23/12/01, at [http://www.observer.co.uk].

Lippman, W. (1992) 'Stereotypes, Public Opinion, and the Press', in Cohen, E.D. (ed.) *Philosophical Issues in Journalism*, Oxford: Oxford University Press, pp. 161–75.

Livingstone, S. and Lunt, P. (1994) *Talk on Television*, London: Routledge.

Lockyer, S. (2001) 'An eye to offensiveness: the discourse of offence and censure in Private Eye', Unpublished PhD thesis, Loughborough University.

Luciani, D. (1997) 'Sweating the details', *Ryerson Review of Journalism Online*, 15/12/97, at [http://www.ryerson.ca/~rrj/archives/features/LockerRoom.html] accessed 21/06/00.

Lull, J. and Hinerman, S. (eds) (1997) *Media Scandals*, Cambridge: Polity Press.

MacArthur, B. (2000) 'An appetite for catastrophe', *The Times*, 28/6/00, S2: 22–3.

MacArthur, B. (2001a) 'Even old pros get unlucky', *The Times*, 13/4/01, S2: 22.

MacArthur, B. (2001b) 'The biggest story', *The Times*, 14/11/01, S2: 20–1.

Macdonald, M. (2000) 'Rethinking personalization in current affairs journalism', in Sparks, C. and Tulloch, J. (eds) *Tabloid Tales: Global Debates Over Media Standards*, Oxford: Rowman and Littlefield, pp. 251–66.

MacGregor, B. (1997) *Live, Direct and Biased? Making Television News in the Satellite Age*. London: Arnold.

Maltese, J.A. (1994) *Spin Control: The White House Office of Communications and the management of Presidential News*, 2nd Edition, North Carolina: University of North Carolina Press.

Marquez, G.G. (1996) *News of a Kidnapping*, London: Penguin.

Martin, W.J. (1995) *The Global Information Society*, Aldershot: ASLIB Gower.

Masters, B. (1985) *Killing for Company*, London: Jonathan Cape.

de Mause, N. (1999) 'Throwing the game: conflicts of interest prevent tough coverage of sports issues', *Extra!*, Nov/Dec, at [http://www.fair.org/extra/].

Mayes, T. (1997) 'Paparazzi snap back', *Living Marxism*, November, No. 103: 22–3.

McCann, P. (2000) 'Celebrity sell-out', *The Times*, 1/9/00, S2: 3–4.

McChesney, R. and Scott, B. (2002) 'Upton Sinclair and the contradictions of capitalist journalism', *Monthly Review*, May, available at [http://www.findarticles. com] accessed 23/04/03.

McCombs, M.E. and Shaw, D.L. (1972) 'The agenda-setting function of mass media', *Public Opinion Quarterly*, 36(2): 176–87.

McCombs, M.E. and Shaw, D.L. (1993) 'The evolution of agenda-setting research: twenty-five years in the marketplace of ideas', *Journal of Communication*, 43(2): 58–67.

McCord, R. (1996) *The Chain Gang: One Newspaper versus the Gannett Empire*, Columbia, Missouri: University of Missouri Press.

McLachlan, S. and Golding, P. (2000) 'Tabloidization in the British Press: a quantitative investigation into changes in British newspapers, 1952–1997', in Sparks, C. and Tulloch, J. (eds) *Tabloid Tales: Global Debates Over Media Standards*, Oxford: Rowman and Littlefield, pp. 75–89.

McLaughlin, G. (2002) *The War Correspondent*, London: Pluto.

McLaughlin, L. (1993) 'Feminism, the public sphere, media and democracy', *Media, Culture and Society*, 15(4): 599–620.

McManus, J.H. (1994) *Market-Driven Journalism: Let the Citizen Beware?*, London: Sage.

McNair, B. (1994) *News and Journalism in the UK: A Textbook*, London: Routledge.

McNair, B. (1995) *An Introduction to Political Communication*, London: Routledge.

McNair, B. (1996) 'Performance in politics and the politics of performance: public relations, the public sphere and democracy', in L'Etang, J. and Pieczka, M. (eds) *Critical Perspectives In Public Relations*, London: International Thomson Business Press, pp. 35–53.

McNair, B. (1998a) *The Sociology of Journalism*, London: Arnold.

McNair, B. (1998b) 'Journalism, politics and public relations: an ethical appraisal', in Kieran, M. (ed.) *Media Ethics*, London: Routledge, pp. 49–65.

McNair, B. (2000) *Journalism and Democracy*, London: Routledge.

McNair, B., Hibberd, M. and Schlesinger, P. (2002) 'Public access broadcasting and democratic participation in the age of mediated politics', *Journalism Studies*, 3(3): 407–22.

McNeill, M. (1998) 'Sports journalism, ethics, and Olympic athletes' Rights', in Wenner, L.A. (ed.) *MediaSport*, London: Routledge, pp. 100–15.

McQuail, D. (1992) *Media Performance*, London: Sage.

McQuail, D.(2000) *McQuail's Mass Communication Theory*, 4th edition, London: Sage.

McRobbie, A. (1991) *Feminism and Youth Culture: From Jackie To Just Seventeen*, Basingstoke: Macmillan.

Media Week (1998) 'ABCs', *Media Week*, 20/2/98, pp. 29–34.

Media Perspektiven (1999) 'Basisdaten'.

Meech, P. and Kilborn, R. (1992). 'Media and identity in a stateless nation – the case of Scotland', *Media, Culture and Society*, 14(2): 245.

Mendes, E.P. (2001) 'Asian values and human rights: letting the tigers free', Human Rights and Education Centre, University of Ottowa, at [http://www.cdphrc.ottowa.ca/publicat/asian_values.html].

Merril, J.C. (ed.) (1991) *Global Journalism: Survey of International Communication*, 2nd edition, London: Longman.

277

Meyssan, T. (2002) *L'Effroyable Imposture*, Chaton: Editions Carnot.

Midgley, C. (1998) 'Loaded and FHM are not for me. They are for kids', *The Times*, 18/12/98, p. 41.

Midgley, C. (1999) 'How Brown self-destructed', *The Times*, 19/2/99, p. 39.

Miller, D. (1994) *Don't Mention the War*, London: Pluto.

Miller, D. (1999) 'Risk, science and policy: definitional struggles, information management, the media and BSE', *Social Science and Medicine*, 49: 1239–55.

Miller, D. and Dinan, W. (2000) 'The rise of the PR industry in Britain, 1979–98', *European Journal of Communication*, 15(1): 5–35.

Miller, D. and Williams, K. (1993) 'Negotiating HIV/AIDS information: agendas, media strategies and the news', in Eldridge, J. (ed.) *Getting the Message: News, Truth and Power*, London: Routledge, pp. 126–42.

Milmo, C. (2003) 'Reporting for duty', *The Independent*, 18/03/03, pp. B8–9.

Mindich, D.T.Z. (1998) *Just the Facts: How 'Objectivity' Came to Define American Journalism*, New York: New York University Press.

Mitford, J. (1963) *The American Way of Death*, London: Hutchinson.

Moncrieff, M. (2002) 'No names ... unless the court decides otherwise', *The Guardian*, 8/4/02, at [http://www.guardian.co.uk].

Moore, M. (2001) *Stupid White Men*, London: HarperCollins.

Morgan, J. (2000) 'Wade's NoW riposte fails to silence Moore and Kelner', *UK Press Gazette*, 18/8/00, p. 2.

Morley, D. (1992) *Television, Audiences and Cultural Studies*, London: Routledge.

Morris, E. (1999) *Dutch: A Memoir of Ronald Reagan*, New York: HarperCollins.

Morrison, D.E. and Tumber, H. (1994) 'Information, knowledge, and journalistic procedure: reporting the war in the Falklands', in Hamelink, C. and Linné, O. (eds) *Mass Communication Research: On Problems and Policies*, Norwood, NJ: Ablex, pp. 211–26.

Murdock, G. (1996) 'Concentration and ownership in an era of privatisation', in Marris, P. and Thornham, S. (eds) *Media Studies: A Reader*, Edinburgh: Edinburgh University Press, pp. 91–101.

Murschetz, P. (1998) 'State support for the daily press in Europe: a critical appraisal', *European Journal of Communication*, 13(3): 291–13.

Naisbett, J. (1982) *Megatrends*, London: Penguin.

Naughton, J. (1999) *A Brief History of the Future*, London: Pheonix.

Negrine, R. (1996) *The Communication of Politics*, London: Sage.

Neil, A. (1996) *Full Disclosure*, London: Macmillan.

Nelson, W.D. (1998) *Who Speaks for the President? The White House Press Secretary from Cleveland to Clinton*, Syracuse, NY: Syracuse University Press.

Nerone, J.C. (ed.) (1995) *Last Rights: Revisiting Four Theories of the Press*, Urbana: University of Illinois Press.

Neumann, A.L. (2000) 'Starting the presses in Cambodia', *CPJ Briefings: Press Freedom Reports*, at [http://www.cpj.org] accessed 25/08/00.

Newspaper Society (2001) 'Top 20 regional press publishers – 1 January 2001', 01/07/01, at [http://www.newspapersoc.org/facts-figures/top20_table.html], accessed 20/07/01.

Nixon, S. (1993) 'Looking for the Holy Grail: publishing and advertising strategies and contemporary men's magazines', *Textual Studies*, 7(3): 466–92.

Nixon, S. (1996) *Hard Looks: Masculinity, Spectatorship and Contemporary Consumption*, London: UCL Press.

Oborne, P. (1999) *Alastair Campbell: New Labour and the Rise of the Media Class*, London: Aurum.

O'Kane, M. (1995) 'Bloodless words, bloody war', *Guardian*, 16/12/95, pp. B12–18.

O'Neill, J. (1992) 'Journalism in the market place', in Belsey, A. and Chadwick, R. (eds) *Ethical Issues in Journalism and the Media*, London: Routledge, pp. 15–32.

O'Rorke, I. (1997) 'Well red', *Guardian*, 3/11/97, pp. B4–5.

O'Rorke, I. (2000) 'Brown in motion', *Guardian*, Media Section, pp. 2–3.

Orwell, G. (1933) *Down and Out in Paris and London*, London: Penguin.

Orwell, G. (1948) *1984*, London: Penguin.

O'Sullivan, S. (1999) 'Change is good for your figures', *Independent*, 16/2/99, p. 12.

Othitis, C. (1998) 'The literary journalists', at [http://www.geocities.com/Athens/Acropolis/3203/litjourn.htm] accessed 14/01/00.

Owen, J. (1999) 'Rory Peck videography winner laments Sierra Leone footage not shown', *Freedom Forum Online*, 20/10/99, at [http://www.freedomforum.org] accessed 30/8/00.

Paige, S. (1998) 'Talking the talk', *Insight on the News*, 9/02/98, at [http://www.findarticles.com] accessed 22/04/03.

Paletz, D. (1990) *Terrorism and the Media*, London: Sage.

Palmer, J. (1997) 'News values', in Briggs, A. and Cobley, P. (eds) *The Media: An Introduction*, London: Longman, pp. 377–91.

Papathanassopoulous, S. (2001) 'The decline of newspapers: the case of the Greek press', *Journalism Studies*, 2(1): 109–23.

Parent, W.A. (1992) 'Privacy, morality and the law', in Cohen, E.D. (ed.) *Philosophical Issues in Journalism*, Oxford: Oxford University Press, pp. 92–109.

Parker, J. (2000) 'The CBS-Viacom Merger: Impact on Journalism', *Federal Communications Law Journal*, 52(3): 519–30.

Pateman, C. (1989) *The Disorder of Women*, Chicago: Polity.

Patterson, T.E. and Donsbach, W. (1996) 'News decisions: journalists as partisan actors', *Political Communication*, 13(4): 455–68.

Pavlik, J.V. (1997) 'The future of online journalism', *Columbia Journalism Review*, July/August, at [http://www.cjr.org].

Pavlik, J.V. (2000) 'The impact of technology on journalism', *Journalism Studies*, 1(2): 229–37.

Pavlik, J.V. (2001) *Journalism and New Media*, New York: Columbia University Press.

PCC (Press Complaints Commission) (1998) 'Monthly Report', No.43, September, at [http://www.pcc.org.uk] accessed 16/05/03.

PCC (2003) 'Witness payments – Important changes to editors' code announced', Press Releases, 19/03/03, at [http://www.pcc.org.uk] accessed 16/05/03.

Peer, L. (2000) 'Women, talk radio, and the public sphere(s)', in Sreberny, A. and van Zoonen, L. (eds) *Gender, Politics and Communication*, Cresskill, NJ: Hampton Press, pp. 299–327.

PEJ (Project for Excellence in Journalism) (2001) 'Gambling with the future', *Columbia Journalism Review*, Nov/Dec, supplement.

Pellechia, M.G. (1997) 'Trends in science coverage: a content analysis of three US newspapers', *Public Understanding of Science*, 6(1): 49–68.

Penman, J. (1997) 'Blair to rethink role of media managers', *The Scotsman*, 29/10/97.

Peters, H.P. (1995) 'The interaction of journalists and scientific experts: co-operation and conflict between two professional cultures', *Media, Culture and Society*, 17(1): 31–48.

Peters, J.D. (1993) 'Distrust of representation: Habermas on the public sphere', *Media, Culture and Society*, 15(4): 541–71.

Pew Research Centre (2000) 'Internet sapping broadcast news audience', April/May, at [http://www.people-press.org] accessed 10/05/01.

Philo, G. (1993) 'From Buerk to Band Aid: the media and the 1984 Ethiopian famine', in Eldridge, J. (ed.) *Getting the Message: News, Truth and Power*, London: Routledge, pp. 104–25.

Picard, R.G. (1999) 'Global communications controversies', in Tumber, H. (ed.) *News: A Reader*, Oxford: Oxford University Press, pp. 355–64.

Pimlott, H.F. (2000) 'Mainstreaming the margins: the transformation of *Marxism Today*', in Curran, J. (ed.) *Media Organisations in Society*, London: Arnold, pp: 193–211.

Pink, S. (2000) 'New law claims Australian radio icon', *The Times*, 1/9/00, S2: 26.

Poole, T. (1996) 'China puts the blinkers on news', *Independent*, 17/1/96: 11.

Popkin, J.D. (1989) 'Journals: the new face of news', in Darnton, R. and Roche, D. (eds) *Revolution in Print: The Press in France 1775–1800*, Berkeley, CA: University of California Press, pp. 141–64.

Price, M.E. (1995) *Television, the Public Sphere and National Identity*, Oxford: Oxford University Press.

Pronay, N. and Wenham, P.D. (1976) *History through the Newsreel*, London: Macmillan.

Putnam, R. (1993). 'The prosperous community: social capital and public life', *The American Prospect*, 4(13): 35–42, also available at [http://www.prospect.org/print/V4/13/putnam-r.html].

Randall, V. (1993) 'The media and democratisation in the Third World', *Third World Quarterly*, 14(3): 625–46.

Rapping, E. (2000) 'U.S. talk shows, feminism, and the discourse of addiction', in Sreberny, A. and van Zoonen, L. (eds) *Gender, Politics and Communication*, Cresskill, NJ: Hampton Press, pp. 223–50.

Read, K.T. (1981) *Truman Capote*, Boston, MA: Twayne Publishers.

Reagan, B. (2000) 'Details, details', *American Journalism Review*, Jan/Feb, at [http://www.ajr.org] accessed 01/06/00.

Reese, S.D. (1997) 'The news paradigm and the ideology of objectivity: a socialist at the *Wall Street Journal*', in Berkowitz, D. (ed.) *Social Meanings of News*, London: Sage, pp. 420–40.

Regier, C.C. (1932) *The Era of the Muckrakers*, Chapel Hill: University of North Carolina Press.

Rehm, D. (1996) 'A tower of babel: talk shows and politics', *Press/Politics*, 1(1): 138–42.

Reinarman, C. and Duskin, C. (1992) 'Dominant ideology and drugs in the media', *International Journal on Drug Policy*, 3(1): 6–15.

Reith, J. (1924) *Broadcast over Britain*, London: Hodder & Stoughton.

Reporters Committee for Freedom of the Press (RCPF) (2001) 'New Jersey appellate court refuses appeal seeking reporter's notes', *The News Media and the Law*, 25(1): 22.

Reporters sans Frontières (RSF) (2002) 'Press freedom situation in france: the french national press federation and RSF appeal to the candidates for the presidency', Press Release, 18/4/02, at [http://www.ifex.org].

Richstad, J. and Anderson, M.H. (eds) (1981) *Crisis in International News: Policies and Prospects*, New York: Columbia University Press.

Robertson, G. and Nicol, A. (1992) *Media Law*, London: Penguin.

Rooney, D. (2000) 'Thirty years of competition in the British tabloid press: the *Mirror and the Sun* 1968–1998', in Sparks, C. and Tulloch, J. (eds) *Tabloid Tales: Global Debates over Media Standards*, Oxford: Rowman and Littlefield, pp. 91–110.

Rosen, J. (1999) *What Are Journalists for?*, New Haven: Yale University Press.

Rosenberg, G. (2000) 'A newsroom lawyer's life: passion and prevention', *Columbia Journalism Review*, September/October, at [http://www.cjr.org] accessed 9/01/01.

Rosman, K. (2000) 'JonBenét, Inc.', *Brill's Content, February*, at [http://www.brillscontent.com] accessed 15/06/00.

Rowe, D. (1991) ' "That misery of stringer's clichés": Sports Writing', *Cultural Studies*, 5(1): 77–90.

Rowe, D. (1992) 'Modes of sports writing', in Dahlgren, P. and Sparks, C. (eds)

Journalism and Popular Culture, London: Sage, pp. 96–112.

Rowe, D., McKay, J. and Miller, T. (1998) 'Come together: sport, nationalism, and the media image', in Wenner, L.A. (ed.) *MediaSport*, London: Routledge, pp. 119–33.

Rule, A. (1987) *Small Sacrifices: A True Story of Passion and Murder*, New York: Signet.

Rumbelow, H. (2001) 'Death is my beat', *The Times*, 15/06/01, S2: 24.

Sampson, A. (1996) 'The crisis at the heart of our media', *British Journalism Review*, 7(3): 42–56.

Santistevan, J. (2000) 'Does Peruvian free press exist or not?', Freedom Forum Online, 8/3/00, at [http://www.freedomforum.org/news].

Saunders, J. (2002) 'CanWest campaign against CBC condemned', *The Globe and Mail*, 21/02/02, p. 8.

Scelfo, J. (1999) 'In their backyard', *Brill's Content, July/August*, at [http://www.brillscontent.com] accessed 15/06/00.

Schechter, D. (2000) 'CNN at 20: from chicken noodle network to global media power', 8/06/00, at [http://www.mediachannel.org] accessed 14/06/00.

Schiller, D. (1986) 'Transformation of news in the US information market', in Golding, P., Murdock, G. and Schlesinger, P. (eds) *Communicating Politics*, Leicester: Leicester University Press, pp. 19–36.

Schlesinger, P. (1978) *Putting 'Reality' Together*, London: Methuen.

Schlesinger, P. (1989) 'Rethinking the sociology of journalism', in Ferguson, M. (ed.) *Public Communication*, London: Sage, pp. 61–83.

Schlesinger, P. and Tumber, H. (1994) *Reporting Crime: The Media Politics of Criminal Justice*, Oxford: Clarendon.

Schlesinger, P., Miller, D. and Dinan, W. (2001) *Open Scotland? Journalists, Spin Doctors and Lobbyists*, Edinburgh: Polygon.

Schloss, G. (1998) 'Sex Spree shows lead to TV fines', *South China Morning Post*, 2/12/98, p. 1.

Schoenbach, K., Lauf, E., McLeod, J.M. and Scheufele, D.A. (1999) 'Research note: distinction and integration – sociodemographic determinants of newspaper reading in the USA and Germany, 1974–96', *European Journal of Communication*, 14(2): 225–39.

Schlesinger, P. and Tumber, H. (1999) 'Reporting crime: the media politics of criminal justice', in Tumber, H. (ed.) *News: A Reader*. London: Routledge, pp. 257–66.

Schönbach, K. (2000) 'Does tabloidization make German local newspapers successful?', in Sparks, C. and Tulloch, J. (eds) *Tabloid Tales: Global Debates over Media Standards*, Oxford: Rowman and Littlefield, pp. 63–74.

Schudson, M. (1999) 'Discovering the news: a social History of American newspapers', in Tumber, H. (ed.) *News: A Reader*, Oxford: Oxford University Press, pp. 291–96.

Seow, F.T. (1998) *The Media Enthralled: Singapore Revisited*, Boulder: Lynne Rienner.

Serafini, D. (1998) 'Robert Irineu Marinho on the future of Brazil's Globo TV', *Video Age International*, January, at [http://www.videoageinternational.com/jan98.marinho.html] accessed 12/07/98.

Seymour-Ure, C. (1991) *The British Press and Broadcasting since 1945*, Oxford: Blackwell.

Seymour-Ure, C. (1995) *The British Press and Broadcasting since 1945*, 2nd Edition, Oxford: Blackwell.

Sherwin, A. (2001) 'The high cost of war reporting', *The Times*, 19/10/01, S2: 19.

Shoemaker, P.J. (1991) *Gatekeeping*, London: Sage.

Shoemaker, P.J. (1996) 'Hardwired for news: using biological and cultural evolution to explain the surveillance function', *Journal of Communication*, 46(3): 32–47.

Shoemaker, P.J. (1997) 'A new gatekeeping model' in Berkowitz, D. (ed.) *Social Meanings of News*, London: Sage, pp. 57–62.

Shoemaker, P.J., Chang, T. and Brendlinger, N. (1987) 'Deviance as a predictor of newsworthiness: coverage of international events in the US media', in McLaughlin, M. (ed.) *Communication Yearbook 10*, Beverly Hills, CA: Sage, pp. 348–65.

Siebert, F.S., Peterson, T. and Schramm, W. (1956) *Four Theories of the Press*, Urbana, IL: University of Illinois Press.

Simpson, J. (1998) *Strange Places, Questionable People*, London: Pan Books.

Sims, N. (1995) 'The Art of Literary Journalism', in Sims, N. and Kramer, M. (eds) *Literary Journalism*, New York: Ballantine, pp. 3–20.

Sims, N. and Kramer, M. (eds) (1995) *Literary Journalism*, New York: Ballantine.

Sinclair, U. (1906) *The Jungle*, Harmondsworth: Penguin.

Sinclair, U. (1928) *The Brass Check*, 9th Edition, Long Beach, CA: Sinclair.

Singer, J.B. (1997) 'Still guarding the gate? The newspaper journalist's role in an on-line world', *Convergence*, 3(1): 72–89.

Sitford, M. and Panter, S. (2000) *Addicted to Murder: The True Story of Dr Harold Shipman*, London: True Crime.

Skogerbø, E. (1997) 'The press subsidy system in norway: controversial past – unpredictable future?', *European Journal of Communication*, 12(1): 99–118.

Snow, J. (2000) 'Journalism, the techno revolution, and the art of disinformation', Hetherington Memorial Lecture, Stirling University, 1/11/00, at [http://www-fms. stir.ac.uk/Hetherington/2000/index.html] accessed 16/05/03.

Soley, L.C. (1992) *The News Shapers: The Sources Who Explain the News*, London: Praeger.

Soley, L.C. (1997) ' "The power of the press has a price" TV reporters talk about advertiser pressure', *Extra!*, July/August, available at [http://www.fair.org/extra] accessed 11/02/02.

Sparks, C. (1992) 'The press, the market, and democracy', *Journal of Communication*, 42(1): 36–51.

Sparks, C. (1996) 'The media and the state', in Marris, P. and Thornham, S. (eds) *Media Studies: A Reader*, Edinburgh: Edinburgh University Press, pp. 84–90.

Sparks, C. (2000) 'Introduction: the panic over tabloid news', in Sparks, C. and Tulloch, J. (eds) *Tabloid Tales: Global Debates over Media Standards*, Oxford: Rowman and Littlefield, pp. 1–40.

Sparks, C. and Tulloch, J. (eds) (2000) *Tabloid Tales: Global Debates Over Media Standards*, Oxford: Rowman and Littlefield.

Splichal, S. and Sparks, C. (1994) *Journalists For The 21st Century*, Norwood, NJ: Ablex.

Sreberny-Mohammadi, A. (1996) 'The global and the local in international communications', in Curran, J. and Gurevitch, M. (eds) *Mass Media and Society*, 2nd Edition, London: Arnold, pp. 177–203.

Staab, J.F. (1990) 'The role of news factors in news selection: a theoretical reconsideration', *European Journal of Communication*, 5(4): 423–43.

Standage, T. (1998) *The Victorian Internet*, London: Phoenix.

Stauber, J. and Rampton, S. (1995) *Toxic Sludge is Good for You*, Monroe, Maine: Common Courage Press.

Steele, J. (1996) 'Television Tsar', *Guardian*, 1/7/96, p. B15.

Sussman, L.R. (1999) *The News of the Century: Press Freedom 1999*, Freedom House, at [http://www.freedomhouse.org/pfs].

Sussman, L.R. and Guida, K. (2001) *Press Freedom Survey 2001*, Freedom House, at [http://www.freedomhouse.org/pfs].

Swain, B.M. (1978) *Reporters' Ethics*, Ames: Iowa State University Press.

Swan, J. (1996) 'I was a "polisher" in a chinese news factory', *Columbia Journalism Review*, March/April.

Tarbell, I. (1966) *The History of The Standard Oil Company*, New York: Macmillan.

Thomas, H. (1999) *Front Row at the White House: My Life and Times*, New York: Touchstone.

Thompson, J.B. (1995) *The Media and Modernity: A Social Theory of the Media*, Cambridge: Polity Press.

Thompson, J.B. (1997) 'Scandal and Social theory', in Lull, J. and Hinerman, S. (eds) *Media Scandals*, Cambridge: Polity Press, pp. 34–64.

Tiffen, R. (1989) *News and Power*, London: Allen and Unwin.

To, Y. (1999) 'Working your sources', *Langara Journalism Review*, at [http://www.langara.bc.ca/ljr/to.html] accessed 25/10/00.

De Tocqueville, A. (1840/1945) *Democracy in America: Vol 2: The Social Influence of Democracy*, trans. Phillips Bradley, New York: Alfred A. Knopf.

Tomlinson, J. (1997) '"And besides, the wench is dead": media scandals and the globalization of communication', in Lull, J. and Hinerman, S. (eds) *Media Scandals*, Cambridge: Polity Press, pp. 65–84.

Tuchman, G. (1999) 'Objectivity as strategic ritual: an examination of newsmen's notions of objectivity' in Tumber, H. (ed.) *News: A Reader*, Oxford: Oxford University Press, pp. 297–307.

Tulloch, J. (1993) 'Policing the public sphere: the british machinery of news management', *Media, Culture and Society*, 15(3): 363–84.

Tumber, H. (1997) 'Bystander journalism, or the journalism of attachment?', *Intermedia*, 25(1): 4–7.

Tumber, H. (ed.) (1999) *News: A Reader*, Oxford: Oxford University Press.

Tunstall, J. and Palmer, M. (1991) *Media Moguls*, London: Routledge.

Tunstall, J. (1996) *Newspaper Power: The New National Press in Britain*, Oxford: Clarendon Press.

Turner, R. (1999) 'Finding the inner swine', *Newsweek*, 1/02/99, pp. 112–13.

Tye, L. (1998) *The Father of Spin: Edward L. Bernays and the Birth of Public Relations*, New York: Crown.

UNESCO (1999) *UNESCO Statistical Yearbook 1999*, at [http://unescostat.unesco.org/statsen/statistics/yearbook/], accessed 01/02/00.

United Nations (1998) *United Nations Human Development Report 1998*, at [http://www.undp.org/hdro/], accessed 01/01/00.

Usborne, D. (2003) 'Christians force Wal-Mart to ban British "lad mags" ', *Independent*, 7/05/03, p. 11.

Verstraeten, H. (1996) 'The media and the transformation of the public sphere', *European Journal Of Communication*, 11(3): 347–70.

Vulliamy, E. (2000) 'Poison in the well of history', *Guardian*, 15/3/00, B: 2–3.

Waisbord, S. (2000) *Watchdog Journalism in South America: News, Accountability, and Democracy*, New York: Columbia University Press.

Wan, C. (1998) 'Chequebook journalism alarm over widower', *South China Morning Post*, 31/10/98, p. 3.

Weaver, D.H. (1998a) 'Journalists around the world: commonalities and differences', in Weaver, D.H. (ed.) *The Global Journalist: News People around the World*, Cresskill, NJ: Hampton Press, pp. 455–80.

Weaver, D.H. (ed.) (1998b) *The Global Journalist: News People Around The World*, Cresskill, NJ: Hampton Press.

Weibull, L. and Börjesson, B. (1992) 'The Swedish Media Accountability System: A Research Perspective', *European Journal of Communication*, 7(1): 121–39.

Weinberg, A. and Weinberg, L. (eds) (1968) *The Muck-Rakers*, New York: Simon and Schuster.

Weinberg, S. (1998) 'Tell it long, take your time, go in depth', *Columbia Journalism Review*, Jan/Feb, at [http://www.cjr.org] accessed 17/01/00.

Westerståhl, J. (1983) 'Objective news reporting: general premises', *Communication Research*, 10(3): 403–24.

White, D.M. (1997) 'The "gatekeeper": a case study in the selection of news', in Berkowitz, D. (ed.) *Social Meanings Of News*, London: Sage, pp. 63–72.

Whittle, B. and Ritchie, J. (2000) *Prescription for Murder: The True Story of Harold Shipman*, London: Time Warner.

Wilkinson, E.J. (1999) 'Consumers, media and marketing: how global trends are affecting newspapers', INMA PANPA Conference, 5/08/99, at [http://www.inma.org] accessed 10/05/01.

Wilkinson, E.J. (2000) 'The state of newspaper circulation', INMA Circulation Summit, 23/03/00, at [http://www.inma.org] accessed 10/05/01.

Willey, D. (2000) 'Italy cracks down on paedophiles', BBC News Online, 25/8/00, at [http://news.bbc.co.uk] accessed 31/08/00.

Williams, K. (1993) 'The light at the end of the tunnel: the mass media, public opinion and the Vietnam War', in Eldridge, J. (ed.) *Getting the Message: News, Truth and Power*, London: Routledge, pp. 305–28.

Williams, L. and Rich, R. (eds) (2000) *Losing Control: Freedom of the Press in Asia*, Canberra: Asia Pacific Press.

Winship, J. (1991) 'The impossibility of *Best*: enterprise meets domesticity in the practical women's magazine of the 1980s', *Cultural Studies*, 5(2): 131–56.

Winston, B. (1995) *Claiming the Real: The Documentary Film Revisited*, London: British Film Institute.

Wolfe, T. and Johnson, E.W. (1973) *The New Journalism*, London: Picador.

Wood, M. (1999) *Legacy*, London: BBC.

Woolner, A. (2000) 'Just doing their jobs', *Brill's Content*, April, at [http://www.brillscontent.com] accessed 19/06/00.

Yelvington, S. (1999) 'The people's journalists', *Press Gazette*, 2/07/99, pp. 16–17.

Yorke, I. (1995) *Television News* 3rd Edition, Oxford: Focal Press.

Zeitlin, A. (2000) 'Draft ethics code for journalists introduced to mixed reviews in Hong Kong', Freedom Forum Online, 03/09/00, at [http://www.freedomforum.org/news] accessed 16/06/00.

Index

NB: Page references in **bold** refer to diagram, *italics* refer to tables.